CW01521414

Corporate Derivatives

Corporate Derivatives
Practical Insights for Real-Life Understanding

By Pablo Triana

Riskbooks

Published by Risk Books, a Division of Incisive Financial Publishing Ltd

Haymarket House
28–29 Haymarket
London SW1Y 4RX
Tel: +44 (0)20 7484 9700
Fax: +44 (0)20 7484 9800
E-mail: books@incisivemedia.com
Sites: www.riskbooks.com
    www.incisivemedia.com

ISBN 1 904339 92 1

British Library Cataloguing in Publication Data
A catalogue record for this book is available from the British Library

Publisher: Laurie Donaldson
Assistant Editor: Hannah Berry
Designer: Rebecca Bramwell

Typeset by Mizpah Publishing Services Private Limited, Chennai, India

Printed and bound in Spain by Espacegrafic, Pamplona, Navarra

Contents

SECTION V – CREDIT DERIVATIVES

SECTION VI – WEATHER DERIVATIVES

To my parents, who gave me the perfect life

*To the memory of Jose Epstein, leading development banker and
visionary academic, who treated me like a son when a
graduate student at American University*

*To the Risk family, that was present all along during
my derivatives upbringing*

*To all the genius minds that have propelled through the years
the derivatives industry to its current place of prominence*

Acknowledgements

I would like to thank Laurie Donaldson, head of *Risk Books*, for his support of my proposals and his confidence in my ideas and writing style. I am also extremelly grateful to Hannah Berry, my main contact person at *Risk* regarding this book, who has shown extreme dedication and effectiveness and who has provided unlimited assistance. Thank you too to the anonymous copy editors who had to ensure that my ramblings made any sense.

Nick Sawyer and Nick Dunbar from *Risk* magazine initially welcomed me into the Risk family, and in an important way contributed to this book becoming a reality.

Of course, I am deeply thankful for the high-calibre outside contributions that have instilled a degree of relevance and quality into the book that would otherwise not have been possible. Didier Hirigoyen, Stéphane Knauf, and Mathew Daniel of Citigroup, Evelio Garay of JP Morgan, Ralf Lierow of Siemens Financial Services, and Alex Pollock of the American Enterprise Institute all kindly offered their pearls of wisdom and devoted a significant amount of their highly valuable time.

About the Author

Pablo Triana was a corporate derivatives banker before choosing to teach and write on the subject. He holds a Master of Science from New York University's Stern School of Business and a Master of Arts from American University's Economics Department. While at Stern he was appointed the president of the Financial Engineering Association. His professional experience includes corporate derivatives coverage for Spain at CSFB London, Madrid-based corporate Red Electrica, Washington DC-based InterAmerican Development Bank, and a US-based e-commerce start-up. He is currently associate professor at Instituto de Empresa, consistently ranked among the best European business schools. During his time at the school he has developed an innovative course entitled "Applied Corporate Financial Engineering" currently not available at any other top international school. He has also lectured at Johns Hopkins University and New York University. He has recently published non-technical papers in the world's two leading derivatives publications, *Risk* magazine and *FOW*.

Introduction

I became obsessed with derivatives about 10 years ago. The late 1990s were a booming time for financial engineering, with the industry having all but forgotten the reputation-destroying episodes of the 1993–95 period that includes the now classical scandals of Procter & Gamble, Barings, Orange County and many others. Swaps and exotic options having become consolidated, new exciting markets were emerging with underlyings such as credit and weather. More and more end-users were joining the party, and every day another university released a new flashy graduate programme on the subject. I became irremediably intrigued by this sector of the financial markets, where extremely smart and mysterious individuals seemed to be making millions. I began to devour everything with the word derivatives on it.

As is probably the case with most outsiders (ie, people whose jobs do not involve derivatives), I immediately concluded from my readings that the derivatives industry was dominated by mathematical geniuses and that a PhD in computer science was needed to get in the door. I imagined that derivatives professionals spent all day solving stochastic differential equations and programming curious models in C++. In fact, it was this notion that pushed me into undertaking a Master of Science, rather than the more common MBA, at New York University's Stern School of Business. If I really wanted to make it in the world of derivatives I had to learn some quantitative stuff, didn't I?

IT AIN'T MATHS
While I don't regret for one moment having pursued a quantitative graduate education (well, that stochastic calculus class was murder),

the truth is that I later came to realise that I had been somewhat naive regarding my perceptions of the derivatives world. In early 2001, I joined a bulge-bracket investment bank that was particularly famous for its financial engineering expertise, and I remember going around asking traders and salespeople about Ito's lemma, GARCH, and implied volatility trees. By far, the most usual response was puzzlement, followed by the (quite forceful) advice to "pick up the phone and start doing some business".

And these seasoned professionals, of course, were right. Derivatives are, above all, a business. It is not a subdiscipline of mathematics, probability theory, or computational physics. It is not even a science, but a key segment of the financial markets where people buy from and sell to each other. While the products and strategies involved can definitely be more complex than your typical stock or bond holdings, you don't need a PhD (or a college degree for that matter) in order to become a highly successful derivatives player. All you need is a good grasp of how the tools work and how they are affected by market movements (along with the right personality). Sure, being good with numbers is a big help, but you don't actually need to do any advanced mathematics while at work. Take a look at any trading floor and you won't find derivatives traders and salespeople solving mathematical problems in their yellow pads. They are too busy doing the only things that directly generate revenue for the bank: closing deals with clients, designing new products, and taking positions in the market.

What explains such a big gap between my early concept of the derivatives industry and the commercial reality? How could I have developed such a wrong idea about the essence of the business? I was honestly shocked to find that very successful, very wealthy derivatives stars did not employ any quantitative methods whatsoever as part of their daily routine (of course, there is an influential group of derivatives professionals that do hold PhDs and that do spend all day solving equations and programming advanced computer code; these "quants" are also inhabitants of the trading floor and their inputs are extremely important, and they too make very good money; but their role is pretty much a supportive one for the players who clinch the big deals). The explanation for my naivety is quite simple: the vast majority of the books and articles that I had read about derivatives prior to me joining the business looked more like mathematics than finance. Integrals, differentials, numerical recipies, and econometric models ruled supreme. This was the case not just of specialised texts written by quants or physics professors, but also of the textbooks used at more wordly outfits such as business schools. Even the high quality titles published by the Risk group (which cannot by any stretch be accused of not paying attention to the real world) were in general filled with complex mathematics. An innocent outsider could easily be forgiven for concluding that, yes, derivatives is maths.

In a way, then, most derivatives literature is catering to only a small proportion of the derivatives universe. They are great sources from which quantitative-minded people could learn the basics of derivatives and how the quant stuff is applied in that arena. But they give the impression that the whole industry is defined by that minority.

One of my key purposes when writing this book was to discuss derivatives-related issues without recourse to technicalities. I wanted to write a book that anybody could read, and I wanted to try to convey the idea that derivatives themes, if properly explained, can be quite easily understood. The fact that the most likely audience will be comprised of leading practitioners reinforces this mission. I wanted to provide jargon-free, to-the-point analysis regarding some of the most critical issues surrounding the derivatives business these days. If you are looking for stochastic calculus, I'm afraid this won't be the right place to look (not that I could even dare to delve in those waters). But if you are looking for detailed information and (hopefully useful) insights on real-life developments, this book could be a good choice. I have attempted to communicate this in an entertaining way; using market anecdotes and case studies to help the reader understand the practical implications of corporate derivatives. Derivatives, entertaining? Well, anything is possible.

WHY CORPORATE DERIVATIVES?

Now that you are aware (warned?) of my desire to offer a non-technical view of the derivatives world, it is time to address the other key point: why corporate derivatives? I could say that my professional experience in the field justifies such choice. I could also say that my research and teaching activities have focused on that field. But this wouldn't be enough to justify a full book treatment that very much aims to grab people's attention. I could have simply chosen the wrong line of work in the past, or I may be inclined to write and teach on weird topics.

The reason why I choose to muse on corporate derivatives is, to put it bluntly, because this is a very important subject. And, to add insult to injury, can also be a pretty interesting one. My professional background and current activities are nice sources to drink from, but I wouldn't have proposed this project to Risk Books if I didn't believe that its contents mattered. I want the book to have a real-life impact, and that may be a little difficult if no one cares about the topic.

The use of derivatives by non-financial companies is, of course, a crucially critical sector of the derivatives business. While it may be a bit less glamorous than the hedge fund or asset management sectors (ever heard of a corporate treasurer receiving a US$500 million bonus?), its influence over the economy (yes, things like company earnings and jobs) is beyond doubt. Derivatives allow firms to control their financing costs, their imports costs, their exports revenue, the losses resulting from defaults on receivables contracts, and even the damaging effects of weather changes. The effective control of those risks may well mean the difference between a good year and a bad one for a company, the difference between healthy earnings and disappointing results, the difference between prosperity and stagnation, the difference between expansion and contraction, the difference between hiring and firing, the difference between placid anonymity and deadly headline-grabbing disasters.

An old example that has current relevance can give you an idea as to the possible negative consequences for corporates of not hedging their risks, and how that can have economic and social ramifications beyond the company itself. Early in 2006, Sir Freddie Laker died in Miami; he was, of course, the founder of Laker Airways, the pioneer of no-frills, low-cost air travel. In the late 1970s, Laker was charging just £118 (US$206) to fly the Laker Skytrain from London to New York. It was an instant success, and one that quickly required expansion. As the existing fleet of aircraft simply could not handle the increasing volumes of transatlantic vacationers, the company purchased a significant number of new planes, all financed in dollars. By 1981, Laker was a highly leveraged firm with a debt of more than US$400 million. This made it disproportionately exposed to a rise in the greenback. Laker incurred three major categories of cost: (1) fuel, typically paid for in dollars; (2) operating costs incurred in sterling (administrative expenses and salaries), but with a non-negligible dollar cost component (advertising and booking in the US); and (3) financing costs from the purchase of aircraft, denominated as we said in dollars. Revenues accruing from the sale of transatlantic airfare were about evenly divided between sterling and dollars. The dollar fares, however, were based on the assumption of a rate of US$2.25 to the pound. The imbalance in the currency denomination of cash flows (dollar-denominated cash outflows far exceeding dollar-denominated cash inflows) left Laker vulnerable to a sterling depreciation below the budgeted exchange rate of US$2.25. Indeed, the dramatic plunge of the exchange rate to US$1.6 over the 1981–82 period brought Laker Airways to default.

Derivatives could have saved Laker, a visionary entrepreneur who revolutionised a very important business. No one can doubt the importance for a vibrant economy of the success of entrepreneurial initiatives. People like Laker are good for the creation of wealth and jobs, so if their ventures fail because their risks prove to be too much to bear, the economic fabric as a whole suffers. By ensuring that those risks are always under control and never fatal, the use of derivatives becomes highly benefitial. What the Laker episode, and other similar stories, clearly tells us is that corporate risk management matters a lot (apparently, when Richard Branson started Virgin Atlantic in 1984, well aware of the Laker experience, he insisted that the aircraft should be leased and, in particular, that the leasing agreement be protected from currency fluctuations).

LET'S BE PRACTICAL

In spite of the subject's relevance, not much has been written about the coporate derivatives business. Perhaps this is due to the fact that mathematics alone won't cut it. That is, one cannot write about corporate use of derivatives without necessarily referring to practical and applied issues. And it is a reality that many of the people who usually write, conduct research, or teach about derivatives either don't have practical experience or have a stronger interest in theoretical matters (yes, many papers have been published that deal with the theory of corporate risk management, arguing whether companies should hedge or not; but in the face of mounting evidence suggesting that, after all, companies have in general been hedging asiduously for a long time perhaps the relevance of the theoretical side of the issue has lost some strength).

Whatever the reason, there are not many books out there dealing with corporate derivatives. The best that can be hoped for are chapters on the issue hidden inside general derivatives texts. In fact, it can easily be claimed that Risk Books already held the leading position thanks to its three other highly acclaimed specialist corporate derivatives tomes (in particular, I must say, the impressive *Corporate Risk*). But comprehensive and wide-ranging as those three books are, Risk's previously existing range has in general a slight bias towards theoretical and technical issues. My book deals exclusively with practical and applied issues, making it complementary to these other publications.

Every single chapter in this book deals with a real-life topic, in most instances covering the very latest and most relevant issues. Even those chapters that focus on past events (such as a brief history of corporate derivatives) should have a significant interest for current market practitioners and analysts, as it is clear that to understand today's financial environment it doesn't hurt to comprehend where we come from. I strongly believe the book's content will prove to be a highly refreshing and informative alternative to the usual theory–filled texts.

The writing in this book is intended to proffer unique insights and analysis rarely covered in any other available sources, and covers a range of pertinent topics such as:

❏ why life is so hard for corporate derivatives marketers;
❏ why hedging is really not riskless;
❏ how an inverted yield curve can affect a company's derivatives strategy;
❏ why DARO options are not very popular;
❏ why quanto swaps became the hot thing to do;
❏ how Sarbanes–Oxley regulations may aid the corporate derivatives business;
❏ why the new accounting rules have had an impact in Italy;
❏ how those accounting rules can cause painful economic and strategic harm to corporates;

❑ how the rules affect the use of exotic options;
❑ how credit derivatives can help corporates and why companies
   have so far not enthusiastically embraced this market;
❑ what kind of deals corporates have executed in the weather
   derivatives arena.

I am also honoured to include here the collaboration of several top-notch practitioners. All are extremely busy people who have been kind enough to share some pearls of wisdom, and they were encouraged to tackle very specific issues of which they have expert knowledge. Thus, a global head of corporate risk solutions contributes a primer on the hurdles that companies face when using derivatives; a pioneer of the derivatives business talks about how it was in the good old days and how things have evolved; a global structuring head pens a lengthy piece on the various tools available for the hedging of year-on-year earnings from the vagaries of the currency markets; a respected outspoken guru goes hard at the new accounting standards; and the maverick portfolio manager who started doing it when most people said it couldn't be done writes about the use of credit derivatives to protect against receivables defaults.

To sum up, what makes this book worth reading:

❑ it is 100% practical, applied, relevant, real-life – 0% theoretical,
   analytical, quantitative;
❑ it uses 100% easy-to-follow language – 0% hard-to-follow jargon;
❑ contributions from leading derivatives professionals;
❑ informative and thought-provoking, rather than scholarly.

I am writing mainly for two groups of people: practitioners (who would mostly appreciate the innovative contents and analysis), and students (who want to learn about the key, hot, current issues in a clear manner). It is only when I detect the approval of the former and the learning of the latter that I consider my work a success.

A GUIDE THROUGH THE FOREST

So, what will this book enlighten you about? I have divided the text into six main sections, each devoted to a major topic that merits separate attention.

Preliminaries deals with the very basics of the corporate derivatives business, the essential information that must be always kept in mind. "Corporate Derivatives: A Brief History" (Chapter 1) walks the reader down memory lane, while also touching on some current key developments. A brief analysis of where derivatives in general came from is also offered. The watershed cases of Gibson Greetings and Procter & Gamble are re-visited, trying to draw conclusions useful for today's corporates. The potential threat of the new derivatives accounting rules are analysed. The chapter concludes with the contribution of Evelio Garay of JP Morgan, a veteran of the derivatives business who shares some memories of the early pioneering days.

"Tough Sell" (Chapter 2) discusses the realities of the corporate derivatives business from the perspectives of both the sell-side and the buy-side. Selling derivatives to corporates is not a walk in the park for marketers and we will see what factors make it so. Didier Hirigoyen from Citigroup helps us understand the obstacles that corporates face when planning to use derivatives.

Quick Product Review provides a window onto the possible corporate applications of exotic, non-vanilla, options and swaps. All treasurers are aware of the value that can be derived from using the simplest hedging tools, but many might not be too familiar with the possibilities afforded by more complex instruments. Again, the discussion will avoid the technicalities and product descriptions. What matters is to provide certain examples of possible real-life corporate applications.

"Plain Vanilla Is Boring (I)" (Chapter 3) deals with how exotic options can be put to good use by treasurers. While it is expected that most readers would be acquainted with the rationale for using popular products such as barrier and Asian options, the degree of knowledge about what can be done with the other members of the exotic family (lookback, digital, chooser, compound, contingent-premium, basket, rainbow) may be less profound, thus requiring a concise primer. Similarly, "Plain Vanilla Is Boring (II)" (Chapter 4) describes some interesting alternatives to plain vanilla swaps that can offer much higher rewards, but in exchange for taking on new risks. The challenge for corporates is to find the perfect balance between the desired extra gains and the potential level of discomfort.

21st Century Developments covers some of the most significant developments and case studies in the corporate derivatives world since the turn of the new millenium. The idea is to provide a (necessarily limited) picture of what has lately been going on in the real business arena. This section therefore focuses mostly on the use of specific products and on the effects of specific market conditions. "An Inverted Era" (Chapter 5) analyses how the presence of an inverted yield curve influences hedging decisions by corporates, and what stratagies would work best under such abnormal scenario. "Hedging Is Not Riskless" (Chapter 6) deals with the case study of South African Airlines and what the substantial losses it suffered in 2003 on its forex forward positions teach us about the true nature of hedging. "DARO-Loving Chicagoans" (Chapter 7) explains the case of medical equipment manufacturer Dade Behring and how its recent embracing of DARO options for the purposes of hedging earnings translation exposures highlights the importance of this otherwise seldom used jewel. Stéphane Knauf of Citigroup contributes an lengthy piece on the hedging of year-on-year results clearly detailing the value added of DAROs as well as other alternative tools. "2001: A Quanto Odyssey" (Chapter 8) takes advantage of the benefit of hindsight and looks at the performance of several real-life structures from the family of quanto swaps, one of the hottest derivatives for corporates in the early part of the 2000s. "Regulatory Incentives" (Chapter 9) makes the case that the new, tough corporate governance regulations symbolised by the Sarbanes–Oxley Act in the US could very well end up providing a boost to the corporate derivatives business.

The *Accounting* section deals, of course, with the new derivatives accounting standards (FAS 133/IAS 39). These days, it wouldn't make sense to write a book on corporate derivatives without devoting a considerable amount of time to the effects and consequences of the new rules introduced in the past few years. Simply put, no other factor has ever had such a potentially destabilising influence on the risk management practices of non-financial companies. Oceans of ink have been written on how the new rules work and what steps are needed for corporates to qualify for hedge accounting. Plenty of analysis has also been done on the historical evolution that has taken us to today's present state. This section will not deal with any of these issues, at least specifically. We will not spend time exactly describing the technicalities involved in applying the new standards. For this, a specialised text written by auditors or accountants would always be a much better reference. Also, it is assumed that most corporates already know by heart how to apply the new rules, or at least they get sufficient feedback in this respect from their bankers and consultants. In this book we will devote our efforts to trying to offer useful insights as to the possible practical effects that the new rules could have on reporting corporates and the financial markets in general. This is an area that has been subjected to relatively less analysis but that is, of course, one of extraordinary importance to treasurers and finance directors. "Accounting Headlines" (Chapter 10) goes over some of the key, headline-grabbings stories involving companies and the new standards. The chapter pays particular attention to how the rules have affected the reported results of several high-profile corporates, including disturbing earnings restatements, and presents the case studies of Poste Italiane and also Italian L'Espresso, two companies that have suffered great turmoil as a result of the accounting treatment of some of its derivatives holdings. "The Four Horsemen of the (Accounting) Apocalypse" (Chapter 11) analyses in detail how the threat of enhanced income volatility that derives from the mark-to-market paradigm at the heart of the new derivatives accounting standards may entrap corporates into situations that yield substantially negative economic and strategic outcomes. "The Anti-Greenspan" (Chapter 12) suggests that the new derivatives accounting rules can conspire to make monetary policy ineffective, through the incentives they place on corporates to enter into certain derivatives structures rather than others. This chapter is a good opportunity to analyse the differences in the accounting treatment of interest rate swaps and options. "Exotic Accounting" (Chapter 13) deals with the accounting treatment afforded to popular non-vanilla options such as asians or barriers, which have proven to be highly valuable to corporates during the past 20 years. "The Pollock Doctrine" (Chapter 14) allows me the distinct pleasure of introducing to corporate treasurers the views of Alex Pollock, an outspoken and well-respected analyst that has called for the elimination of the new standards. I believe that his message, whether one agrees with it or not, should be heard.

Credit Derivatives talks about – you guessed it – the possible corporate applications of credit derivatives. "Addressing Concerns" (Chapter 15) argues that while corporates still account for only a tiny proportion of the overall credit derivatives market, and with the sector growing in size and liquidity, treasurers should reconsider their aversion to hedging receivables with credit derivatives.

Ralf Lierow from Siemens Financial Services provides a primer detailing how the German giant led the pioneering efforts in this field. "Beyond Receivables" (Chapter 16) discusses all the other things that companies can do with credit derivatives, apart from hedging receivables risk.

Weather Derivatives attempts to give an overview of the latest developments surrounding the weather derivatives market and corporate use of its products. The section provides comments regarding the evolution, present state, and future of the market, "Weather Update" (Chapter 17), as well as a comprehensive analysis of some of the deals closed since the market began, "Weather Deals" (Chapter 18).

Section 1

Preliminaries

1

Corporate Derivatives: A Brief History

What a long, strange trip it's been

Over 90% of the world's 500 largest companies use derivatives to manage their risks, so said the International Swaps and Derivatives Association (ISDA) at its 2003 annual meeting held in Tokyo. After reading that piece of news, any doubts regarding the pre-eminent place that derivatives have achieved inside non-financial corporations should be instantly erased.

According to ISDA's survey (which covered the 500 largest companies worldwide ranked by revenues as of year-end 2001), 92% of these firms use derivative instruments to manage and hedge their risks more effectively. The companies using derivatives are located in 26 countries around the world and represent a broad variety of industries, ranging from the aerospace industry to wholesalers of office and electronic equipment. "The survey demonstrates that derivatives today are an integral part of corporate risk management among the world's leading companies", said Robert Pickel, Executive Director and Chief Executive Officer of the ISDA, adding that: "Across geographic regions and industry sectors, the vast majority of these corporations rely on derivatives to hedge a range of risks to which they are exposed in the normal course of business."

How did we get here? What explains the resounding popularity of derivatives in the corporate arena? In order to understand the evolution of corporate derivatives we must first understand the evolution of derivatives themselves. In this context, it is critical to have a notion as to the timeline of key market events. How old are derivatives? How did they evolve through the years? When did the essential products begin to emerge? Equally important is to grasp the tectonic forces that made the boom in derivatives trading possible in the first place. In today's free-wheeling market economies and high-tech realities it is easy to forget that things were not always so and that we are in fact living in a derivatives wonderland, where all the right pieces are in place to provide the ideal platform for the blossoming of financial engineering practices.

As the over-the-counter (OTC) derivatives industry matured, corporates came knocking. It is basically impossible to detail when exactly company A started using options or when company B began embracing swaps. However, sufficient anecdotal evidence suggests that not only were corporates among the very first players to jump on the derivatives bandwagon, but in fact that some of the more sophisticated products were originally designed with corporate needs in mind.

What we do know is that the corporate derivatives business suffered a mild heart attack in the mid 1990s, when well-known companies incurred large losses on highly exotic structures. It wasn't fatal, and the patient is now alive and well and enjoying extraordinary health. However, it was a hard blow nonetheless, and one that should never be entirely forgotten. As the philosopher George Santayana so famously stated, "Those who forget the past are condemned to repeat it". Unlike most other sources on this topic, however, we do not solely refer to corporate treasurers and their bankers. Yes, some mistakes were committed on both sides of the aisle. Some corporates entered into structures that (while hedges, not speculation) were too risky and inappropriate. A few bankers probably didn't behave as well as was expected. However, other people were guilty of even greater sins. I am pointing my finger at those who, fired up by the size of the losses involved and the high-profile names of the players, started a relentless and quite ill-informed derivatives-bashing campaign. Suddenly, derivatives (of which not many regular folks had heard of previously) were grabbing the headlines of the world's most influential media outlets, and it wasn't pretty. Name-calling was aplenty. Derivatives, said some, are the financial instruments of the devil. Others said that their booming market was an "electronic Ponzi scheme". Dealers were accused of racketeering practices. Lengthy and controversial legal disputes took place. Famous investors proposed that some exotic products be made illegal.

For a period of time, derivatives became such a dirty word both outside and inside corporate boardrooms that many companies that had profitably used the tools in the past stopped in their tracks; at least until the public relations storm had calmed. Other companies contemplating their debut in the derivatives arena probably postponed their plans until further notice.

In the end, the waters receded. People, and specially the media, forgot the old scandals and concentrated on what really mattered: can derivatives help me manage my risks in an economical and efficient way? Since the answer is, most definitely, yes (when combined, mind you, with responsible use), the corporate derivatives business flourished. In a 1998 survey of the corporate use of derivatives in the US by the Wharton School of Business, half of respondents (some 400 firms, mostly randomly selected) reported using derivatives. This was up from 35% in 1994 and 41% in 1995. Of derivative users, 42% indicated that their usage had increased over the previous year, with only 13% reporting a decrease.

Today, corporate financial engineering faces another major threat. Contrary to the mid-1990s malaise, which in essence was a problem of "perception" (though it wouldn't be unreasonable to argue that some strategies went too far in their exoticness), the current menace is very much real. Of course, we are talking about the new derivatives accounting rules recently introduced, first in the US (FAS 133 in early 2001) and then in Europe (IAS 39 in early 2005). The rules, which are of course mandatory for any public company (thus the dabbing of the threat they present as "real"), present a double blow to the corporate derivatives business. On the one hand, they can introduce potentially devastating volatility into the income statement. Unless the derivative qualifies for special treatment (so-called "hedge accounting"), changes in its market value must be recorded into earnings. Since the mark-to-market of derivatives can swing widely, the effects on reported results can be devastating. It shouldn't be surprising, then, that stability-loving corporate executives would want to enter only into structures that qualify for hedge accounting. The problem is that achieving such status is a time-consuming and cumbersome process, which successful undertaking is by no means guaranteed. Many corporates have found that complying with hedge accounting for even simple instruments can be difficult, and utterly impossible for some exotic products. There have been several cases of large results restatements due to technical errors when applying the new rules (even in situations where auditors had given the OK).

Since income volatility, enhanced workload (with no guarantee of successful results) or earnings restatements down the road are desirable things for corporate bigwigs and the concern is that some companies may simply decide to forgo the use of derivatives. Or, at the very least, to limit that use to the most vanilla accounting-friendly strategies. In the post-Enron Sarbanes–Oxley age, the number of executives who would risk having their names make the headlines next to the D word and to phrases such as "big losses", "scandal and turmoil" and "shocking restatements" must surely be quite limited.

In the following paragraphs we will take a look at how and why derivatives evolved and came to be the biggest and most important market in the world. We will also re-visit the mid-1990s scandals and see what lessons can be drawn from them. Then, the new accounting standards will be briefly introduced together with some evidence as to their effects so far on corporate derivatives activity. The chapter will end on a very high note with the special contribution of veteran derivatives professional Evelio Garay of JP Morgan who is wonderfully suited to share insights and experiences from the early days of the market and its subsequent development.

WHERE DID DERIVATIVES COME FROM?

Nowadays we take the availability of options and swaps for granted. They are as much part of the financial landscape as bonds and stocks. Irretrievably mainstream. Such familiarity blinds us to the fact that only 20 years ago the OTC derivatives market (where corporates generally operate) was very limited, with outstanding notional amounts 200 times smaller in 1988 than in 2004 (according to the ISDA). Just 30 years ago swaps didn't even exist. Options, while much older, also took a long time to shine. The paradoxical truth is that despite all the glamour and well-deserved fanfare that currently surrounds the derivatives business and its players, the popularity of derivatives is quite a recent phenomenon. Why is this? If derivatives offer a valuable service, why did they take so long to reign supreme in the financial markets? In order to understand where we are today, we need to appreciate where we came from. In the following paragraphs we will list some of the breakthrough historical moments in the derivatives world, as well as describe the tectonic forces that have only recently prompted derivatives to the top.

We can highlight the following key dates in the evolution of the derivatives market:

❏ Ancient Times – There is ample evidence of early derivatives use by ancient civilisations from many years ago (most popular example is that of Thales of Greece, but it seems that oldest reference to derivatives could be the Code of Hammurabi discovered in Iraq in 1902 and now some 4000 years old). Other famous old timers include the use of options during the tulip bulbs craze in Holland in the 17th century, the appearance of options in the US in the 1790s during the beginnings of the NYSE and the widespread use of "puts" and "calls" by railroad speculators during the late 19th century.

❏ 1848 – The Chicago Board of Trade (CBOT) is founded as a commodity derivatives exchange, originally for futures contracts and then also for "privileges" (options). The CBOT becomes a key factor aiding the North win the US Civil War.

❏ 1934 – The CBOT falls into disrepute as excessive speculative activity takes place and Congress bans the trading of commodity options. After 1934, the only type of options that would remain legal would be stock options traded OTC by a handful of traders in New York who conducted business from a restaurant and got customers by advertising in newspapers.

❏ 1972 – The Chicago Mercantile Exchange (CME) starts trading currency futures.

❏ 1973 – The Chicago Board Options Exchange (CBOE) is set up to trade stock options, and traders start using the Black–Scholes formula.

❏ 1975 – The CBOT introduces the Ginnie Mae future, the first exchange-traded interest-rate derivative, based on mortgage backed securities (bonds issued by federal mortgage agencies).

❏ 1976 – The CME launches a future on six-month Treasury bills.

❑ 1977 – The CBOT launches a future on 30-year Treasury bonds.

❑ 1981 – First cross-currency swap transacted between The World Bank and IBM, brokered by Salomon Brothers first interest-rate swap transacted between Deutsche Bank and an undisclosed counterparty.

❑ 1982 – The CME launches Eurodollar futures, allowing the hedging of the interest-rate risk of a Eurodollar deposit.

❑ 1982 – Stock Index futures, options on futures make an appearance.

❑ 1982 – The London International Financial Futures and Options Exchange (LIFFE) is established, and starts trading futures and options on interest rates.

❑ 1982 – The Philadelphia Stock Exchange starts trading currency options.

❑ Early-1980s – Interest rate options start to be transacted OTC.

❑ Late-1980s – Equity swaps.

❑ Early-1990s – Exotic options boom, in particular of the path-dependent variety (barriers, Asian, etc), with the foreign exchange (FX) market being the usual breeding ground: Credit Suisse develops "correlation derivatives".

❑ Mid-1990s – Derivatives start to be applied to more esoteric underlyings (credit, weather, energy, etc).

❑ Late-1990s – Volatility swaps.

❑ Early-2000s – Economic derivatives, developed by Goldman Sachs and Deutsche Bank.

We can clearly see that after the backlash against the CBOT and options in 1934, there was a gap of almost 40 years before any new notable development took place. However, from that point on, there was an unstoppable rush of activity, with new exchanges and new products being continuously launched. The outburst of creativity and innovation that began in 1972 continues to this day. So the real question is why 1972? Why not earlier? Later? What was it about the early-1970s that created the perfect conditions for the derivatives boom?

The key tectonic forces that set the stage for the emergence of financial engineering as an essential part of modern finance were:

Increased market volatility

The international financial system devised after World War II (based on the Bretton Woods guidelines), together with the new monetary policies put consensually in place by the most advanced economies (based on the Keynesian doctrine), ensured that the major currency and interest rate markets would show very limited instability, if at all.

Bretton Woods established the rule that FX rates between different countries were to be permanently fixed in relation to the dollar, which in turn would be fixed in relation to gold.

Keynesian monetary policy was based on the notion that unemployment, not inflation, was the main enemy and governments should be ready to act at all times to guarantee full employment.

Such an interventionist monetary policy kept interest rate volatility in check. In the US there was even a law that put a limit on how much interest savings and loan banks could pay on deposit accounts. At the same time, if yields rose in the bond market, the Federal Reserve was always standing by ready to flood the economy with money, to keep interest rates constant at a lower level and so keeping unemployment at bay.

This non-volatile environment made the existence of hedging tools pretty unnecessary. What risk is there to hedge when there is no volatility?

In the 1970s, this comfortable system started to blow itself apart. The first to go was Bretton Woods, replaced in 1971 by a system of flexible exchange rates (at the instigation of European governments, tired of having to import Vietnam War-induced inflation from the US).

Then, the oil shocks of 1973 and 1979 contributed decisively to a sharp increase in inflation, which in the case of the US was over 10%. Fighting inflation, not unemployment, became the main focus of monetary policy. Conservative groups that included the University of Chicago Economics Department seized the opportunity to end 40 years of Keynesian activism and lobbied aggressively to have monetary policy changed. Congress listened and rescinded the law keeping deposit account rates fixed.

The final punch came on Saturday 6th October 1979, when then Fed chairman Paul Volcker decided to stop trying to control the yield curve. From then on, interest rates would find their own level in the market. The more immediate outcome of what came to be known as the "Saturday Night Massacre" was that on the following Monday, when Treasury bond prices fell 11% causing huge loses for holders of long positions. The era of high interest rate volatility had begun.

Since the dramatic shifts of the 1970s, the world has experienced tremendous levels of volatility in currencies, interest rates, commodity prices and stock markets. Obviously, the increased uncertainty brought about by exploding volatility levels made the appearance of hedging tools extremely necessary. It is surely not a coincidence that the first exchange-traded financial future was offered in 1972 and that in the next few years many others came to life.

Derivatives, thus, became a godsend for market participants and businesses that now had a shield against the monster of volatility.

Technological developments (capacity to satisfy that need)

The development of the derivatives market has been greatly (some might say decisively) aided by advances in financial theory, and by the successful application of quantitative and computational techniques to finance.

Particularly in the case of options, it would have been extremely challenging to reach the current market size without the appearance of acceptable pricing formulas, in particular the Black–Scholes–Merton model which was published in 1973. The crucial models, especially at the beginning of the revolution, came from academia such as B-S-M and the Cox–Ross–Rubinstein binomial tree model (1979), two early successes that had a critical real-life impact. These and other models made use of advanced mathematical techniques the likes of which had never been seen in the financial markets. As the need for derivatives expertise grew, those with the skills to understand, implement and improve the models were suddenly in great demand. Thus, in the 1980s investment banks started to hire massive amounts of quantitative people from different disciplines (physics, maths, engineering, etc). These so-called "quants" added rigorous thinking to the trading floor and provided essential technical support to deal-makers in those key early days of the financial engineering revolution. It is certain that quants, while clearly not the leading players in the derivatives team, made a decisive contribution towards the launch of the derivatives business into the stratosphere. Some of the people that joined banks as quants in those pioneering times are to this day considered among the most influential derivatives thinkers ever. Fischer Black, for example, joined Goldman Sachs in 1984.

The impact of technology on the growth of the derivatives market has been as dramatic as that of electric light bulbs on our living standards. Until the advent of personal computers in the 1980s, computers were too slow to be used in the context of the capital markets. It is precisely the new power of computers that allowed sophisticated mathematical techniques and advanced theory to be applied to finance. For example, the binomial model for pricing options could have never been used in practice without the proper computing capabilities. The same, of course, goes for simulation methods such as Monte Carlo, nowadays widely used to price complex options. Crucially, technological advances also have enabled a shortened cycle of innovation, as the time lag from insightful idea into implementation gets reduced.

As the theoretical and technological breakthroughs became widely adopted by the financial community, not only did the range of products that could be designed grow spectacularly but even more significantly the price at which they could be offered became lower and lower. In fact, one could argue that the single most important factor contributing to the phenomenal growth of derivatives is their low prices. Derivatives offer a cheap way of managing the risks that have plagued businesses for decades, if not centuries. This cheapness is basically due to the contractual nature of derivatives (which, in the words of legendary academic Merton Miller, "entitle the owner only to the price change of the underlying asset and nothing else"), but technological factors guarantee that prices are even lower that they would otherwise be (especially in the case of more exotic products).

Regulatory issues

There can be no doubt that the market has been greatly aided by two key facts regarding regulation:

❏ Non-disclosure – OTC contracts have historically been off-balance sheet; ie, there was no way for outside parties to know the amount of derivatives activity of a corporation, bank or fund. This has clearly encouraged the use of derivatives, be it because of the lack of concerns about the impact of volatile derivatives values on balance sheets or because of the possibility of taking non-authorised exposures.

❑ Self-policing – OTC derivatives have generally been free of regulation, and dealers have been allowed to police themselves. For example, in January 1993, Wendy Gram, then chair of the Commodity Futures Trading Commission (or CFTC, the body that watches over derivatives), signed an order exempting most OTC derivatives from federal regulation. In 2000, this exemption was made permanent by Congress

While new recently introduced accounting rules have eliminated derivatives non-disclosure, the market continues to be pretty much unregulated. In 1994, the very high profile derivatives disasters (huge losses at Procter & Gamble, Gibson Greetings and Orange County, among others) severely damaged the public reputation of derivatives, and the industry faced mounting pressure to introduce sweeping federal regulation. However, at the end of the day nothing substantial happened. For example, then SEC chair Arthur Levitt suggested that it would be better for dealers to regulate themselves, and that they should form a self-regulatory "Derivatives Policy Group" and said any legislation should wait until that group had decided on a plan. Several congressmen proposed new legislation to regulate derivatives, but they were defeated.

In 1995, four new bills were proposed to, among other things, require companies to disclose their derivatives positions, prevent federally insured banks from using derivatives and bring derivatives dealers into a regulatory framework similar to that for securities generally. All the bills were again defeated. Perhaps more importantly, the banks had responded to Levitt's requests for self-regulatory reforms and the Derivatives Policy Group agreed to a "Framework for Voluntary Oversight", a document in which they agreed to improve internal controls and risk management. Self-regulation, then, had been preserved.

Ironically, while de-regulation clearly helps the OTC market, in the case of exchange-traded markets one of the key reasons for their success has been the very tough regulation in place that guarantees the enforcement of rules and participant's protection.

SPRING OF 1994: "IT WAS THE BEST OF TIMES, IT WAS THE WORST OF TIMES"

Anyone who follows the political scene is aware of the polemic that has recently dominated media attention in the US with regards to the wiretapping of people's telephone conversations. Some observers believe that such practices are justified as a way to fight terrorism; others beg to differ and point to the potential violation of civil liberties. The relentless protests by the latter group may prompt the government to put an end to its eavesdropping practices. Had derivatives salesmen been able to count on such activist support back in the mid-1990s, the corporate derivatives business may not have been immersed in a potentially life-threatening mess. Taped phone conversations originating in the trading floor, later used in court proceedings and made publicly available did as much as anything to deliver a devastating blow to the public image of derivatives, and to send corporate use of financial engineering tools into a catatonic state (if only temporarily).

By the late 1980s, Bankers Trust had become the world's leading derivatives powerhouse. Just another staid commercial bank a few years earlier, it had aggressively transformed itself into the most innovative and sophisticated player at the new red-hot game of exotic derivatives. In 1989, the equity derivatives group alone made one-third of Bankers Trust's overall profits. By the first quarter of 1994, three-fourths of the bank's profit came from derivatives sales. Back in those days, Bankers Trust was derivatives and derivatives was Bankers Trust. It shouldn't be surprising, then, that the bank was involved in some of the most daring transactions entered into by companies in those wild-frontier days of ceaseless inventiveness and experimentation. Unfortunately, some (many) of Bankers Trust's corporate clients got burned.

If the spring of 1912 symbolises the real sinking of the Titanic after being hit by an iceberg, the spring of 1994 marks the metaphorical sinking of the corporate derivatives business after being hit by headline-grabbing losses. In both cases, safety measures were found not to have been properly implemented. In both cases, danger signals were not promptly reported to superiors. In both cases, awe-inspiring human inventions became involved in mayhem. The only difference between both episodes is that, while the ship rests forever at the bottom of the ocean, corporate derivatives recovered and not only stayed afloat but speedily sailed towards unprecedented success.

Many corporates (and countless other entities, both from the financial and public sectors) suffered derivatives related losses in the spring of 1994, but the legendary names that have become forever part of financial engineering folklore are of course those of Procter & Gamble and Gibson Greetings. The former owes its notoriety to the fact that it was (and is) a very famous company, that the losses were quite substantial, that hard-fought legal litigation was involved (including racketeering charges) and that, frankly, the details that emerged were extremely juicy. The latter's claim to posterity is not explained by the gross amount of its losses (other companies, such as Air Products and Sandoz suffered much larger gross losses in May 1994), but rather by the facts that the shortfall was so vast in relation to the size of the company that it threatened its very survival (Gibson's net income in 1993 had been about US$20 million, well below the US$27.5 million derivatives-provoked losses) and that the level of complexity and number of structures were simply mind-boggling. All of these corporates were Bankers Trust clients.

So, what exactly happened at Procter & Gamble and Gibson Greetings and why should today's corporate treasurers and other executives care?

In 1991, Gibson Greetings was a Cincinnati-based company that sold (what else?) greetings cards. Probably the only derivatives professionals that had heard of the company up to that point were those in the habit of buying Valentine's Day cards for their loved ones. Only three years later, Gibson had become a household name for anyone remotely involved in the derivatives business. To this day, the case study of how even a smallish outfit from America's heartland can be sucked into a nightmarish death spiral with no apparent ending simply as a consequence of using financial engi-neering products lends very powerful ammunition to those who would like to completely ban derivatives from the corporate landscape. What better case than Gibson's, a traditional maker of birthday cards ruthlessly abused by slick investment bankers, to point at the unaffordable dangers of using these devilish instru-ments? What better poster child for those campaigning for deri-vatives abstinence inside corporate boardrooms? What better justification for tougher regulation of the market? The problem with these arguments is that if the Gibson episode really proves something, if there really is one key lesson to be learned, it is, as derivatives dealers have been saying all along, "derivatives don't kill companies, companies kill companies". When a corporate treasurer enters into a derivative transaction where the potential for blowing up (ie, suffering huge losses, huge enough to have a Spanish author write about them more than a decade later) is substantial depending on market movements, and is openly portrayed as such for everyone to see and appreciate, is it really honest to blame someone else when markets in fact move against the structure and the company begins to incur the feared downfall? Yes, bankers have often behaved badly, and they apparently did behave badly when dealing with Gibson, but that bad behaviour did not include pointing a gun to the company's head and making it an offer that it couldn't refuse. When Gibson decided to enter into super exotic (and potentially very dangerous) transactions that did not look like hedges, the corporate was exercising its free will. While bankers seem to have lied about the market valuation of the structures, this was done after the fact, ie, after the structures had been entered into in the first place. Therefore, the ultimate responsibility for that remains, of course, with the company. Remember this before asking for the burning of derivatives dealers at the stake: Gibson could have said no.

The whole Gibson Greetings saga began in May 1991, when the Ohio firm borrowed US$50 million from the capital markets. Its financing cost was a fixed rate of 9.33%. Since short-term went down in subsequent months, this fixed cost started to look funny in the company's eyes. In order to stop the negative carry bleeding, Gibson's treasurer, Jim Johnsen, began to explore the idea of swapping into floating. Apparently, the company had never used derivatives before. Since Gibson had a long-standing commercial banking relationship with Bankers Trust, it was only logical that Bankers Trust's number was dialled when looking for a quote on the swap. The salesmen must have made an impression because Gibson decided to execute only with Bankers Trust and to enter into not just one, but two interest rate swaps.

On 12th November 1991, Gibson entered into two plain vanilla swaps that somehow overlapped each other. Let us call them Swap A and Swap B. Here is what they looked like.

Swap A:
❏ US$30 million 2 years;
❏ Gibson Greetings pays 5.91%;
❏ Bankers Trust pays six-month Libor.

Swap B:
❏ US$30 million 5 years;
❏ Gibson Greetings pays six-month Libor;
❏ Bankers Trust pays 7.12%.

That is, this was free money for Gibson during the first two years. The net 1.21% that it would receive every six months during that initial period would go a long way towards alleviating the pain of the 9.33% coupon owed to investors. In effect, Gibson had transformed its financing cost from 9.33% to 8.12% for years one and two (on US$30 million). What's going on? Was Bankers Trust in the habit of giving away freebies? Was Bankers Trust a charitable organisation, not a take-no-prisoners derivatives powerhouse? Of course not. While it is obviously nice to receive a net guaranteed payment and the optics of the trade look fabulous, what Gibson was basically doing is fix its financing costs again (OK, at a lower level than before). It went from fix to fix for the first two years. The point I am trying to make is that while 8.12% is of course much better than 9.33%, it could end up being higher than having paid floating from the beginning had Gibson entered into a single five-year plain vanilla swap (six-month US Libor was around 5% at the time the deal was made). Of course, from Bankers Trust's point of view, two swaps are better than one. In the available literature on the Gibson case, it is usually taken for granted that the initial two-swaps strategy was a success and that anyone should have entered into such hedging structures. It would be more accurate to say that the strategy had the potential of being a success in case Libor went up for the first two years. Gibson was not the recipient of an unsuspected gift in the form of a 1.21% giveaway. Gibson was very much taking a view on future Libor (which, in fact, did go down).

In mid-July 1992, Gibson decided to cancel the two vanilla swaps, at a profit of US$260,000 (the mark-to-market was positive to the company to the tune of that amount, according to Bankers Trust). It seems that treasurer Johnsen did not shop around the market value of the swaps with other dealers, as a way to check if Bankers Trust's valuation was correct and fair. He decided to fully trust Bankers Trust's salesmen and to take home the quarter million dollars. Later on, it emerged that the real market value of the position was closer to three quarters of a million dollars.

Why did Gibson close out the vanilla swaps? This is crucial in order to understand the mess that was about to unfold. It is, in fact, one of two (closely related) key questions regarding the Gibson Greetings saga. Had Gibson not unwound these transactions (which, mind you, were really hedging an underlying interest rate exposure), it would most likely had never entered into exotic and super exotic structures later on and few derivatives bankers today would be familiar with the company's name. It is clear that the vanilla swaps were helping the company reduce its financing costs, at least in the short term. However, it is also clear that Libor was going down, so perhaps Gibson's treasury team hated the fact of remaining fixed all the way to the end of 1993. It is possible that this was the reasoning prevalent inside the company at the time. While the cost savings afforded by the vanilla strategy were surely nice, they perhaps seemed too modest in light of market developments. What is more difficult to know is whether such conclusions were independently reached by Johnsen and his team or if relentless whispering from Bankers Trust's salesmen played a bigger role (the salesmen, obviously, savoured the perspective of taking the company into exotic land).

Once the vanilla swaps were terminated, Gibson had two alternatives: to remain unhedged (ie, facing a 9.33% financing cost till the bonds matured), or to return to the hedging arena. In case that the latter route was taken, there were also two choices to select from: go back to the vanilla world, or try something else. It only took three months for the company to reach a decision. In October 1992, Gibson agreed with BT to enter into a so-called "Ratio Swap" and a so-called "Periodic Floor", two swaps each for a notional of US$30 million. The former, which will be explained in a moment, is the structure that truly killed Gibson. After that contract was signed, the company's fate was sealed. While the final losses that led to a lawsuit and an out of court settlement derived from other transactions, the ratio swap was the origin (and the primary cause) of all the mayhem that eventually ensued. Just as the Titanic's slight lateral impact with the iceberg did not initially look too worrisome to the untrained eye, no one at Gibson Greetings would have in their wildest dreams ever imagined that an encounter with a ratio swap would unleash two years of chaos, pain and despair.

What exactly was this ratio swap thing? It was temptation incarnated. It offered Gibson the chance to obtain spectacular financial cost savings. However, as with most temptations, there was scope for a parachute-less fall. That is, the ratio swap had the potential to destroy its end-user. Let us take a look at the numbers.

Ratio Swap:
❑ US$30 million 5 years;
❑ Gibson Greetings pays six-month Libor squared and divided by six;
❑ Bankers Trust pays 5.50%.

Periodic Floor:
❑ US$30 million 5 years;
❑ Gibson Greetings pays six-month Libor;
❑ Bankers Trust pays six-month Libor +28 bps subject to Libor not being 15 bps lower than its previous level.

Again, forget about the second swap. The former should capture our attention. Through the ratio swap, what Gibson was essentially doing was leveraging to the tilt its exposure to floating rates. Its net financing cost was now a mix of fixed and floating, as it was facing net disbursements equal to 3.83% (9.33 – 5.50%) plus the floating leg of the swap. If Libor were to remain relatively low or even go down from its 3.25% level, the company's floating payments would be lower than Libor itself (as can be seen from Table 1) and, crucially, total net financing costs would be below the 9.33% bond coupon. That is, Gibson would have achieved its objective of lowering costs.

However, were Libor to go up fast and hard, the company would be in deep trouble. Since the payoff formula of the ratio swap magnified any up movement experienced by Libor, the risk was that in an upward market Gibson would end up paying above Libor itself and adding (not subtracting) to the 9.33% fixed cost. It is easy to calculate that the breakeven point was when the company had to pay 5.50% as part of its floating obligations on

Table 1 Payments implied by the ratio swap under different Libor scenarios

Libor (%)	Gibson greetings (%)	Bankers trust (%)	Gibson net (%)	Gibson net fin cost (%)
3.00	1.50	5.50	4.00	5.33
3.50	2.04	5.50	3.46	5.87
4.00	2.67	5.50	2.83	6.50
4.50	3.38	5.50	2.13	7.21
5.00	4.17	5.50	1.33	8.00
5.50	5.04	5.50	0.46	8.87
6.00	6.00	5.50	−0.50	9.83
6.50	7.04	5.50	−1.54	10.87
7.00	8.17	5.50	−2.67	12.00
7.50	9.38	5.50	−3.88	13.21
8.00	10.67	5.50	−5.17	14.50

the swap; ie, when Libor had reached 5.75%. If Libor surpassed that critical level, then the ratio swap would start being a disappointing trade from an economic point of view (it would again cause an increase in total net financing cost, not the desired reduction). If Libor shot to the moon, the economic downfall could be spectacular.

Is this an appropriate hedging strategy for a non-financial corporate? Most likely, the answer is a resounding no. Such structure forces treasurers to take too much of a view on future market developments. They expose the company's fortunes too greatly to those market developments. In a way, treasurers would be betting the farm on short-term rates not going up. Clearly, this should not be their mandate. While it is desirable that treasurers are informed enough and smart enough to design their hedging strategies in accordance with some views about what's around the corner, it is definitely not desirable to be put in a position where all hell breaks loose if those views are proved wrong. Such an outcome might be acceptable in the case of hedge fund managers, who after all make their living precisely out of placing huge bets on market movements. That's how they can make millions, or lose their shirts. However, they have to take big risks in order to reap big rewards. Corporate treasurers, of course, do not need to reap big rewards, especially when the stakes are very high. What they need to do is shelter the company from disaster. If financing costs can be low-ered through the use of intelligent risk management strategies, that's wonderful (some creativity and innovation on the part of treasurers should be expected and demanded). However, the main priority should be to prevent those costs from reaching the stratos-phere, not to focus on them hitting the floor. In this light, any trans-action that has the potential of blowing up the company contingent on market events should be discarded as a prudent hedge. It is OK to take some informed leverage when using derivatives as a way to obtain value, but there should be a limit to the amount of leverage that corporate treasurers can indulge themselves in.

Before being accused of being an unrepentant exoticness-bashing conservative, let us remind ourselves of the potential sorrow that a derivative position can bring to its holder is not limited to its purely economic outcome (ie, the actual cashflows that take place), but also, some may say especially, to its accounting (or mark-to-market) num-bers. It was through the mark-to-market conduit that the ratio swap caused the initial damage that would eventually cascade into Gibson's precipitous descend into the abyss.

In early February 1993, Gibson asked Bankers Trust for the mar-ket value of its derivatives portfolio as of 31st December 1992, so that the information could be included in the company's 1992 year-end financial statements. Bankers Trust came back with a figure of US$1,025,000. This mark-to-market loss corresponded, of course, to both the ratio swap and the periodic floor but was disproportion-ately skewed towards the former, which contributed US$975,000 mark-to-market losses to the overall figure. Again, Bankers Trust's reported numbers were later shown to have been wildly off the mark, with the real losses being above US$2,100,000. What explained such a big decline in market value for a transaction that had been in place for barely three months? Quite simply, the for-ward curve moved against Gibson Greetings. That is, it shifted upwards. The yield on the five-year US Treasury bond went from around 5.25% at the beginning of October to around 6.10% by the end of the year. What this meant is that forward rates (the magic tool used when calculating the market value of swaps) were now "indicating" that those paying floating as part of a swap would face higher outflows of cash during the transaction's lifetime, while obviously the inflows received from the fixed payer remained constant. In other words, losses were expected for the floating payer. These losses were greatly magnified in the case of the ratio swap through the squared feature, as the steeper curve was saying that Gibson would at some point be facing those very dangerous above 6% levels for Libor. Thus, only 90 days after transacting, the ratio swap was already wreaking havoc, if only from an accounting point of view (paradoxically, and interestingly, the first scheduled floating payment on the swap, to take place on April 1993, was set at just 1.581% and thus promised a very significant economic gain).

This was most definitely an unwanted result for Gibson. Something very unpleasant, particularly for a company that was essentially making a debut in the brave new world of derivatives. From the day when Gibson was told about the large mark-to-market loss on the ratio swap, the number one priority for the treasury team became the restructuring of that position so as to try to eliminate the annoying downfall. Restructuring a derivatives position can mean two things: an amendment to the original trade, or its cancellation and either a cash settlement based on the prevalent market value or the rolling out of that market value into a new completely different structure that hopefully will evolve more positively. Dealers love restructurings because it gives them another opportunity to make money. The minute after Gibson showed concern about its mark-to-market losses, Bankers Trust's salesmen went to work on proposals for restructuring the ratio swap.

On 19th February 2003, Gibson did the first restructuring, entering into a so-called Treasury-linked swap with a very complicated payoff formula. This didn't look anymore like a hedge on a fixed coupon bond issue. For starters, its maturity was only eight months. Its whole purpose was to shorten the maturity of the ratio swap from five to four years (this was important in terms of market losses reduction since under a steep curve the highest expected rates are those situated at the longest maturities). That is, Gibson was sheepishly agreeing to this complex deal only as a desperate attempt to stop the bleeding from the ratio swap. The risk that Gibson was running by doing this is that eventually the whole thing would resemble that old saying: "bread for today, hunger for tomorrow". Also in this case it appears that Bankers Trust's salesmen gravely deceived their client. Apparently, the negative value of the ratio swap had by mid-February 1993 improved to US$138,000 (this was due to a downward shift in the curve, with five-year yields receding to about 5.50%) but the bankers failed to inform the company of this fact, even while (or precisely because) concurrently they were trying to convince the company to enter into new restructuring transactions. What we are saying here is important: by mid-February, Gibson could have gotten out of the ratio swap nightmare by simply paying up US$138,000 and without any need for embarking on highly complex transactions that bore no resemblance to its original hedging aims.

The Treasury-linked swap itself went underwater and had to be restructured into something called a knock-out (KO) call, and so on and so on. In total, between November 1991 and March 1994, Gibson Greetings entered into approximately 29 derivatives transactions, including amendments to existing trades, with some deals being amended within weeks of execution. The vast majority of these transactions represented desperate attempts to get rid of the negative mark-to-market nightmare that originated with the ratio swap (which was the last structure that could be reasonably deemed a hedge to the underlying bond exposure).

On 21st December 1993, Bankers Trust told Gibson that total losses were US$2.9 million (the real number was US$7.47 million). On 23rd February 1994, Bankers Trust told Gibson that total losses were US$8.1 million (real number was US$15.45 million). By 25th February the number had gone up to US$13.8 million (real number US$16.25 million). On 4th March 1994, Gibson and Bankers Trust transacted their very last derivatives deal, the so-called Swap S10044. This was essentially a way to cap Gibson's possible losses at US$27.50 million, and to replace all outstanding (uncapped) positions. As per this swap Bankers Trust agreed to cancel all losses incurred in outstanding transactions; in exchange, Gibson agreed to make payment based on a complex formula linked to the level of six-month Libor on June 1995. The amount of that payment could be as low as US$3 million or could be huge, but capped at US$27.50 million, if six-month Libor quoted above a certain level. Why this trade? According to Gibson, Bankers Trust issued an ultimatum: either agree to the trade or pay up immediately US$17.5 million (which was, finally, a correct representation of the company's real mark-to-market malaise).

By 30th June 1994, the market value of that last swap was US$23 million (cost of unwinding the position). The following September, Gibson sued Bankers Trust and demanded compensation for US$23 million in derivatives losses plus a larger amount in punitive damages. Two months later, an out-of-court settlement was reached, allowing Gibson to pay just US$6 million to get completely out of the whole mess. In parallel consent decrees issued by the SEC and the CFTC, Bankers Trust Securities was found to have violated reporting and antifraud provisions of federal securities laws and antifraud provisions of federal commodities laws by providing Gibson with inaccurate and understated values of the losses it had suffered on its derivatives transactions. The consent decrees required Bankers Trust Securities to pay a US$10 million civil penalty, to cease and desist from violations of federal securities and commodities laws and to conduct a review of its OTC derivatives business.

What are the key lessons from the Gibson Greetings affair for today's corporates? Well, as has been already mentioned, much of the blame has to lie with the company itself. The derivatives gun should not be singled out; the treasury team that misused it should.

In order to bring this point home, let us spend some time trying to analyse the motivations behind Gibson's decision to jump into the arms of the ratio swap. Since this structure originated the troubles, and since it seems so recklessly inappropriate to a corporate hedging risk, it is essential that we try to understand the rationale behind it.

Why did Gibson enter into the ratio swap on 1st October 1992? To me, this is the key question of the whole saga. There are only two plausible explanations: extreme greed, or extreme fear. Recall that the ratio swap could deliver paradise, but it could also deliver hell. Most derivatives transactions live in the middle: they can offer attractive (though not super spectacular) gains, while subjecting the end-user to the possibility of bothersome (though not life-threatening) losses. Thus, the only reason one enters into something like a ratio swap is because you definitely need to obtain the benefits derived from making it to heaven, and such need blinds you to the infernal menace. Whether this need is internally created (ie, irrepressible greed) or forced upon by outside factors (ie, fear) does not really matter. The important issue is that you must obtain large economic gains, pronto.

It is not difficult to see why Gibson would greedily eye the ratio swap. As was indicated in Table 1 when discussing the structure, were US Libor to remain calm or even to go down the gains from the trade would be outstanding. The resulting savings in net financing cost would be truly amazing. For instance, as long as Libor did not reach 4%, Gibson would obtain savings of at least 2.8% (taking the 9.33% original financing cost down to 6.50%). Here was a chance for treasurer Johnsen to become a hero inside the company. That may have proven to be a very difficult prospect to run away from.

The possible fear motivator to enter into the ratio swap might have been explained by the bankruptcy of Gibson's largest customer, Phar-Mor, in August 1992. Gibson was forced to incur massive write-offs on receivables related to long-term sales agreements with Phar-Mor, resulting in a Q3 loss of US$20.1 million. This eventuality may have added a renewed sense of urgency (to put it mildly) to lowering all types of costs, especially financing costs. The ratio swap could clearly have been seen as a godsend in this respect.

Fear and greed, particularly when intense, should never be the guidelines that delineate the configuration of corporate hedging strategies. If they are, companies may end up entrapping themselves into transactions that can cause irreparable harm, whether economic, accounting or both. In other words, into transactions that have the potential of blowing up.

Corporate risk managers should never expose their companies to the eventuality of blowing up. If anything, their job should be the prevention of such outcomes, not their origination. The ratio swap entered into by Gibson Greetings was the type of derivative product capable of blowing up its end-user. The outrageous built-in leverage to short-term interest rates guaranteed that any relatively significant move in monetary policy and/or in the shape of the forward curve would cause poisonous malaise. The derivatives position that Gibson eventually entrapped itself into was at one point worth US$23 million. This contrasts with net income of just US$50 million for the prior five year period (1989–1993). Clearly, a corporate should never allow itself to be involved with structures that can result in losses that represent almost half of the income generated in the previous lustrum.

Putting the final blame on Gibson does not mean that Bankers Trust's behaviour should be condoned. Its salesmen gravely misled the customer when it came to the crucial issue of mark-to-market valuation. Most of the proposed transactions (if not all) were too complex for a non-financial environment and they probably knew that. They could have offered simpler solutions, but then again those make far smaller profits.

In the end, however, Bankers Trust did not force treasurer Johnsen to sign on the contract that bound his employers to the ratio swap deal. He acted as a free man in the land of freedom. He willingly and eagerly entered into a structure that could take the company into a dark passage of chaos. By the autumn of 1992, Gibson Greetings did not owe a penny to Bankers Trust and had no derivatives outstanding. It could perfectly well have entered into any simpler hedging instrument of its liking. It chose one of the most exotic instruments possible, and it paid the price. The only excuse that Jim Johnsen could allege in his defence is that he didn't really know that the ratio swap could produce such damage. That it took him completely by surprise. That no one had warned him about such things. The problem with these arguments, of course, is that for them to be acceptable we are forced to believe that Johnsen or anyone else at Gibson's treasury did not understand what "squared" meant when reading the discussion term sheet presented by Bankers Trust's bankers, and that they were too shy to ask. Is this plausible? As much as the notion of those salesmen ever receiving a greeting card from Cincinnati.

The Procter & Gamble story shares some characteristics with that of Gibson Greetings, but also some key differences. In both cases, the mess was originally caused by hyper-leveraged structures. In both cases, the treasury people knew pretty well what they were doing (or at least is very hard to reasonably think otherwise). In both cases, lawsuits and settlements became part of the picture. However, Procter & Gamble faced real (economical) losses, while Gibson's were basically of an accounting nature. In fact, while the underlying market (ie, interest rates) moved against Proctor & Gamble, in the case of Gibson it didn't (Libor remained below or well below 6% during most of the period; actually the ratio swap would have worked out pretty well from an economic point of view).

If someone ever cames up with an idea to organise a "derivatives olympiad", the P&G episode would surely end up in the podium for the category of best-known and most influential historical events. The soap maker would be competing for gold head-to-head with those other two big names that will forever be associated with the D word, Barings Bank and LTCM. And, contrary to what many might think, P&G would have a real shot at the crown. For while Barings and LTMC definitely have a much more recognisable "brand name" among the public, especially at an international level, the P&G situation had a more profound effect within the derivatives industry itself. Yes, Barings' downfall led to important reforms in the way financial institutions organise their internal controls. Yes, LTCM's demise highlighted the limitations of certain theoretical assumptions regarding financial markets. But only P&G's scandal can claim to have significantly influenced (and altered?) the way people actually use derivatives, as well as the way market participants interact with each other. Its gold medal candidacy would count on endorsements such as "the derivatives market has never been the same" and "it was a critical turning point in the derivatives market".

What made the P&G case such a watershed? Simply put, disclosure. Without the contents of the taped phone conversations that were alluded to at the very beginning of this section, the episode would not have grabbed so much attention. It would have still been a key example of excessive risk taking by a corporate through the use of leveraged derivatives and of lack of management involvement, but it probably wouldn't have reached the mythical proportions that it did. The tapes, recording internal exchanges by BT professionals, became gold in the hands of those eager to portray the derivatives industry as an evil enterprise. Perhaps jealousy played a part too, as outsiders learnt of the tremendously large amounts of money that derivatives people can make and about their boastful personalities (and, why deny it, about the fun they can have while at work). More to the point, they became a key resource during court proceedings.

Conventional wisdom has it that the tapes prove that P&G's bankers behaved improperly and that exotic derivatives are a toxic thing for companies to play around with. Maybe so. But in my view, those taped conversations are not, by a long stretch, the key lesson to be derived from the story. Or at least, not the one that can bring more value to today's corporates. After all, treasurers, finance directors, and senior managers already know that dealers can sometimes be a bit shy about sharing the true market value of a derivatives position, and that they prefer making large profits to small ones. And they surely know about big egos and bigger pay-checks inside trading floors. Unfortunate though some of these attributes may be, they are, in a way, the cost of doing business. Besides, companies these days use plenty of defenses to fight back. For instance, by putting several banks in competition for a single trade they guarantee that the price obtained is not abusive, and they also get several opinions as to the risks underlying the structure.

No, the real lesson from the P&G debacle is that, just like in the case of Gibson Greetings, non-financial companies should really not enter into structures that can reasonably blow up. Again, let me remind you of my motto: "exotic stuff is good, not bad, but too exotic stuff is bad, not good". A hedge fund can blow up (some may say there is even a degree of mystique attached to a speculator that blows up) because it is in its nature to bet big on market developments. Its very reason for being is to make lots of money, and quite often this requires the taking of large risks. Taking those risks should be seen as acceptable in the case of a fund, where the goal is not to minimise risks but to maximise gain. A corporate risk manager, on the other hand, faces the complete opposite set of incentives. It must first and foremost limit possible damage, without an obligation to create mythical gains.

On 2nd November, 1993, P&G and BT entered into the legendary 5/30 leveraged swap that would change the history of derivatives. The objetive of P&G was to achieve a desired low financing costs target of US commercial paper (CP) minus 40 bps. The structure assembled by BT offered that and more. Through the 5/30 swap, P&G could obtain CP – 75 bps for as long as five years. In exchange, P&G exposed itself to extremely high financing costs were the US yield curve to shift upwards. This trade is a clear-cut example of the "heaven and hell" dicotomy that only derivatives can offer. Could P&G have said no? Sure. Did they? No, they were too busy looking at that −75 thing.

This is what the deal looked like:

5/30 Swap:

❑ US$200 million 5 years

❑ P&G pays CP − 75 bps for first six months, CP − 75 bps + spread for the following 4, 5 years

❑ BT pays a fixed rate.

The alert reader may be wondering what that "spread" that the company was facing after the first six months was all about. This spread, of course, is where P&G's risk resided. It was calculated using a long and complicated formula, but suffice to say that it depended on the levels of the yields of the five-year and thirty-year Treasury bonds. If both yields rose, it could be very bad news. Specially damaging were increases in the five-year, since they were leveraged 17 times (ie, in the formula the level of the five-year yield was multiplied by the number 17). Ok, let me give away the formula in easy-to-understand terms: the spread that P&G would face for the last four to five years of the trade (and which could be locked-in by the company at any point during the six months window) was roughly calculated as 17 * five-year yield − thirty-year price. As the price of a bond and its yield move inversely, P&G was exposed to the five-year yield and the thirty-year yield going up. Now, it is important to note that this spread had a floor of zero, ie, it didn't count if the formula turned out negative numbers. What this implies is that the lowest possible financing cost that the company could achieve from the swap was CP − 75 bps (not CP − 100 bps, not CP − 234 bps). But, hey, who's complaining? P&G certainly didn't as −75 was already more than good enough.

Thus, we see that the company stood to make fantastic gains through the 5/30 swap as long as the US yield curve did not shift upwards too much in the six-month period following the signing of the contract, with particularly strong sensitivity to the five-year maturity due to the very high degree of leverage at work there. But were the company's views on interest rates to prove wrong, even mildly wrong, the losses could be devastating. Blow-up caliber. Calculations done by other authors show that assuming parallel shifts in the curve (all yields increase by the same amount), it was simply required for five-year yields to climb from 4.95% (the level prevalent at initiation) to 5.65% for the spread to equal +243 bps, resulting in a net financing cost for the last four to five years of

CP + 168 bps. Yes, 243 bps above the enchanting −75 promise and 208 bps above the original target of −40 bps. Were five-year yields to shoot to 5.95%, the spread would then be +1110 bps, delivering net financing costs of CP + 1035 bps, 1075 bps (10.75%) above the original target. A trade that was supposed to take P&G into heaven, would instead be opening the gates of hell.

At this juncture it is crucial to point out that some of those infamous taped phone talks unequivocally show how a BT salesman warns a P&G's treasury person, prior to entering into the transaction, that "the only way that you would run into trouble with the five-year is if you saw an absolute shift-up in the entire yield curve of about 75 or 80 basis points". Some people have claimed in subsequent years that P&G did not understand the mechanics of the 5/30 swap and the risks that it was facing. At least this particular conversation seems to contradict such claim.

The 1994 bond market meltdown that was ignited by Alan Greenspan's surprising 4th February move into a tightening cycle for interest rates caused countless victims among investors and traders. It also devastated P&G's prospects in the 5/30 swap. As the yield curve jumped upwards in response to the massive and sudden sell-off, so did the level of the spread. As P&G's treasury team realised that their view of stable future monetary policy had been spectacularly proven wrong, they tried to exercise the early bail-out option and lock-in the spread before further action by the Federal Reserve took place. But P&G was in for a surprise, as it learned that the early exercise option would not be priced below CP, as it had apparently assumed all along. BT's quote reflected the latest market conditions, and that put it at CP + 100 bps until maturity. Remarkably, and somewhat inexplicably, P&G did not exercise the option and walk away from the deal (at only a relatively small cost). The most likely explanation for this is that having tasted the prospect of CP − 75, the treasury team was not ready to throw in the towel at CP + 100. It would not only be an early admission of defeat, it would represent the irrevocable shattering of a beautiful dream. Thus, P&G decided to wait it out, hoping that the bond market had overreacted and that soon yields would return to calmer waters.

Things did not improve. By 22nd February the spread was at CP + 465 bps, P&G now clearly suffering the leverage punishment.

The company's negative mark-to-market on the option it had sold to BT (for that is what the spread formula stood for) was almost US$40 million. Still, P&G's treasury staff wouldn't lock-in, seemingly still believing that eventually they may be able to walk away at CP flat. Incredibly, they still hoped for a market sell-off before the May deadline for fixing the spread. P&G's predictions turned out to be flat wrong. Rates kept surging. By 1st March, the quoted price of an early exit had now gone up astronomically to CP + 844 bps (the sell-off on the long bond had been particularly brutal that day). The losses were now higher than US$50 million.

On 3rd March, with the 5/30 reportedly down US$120 million, P&G's treasurer Rymond Mains decided to inform CFO Eric Nelson. But Nelson did not notify CEO Edwin Artzt, or the P&G board, of the loss for nearly a month. On 10th March, P&G finally gave proof that its treasury team wasn't brain-dead and gave BT an order to unwind US$50 million of the 5/30, which got done at CP + 1055 bps. The company justified not tearing the whole US$200 million by ratifying its belief that the market was behaving irrationaly and should soon return to more normal levels. It is essential to emphasise that since the bond market massacre started, BT's salesmen all along encouraged the company to lock-in and get out. In effect, they went home everyday praying for a rally the following morning.

On 14th March, a second unwind for US$50 million got done at CP + 1198 bps with a third, for US$100 million, to follow on 29th March at CP + 1697 bps. By mid-April, P&G made a public announcement of losses totaling US$195 million from two BT-engineered swaps, with the biggest portion corresponding by far to the 5/30 structure. The company also announced its decision to sue.

In October 1994 P&G sued Bankers Trust for US$195 million (the company recorded a US$102 million charge against fiscal 1994 earnings to cover losses from derivatives transactions), claiming that the bank had failed to fully inform it with respect to the risk involved in the transactions. BT countered that it was not acting in an advisory (or "fudiciary") role to P&G, but merely as a business counterpart. It also claimed that P&G's reputation for using cutting-edge financing techniques cast doubt on its claims to be naive in this matter. In May 1996 an out-of-court settlement was reached whereby P&G agreed to pay US$35 million of the US$195 million it owed to BT.

What should we learn from this saga? Just like in the Gibson Greetings epic, P&G's treasury people most likely got greedy. They were presented with a devilishly tempting tool that could make them heroes, not just inside their own company, but also among competitors (who else could claim to be financed at CP − 75 bps?). This rosy perspective probably blinded them to the deadly exposures that they were taking in return. The other (popular) explanation which argues that the company was misled into super complex transactions that it didn't understand is simply not plausible. Just like Jim Johnsen must surely have noticed the little "2" right above Libor in the payoff formula for the ratio swap, it is unseemgly that P&G's treasury did not realise that the five-year Treasury yield was being magnified 17 times. P&G simply made a huge bet on the yield curve not shifting up, and it lost. The point is that a non-financial company shouldn't enter into such bets when the original problem relates to hedging financing costs. A super hedge is not worth it if the price includes the possibility of blowing up in case the market takes the wrong turn.

But not all the ramifications of the P&G story need have a negative tone. Some positive developments emerged as a result. Perhaps, many argue, the most dramatic consequence of the disaster was the apotheosis of risk management. Oversight improved, best practices were developed and the industry matured. Dealers became a lot more careful about what they sold and they engaged in more thoughtful and analytical discussions with end-users about the risks, nature, and behaviour of instruments under different scenarios. In the wake of the P&G fallout, corporates took a hard look at what they were doing. Many of them probably realised that rather than hedging exposures, they had been basically trading. While companies, in particular large ones, may have had the relevant product knowledge, risk management procedures were often lax. In order to avoid becoming the next P&G, corporates understood that things had to change, and that policies regarding derivatives had to improve. It is thus not unreasonable to trace at least part of the impressive growth in volume of derivatives transactions over the past decade back to the P&G affair, since that was quite possibly the fount of better risk management practices.

THE ACCOUNTING THREAT

Historically, as we have already analysed, a heavily promoted feature of derivatives were that they were off-balance sheet and quite well hidden from shareholders and other interested parties. The new FAS 133/IAS 39 accounting standards put an end to that practice: all assets and liabilities created by derivative contracts must now be disclosed in the balance sheet.

With the new rules on derivatives, accounting authorities have done something that goes beyond what we would normally expect of an accounting standard setter. FAS 133/IAS 39 do more than just define how the debits and credits should be recorded, since they implicitly go a long way in describing how internal policies and processes of companies hedging ought to look. This looks more like regulation than accounting and is almost certainly a reaction by regulators to a perceived failure by the market to properly control derivatives activities ("accounting as a driver for derivatives control", or "accounting as regulation in disguise").

Under FAS 133/IAS 39 a derivative instrument is considered an asset or a liability and must be carried on the reporting entity's balance sheet at fair market value. This holds true whether or not the derivative qualifies as an effective hedge. The key issue is that changes in fair value for derivatives not designated as hedges will be immediately recorded in earnings. On the other hand, if the derivative qualifies as a hedge its gains or losses will be recognised exactly in the same period as the income effects of the underlying hedged item. Thus, not qualifying for special hedge accounting will present a picture of income statement volatility that poorly reflects the underlying economics of the hedging activity. Given corporates and analysts obsessive focus on short-term financials, there will be a strong desire to achieve special hedge accounting treatment.

However, stringent and burdensome reporting and valuation requirements will be placed on derivatives users that want to take advantage of hedge accounting. In fact, the complexity of the hedge accounting requirements has meant that several companies have elected not to avail themselves of hedge accounting treatment under FAS 133/IAS 39 and have elected to use a mark-to-market accounting methodology for derivatives with all changes in fair value flowing directly into current period earnings.

The risk is that corporates would be discouraged by the new accounting standards so much that they will reduce or stop their derivatives activities. Thus, the new standards threaten to derail (or at the very least to slow down) the previously unstoppable derivatives juggernaut. Without a doubt, one of the key financial markets-related questions of our time is: will derivatives accounting kill corporate financial engineering?

There is not a lot of empirical evidence available regarding the effects that the new rules have had so far on corporate derivatives activity. Perhaps the best-known surveys are those conducted by the US-based Association of Finance Professionals (AFP), which in 2001 and 2002 tried to measure the impact that FAS 133 had had on hedging strategies among US corporates. The first survey, conducted in May 2001, released the following results.

❑ More than 200 respondents, from a wide-cross section of sectors and revenue sizes. Two-thirds of the companies were public, one-third private.
❑ Two-thirds of respondents stated that FAS 133 had imposed an "excessive burden" on reporting companies.
❑ A quarter of respondents said that they expected to apply regular accounting as opposed to hedge accounting (ie, to have the mark-to-market of the derivative immediately hit earnings) for a significant portion of their derivatives use, rather than devoting time and expense to the process of trying to qualify for hedge accounting.
❑ In virtually all categories of risk, the new accounting requirements fostered (or was expected to foster) a small reduction in hedging activity (see Figure 1). Even so, a significant number of respondents who didn't use derivatives to manage risk planned to do so in the future.
❑ Prior to the adoption of FAS 133, hedgers showed a marked preference for interest rate swaps to hedge interest rate risk and for forward contracts to hedge currency and commodity risk. Although the change in instrument preferences post-FAS 133 seemed to be minimal, in general the original preferences for swaps and forwards were enhanced; mostly at the expense of options.
❑ Only a quarter agreed with the view that FAS 133 imposed a beneficial discipline on risk management activities: 47% disagreed.

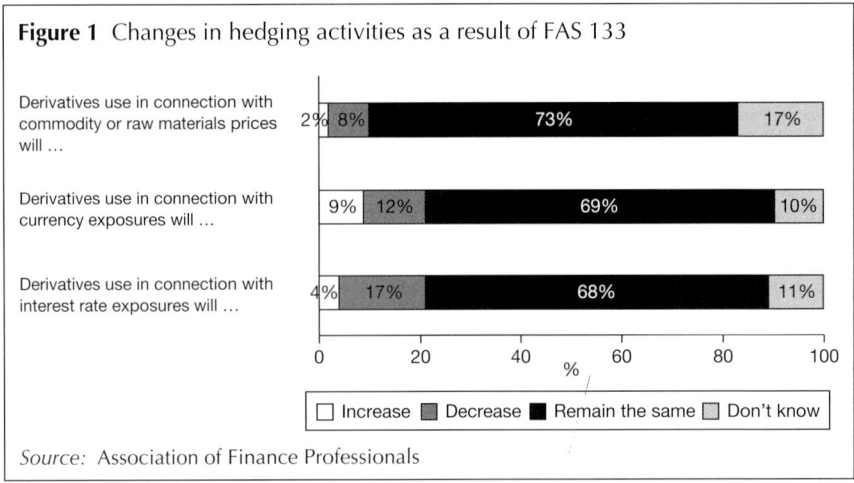

Figure 1 Changes in hedging activities as a result of FAS 133

Derivatives use in connection with commodity or raw materials prices will ... : 2%, 8%, 73%, 17%

Derivatives use in connection with currency exposures will ... : 9%, 12%, 69%, 10%

Derivatives use in connection with interest rate exposures will ... : 4%, 17%, 68%, 11%

☐ Increase ▨ Decrease ■ Remain the same ▨ Don't know

Source: Association of Finance Professionals

❑ Two-thirds of firms that had formal risk management policies in place before the adoption of FAS 133 reported that those policies had to be amended to accommodate the new standards.
❑ Auditors and consultants were reported to be the most favoured source of information about FAS 133; bankers the least favoured source.

The second AFP survey, conducted in September 2002, produced the following conclusions.

❑ 175 corporates responded, again from a wide spectrum in terms of activity and revenues.
❑ Respondents indicated lower levels of hedging activity compared to the previous year's survey (see Table 2).
❑ Even after the process of initial implementation of FAS 133 had been completed (a process that imposed special, one-time costs) nearly half of all respondents still reported that complying with the rules was "excessively burdensome". This result was especially significant in that it came despite an overwhelming reliance on and preference for the simplest plain vanilla instruments.
❑ Again, a quarter of respondents reported that they had decided to forgo hedge accounting on significant portions of their derivatives portfolio; mark-to-market into earnings seemed more acceptable to this companies than extra workload and expenses

Table 2 FAS 133's impact on companies' use of derivatives (percentage distribution)

	Increased	Remained the same	Decreased	Don't know
Use of derivatives for interest rate exposures has …	7%	69%	21%	3%
Use of derivatives for currency exposures has …	12	74	13	1
Use of derivatives for commodity or raw material price exposures has …	7	71	15	7

Source: Association of Finance Professionals

What about IAS 39? Well, in this case we must rely on anecdotal evidence rather than well-defined surveys *à la* the AFP. The lack of comprehensive evidence regarding the effects of IAS 39 is understandable given that the standard did not become enforceable until January 2005. Perhaps in the very near future, once enough water has passed underneath the bridge, comprehensive factual reports will be made available. Anecdotal evidence suggests that European corporates have cut back on derivatives use and there has been a growing trend towards the use of less complex structures. When selecting hedging instruments, many seem to be placing more emphasis on the accounting impact rather than the economic rationale. A lot of portfolio restructurings have been reported as companies try to gear their derivatives positions towards IAS 39 compliance. And yet, there have been several instances identified where high-profile corporates have refused to give into the accounting threat and have decided to maintain their hedging policies unaltered. Among these brave mavericks we can highlight the names of Rolls Royce, Vivendi Universal, and BASF. Do they represent just a minority group of rebels or are such decisions expected to be widespread? Some people argue that the introduction of IAS 39 need not produce the same results as FAS 133 in the US (where, as we saw earlier, a not insignificant proportion of companies reduced their derivatives usage and vanilla instruments gained in pre-eminence). The idea is that since Europe's investing culture is less focused on quarterly results, European companies may have a greater tolerance of profit and loss (P&L) volatility than their US counterparts.

The main point is that since enterprises seem unable to take their eyes off short-term reported earnings, FAS 133/IAS 39 will probably change how corporates hedge. Given the unpleasant trade-off faced by companies between the heavy workload involved in making a hedge compliant and the earnings volatility resulting from not following the guidelines, there is a substantial risk that in the end corporates will choose neither and simply reduce or stop hedging altogether.

Another possibility, of course, is that enterprises will continue using derivatives and try to find ways not to have to account for them, ie, try to find ways to get around FAS 133. One recent very high-profile case has been that of Freddie Mac. Interestingly, this accounting scandal involved the firm understating, rather than overstating, earnings.

Apparently, Freddie entered into trades that were specifically designed to offset the impact of the new derivatives accounting rules. Some of the things that were done clearly violated accounting rules, while other transactions were more creative and therefore bending the rules without breaking them.

Rather than disclosing the market value of their derivatives, Freddie devoted vast resources to a "transition" strategy designed to ensure that FAS 133 would have as little impact as possible on the financial statements issued to investors.

That was no easy task because Freddie Mac was sitting on billions of dollars of gains in the market value of its derivative portfolio, a condition that would have ballooned its profit.

Freddie didn't want to report that windfall all at once, as accounting rules required, but wanted to move the "profit" into future quarters when it wouldn't just be seen as a fluke of accounting but real sustained growth in the bottom line. Investors and analyst wouldn't understand the one-time gain, Freddie feared. The key goal was to smooth earnings and avoid excessive volatility (a practice known as "steady Freddie"). Apparently, there was a long-standing practice at Freddie Mac of making discretionary accounting judgements with a view to producing financial statements that more closely approximated analysts' estimates (and preferences for steady results). FAS 133 can be a scary proposition for an entity with a very heavy usage of derivatives dislike and an aversion to earnings surprises. Rather than face the possible consequences of the new standard, Freddie chose to get around it.

The key lesson from the Freddie Mac episode is that some people really find FAS 133 and its implications very inconvenient and troublesome, clearly seeing the standard as a bringer of earnings volatility, and will do almost anything not to be affected by it. The risk for the continuing growth and evolution of financial engineering is that that "almost anything" would turn out to be a radical decrease in derivatives activity.

At the same time, given most companies' recognition of the usefulness of derivatives and their desire to continue using them for hedging purposes, together with bankers' proven ability to tackle difficult challenges, it is also possible that eventually the impact of the new accounting rules will be quite limited as investors and analysts learn to cope with the extra earnings volatility and/or bankers come up with ways to tame the effects of the new standards. For the sake of the continuing evolution of the corporate derivatives business, let us hope that this will be the case.

A Practitioner's View: Evelio Garay

Evelio Garay is currently Managing Director at JP Morgan in London. He belongs to the small and select group of pioneers who participated in the early days of the derivatives revolution, having started in the business in 1992. He was for many years head of derivatives sales for Spain at financial engineering powerhouse Credit Suisse Financial Products, and as such was involved in some of the very first hedging transactions with corporates in that market. Mr Garay holds an MBA from Columbia University's Graduate School of Business.

A personal historical perspective

The early 1990s was a particularly exciting period in the financial derivatives industry in general and particularly in the less financially developed markets such as those of Spain, Portugal, Greece and Italy. As far as the Spanish market is concerned, the corporate and public sectors were the first to embrace the use of derivatives.

Back then, the derivatives marketer/structuring professional was confronted with a very limited market in terms of credit lines, yield curve and volatility. On the other hand, the accounting limitations were almost non-existent, with the accounting treatment of derivative structures being left to interpretation and negotiation between Chief Finance Officers (CFOs) and auditors.

The peseta (Spain's pre-euro currency unit) yield curve was inverted at the time, due to the high short-term rates the Bank of Spain had to impose in order to keep the currency within the fluctuation bands imposed by the European Exchange Rate Mechanism (ERM), the precursor of the current single currency area. In fact, the peseta yield curve did not adopt a positive slope until it suffered a second devaluation in 1993.

However, the absolute high level of interest rates was not so much the result of Bank of Spain monetary policy tightness as of the poor credit quality the market attached to the Kingdom of Spain. This was reflected by the higher yields displayed by most government bonds when compared to the equivalent tenor peseta swap, ie, the market was attaching a higher credit quality in pesetas to the banking community than it was ready to attach to the ultimate issuer of pesetas!

This was not a pretty scenario for corporate and public sector borrowers and importers. In fact, the Spanish Treasury was forced to fund most of its deficit in the short-term part of the curve and in domestic currency given the limited appetite investors had to invest in Spain's credit risk beyond three years in a currency other than pesetas (this factor has in fact played in Spain's favour in the process to comply with the Stability Pact in an environment of falling rates).

Under these circumstances the role of a derivatives marketer to corporates and the public sector was very challenging. Borrowers and importers where exposed to considerable strain given the spot and forward variables they had to deal with. Furthermore, derivatives-based solutions were looked at with suspicion due to the innovativeness of the structures.

The most basic instrument used by borrowers in order to overcome the then prevailing high peseta interest rates was to borrow in a low coupon foreign currency. Alternatively, for lesser-known borrowers that could not access the foreign currency markets, they could enter into a cross currency swap where the borrower would take a bet against the peseta forwards *vis-à-vis* the low coupon currency. In essence, borrowers were ready to assume the risk of a depreciation of the peseta against the low coupon currency in exchange.

The high level of interest rates was a major problem for some business with high exposure to long interest rates such as toll road operators. These were encouraged by the Government to borrow in low coupon currencies such as yen and Swiss francs. That "encouragement" took the form of a FX guarantee, ie, the Spanish Treasury guaranteed the initial exchange rate between pesetas and the low coupon currency: the State was, therefore, giving away deep in the money peseta puts/low coupon currency calls for free! The author made several attempts to purchase these options from a number of these companies with no success. They were extremely valuable due to their long tenor and large intrinsic value. However, CFOs were adamant to write options on the back of these guarantees since it would have been difficult to be recorded in the company's results and justified to auditors.

A number of borrowers were extremely successful in taking advantage of the interest rate differential between pesetas and low coupon currencies such as the Japanese yen. One of them was the Spanish Treasury. Spain launched a number of JP¥ issues during the first half of the 1990s. Most of these issues were left unhedged creating a *de facto* short JP¥ position. A number of them have matured recently and the implied ESPts/JP¥ rate was basically the same prevailing at issue date. Thus, Spain has basically benefited from the interest rate differential in most of these borrowing exercises.

However, most of the derivatives exoticness in the early-1990s was found in FX structures. During this period of time, the peseta had two different interest rate curves: the domestic (Mibor curve), and the ESPts Libor curve. The existence of two curves imposed restrictions in developing exotic interest rate derivatives. Most of corporate Spain's peseta liabilities were Mibor based. On the other hand, most of the banks behind the development of exotic derivatives were London based and had no access to domestic Mibor rates. Thus, peseta interest rate derivatives did not achieve the degree of development of other currencies such the Italian Lira.

The peseta FX space was, however, a different story in terms of development and sophistication. Importers suffered dearly the various depreciation episodes the peseta underwent against most of the currencies of Spain's trading partners. Therefore, corporates that were active importers were not shy of analysing and entering into relatively sophisticated and exotic structures.

The application of knock-in and knock-out (KIKO) features were rapidly accepted among Spanish corporates in their hedging structures. An application of the KIKO technology that became widely spread was into the construction of ESPts forward contracts against other currencies. The corporate would enter into a forward rate below that prevailing in the market rate as long as it was ready to accept the risk of that "improved" forward contract knocking-out at some stage should the referenced currency pair reach a KO level at some point between inception and maturity of the structure. The corporate would establish a KO level at which it would feel comfortable. As the experienced reader could figure out the "outperformance forward" (as the structure was christened at the beginning) was built through the combination of a in-the-money KO peseta put and an out-of-the-money KO peseta call with the same KO level, strike and maturity. The importer would buy the peseta put and sell the peseta call, which is equivalent to entering into a forward agreement contract in which the client has the obligation to sell peseta forward subject to the KO risk. The KO would be established at a level at which the peseta put would be in-the-money and conversely the peseta call would be out-of-the-money. Therefore, the KO feature would cheapen the peseta put more than it would reduce the cost of the peseta call being sold to finance the purchase of the put. As such, the Spanish corporate could improve the terms of the traditional forward by assuming some KO risk that could make its hedge cease to exist.

The large interest rate differential levels between the peseta and most of the demanded currencies by Spanish corporates coupled with the high levels of volatility witnessed in FX markets during the early-1990s made the KIKO technology a very useful and widespread tool among corporate clients. With a pinch of creativity coming from the banks and a more active risk management attitude displayed by some of the corporates the KIKO technology became a common tool in pricing FX hedging structures.

The FX space was also the area in which the author was first exposed to correlation as a risk variable. Corporates with large FX forward exposures started to analyse both FX spot and interest rate differential as separate variables, due to the high levels of FX spot volatility and the very large interest rate differential between peseta interest rates and other currencies. As a consequence, customers were ready to enter into structures that would allow them to hedge both variables with some degree of independence. One example of such a structure was the Forward Points Agreement (FPA). A company with a view that FX spot would move in its favour but that was happy to assume the existing interest rate differential could enter into a FPA in which it would lock-in a fixed number of forward points to be applied to a spot FX level, which had to be picked at a moment between the inception date of the transaction and its maturity. As such, a corporate with a view on any of the two variables or on both of them could hedge the two components of the forward at different moments in time. Institutions offering these structures had to be in a position to actively manage the correlation between the FX spot and the interest rate differential of the two currencies.

In any case, these more actively managed exposures were aimed at improving the variables that had a direct influence in their underlying business. They were not in themselves means to take on financial risks in order to profit from them. The core activity of the company was always present when designing or deciding on the best possible hedging strategy. As such, the risk of situations such as those triggered by the Proctor & Gamble and Gibson Greetings scandals was minimised.

This prudent attitude by the Spanish corporate space coupled with limited product knowledge demanded a marketing coverage with a significant content of education and advisory role. The marketer needed to be well versed on structuring and pricing and capable of building bespoke models to accommodate the needs and requirements of each individual client needs. As such the successful marketer tended to have more of a trader/structurer skills set and less of those of a salesman.

The Spanish corporate space was significantly less aggressive in its use of derivatives than its European counterparts. However, the use and applications of derivatives was always intended to complement the core business. The strategic angle was always present. A transaction executed by the author that demonstrated a high degree of strategic content was a sale and lease back of a physical platinum stock. A chemical company had to maintain costly physical platinum stocks to be used in their catalytic converters. The stock used up a considerable amount of resources. The structure proposed implied the chemicals company selling the stock of platinum to the bank, and then the bank would lend back the platinum so the company could continue using it up in its catalytic converters. This is an example of how derivatives assist corporates in optimising the use of otherwise scarce resources. The mere existence of a term structure of platinum forward prices made this possible. This example demystifies the status of derivative transactions as complex and obscure tools whose effects can't be predicted and could eventually destroy shareholder value and ultimately the whole company.

A prestigious and well-known investor has called derivatives "financial weapons of mass destruction". Events such as Proctor & Gamble and Gibson Greetings did not do much to help the industry either. These and other cases in which derivatives have caused damage to corporates and investors have contributed to an environment where the blame is put on derivatives instruments *per se*, thus ignoring the real cause behind the scandals: mismanagement, and, in some instances, fraud.

Derivatives themselves are very useful tools that allow managers to optimise the use of resources and address those financial risks that require specific management in order to focus on the core underlying business.

In the author's experience as a structurer and marketer of derivates to Spanish corporates and public entities, in the vast majority of situations prudent and sensible management has always being the norm. Derivative transactions have not been an end in themselves, but always analysed in the context of an underlying business.

The learning curve in the Spanish corporate and public sector spaces in the management of financial exposures through derivatives has been very steep. Behind this rapid and widespread use of derivatives are the adoption of the euro, the improvement of credit standards, the increased importance of the role played by domestic banks and the overseas expansion undertaken by many companies (mostly into Latam countries). The use of derivatives as a risk management tool has become a standard in corporate Spain. Treasurers across companies are well-versed derivatives professionals. The market has now turned into a distinctively two-tier market: flow activity, which involves daily risk management, and more strategic deals. As such, corporate derivatives marketers have specialised around these two types of activities. Derivatives marketers involved in the more strategic part of the business are becoming more like corporate finance practitioners. The corporate derivatives strategic transactions have similar characteristics to the pure corporate finance ones in terms of lead times, legal work, tax work and accounting implications.

As far as the flow business is concerned, corporates have started to operate more like banks. Corporate treasurers have pricing tools, are sensitive to credit risk and have built a separate back-office activity. The increase in the number of banks competing for business, and the efficiency and proficiency that local banks have built over the years, has resulted in industry margins falling significantly. However, part of this margin reduction has been compensated for by larger volumes.

The new accounting rules have had a major impact in the way corporates manage derivatives. The introduction has been slightly traumatic for a few companies but for the vast majority it has not been a major issue. Going forward, new accounting rules should have a positive impact in business volumes since they create a level playing field where the effect of sensible risk management can be more easily spotted by analysts and investors. This is not to say FAS 133/IAS 39 will not cause additional P&L volatility. However, additional volatility caused by the application of the new accounting rules can be identified more easily analysed in the context of its effect in the corporate's core business.

Structuring, marketing and selling derivatives to the corporate and public sector spaces is still a very attractive activity in the financial industry. Whilst the traditional corporate finance business has barely changed, new ways of addressing risk management and new technologies to hedge previously unhedgeable risks are coming into the market on a daily basis. Credit risk and bid-contingent hedges, for instance, were concepts no one in this industry would have thought about a few years ago and now represent mainstream business.

Very few professional activities provide the excitement this industry does. The combination of technical knowledge and creativity is part of the job description. The coexistence of these occasionally antagonist concepts is what makes this the exciting activity it is.

2

Tough Sell

Why the corporate derivatives business is plagued with obstacles

When a young and ambitious newly minted b-school graduate is lucky (and skilful) enough to land a highly coveted derivatives sales job at a top-notch investment bank, they face one major initial choice (on top of how to spend the generous sign-in bonus), namely deciding whether they want to sell to financial institutions (including hedge funds and asset managers) or to non-financial corporates (which may also include government agencies). The new master of the universe may naively think that it doesn't matter. They just want to start selling and make big profits for the bank; the identity of their client is ultimately not something to be concerned about. They are totally indifferent as to which desk they are ultimately placed on by their new employers. Is this indifference justified? Is it really the same to sell derivatives to George Soros than to Bill Gates? Of course not. In real life there are big differences between covering financial customers and covering corporate customers. These differences are so large that they could eventually force our young salesman to deeply regret having landed on the corporate derivatives coverage group.

To put it bluntly, selling derivatives to non-financial companies can be a tough, difficult and obstacle-filled activity where economic rewards may be dwindling. This doesn't mean that people should be entirely discouraged from taking on such a job. After all, fame and fortune have been historically linked to the corporate side of the business, which has witnessed some of the most well-known and profitable derivatives transactions ever. And there are other obvious perks, such as the regular access to and capacity to influence senior company executives, as well as the possibility of being involved in high-profile, complex, strategically important deals. In fact, one could think of a corporate derivatives coverage job as one that allows you to interact with important decision-makers just like an investment banker, while at the same time working on more interesting, high-tech solutions (the "investment banker with a brain" simile could be fitting if it wasn't so obviously demeaning). No, the purpose of this chapter is not to prevent young impressionable minds from pursuing a career peddling financial engineering products to treasurers. Rather, it is to acknowledge the undeniable reality of a market that presents serious hurdles to deal making and to try to analyse the nature and severity of those hurdles.

The chapter is divided in two main parts. The first deals with the perspective from the sell-side and takes a look at the obstacles that derivatives bankers face when it comes to transacting (ie, here we would be assuming that the corporate is willing and able to transact). The second part, specially written for this book by leading derivatives practitioner Didier Hirigoyen from Citigroup, deals with the perspective from the buy-side and lists the challenges corporates face when designing a derivatives strategy (these challenges, of course, also add an extra burden to the sell-side). Once this two-sided analysis is complete, it will be easier to realise just how complicated the corporate derivatives business really is and, crucially, how on many occasions companies make things harder than they should be by refusing to modify deal-unfriendly internal procedures and methodologies and by succumbing to the pressures of potentially negative external forces.

THE SELL-SIDE: IT'S A HARD LIFE

As stated earlier, selling derivatives to a corporate treasurer is not the same as selling them to a financial firm. On the plus side, corporate deals tend in general to be of a much larger size (think the hedging of a new bond issue) and thus, in theory, provide an opportunity for fatter profits. While those salespersons covering, say, retail banks that distribute structured products need to close lots of margin-deprived deals in order to accumulate some decent profit and loss (P&L) numbers, those covering corporates may earn the same with just a couple of transactions. On the minus column, the amount of work and time involved in closing a corporate deal is usually much larger, particularly if the trade offers strategic benefits (ie, tax or accounting driven solutions, structured financing). Someone covering an asset manager or a retail distributor can sell an exotic equity derivative over the phone without ever having met the client in person to pitch the trade and without having had to provide much analysis and guidance. In this case, the salesperson is basically a price giver in an auction where the buyer already knows what they want to purchase and wishes to select the best quote from several competing banks. The life of the transaction, from the time that the client first shows interest till the time of closure, could take less than an hour. In the case of corporate derivatives, this type of deal would be extremely rare. The life of the transaction could take, and does take, months. Face-to-face meetings with the client (possibly involving long-distance flying) would be an absolute must, as would be continuous dialogue and amendments to the original proposal depending on changing market conditions and customer desires. It is not rare to find lots of corporate marketers with crowded deal pipelines but no real kill yet.

For those looking for action and the thrill of scoring, such arrangement may seem boring. But if you don't mind endless discussions and changes (not just with your client, but also with your traders) and you are OK with spending half the week on the road, then the lifestyle of a corporate derivatives salesperson should not be a bother. The real problem is that all that hard work, all those long hours, all those promises may end up in bleak disappointment as the client either finally decides not to transact at all or chooses a rival bank as counterparty. In other words, when it comes to corporate derivatives there is a big risk that diligence and personal attention will not be rewarded. With so many different houses having the capacity nowadays of quoting a price for almost any derivative product, it is quite tempting for treasurers to take advantage of the creativity and labour of a particular salesperson and set-up a multiparty auction around the designed structure with the sole purpose of obtaining the very best possible price, rather than the very best possible price that the hard-working marketer could offer.

The following, real-life example may help clarify the unfairness of it all: in early 2001 a corporate derivatives salesman discovered that an important customer had been exercised into a plain vanilla interest rate swap with very large negative mark-to-market as a result of a receiver swaption that it had sold to the bank a few years earlier. What was puzzling was not so much the vast losses but the fact that the corporate did not seem to be aware of the situation, as no alarming phone call had been made to the bank begging to restructure the original swap. So the salesman, smelling a profitable opportunity as well as complying with his responsibility to alert a client, contacted the company's treasury people and duly informed them of the negativity of the trade and offered to fly to see them and perhaps discuss a possible solution. During a period of two months or so, the banker presented several ideas that substantially reduced the negative carry for the corporate, putting many hours into the effort and overcoming several obstacles, chief of which was the fact that the company had recently launched a no more derivatives policy. Mixing charm with financial necessity, the marketer finally managed to convince the client to make an exception and to restructure the nightmare-inducing swap position (the notional amount was quite substantial). Even better, he got them to choose an exotic structure (a quanto swap) as a substitute. Everything seemed rosy. The day before transacting, the client called the salesman and coldly informed him that he was going to be put in competition with other banks, which until that day had no idea that such deal was on the cards. In other words, for those other banks the corporate was offering them a golden opportunity: the chance to enjoy a free lunch, in the shape of a potentially highly profitable transaction that did not require too much work or time. The marketer who effectively discovered the problem and provided the assistance to solve it was suddenly transformed into a mere price giver at an auction, with the same weight as anybody else. What happened? A rival bank closed the deal. And, to add insult to injury, at a level at which it was losing money (ie, the market value of the quanto swap was negative for the bank at the level at which it was entered into). It is quite possible that the winning bank (which most likely enjoyed a strong relationship with the company) was brought into the auction with the sole objective of quoting a price so low that no matter who won the bid the corporate was walking away with a subsidised structure. The hardworking salesman was left not only with no deal but he also had to face the wrath of his bosses who accused him of not having been able to "anticipate" the fact that the corporate may put him in competition. Not that this helped him better understand what had happened. He had done all the right things. He had earned his bank a chance to profit from a juicy trade that would have remained hidden had he not discovered the problem and devised a solution. Even if he had known or suspected way beforehand that other banks would be competing that still does not change the fact that he was the only one who put time and effort into the restructuring and that had he won the bid the transaction would have had a negative, not positive, mark-to-market (courtesy of the corporate's banking accomplice).

Another major potential drawback of covering corporate clients is the fact that many of them can be quite conservative when it comes to selecting hedging strategies. This is explained by several factors, such as lack of product knowledge (which is covered at length in the next section) or the bad reputation that derivatives may carry inside some executive offices (no one wants to be accused of being the next Procter & Gamble, Enron or Parmalat, even if on most occasions the proposed trades have nothing to do with what these companies entered into). If you are a derivatives salesperson you want your customers to be aggressive and daring, not conservative. Conservative means thin-margin structures, such as vanilla swaps or forwards. To this day, several very important companies would not use options when hedging their currency risks, or would not touch exotic options when it comes to hedging interest rate risks. The new derivatives accounting rules, which will be analysed in the next section, reinforce this conservativeness and further reduce the scope for sophisticated, high-margin trades.

The ill of conservativeness need not be initially present to do damage to profit-hungry salespeople, but, worse, could suddenly present itself and threaten the viability of an exotic structure that may had been negotiated for a long time. Another real world example can illustrate this point. In late 2001, a telecom company that had recently obtained a large floating-rate syndicated loan and that wanted to hedge the subsequent interest rate risk, started soliciting ideas from its derivatives providers. While it decided to base around 75% of its hedging strategy on vanilla or semi-vanilla products, the company also wanted to enjoy the added value that more exotic tools could provide. It particularly liked a structure presented by one of the banks that would allow it to benefit from lower interest rates while affording attractive protection from rising rates. This so-called "knock-in collar" structure was a potentially high-margin trade and thus made the marketer quite eager to transact. He spent the next weeks fine-tuning the structure in conjunction with the treasury team and adapting it to changing market conditions and forecasts. When everything seemed ready to go disaster struck in the form of a new, conservative finance director, joining the company. This person had never entered into non-vanilla derivatives transactions before and was determined to kill the knock-in idea and instead replace it with a plain vanilla swap (against, it must be said, the advice of his treasury team). The swap, as opposed to the exotic alternative, would fix the corporate's financing cost thus not allowing it to benefit from low interest rates. In fact, with the swap the company would suffer negative carry from the beginning while the knock-in collar offered instant positive carry. As with the previous example the salesman had been the victim of customer disloyalty, in this case the banker was about to see weeks of hard work fall down the drain because of the ruthless conservativeness of a suddenly appointed corporate executive who wouldn't listen to his own, innovative underlyings. Just as in the previous example, the marketer had done everything right: he had managed to put forward an attractive, value-adding hedging strategy and to convince his clients to buy into it. It would be unreasonable to demand more from him. That an unappreciative treasurer would decide to entrap him into an auction or that the company would decide to switch finance directors are, of course, factors that were totally out of the salesman's control.

This is, clearly, the key lesson. In the corporate derivatives world, the long hours and personal attention that each potential transaction requires don't guarantee success, even when the banker has performed admirably as a marketer. Too many external factors can conspire to derail things. After all, whether a price auction is won or not would ultimately depend on the trader, not the salesman. Similarly, whether a stubbornly conservative new decision-maker is forced to change his mind ultimately depends on internal pressure from his less short-sighted colleagues, not on whether the salesman again pitches him the trade for the umpteenth time.

What is worse, a salesman may not even be given the chance to earn himself a slot at the price auction. This is because corporates have, in general, a very clear and direct discriminatory policy when it comes to their hedging activities: only those banks with an existing lending relationship may apply. Unless you work for a bank that lends money to the company, your chances of gaining derivatives business are very slim. In effect, corporates use derivatives as a carrot that makes lending more attractive (perhaps a must) for bankers. It doesn't really matter much if you are a new lender or already established. As long as you put up some cold hard cash, your derivatives people are welcome to show ideas and to bid. In the knock-in collar example that was discussed earlier, the bank for which the salesman worked had never lent money to the corporate before and had just joined the syndicate at the very last moment. In spite of this novelty, the marketer was awarded the same treatment as his counterparts at other institutions with a much longer history as creditors.

This lending discrimination reality has been known to bankers for years, if only because their corporate clients never shied away from emphasising it at meetings. However, thanks to the laborious efforts of US-based premier consulting firm Greenwich Associates we now have hard evidence in print for all to see. Based on an April 2005 survey of almost 1,500 firms, Greenwich concluded that almost two thirds of currency derivatives users and nearly three-quarters of those using interest rate derivatives did business only with banks that lent them money. Of those who did use banks other than lenders, the vast majority of their trading still went to the lending banks. According to the report, nearly twice as many users of forex products felt that lending relationships were becoming more important than thought the contrary. Among interest-rate derivatives users, three times as many believed that the influence of credit in their decisions was growing.

Other anecdotal evidence that illustrates the predominance of lending banks in the corporate derivatives business comes from the several end-user rankings that are regularly published. Without exception, those institutions with strong lending arms are the institutions considered as best derivatives providers by corporate treasurers. Pure investment banks are almost never highly ranked. For instance, in Risk magazine's 2005 corporate end-user rankings only one of the top 10 choices was a pure investment bank with no commercial lending division or ties to a commercial bank. The 2004 rankings delivered the same result (although the lone ranger here was a different name than in the 2005 rankings). While no one doubts the derivatives capabilities of those banks that lend, it is clear that non-lending pure investment banks (Goldman Sachs, Morgan Stanley, Merrill Lynch, Lehman Brothers, etc) also posses world-class financial engineering expertise as well as highly-skilled sales forces. On a pure product and coverage platform, these houses have nothing to envy from their lending competitors. If they are not being ranked among the very best by corporates it is simply because one can only rank what one knows. If corporates as a general rule don't do lots of derivatives deals with the likes of Goldman then they really don't have many arguments on which to base their judgement of Goldman as a derivatives provider. On the other hand, since, as a general rule, corporates enter into most of their derivatives deals with Citigroup and the like, then it is not surprising that Citigroup enjoys a very high average score from the surveyed companies (of course, if Citigroup or other heavy lenders had mediocre derivatives units then they would be ranked low, no matter the amount of financing that they provide to corporates; the point is that while Citigroup, Deutsche Bank or JP Morgan Chase obviously present top-notch derivatives teams so do Goldman, Morgan Stanley or Merrill; the difference is that the latter group is not in the habit of lending money to companies and thus their derivatives marketers have a hard time getting invited to the corporate hedging fest; as such, their skills remain somewhat undiscovered by potential end-users).

The conclusion of all this must be that transacting derivatives with corporate clients, and making it a profitable activity, is no walk in the park. The issues of ruthless price competition (according to the same Risk 2005 survey mentioned above, pricing is the number one consideration for corporate treasurers when choosing dealers) and disloyal customers, which are common to all derivatives salespeople, are accentuated in the corporate arena because of the larger amount of time and work required to complete the transaction. In addition, the corporate derivatives business presents two extra, inherent obstacles to making money for dealers. On the one hand, the potential for high-margin exotic trades is limited by a tendency among corporate bigwigs to err on the side of caution and conservativeness when establishing risk management guidelines. When entering into hedging structures, most companies simply tend to go for the vanilla options. The 1998 Wharton survey of financial risk management by US non-financial firms showed that while almost 70% of respondents used options, only a minority used exotic contracts, with less than 20% employing Asian options and less than 15% using Barrier options. The more recent Bank of America 2004 FX survey showed that when it comes to hedging currency exposures the most widely used tool by US corporates is by far the simple forward. Apart from this relative lack of high-margin opportunities, the other obstacle to deal making that is particular to the corporate sector is, of course, the lending requirement.

Slightly over a decade ago, working as a corporate derivatives salesman at a big investment bank seemed like a very tempting job. That was a time when treasurers were willing to enter into very exotic structures (such as highly leveraged interest rate swaps) and when huge margins could be obtained (with some marketers reportedly making several million dollars in profits from a single transaction). It was, then, a period of both exciting product developments and sensational profit opportunities. Today, things don't look so easy at first glance. Gone are the days when Bankers Trust or Credit Suisse Financial Products were the only banks to be able to price a particular product. Competition has increased dramatically and margins on traditional structures (both vanilla and exotic) have fallen in tandem. However, at the same time, new products and in some cases whole new markets have emerged and with them, new opportunities for profitable dealings. Making money on currency and interest rate derivatives might prove to be a tough challenge for salespeople, but these days they can also try their hand at newer tools such as equity derivatives, credit derivatives and even weather derivatives. As long as financial engineering continues to evolve, marketing derivatives solutions to corporates would remain an attractive way to make a living, in spite of the undeniably abundant number of obstacles.

A Practitioner's View: Didier Hirigoyen
The Challenges of Using
Derivatives in a Corporate Setting

Didier Hirigoyen is Managing Director and Global Head of Corporate Risk Advisory with Citigroup Foreign Exchange

Introduction

When managing their risk, corporations face a variety of challenges that are often either unknown or underestimated by their bankers. For a long time, corporate derivatives coverage focused on the risk–reward profile of product-based solutions, an approach that was born from the nature of financial markets where priority is given to returns. However, such a bias often missed accounting for some of the hurdles companies face when trying to develop and implement derivatives-based risk management programmes.

Without much effort it is easy to classify these challenges under two broad categories: endogenous and exogenous. We will now look at these two categories in detail.

Endogenous challenges

The path to implementing a derivatives programme in a corporate setting is often full of obstacles that are created by companies themselves.

Building a knowledge base

The first problem that comes to mind, while not the most common, is the lack of knowledge about derivatives products. This lack of knowledge can be experienced at different levels of a corporate organisation. One place where you may expect it the least is in a treasury firms' department. However, this often has nothing to do with the staff's ability to learn, but more with how much time they have to do so. This issue is probably more acute in the US than anywhere else in the world. The main reason for this situation has to do with the fact that in many US companies, knowledge of a firms' treasury is only one step on the path to learning about and understanding the firm. It is therefore not rare to see some large multi-national companies have rotation programmes whereby the staff only spends two to three years in risk management before moving on to another position. This is barely enough time to learn about market mechanisms, let alone to learn about the more sophisticated derivatives products that could really make a difference in how companies manage risk. Corporations that have this approach should really reconsider their position. Managing risk is a challenging responsibility that requires highly trained, motivated and experienced professionals. This is an area of the firm where value can truly be added and where a well-designed and efficient implementation can make a difference even from a business perspective.

Beyond treasury it is also not rare to find a lack of understanding and misconception about derivatives instruments at corporations' senior management level. Whether because of limited exposure during their career or because of their sensitivity to the bad press some of these products received in the past 15 years (especially after the 1994 Bankers Trust – Proctor & Gamble story), senior managers are often the most reluctant to consider, let alone implement, more advanced derivatives products as part of their company's risk management toolkit. Therefore, they may limit their treasury's utilisation of instruments to the most basic choices, even if that means preventing the company from using what it really needs to mitigate its risk profile. This also means more difficulties for the treasurer and their staff to internally promote ideas that may be consistent with corporate objectives but too sophisticated or innovative. In any case, such an approach means a longer approval process and more uncertainty around its outcome.

Pricing capacity

A second issue that somewhat relates to the first has to do with the existence, or lack thereof, of pricing capacity within companies. While the pricing of most vanilla instruments is usually well mastered, the second and third generation of products often challenges corporate treasuries in this respect. From a control perspective, corporations' policy frequently prohibits, and rightly so, the usage of derivatives instruments that cannot be priced internally. Because corporate treasury resources are often stretched, it is common for companies to never undertake such projects, therefore severing themselves from the possibility of implementing more complex products when needed. Since many risks do not have a linear profile, the lack of such capacity may prevent a firm from adequately mitigating their exposure, thereby leaving an unidentified amount of risk on the table.

Beyond the scope of this chapter, such a situation actually raises the broader issue of adequate resources, which many corporate treasuries lack. While this may not impact the appropriate implementation of a risk management programme, it certainly affects the treasurer's capacity to drive the improvement of the existing programme. While in the largest multi-national companies a specific effort has been made to remedy this problem and slowly drive corporate treasury to become an advisor to the various businesses, this situation is still more the exception than the rule.

Financing the cost of derivatives

A third internal hurdle companies face regarding the implementation of derivative instruments has to do with the reluctance many corporations show to paying the upfront cost that may be attached to them. Options are a good example of that situation. A recent survey conducted by Citigroup's Foreign Exchange department showed a fairly low usage of options as a currency management tool. This can be surprising considering that options combinations can be more easily designated as hedges of forecasted cashflows under FASB Statement No 133 (FAS 133): "Accounting for Derivatives Instruments and Hedging Activities" and more specifically Derivatives Implementation Group (DIG) Issues G-20 than they could before that. Unfortunately, the decision to use forwards over options choice is often made independently from any consideration around the underlying risk profile, businesses' pricing processes or peer competitive pressures. It is also often the result of corporations' internal structures, as business units' performance measurements frequently pushes them to make decisions that favour their own individual performance over that of the company as a whole.

The best way around this problem is to define, at the corporate level, a budget to allocate specifically to the implementation of hedge derivatives. This will solve both the issue around cash disbursement by the businesses themselves, as well as that of poor utilisation of efficiencies across the various divisions of a company.

Now that we have highlighted some of the internal obstacles companies may face to utilise derivatives instruments, let us turn to some of the external factors that influence their behaviour in this domain.

Exogenous challenges

Corporations' strategic decisions are often subject to external influences that not only reflect pure business constraints but also regulatory conditions, as well as the equity market sentiment and expectations. It is therefore not surprising that corporate risk management practices are also affected by similar forces.

The impact of accounting

However, when it comes to the usage of derivatives, the most influential exogenous factor is undoubtedly accounting. In the US, that "trend" started with the release in December 1981 of FASB Statement No 52 ("FAS 52"): "Foreign Currency Translation". This standard, which affects the financial reporting of most companies that operate in foreign countries and directs how to account for various types of foreign operations and transactions, played a major role in the hedging decisions made by US companies until the publication of FASB Statement No 133 ("FAS 133"): "Accounting for Derivative Instruments and Hedging Activities". A similar trend is slowly appearing in Europe with the implementation of IASB Statement No 39 ("IAS 39"): "Financial Instruments: Recognition and Measurement".

The impact of accounting can be felt on different levels but in the risk management arena it affects decisions such as whether to hedge or not as well as the type of hedge instruments or hedge tenors used. This situation can be explained by the clear desire that companies have to match the impact of an exposure on their income statement with that of the hedge instrument they employ. If hedging is likely to generate a mismatch of any kind, thereby creating an unexpected shock on their bottom line, the decision to hedge is likely to be rejected. Similarly, the type of derivative instruments that may be used is generally a function of its impact on the P&L of the firm.

This situation is best illustrated by how the use of currency options has changed in the US since FAS 133 was released. This is mostly explained by the fact that although FAS 133 (and DIG issue G-20, which dealt with effectiveness issues around time value) somewhat facilitated the usage of options by allowing to use hedge accounting for options combinations as long as they met certain criteria, it also permitted, unlike under FAS 52, to designate a forward contract as the hedge of a forecasted transaction. This prompted many US companies to choose forwards over options as their primary hedge instruments, as forward contracts have no immediate cash implication.

However, this is somewhat surprising considering the forecasting inaccuracies that often exist in the corporate world. Options offer the flexibility needed in this type of an environment, as they do not have the same negative implications as forwards should the underlying risk fail to materialise and the market move against the hedge.

Interestingly enough, the problem that effectiveness testing created around the time value of options under FAS 133, later solved to a certain extent by DIG issue G20, seems to wreck havoc amongst European companies as IAS 39 is creating a similar problem, and no amendment "*à la* DIG" exists to this day. This means that European corporations that hedge anticipated foreign currency denominated cashflows will have to take the change in the time value of their options portfolio to P&L. This is likely to raise many questions around the usage of options as part of the risk management toolkit, in the same way it did in the US before G20.

Such a situation is only one example of how accounting can impact the use of derivative instruments but many others exist. Absence of hedging of forecasted foreign currency denominated dividends before they are declared or a lack of hedging of cross border acquisitions for example can both be attributed essentially to accounting constraints. In general, any transaction that has the potential of creating unexpected volatility in the bottom line is a "big no-no" for most companies around the globe.

In a similar way, another factor that may impact the usage of derivative products by a corporation is the perception that investors and equity analysts have of the firm from various points of view. Although the scandals of the early 2000s stained some analysts' rating fairness reputation, companies still focus on the market's expectation and assessment of their performance. Therefore, unless analysts and investors really understand the purpose of certain risk management products or techniques, they may shy away from companies that are too creative in this line of activity.

Issues around credit

Another important obstacle to corporations using derivatives has to do with credit. Although these products are nowhere as credit intensive as loans may be, most of them still consume lines from banking partners. This means that unless a company has a decent creditworthiness (ie, investment grade), its access to the derivatives market may be limited. This is especially important when looking at implementing long-term hedges, as extended horizons translate into increased risk for the banking counterpart. It is important to highlight that in this sense lack of credit can raise major problems for companies, as long-term risk management is truly the most effective way to smooth the impact of financial markets on a corporation's bottom line over time. Certainly, risk assessment methods used by banks have evolved substantially in the past few years and, with an ISDA in place, netting of a bank's exposures to a specific firm can help dramatically reduce credit consumption. Furthermore, the development of a credit default swap (CDS) market may allow a bank to unload onto another institution some of the risk it has on a particular name: in a way, a derivative to the rescue of derivatives!

This being said, not all derivatives are equally credit intensive. Certainly cross-currency swaps and forward contracts are up there. Options sold by a company within the frame of a structured product also consume credit, although how much is a function of the money-ness of the strike price. Purchased options on the other hand only have limited credit implications, essentially around the payment of the premium and the settlement process. This can offer a valuable alternative for companies that experience credit difficulties but still feel that managing risk plays an essential role in delivering expected results and in supporting the businesses in achieving their objectives.

This being said, credit made available by banks is only one side of the equation. In reality, companies also need to monitor how much exposure they have to banking partners. This may be sometimes challenging, as it requires resources of various kinds. This leads us to another factor that is likely to affect companies' appetite for derivatives products: systems.

Treasury systems

Systems play a very important part in how corporations manage their risk on various levels. Therefore, making the right choice in this respect is crucial.

The capacity to capture certain derivative instruments, for example, may determine whether they will be used or not within a risk management programme. Booking ability is truly essential because it drives the monitoring of derivatives contracts on several levels:

❑ revaluation, which determines the mark-to-market and P&L implications of the change in the value of the instrument;
❑ documentation and effectiveness testing, which, if automated, allows for a painless accounting designation as a hedge;
❑ control and reporting, which have undergone increasing scrutiny under Section 404 of the Sarbanes–Oxley Act of 2002.

The initial decision is especially important since, once implemented, a system is unlikely to be changed soon thereafter. Large multi-national corporations often see a treasury system as a strategic investment and may spend substantially to ensure that it delivers comprehensive functionality and offers room for expansion. It is also important that it allows for some degree of customisation, so that certain utilities may be developed as needed. This last characteristic is obviously essential when implementing complex derivative instruments or structures. Without the right system in place, the nature of derivatives contracts used within the risk management programme will probably remain limited. Although system vendors all offer features that satisfy basic requirements, not all provide enough flexibility to pursue booking and monitoring of advanced financial instruments. Any company that would like to pursue innovative risk management methodologies or has complex risk profiles should be aware of a system's deliverables and ensure of its suitability to present and future uses.

Conclusion

I have highlighted the major hurdles that companies face in the implementation of financial derivatives from various perspectives. While internal limitations can be resolved with some degree of self-assessment and, most importantly, with the increased involvement of senior management, external constraints are likely to survive and evolve in spite of the demands they impose, rightly or not, on corporations. Depriving itself, for one reason or another, of the capacity to use certain risk management tools could have unexpected consequences on a company's ability to mitigate hidden or future exposures.

Through a more stringent control over financial markets' impact on a company's bottom line, risk management has become increasingly important to deliver earnings growth. Derivative products of all kinds can prove useful in a variety of circumstances; discarding some to avoid some implementation implications may prove short-sighted in the long run.

Section 2

Quick Product Review

3

Plain Vanilla Is Boring (I)

A guide to the possible corporate applications of
exotic options for adventurous treasurers

The exotic options revolution began in earnest more than 15 years ago. In the period of time sandwiched between the end of the 1980s and the beginning of the 1990s, the markets witnessed an unparalleled explosion of creativity and innovation that almost overnight transformed the corporate risk management scene. From a business dominated almost entirely by forwards and vanilla contracts, corporate derivatives became an exciting testing ground for alternative structured financial engineering solutions. Companies that previously had to resign themselves to facing the potentially devastating negative carry implied by currency forwards and interest rate swaps could now enter into highly economical and tailor-made option structures. Barrier options allowed treasurers to purchase cheaper protection. Asian options also reduced the cost of hedging very particular exposures. Basket options too proved a money-saving and less cumbersome way to cover risks that were previously covered with vanillas. Contingent-premium options allowed companies to pay for protection only if this was needed. Chooser options let the user decide if they wanted upside or downside protection. Compound options provided a pre-hedge for those companies not sure about the existence of a future exposure. Digital options provided a fixed amount of money at precisely the right time. Rainbow options were a godsend for those interested in the relative performance of several assets. Lookback options afforded treasurers the privilege of always enjoying the best possible hedge. And so on.

This revolution came briefly into disrepute in the mid-1990s, after a series of derivatives-related scandals involving some very high-profile institutions struck a devastating blow to the public reputation of financial engineering. The suspicion towards exotic solutions that was first generated then has not been entirely extinguished. To this day, many corporates are still wary of using non-vanilla technology. The fear of headline-grabbing troubles is surely one factor behind such shyness. However, other factors are as important, if not more so. The new derivatives accounting rules, with their confused treatment of anything exotic, have surely not helped matters. At the same time, it is quite likely that even today many corporate treasurers and other executives are not entirely aware of the many possibilities afforded by the exotic spectrum. The reluctance seen in many companies to have a taste of the exotic menu may be explained by old-fashioned ignorance. It may simply be that they don't really know what exotic options can do for them. The hope is that, while providing a refresher for their exoticism-embracing colleagues, this chapter would aid those treasurers who are unfamiliar with the exotic terrain and perhaps open a new world of value-adding possibilities for them.

BARRIER OPTIONS

Barrier options are derivatives that either cease to exist at a certain spot level (knock-out (KO) options) or start to exist at a certain level (knock-in (KI) options). Since it makes a difference whether the settlement price is breached from above or below, there are down KIs and down KOs as well as up KIs and up KOs.

It can be argued that the main reason for the creation of barrier options is the fact that they provide means to hedge or take exposures without having to pay for the price ranges that the end-user believes to be unlikely to occur. This ensures that barriers are cheaper than the corresponding vanilla options, especially for high-volatility situations. The economical and tailor-made protection that they offer has made barriers the most popular exotic option among corporate end-users. Furthermore, they are not just purchased; corporations routinely sell barrier-type structures as a way to lower the cost of a hedging strategy.

A KO option is a regular vanilla option with a second feature, called the "trigger" or "barrier". A KO is considered to be immediately void when the barrier is triggered. The barrier can usually be triggered at any time from the trade date of the option up to the time it expires. If the KO option gets knocked out the end-user can sometimes receive a cash rebate. Although market terminology may vary, KO options are generally defined by where the barrier is in relation to the strike. An option that knocks out when it is out-of-the-money (OTM) is called a "regular KO"; an option that knocks out when it is in-the-money (ITM) is called a "reverse KO". An option with both an ITM and an OTM barrier is called a "double KO".

A KI option is also a regular vanilla option with a barrier feature. Initially, the KI does not exist: it is considered to be live only when the barrier is breached. This option cannot pay out unless it has knocked in first. The same conventions as above apply.

OTM KO options are cheaper than vanilla options and are used for speculation and hedging. ITM KO options are usually significantly cheaper than vanilla options, which can allow for a high return on investment; this structure can make the owner short volatility (negative vega). The basic reason why reverse KOs are cheaper is because the end-user gets killed "in paradise". They are really enjoying life at that point and certainly don't want to die. Not many people would pay much for the privilege of having something similar happen to them. In contrast, in the case of normal KOs the end-user gets killed when "in hell". They are not a happy camper at that point, so leaving this world doesn't look so bad. Thus, the discount for the possibility of getting knocked out should be small.

The intuitive reasons for the sometimes disconcertingly low prices of reverse KOs are hard to accept at first, but they make sense the more you think about them. Take the example of a € call/US$ put reverse KO (and up-and-out, or UAO) with a strike of 1.20 and a trigger of 1.40. Despite the fact that this option could end up with as much as 200 points of intrinsic value it is worth little, regardless of where spot is. That's because any time it gets intrinsic value the likelihood of it being knocked out, and therefore becoming worthless, is also increasing. This is in contrast to a straight vanilla that has unlimited upside, or a 1.20–1.40 call spread, with also a limit of 200 points of intrinsic value but does not lose that value when spot goes above 1.40. At the same time, a regular KO has just as much upside as a vanilla and only gets knocked out when it's already OTM and is thus already of little value.

OTM KI options are rare but are sometimes used with a very precise spot view. ITM KI options are usually valued at only a small discount to the vanilla, and are consequently often sold to finance the purchase of another option in a structure. Again, reverse KIs are more expensive because you are born "in paradise". You show up into this world with a silver spoon, a member of the aristocracy. Such privilege should be paid for. Normal KIs are cheaper because you are born "in hell". With no aristocratic entitlements, you have to work your way up from modest upbringings and there is no guarantee that you will ever make it into the upper class. Clearly, few would pay much for such prospects.

The values of reverse KIs are thus virtually indistinguishable from vanilla options unless the trigger is fairly deep ITM. The vanilla and the reverse KI have the same downside: if the option expires OTM it doesn't matter whether it was knocked in or not. Also, when the reverse KI gets knocked in, it has the same upside and intrinsic value as the vanilla. The only time it is worth less is if the spot is in between the strike and the trigger, having never reached the latter during the life of the option. If the trigger is reasonably close to the strike, this likelihood would be fairly low.

Table 1 provides a summary of the advantages and disadvantages of each class of standard barriers.

Barrier options came negatively into the limelight during the 1994–96 period. The exchange rate between the US$ and the German mark was then between 1.50 and 1.70. Since the all time low before 1995 was 1.387 (on 2nd September 1992) there were a lot of down-and-out barrier contracts written with a lower KO trigger of 1.38. The sudden fall of the dollar at the beginning of 1995 came unexpectedly, and the 1.38 rate was hit at 10:30 am on 29th March 1995. From that point the dollar fell even more to its all-time low of 1.35 on 19th April 1995. Numerous barrier option holders were shocked to find that losing the entire option is something that can really happen. The shock lasted for more than a year and barriers became temporarily unpopular (especially notorious was George Soros' criticism of barrier options, and subsequently derivatives in general). Even the use of exotics as an asset class came temporarily into question. The lesson to be learnt from this episode is that while complicated products can indeed lead to unpleasant surprises, to cover risk in an individual design at minimal cost requires exotic

Table 1 Advantages and disadvantages of each class of barrier options

	Advantages	Disadvantages	When to consider
Buy KOs	Cheaper way to express a view (especially ITM KOs) The hedger can put on cash hedge if knocked out (OTM KOs) Speculator can express directional view with unlimited upside (OTM KOs) Facilitates very cheap speculative plays (ITM KOs)	Risks of getting knocked out and: (1) for OTM KOs, getting whipsawed (market rallies against you, making vanilla protection very expensive), (2) for ITM KOs, giving back your gains	When you expect volatility to: (1) go up in the direction of the strike, (2) go down in the direction of the KO
Sell KOs	Less risk of being exercised, hedger may use to write covered calls Speculator may use to earn income Good for choppy market	Earn less premium than from selling a regular option Since option inexpensive it is difficult to find natural sellers (eg, customer rarely initiates from short side)	When you expect volatility to: (1) go down in the direction of the strike, (2) go up in the direction of the KO
Buy KIs	OTM KIs can be a very cheap way of expressing a path-dependent view ITM KIs cheaper way to buy disaster protection	Difficult to sell to hedger (spends premium without receiving a certain hedge) In case of OTM KIs you have to be right twice: (1) the market quickly moves away from the strike and knocks you in, (2) the market then whipsaws back through the strike	When you expect volatility to go up
Sell KIs	Selling an ITM KI can earn you almost as much as selling the vanilla, with less risk of being exercised (thus good for natural writers of covered calls)	If you get knocked in you take a sudden large hit at once	When you expect volatility to go down

solutions. It is essential to understand and embrace this trade-off before jumping into the exotic options arena.

From a corporate hedging standpoint, normal KOs are the most appealing of the barrier classes. Assuming that the customer is buying the underlying vanilla option for hedging purposes it is clear that when the trigger is reached, the underlying has moved in his way and the protection may no longer be needed. For example, consider a corporate customer who is long Sterling against US$. Say the exchange rate is currently at 1.60 and the client's level of pain on the downside is 1.55. He could buy a three-month UAO Sterling put with the strike at 1.55 and a barrier of 1.70. For the trade to work against the company, Sterling must first rise by 6.25% to trigger the KO and then it must go down 8.82% to reach 1.55. This is some volatility for just three months. In any case, if £/US$ reaches 1.70 the client would be more than happy to sell Sterling at that level so the protection would no longer be necessary anyway. Alternatively, the client could buy at that point a vanilla 1.55 put at what presumably would be a very low cost.

The corporate hedging rationale for the other classes of barriers is not so clear, particularly for reverses that get knocked in or out when the option has intrinsic value. Reverse KIs seem appealing until you realise that the barrier has to be so far ITM to realise meaningful costs savings that the risk of the option to never KI is too great to bear.

We previously said that there are two main reasons to use barrier options as hedging instruments: as cheaper ways to buy protection, and as tailor-made ways of financing (in part or in total) the purchase of protection. Let us analyse this in detail through the use of some examples, both derived from real-life situations taking place in different market contexts.

In the first example, which will give us a clear picture of how employing barrier technology can lower hedging costs for a corporate, we have a Japanese company with a bullish US$/JP¥ three-month view that believes that the US$ will reach a maximum level of around 112, at a time when spot is at 105 and volatility is 12%. This client imports heavily from the US, and would like to hedge its short US$ position. The client approaches their favourite derivatives dealer and asks for the price of a vanilla US$ call/JP¥ put. The

Table 2 How adding barrier options reduces the cost of a hedge

Strategy	Description	Cost (%)
Premium reduction strategies		
1. Vanilla option	Buy three-month 106.25 US$ call	1.82
2. Risk reversal	Buy three-month 106.25 US$ call Sell three-month 99.50 US$ put	1.20
3. Call spread	Buy three-month 106.25 US$ call Sell three-month 112.00 US$ call	1.39
Barrier strategies		
4. US$ call with KO	Buy three-month 106.25 US$ call KO 102.00	1.47
5. Risk reversal with KO	Buy three-month 106.25 US$ call KO 102.00 Sell three-month 99.50 US$ put	0.89
6. KO call spread	Buy three-month 106.25 US$ call KO 102.00 Sell three-month 112.00 US$ call KO 102.00	1.08
7. ITM KO risk reversal	Buy three-month 106.25 US$ call KO 112.00 Sell three-month 99.50 US$ put	Earn 0.28

next day the banker sends the vanilla levels together with a lengthy list of alternatives, as shown in Table 2.

Before analysing the merits of each proposed structure, it is crucial to understand what the client truly wants. In this case, the Japanese importer is looking at obtaining a dollar call struck at 106.25 so as to be protected from any further yen depreciation after that point. One way of making his wish come true is to part with the vanilla premium and simply buy the option. However, this may be considered too expensive. Ideally, the client would like to incur an inferior cost. This desire can be accommodated but only if the company is willing to take on some risk, either through the selling of options to the dealer or through the addition of barrier technology to the purchased option. The value of such risk would be amortised in the form of a cheaper upfront premium. The corporate's cash reserves would now be more plentiful, but its level of risk would be enhanced. As the saying goes, there is no free lunch.

The key, of course, is to decide with risk-reward trade-off makes more sense and is more acceptable.

The vanilla US$ call (1) is the most expensive structure, but also is the most "constraint-free" in the sense that it allows the client to be hedged in an unlimited way from a rising US$ while at the same time not having to give up any bottom line benefits derived from a weaker US$.

The risk reversal strategy (2) costs 62 bps less and provides the same full hedge, but it constrains the bottom line profits if the US$ falls below 99.50.

The call spread (3), on the other hand, eliminates the bottom line constraint embodied by the short put position, but constraints the protection from a rising US$ by capping it at 112. The savings are 43 bps with respect to the vanilla.

To all these three basic structures we can add a barrier feature that would cheapen them all.

For example, the KO call (4) represents savings of 35 bps over the vanilla call. It offers the same hedge from a skyrocketing US$, but of course if the 102 barrier is reached then the hedge disappears.

The risk reversal KO (5) is 31 bps cheaper than its simpler sister, but it also runs the risk of a US$/JP¥ at 102, in which case the client will find themselves not only unhedged but with a short US$ put position at a time when the US$ is going down. Imagine the client's face if the barrier is triggered: "So, I paid 0.89% premium and now I don't own any option but have also given a free option to the bank. Not only I am unprotected from a higher US$, I might have to give up my bottom line profits if the US$ goes down". This example illustrates the controversies that can surround real-life contracts when clients are knocked out of protection.

The KO call spread (6) is 31 bps cheaper than the plain call spread, but if 102 is reached the client is unhedged ("as if the structure had never existed").

A final alternative would be to enter into the KO risk reversal but with the barrier struck ITM (7). In the previous example the barrier was at 102, ie, OTM so that if the client is knocked out it is bad news but not so bad (the protection is lost at a time when there is no immediate need for such protection). However, if we set the barrier at 112 the risk is that the protection will be lost right when it is mostly needed, and the bottom line effects of this could be serious. That is why the new structure not only does not cost anything to the client, but they are the one receiving money. Such is the value of selling an ITM KO feature.

Which structure should be chosen ultimately comes down to a few points.

❏ Is the client willing/able to pay large premiums for protection?

❏ Is the client willing/able to sell options to finance the purchase of protection?

❏ Does the client allow their views to play a part in selecting hedging structures?

❏ Would the client be more comfortable giving up upside protection or downside gain?

❏ Is the client willing to sell KO features?

Obviously, choosing structure (7) requires a treasurer sophisticated enough (and "gutsy" enough) to develop a reasonable view on future US$/JP¥, to be willing to let go some bottom line benefits in case US$ is below 99.50 in exchange for purchasing upside protection, to understand the consequences of breaching the barrier and to be able to react accordingly. In our particular example, the client seemed to believe that the US$/JP¥ would not reach 112 in the next three months. Thus, they could comfortably enter into the ITM KO risk reversal, earn the initial premium and obtain the same hedging benefits as the vanilla call if their views are proven correct. In fact, if during the three-month period US$/JP¥ trades in the 99.50−112 range, the treasurer could proudly boast that they achieved the desired protection and saved the company 210 bps.

The second example involving barrier options focuses on the construction on zero-cost hedges and emphasises more deeply the value to be derived from selling barriers.

Here again we have a Japanese importer of US merchandise, at a time when the spot rate is 125 and volatility is around 16%. The corporate, as in the previous example, would like to hedge its exposure to a higher dollar against the yen. However, crucially, it doesn't want to spend any money whatsoever. For this corporate, a mere reduction of vanilla premium won't do. Only paying no premium will.

What this means is that in this scenario the more structured strategies are to be compared not to the benchmark of the vanilla option but to the benchmark of the (zero-cost) currency forward, which for this three-month exposure was 123.40 (ie, the corporate could fix at this rate the price of buying dollars three months from now). The first structure to consider is the vanilla risk reversal, in this case:

1. buy US$ call JP¥ put K = 130.50 and sell US$ put JP¥ call K = 117, net zero cost;
2. participate in gains from a lower spot rate but caps potential profits below a set level (117);
3. faces losses from a higher spot rate but provides a floor against further potential losses above a known level (130,50).

On top of this basic strategy, let us begin to add some barrier technology:

1. buy US$ call JP¥ put K = 130.50 and sell US$ put JP¥ call K = 118.00 RKI (reverse knock-in) = 113.00, net zero cost;
2. participate in gains down to a set level (113.00) that is better than the vanilla risk reversal cap (117.00) but potential gains are capped at a slightly worse rate (118.00) if 113.00 should trade.

And some more:

1. buy US$ call JP¥ put K = 130.50 and sell US$ put JP¥ call K = 120.00 KO = 127.75, net zero cost;
2. participate in gains from a lower spot rate but caps potential profits below a set level (120.00) that is worse than the vanilla risk reversal cap (117.00), but should the spot rate reach the trigger (127.75) then the cap on any gains disappears completely.

Other possible strategies include the so-called "forward extra":

1. buy US$ call JP¥ put K = 125.00 and sell US$ put JP¥ call K = 125.00 RKI = 113.50, net zero cost;
2. provides a known hedge rate (125.00) slightly worse than the forward rate (123.40);
3. participate in gains from the hedge rate down to a set level (113.50), but should the spot rate trade through this level then the underlying position will be locked into the hedge rate (125.00) with no further opportunity for profit potential.

And the "enhanced forward extra":

1. buy US$ call JP¥ put K = 126.00 KO = 113.50, buy US$ call JP¥ put K = 123.40 KI=113.50, and sell US$ put JP¥ call K = 123.40 RKI = 113.50, net zero cost;
2. provides a known hedge rate (126.00) slightly worse than the Forward Extra hedge rate (125.00);

3. participate in gains from the hedge rate down to a set level (113.50), but should the spot rate trade through this level then the underlying position will be locked into the outright forward rate (123.40), which is better than the hedge rate (126.00), with no further opportunity for profit potential.

In summary, we see how barrier options can be combined in endless ways to provide free (although not riskless), tailor-made and highly flexible protection. No wonder, then, that if there ever was a popularity contest for exotic derivatives among corporate treasurers, barriers would come up as winners by a landslide.

ASIAN OPTIONS

Asian options are those whose payoffs depend on the average value of the underlying during a pre-determined period. There are three main members of the Asian family. Average-rate options (AROs) are those where the strike is fixed, and pre-set and the settlement price at maturity is the average spot level during the totality or a portion of the life of the contract. That is, while for a standard vanilla option the payoff at maturity is the difference between the strike price and the underlying spot price on the expiry date, the payout for an ARO is the difference between the strike price and the average spot level.

Average-strike options (ASOs) are those where the strike is not pre-set and will not be known until maturity, its level being determined by the average spot price. That is, here we have a permutation of the averaging process that allows the buyer to choose to average the strike and not the spot level. The payout for an ASO is the difference between the final spot level and the average spot level.

Double average-rate options (DAROs) combine the characteristic properties of both ARO and ASO. A DARO is thus basically an option that covers the difference between two averages of the same underlying. Each average, of course, refers to different sample periods, and both are unknown by the time the contract is transacted.

Asian options are among the most widely used of all exotic products, particularly when it comes to the corporate arena. However, it is crucial to point out that there exist vast differences in usage intensity between the three major types of Asians. AROs are much more prevalent than ASOs, and DAROs are rarely employed (although they have been adopted by some of the most important multinational corporations, such as Microsoft and McDonald's). Let us try to analyse in following paragraphs how a corporate treasurer could profitably use these tools.

AROs are used almost exclusively as a way to hedge a stream of cashflows. The weighting of the average can be customised to fit the actual stream of cashflows received over time. That is, the ARO can exactly match the actual exposure of a client that does not care about the level of the underlying on specific dates.

For instance, a US importer that has agreed to make several Euro-denominated payments at regular intervals in the near future is exposed to the average of the exchange rates prevalent at each payment period. Such company could purchase an ARO US$ put/€ call to hedge its exposure. Similarly, an airline that has to buy oil every day is exposed to the average daily price of oil for the relevant period. When determining profits for that period, what matters is not so much the price per barrel on a particular day but the average cost that the airline faced. Finally, a Japanese exporter to the US that is concerned with an appreciation of the yen that may lower the base currency value of expected dollar receipts, could also profitably use an ARO. The company estimates 12 monthly sales receipts of US$1 million each for the upcoming year. The target budget exchange rate has been established at 120 yen per dollar. Thus, an ARO JP¥ call/US$ put with a notional value of US$12 million struck at 120 and with monthly fixings could take care of the risk that the exporter faces.

AROs are cheaper than the corresponding European vanilla (because in the case of the former, volatility is smoothed out through the averaging process: also, it is easier to predict an average than a single final spot level), but this doesn't really matter much. The real competitor of an ARO would generally not be a single standard option, as of course the payout profile of both contracts is diametrically opposed. The exposure that would be hedged with an ARO simply cannot be hedged with a regular vanilla.

The real alternative to an ARO as a hedge for a stream of cashflows would be a strip of vanilla options, as many as averaging dates are included in the ARO (daily, weekly, monthly, etc). In the case of the Japanese exporter that was mentioned earlier, instead of going with the ARO the company could have chosen instead to purchase a strip of twelve US$1 million one-month European yen puts all struck at 120. The hedge provided by the strip would be at least as good as that of the US$12 million ARO (net of premium).

Both the ARO and the strip of vanillas present key advantages over the other. The ARO would still be cheaper, since there is a chance that several of the vanillas expire in the money while the average spot level finishes OTM. That is, the strip strategy could very well deliver a payout while the ARO expires worthless. For example, the average JP¥/US$ exchange rate for the one-year period that concerns our Japanese exporter may turn out to be lower than 120 (say, 116). The ARO yen put would have expired OTM. However, given that the exchange rate may have followed a volatile path, some of the vanilla puts could have expired in the red. While the strip would have provided a payout, the ARO would not. The holder of the ARO needs to be initially compensated for this eventuality.

In some texts it is usually inferred that since the ARO is cheaper, it should automatically be chosen over the strip. This, of course, is nonsense. What matters is not the initial relative costs, but the final relative payouts. As we have seen, a key reason why AROs are cheaper is precisely because of the substantial risk that its final payout would pale in comparison to that of the strip. Before choosing between an ARO or a strip, then, a corporate must do a little thinking about the circumstances under which one would outperform the other in the battlefield. Although at initiation the ARO seems to be holding the high ground, nothing guarantees that by the end of the day its flag will still stand tall.

Whether the strip delivers a better gross payout than the ARO or not will be dictated by the path followed by the underlying asset during the life of the transaction. If the treasurer believes that the underlying asset would move in such a way that all the vanilla options expire either OTM or ITM then, from an economic point of view, going with the single ARO would have been the wisest choice as its gross payout would exactly equal that of the family of vanillas while its initial cost was inferior (perhaps by a wide margin). Alternatively, if the view is that the market would experience volatile swings that make some vanilla options expire ITM and others to expire OTM (preferably deeply so) and that it delivers an average spot level at maturity that is only slightly ITM (if at all), then the gross payout of the strip could outperform that of the ARO (which may well be zero) by a margin large enough to cover for the initial difference in premium.

The conclusion is that only if the underlying follows a path that results in some ITM vanilla options and some OTM vanilla options would the strip strategy be more profitable (in net terms) than purchasing the Asian option. The deeper the out-of-the-moneyness is, the greater the advantages of the strip strategy (obviously, starting from an already OTM situation the larger the option is in the red the lower the final average: this will diminish the final payoff of the Asian option while keeping constant that of the strip of vanillas because they were not being exercised for those particular periods in any case). Our Japanese exporter should choose the strip strategy if it believes JP¥/US$ will experience a bumpy ride in the following year that will cause some options to finish ITM and others OTM. It should also choose the strip of vanillas if it believes that most of the time the options will be ITM, even deep ITM, but that for a few periods the options will be deep OTM (this could be a situation where the yen depreciates for most of the year but extremely good news regarding the Japanese economy or renewed concerns regarding the US unsustainable current account deficit prompt the yen to recover spectacularly in the final part of the year).

The company should choose the Asian strategy if it believes that all the options will be either ITM, OTM, at-the-money or there will be a very few exceptions to the trend and very minor in strength (such as the options being OTM for the first 10 months and then turning ITM for the last two months but very slightly so).

In brief, the choice of the optimal hedge would very much depend on the company's view of the path to be taken by the underlying. If it foresees a clear and sustained trend for JP¥/US$ (the yen either clearly appreciating or depreciating), then the Asian structure should emerge as winner. If, on the other hand, it forecasts a volatile bumpy ride full of ups and downs then the strip strategy should be chosen.

What about ASOs? Under which circumstances would a corporate use this type of option? Well, obviously, an ASO allows the end-user to hedge the exposure that the final level of the underlying would be higher (lower) than the average level in the case of a call (put). That is, while ARO users tend to be more concerned with the risk of the average level of the underlying reaching a certain number, ASO users are more concerned with the risk that at maturity the underlying spot level would be different from the underlying average level. Thus, ASOs are ideal for people who have to buy/sell something at some future time and don't want to pay more/receive less than the average price. In that sense, ASO options allow the user to always buy/sell at no more/no less than the average price.

A typical example of the corporate use of ASO is the following: assume a German company that has a manufacturing facility in the US. Each month the plant incurs dollar-denominated expenses of US$1,500,000, which are duly remitted by the parent company (which has to sell euros to buy those dollars). By year-end, a large project should be completed at the US-based plant, resulting in a lump-sum payment of US$24 million. The profit margin in euros is clearly exposed to the exchange rate at the end of each month and, particularly, at the end of the year. More precisely, if by the time the US$24 million are received the dollar has tanked against the euro while having shown strength during the previous monthly intervals, the company's bottom line could suffer a severe blow. The whole American adventure may suddenly look like a failed affair. In order to hedge such unpleasantness, the German corporate should consider buying a one-year US$24 million ASO US$ put/€ call with monthly fixings.

Lastly, a DARO option basically allows the end-user to hedge the gap between two different averages. The payoff formula combines the characteristic (ie, exotic) features of both ARO and ASO options, ie, the strike of a DARO is an average (ASO influence) and the settlement price is also an average (ARO influence). Both averages are calculated using pre-defined (and different) sampling periods.

DAROs are mostly used by multinational corporations wishing to hedge their forex exposure. In particular, DAROs can assist to reduce reported income volatility. Assume a US multinational that wants to ensure that currency movements will not make Q3-2007 results look poor when compared to Q3-2006. The company could purchase a DARO with a strike level based on the average monthly rate for the three months of Q3-2006 that will settle based on the average monthly rate for the three months of Q3-2007. Thus, earnings would be reported on an "equal currency basis" regardless of fluctuations in the forex market. Obviously the option is transacted prior to the end of Q3-2006, otherwise the corporate could just buy a regular ARO with the Q3-2006 known average rate as the fixed strike level. The main rationale for using DAROs as opposed to simply waiting till the strike is known and then purchasing an ARO is the possibility of obtaining a cheaper premium.

DARO are also used to hedge the risks that account receivables might not be collected in the relevant period, but in the following period. For example, a multinational might not collect the money during the month it has been billed but during the following month. This creates a mark-to-market exposure represented by the difference between the accounts receivable on the books, based on the current month's average exchange rate compared to that of the prior month. A DARO can help manage such a risk, by hedging the difference between both averages.

DIGITAL OPTIONS

A digital option (also called "binary") is a bet on the spot level being higher or lower than a certain level at expiration, with the investor being paid a pre-determined fixed amount independent of the magnitude of the difference between spot and strike. For example, someone could enter into a digital call that pays US$1 million in case at maturity Google's stock price is above US$300. The purchaser of the option would receive US$1 million whether Google is trading at US$301, at US$375 or at US$1000. Typical users of digital options are people who are mainly concerned with the underlying reaching some specific level and wish to obtain a large payoff in that situation. They do not care about other levels of the underlying, and thus do not wish to pay for protection/exposure at those points. As binary options give up some upside potential and they deal with low-probability and high-payout situations (thus, eliminating high-probability outcomes) they tend to be cheaper than similar vanilla options. Thus, binary options are suitable for traders who want to make a big bet but don't want to lose much in case they are wrong, and are willing to give up some upside potential gain. They are also used by corporate treasuries wanting to hedge extreme events (eg, a 30% devaluation in the yen) at a reasonable price.

For the purchaser, the major advantage of a digital option is that the payoff is a known constant amount. This amount may be related to some fundamental amount related to the underlying hedging transaction. In addition, it overcomes the problem where the option expires slightly ITM and the resultant payoff does not cover the cost of the option premium paid.

Digitals are also often sold to finance the purchase of other options, since selling these instead of vanilla options allows the end-user to set a maximum loss scenario. This applies particularly well to corporates, which can finance zero-cost hedging structures by taking on limited (or at least acceptable) levels of risk via short digital positions. Similarly, a treasurer can sell digitals as a way to improve the levels of hedges that are already zero-cost, such as swaps. For example, a company that issues fixed-rate debt and then swaps into floating could reduce the spread on its floating leg by selling one or more digital options where the risk is that in case interest rates reach a certain (presumably quite high) strike then the corporate's net financing cost immediately jumps up by a pre-determined amount (say, an extra 1%). If the digital strike(s) is (are) never reached then the structure would have positively delivered reduced financing costs. Otherwise, the corporate would be pena-lised through the addition of a lump-sum amount to the floating rate costs that it faces, precisely at a time when floating rates are on the way up. By setting the digital strike(s) at a historically high level, corporate treasurers could obtain instant financing cost sav-ings while at the same time avoiding excessive worries.

We see why selling digitals would make sense for a corporate. When would buying digitals make sense? Perhaps the two major goals that purchasing binary options can accomplish for a com-pany are, on the one hand, economical and tailor-made disaster protection and, on the other hand, guaranteeing the obtention of a certain exact payout in case the underlying reaches a critical level.

An example of the first type of key application was mentioned earlier. Real estate developers have been known to use deep OTM digitals in order to hedge, at a good price, the contingency of a large currency devaluation. Builders often finance their projects in currencies other than that of the country in which the project takes place. That is, their costs and revenue are denominated in different currency units. This creates a potentially devastating mismatch in case the local unit suffers a large devaluation. This risk may be more acute the less stable the project-hosting nation is. Realtors are not too concerned about currency swings around a modest range (say, 5–10%). These losses can be absorbed and in fact could be considered as part of the normal cost of business. The worries are centered on disaster-like movements, such as a 30% depreciation. Were such scenario to take place, the project may no longer be viable. Under these circumstances, the corporate would need to receive a large compensating lump-sum payment in order to keep things going. A normal vanilla put that paid out the same amount at the digital strike would provide protection against both smaller and larger devaluations. Since the realtor does not care about these devaluations (devaluations below 30% being not deemed a problem, those above 30% being deemed irrelevant as 30% would be damaging enough) they do not want to pay for protection against them. Thus, the vanilla option would fail at addressing the specific needs of the company. The digital, in contrast, would be a perfect solution for its very particular problem.

An example of the other type of key rationale for corporates to purchase digital options is the following. Imagine a Mexican firm that has concluded that if the US dollar appreciates to be worth at least MX$10 pesos in one year, then building a new plant costing MX$1 billion will be a positive Net-Present-Value project (because a cheaper peso would significantly boost exports to the US thus making the business viable).

The company wants to make sure that the money required to build the profitable plant will be available. They could enter into an arrangement today to borrow MX$1 billion. However, borrowing today might be expensive or even impossible. The current credit quality of the company may make external financing unfeasible. The economy may be going through a general credit crunch. International investors could shy away from Mexican risk. The lenders could worry that, having the money, the firm might build the plant even if it is not likely to be profitable. A conditional loan agreement to make the money available next year if the peso depreciates would solve the problem for the lenders. Yet, if the firm faces financial difficulties in one year, the lenders might choose not to fund the plant. In other words, relying on bank financing cannot guarantee for sure that the company would be able to finance the project.

The firm therefore considers taking a derivative position that provides the required funds if the dollar appreciates sufficiently, regardless of its financial condition at that time, the credit appetite of banks or the reputation of emerging markets.

A European call on US$100 million with exercise price of MX$10 could be considered. It only pays-out if the dollar is at least worth MX$10. However, for the firm to get MX$1 billion the exchange rate must be 20. If one year from now US$/MX$ stands at, say, 15 then building the plant would be profitable but the firm won't dispose of the necessary cash. This is a paradox where owning an ITM call not only does not cause gratification to the holder but it could turn out to be a disaster (not being able to finance a profitable business because the company chose the wrong instrument to guarantee the funds). In summary, there is no way that a plain vanilla call will yield with the payoff corresponding exactly to the investment the firm has to make.

The solution to the firm's problems is to use a cash-or-nothing digital call option that pays MX$1 billion if the US dollar exceeds MX$10 in one year.

This example can also be used to analyse the tremendous risks that digital options can pose for the dealers that sell them. In particular, it highlights the difficulties involved in hedging their short positions. Imagine that an instant before maturity the dollar is worth MX$9.9999. The digital option would pay nothing if the price stays the same over the next instant. However, if the dollar rises slightly to MX$10.0001, then the option pays MX$1 billion. In other words, close to the strike very close to expiration the delta of the digital option is huge and dynamically unhedgeable by traders.

LOOKBACK OPTIONS

The payout of a regular lookback option is based on the best prevailing spot level that existed during the life of the option and a strike that is fixed at the beginning of the option.

For instance, imagine a six-month lookback call on Google struck at US$300. At maturity the stock is trading at US$292. OTM blues? Only for vanilla people. In the case of the lookback, what matters is not so much the level of spot at maturity but the most favourable level that spot ever reached during the six-month window. As long as Google traded once above US$300, the lookback would end up ITM and thus deliver a payout. In the case that Google traded above US$300 several times, then the highest of those levels would be picked as the settlement price at expiry. Say that Google caught on bullish fever right after the option was transacted, reaching a peak of US$400 after four months only to embark on a wild descent for the final two months that takes it to the unfortunate US$292 mark. The final payout for the end-user would be US$400 − 300 = US$100, which clearly beats the vanilla alternative (US$0).

One variation from the regular structure is the lookback strike option. This option is settled using the spot level at expiry and the best prevailing spot level that existed during the life of the option for the strike.

Again, let us Google. Now the strike of the call is unknown until the maturity date. Six months from now, the price of the stock is US$292. What do we need for this option to be ITM? Exactly. We would love to have a strike level below US$292 (and as far below as possible, please). So we look at the rear-view mirror and full of hope investigate the path that Google's stock has taken over the last six months. We gladly find that when the contract was initially transacted, Google was going through a lacklustre period (perhaps explained by their scandal-ridden Chinese operations) and was quoting at just US$250. As this is the lowest level that the stock had reached during the relevant period, and since we are talking about a call option, this would be our chosen strike price. Thus, the lookback would deliver a payout equal to US$292 − 250 = US$42.

As the end-user realises the maximum benefit of the spot movement over the life of the option, lookbacks tend to be much more expensive than comparable vanilla options. In a low volatility environment, however, lookbacks can be a good value (since the chance of very favourable spot levels gets reduced). Owing to their character, lookback options are also referred to as "no regrets" or "hindsight" options. They can basically avoid painful moments of reflection dominated by thoughts such as "I should have...", "I could have...", "If only I had...", etc.

The lookback structure is ideal for those who wish to be absolutely certain of the best asset price and are prepared to pay for that right. It is appropriate also for those who believe that there will be a sharp move in the underlying, but are unsure of when and for how long the price will move.

Why would a corporate find lookback options attractive? This is not an easy question to answer. Simply put, not many corporates are likely to have the type of underlying exposure that lookbacks are good at hedging. If a company has clients with contractual obligations that give them the "best price" then obviously lookbacks would be natural hedges for this kind of situation. However, how often do we find such exposures in real life? In fact, several prominent corporate derivatives experts claim to have never in their long careers witnessed the use of lookbacks by a non-financial firm.

Perhaps the major attraction of lookbacks for a treasurer lies in their technical advantages, namely that they provide the capacity to implement a hedge that once established will always perform optimally. All hedges require a certain degree of continuous management. The value-added of the lookback option is that it structurally eliminates the need for this. The purchaser is always guaranteed optimal performance, thereby eliminating the risk of errors in timing entry into particular option strategies. In essence, the lookback allows one to always buy at the cheapest possible price and sell at the highest possible price. Before we saw how the lookback-strike call allowed us to effectively buy Google stock for only US$250, rather than the US$292 level quoting at maturity. Similarly, a lookback-strike put would have allowed us to sell at the peak-establishing price of US$400, again much better than US$292. The key, of course, is whether such superior gains justify the superior premium paid for the privilege to look back.

A lookback option could be marketed over a vanilla option as one where the chances of being considered a "wasteful contract" by corporate executives would be drastically diminished. If the exposure being hedged is a sale/purchase taking place at maturity and by that time the underlying has moved in the company's favour and the option thus expires worthless, the whole hedging option may be considered a fancy way of throwing valuable cash down the drain. Were the spot to embark on a sustained positive trend and force a series of vanilla covers to never deliver a payoff, the treasurer who put them in place might have to answer to his concerned superiors. A lookback option, by almost certainly guaranteeing a final payoff (although perhaps not a net payoff, after the high premium is taken into account) could in this sense free the treasurer from those stress-inducing eventualities. His hedges would, after all, deliver a payout with remarkable consistency.

Another possible advantage of using lookbacks is that they could end up delivering the same protection as a vanilla but at a cheaper cost. That is, buying a lookback could be seen as a way of obtaining a free (or almost free) vanilla hedge. Assume a company that is exposed to the Japanese yen going up six months from now. If at expiry the US$ is worth less than JP¥105, the corporate gets hurt. One straightforward hedge is to purchase a plain vanilla US$ put/JP¥ call struck at 105. Alternatively, one could buy a lookback put where the settlement price at maturity would be the lowest level that the dollar has achieved in the six months period. If the dollar tanks well in advance of expiration (say, go to 95), then the payoff from the lookback may be large enough to cover both the lookback premium and the payout that would have derived from the vanilla put (if any). This way, vanilla protection (the vanilla payout) would have been delivered free of charge (or, more precisely, with the initial cost entirely reimbursed at expiry).

Lookback options are possibly more of a competitor to Asian options than to vanilla options when it comes to winning the hearts of corporate risk managers (after all, they are both members of the path-dependent family). Given that Asian options are even cheaper than vanilla, the relative costliness of lookbacks is dramatically intensified. In this light, convincing a corporate to use a lookback rather than an Asian becomes more difficult. However, still it is possible to think of ways in which a lookback could be quite attractive, in spite of the price. For instance, let us consider the case of a company that gradually purchases a particular type of asset or commodity (paid for in foreign currency) with the purpose of then selling those purchases at a pre-set future date. The company is exposed to the average cost of the asset or commodity, rather than a single spot level. Thus, a vanilla option would not be appropriate. An ASO put would be a better fit, with the strike price being determined by the average cost incurred during the purchase period. On expiry date, the corporate would sell at the then current spot price. The ASO would cover the risk that the sale price falls below the average cost (both expressed in the same currency). By guaranteeing that the price charged to customers is never below the relevant average purchase price, the company is basically making sure that it never suffers a loss.

Using a lookback-strike put could afford the corporate even more sunshine. Since it can safely be assumed that the highest purchase price would always be above the average purchase price, the (gross) payout from the lookback put would be higher than that from the ASO counterpart. In other words, while the ASO would guarantee the absence of losses, the lookback would guarantee the presence of profits. Of course, these are gross results. Once the premiums are deducted the strategies, in particular the latter, may appear less attractive. However, in principle, it can be argued that a possible rationale for using lookback options in a corporate environment is that they may help guarantee the existence of profits as part of a commercial transaction.

The main idea is that a lookback would almost certainly always outperform an Asian in gross terms given that the maximum/minimum level of the underlying is bound to be superior/inferior to the average level (this is not necessarily the case when it comes to vanilla options: the gross payout of a vanilla and a regular lookback could very well end up being the same if the underlying is experiencing a substantial rally or decline by maturity date). Thus, a corporate that wants to outperform the Asian hedge would be interested in using lookbacks. Another possible application concerns the quarterly translation of net foreign income into consolidated earnings. This is usually done by using the average daily exchange rate during the quarter. An ARO put on the foreign currency (with the strike set at the firm's budget forex rate) is the natural hedge for this exposure. A lookback would likely deliver an enhanced payout and thus possibly improve the corporate's reported results.

Finally, lookbacks may be helpful for those treasurers who would like to protect themselves from forecasted temporary extreme movements in the underlying. Let us illustrate with an example. A US company that exports heavily, continuously and somewhat randomly to Japan is concerned that the dollar might appreciate against the yen, thus potentially harming its price-sensitive business. The company ships right after an order is received and receives payment via bank transfer one week after shipment. Thus, any yen depreciation is immediately felt. The company estimates that its volume of exports is relatively safe as long as the dollar does not go above 120 on average, and, crucially, there are no big spikes in the interim. While any dollar strengthening is bad news, the company believes that levels above 135 would be disastrous since at that point all sales would cease. Demand from Japanese customers would suddenly stop, as at that forex rate they would be exceeding the maximum local currency-denominated price limit that their domestic market accepts. These customers may be willing to sell the products to their domestic clients at ever tighter margins as the dollar goes up, so as to keep their good image and reputation ("you don't sell this item?"), but they surely won't sell any longer if the price of ongoing activity is negative profits. In a way, then, the demand from these Japanese firms is somewhat digital: a slow drop in purchases up to US$/JP¥ = 135, after which point all purchases dry up.

For the American exporter, buying an ARO dollar call struck at 120 may be irremediably risky. The option could very well end up OTM, with lower rates compensating higher rates. This may be all right if the currency rate has been trading inside a decently narrow upside band (with the yen never reaching, say, 127). However, if the dollar happened to surpass the 135 deadly mark, then the exporter would have suffered a decisive bottom line blow (zero exports for what could have been a long time) without eventually receiving any derivative-related compensation.

Clearly, were the American firm to believe that a drastic dollar rise was in the horizon it would most likely decide not to enter into the ARO. Lookback technology could be appropriate, though. By entering into a so-called lookback Asian call, the exporter would be entitled to select at maturity the most favourable average (on a rolling basis) for settlement purposes; ie, the highest average. In the eventuality that the yen does dive all the way to 135 and beyond, it is likely that this would be reflected in a highest average well above the 120 strike, thus guaranteeing the end-user a much-needed final payout.

Given the high cost of lookbacks, a number of structures have been developed that seek to use the advantages of path dependency and extend it to provide many of the benefits but with a lower cost. These structures include Ladder options (the strike periodically resets when the price of the underlying trades through pre-specified levels), Cliquet or Ratchet options (conceptually very similar to ladders) and Shout options (the purchaser has the right to lock-in a minimum payout from the option, while retaining the right to gain from further favourable movements in the underlying). All these structures could be put to use in a corporate setting.

Let us analyse a possible corporate application of shout options. Consider a German importer of basketball merchandise from the US. The European company wants to limit its exposure to a weaker euro (stronger dollar) over the next three months. In truth, it wants to do more than that: it actually would like to obtain the best possible rate during the period. Buying a lookback is considered, but the treasurer sees the premium as too high. In light of this tight-pocketedness, the treasurer's favourite derivatives dealers offers what looks like a more suitable alternative: to purchase, at a cheaper price, a shout US$ call/€ put struck at US$1.20. The German treasurer complies, and the shout option is transacted. One month into the trade, the euro has descended into an exchange rate of US$1.14. Not believing that the euro could sink further, the treasurer "shouts". What this means is that the treasurer ensures a final payout at expiry of US$120–1.14 = US$0.06. That is, moneyness has been locked-in and at a level that seems optimal. The next two months would be spent in a relaxed mood, confident that an acceptable degree of protection has been achieved and hopeful that an improvement could be obtained if the market swings in the right direction. If at maturity the dollar has strengthened beyond US$1.14, then the importer would enjoy that better level as the settlement price. For instance, if the currency trades at US$1.11 then the payoff from the shout put would be US$1.20 – 1.11 = US$0.09.

On the other hand, were the dollar to quote weaker than US$1.14 at expiration there would be no last-minute improvement to the previously locked US$0.06 payout. If the currency trades at US$1.22 then the payoff from the shout would be US$1.2 0 − 1.14 = US$0.06.

We see that a shout option can present highly desirable features. As with a lookback, it can offer a way to improve vanilla and Asian protection. There is even a chance that it delivers the same protection as the costlier lookback, provided that the end-user perfectly times the shouting point. However, it must be obvious that the probability of outperformance is, in the absence of perfect forecasting powers on the part of end-users, much more remote than in the case of lookbacks. In essence, a lookback allows for plenty of shouting rather than a one-time outburst. This limitation to free speech is, of course, what makes the shout option cheaper.

In principle, the sales pitch of shout contracts to corporate treasurers has a nice ring to it. Here would be a hedge that promises a minimum guaranteed level of protection that could be bettered at maturity.

Having said that, shouts present a major drawback that may drive treasurers away. With a shout, as opposed to a lookback, there is a need for continuous monitoring. End-users must be constantly alert, constantly on the lookout, constantly thinking about possible future movements in the underlying. Will the dollar go up or down? Will it go above today's level? Is this a maximum? A minimum? What do the latest Wall Street reports have to say? I feel like shouting, should I? Did I miss a once-in-a-lifetime chance by not shouting a week ago? Will I be judged a poor trend-spotter? Can I get forex news on my BlackBerry?

In summary, the shout could end up requiring too much time and inducing too much stress. Faced with the prospects of sleepless nights and nail-biting working hours, many treasurers may simply decide that paying the extra cash for a lookback or going plan-vanilla would be the sensible things to do.

To conclude this section on lookbacks, let us do some comparative analysis. As has been repeatedly said in previous paragraphs, lookback options compete with standard vanilla options and Asian options as hedging instruments. A famous case study highlighting the comparative performance of lookback-strike options, European vanillas and AROs was conducted by Leland, O'Brien Rubinstein Associates using the US$/£ exchange rate as underlying, during the period from 2nd January 1989 to 29th June 1990. Tables 3 and 4 display the data used in the analysis, and the net profits obtained. All values for options represent the annual purchase of an option on £100.

During the first period, the exchange rate fell constantly (ie, the dollar strengthened), the maximum rate was obtained on 3rd January, the minimum rate on 14th June and with the average rate ending above the final rate at maturity. Over this market scenario, the holders of the vanilla and Asian call options lost their entire premium. However, because the dollar weakened during the last two weeks the lookback call retained 40% of its initial premium.

While this period clearly favoured put holders, the lookback put (which had the highest final payout) did not experience as big a

Table 3 Comparison analysis between European, Asian, and Lookback (LOR Associates 1990)

Period	2nd January–29th June 1989	29th June–29th December 1989	29th December 1989–29th June 1990
Starting rate	1.8085	1.5490	1.6145
Ending rate	1.5490	1.6145	1.7450
Average rate	1.6870	1.5910	1.6650
Strike rate	1.8085	1.5490	1.6145
Volatility (%)	10.7300	12.6500	7.8200
US interest (%)	9.3750	9.0625	8.1875
UK interest (%)	13.1250	14.1875	14.9375

Table 4 Comparison analysis between European, Asian, and Lookback (LOR Associates 1990) (continued)

Period	European call	European put	Lookback call	Lookback put	Asian call	Asian put
2nd January–29th June 1989						
Option cost (US$)	3.85	6.69	8.72	12.04	2.31	3.74
Final pay-out (US$)	0	25.95	3.45	27.35	0	12.15
Net profit (%)	−100	288	−60.4	127.2	−100	225
29th June–29th December 1989						
Option cost (US$)	3.72	7.08	8.6	12.54	2.24	3.94
Final pay-out (US$)	6.55	0	7.7	5.15	4.2	0
Net profit (%)	76.2	−100	−10.5	−58.9	87.3	−100
29th December 1989–29th June 1990						
Option cost (US$)	1.55	6.17	4.65	9.5	1.01	3.33
Final pay-out (US$)	13.05	0	15.05	0	5.05	0
Net profit (%)	740.1	−100	223.8	−100	399.6	−100

percentage gain as the vanilla puts. With only one day's rate exceeding the initial rate, the lookback feature provides a final pay-off that is only US$1.40 higher than the vanilla. This is not enough to offset the US$5.35 higher premium cost of the lookback.

During the second period from 29th June to 29th December 1989 the highest volatility was witnessed, with no clear trend emerging after an early initial rise in the exchange rate. The rate hit its peak almost in the middle of the period. The final rate settled narrowly above the average for the period. This period provided a solid return to the buyers of calls. Once again, the lookback suffered from the minimum experienced asset value being insufficiently lower than the vanilla strike to offset its higher premium costs. The best result was obtained by the Asian option because of the lower initial cost.

The third and last period was the least volatile, with a strong upward trend in the exchange rate. All of the call buyers received excellent returns. The period was interesting in that the last day established a new high for the underlying. This had the effect not only of making the lookback put expire worthless but also of making the final delta zero. This can only happen to the lookback put (call) if the last value establishes a new high (low).

The conclusion of the case study is that the results are highly dependent on the dates selected. However they do highlight the fact that, while the lookback clearly tends to outperform in terms of final payouts, its much higher cost makes it very challenging to outperform on a net basis. The lookback would be relatively very beneficial in those situations where extreme high and low values are experienced prior to maturity.

CHOOSER OPTIONS

A chooser option is a vanilla option with the added feature that on a predetermined future date the holder can choose whether the option is a put or a call. Once the choice has been made the option acts just like a single vanilla option. Under standard chooser options the call and the put have identical strikes and expiration dates; more complex choosers present different strikes and expiries.

For example, one could enter into a Google chooser today with a choice date three months from now and an expiration date six months later. The end-user would be entitled on choice date to select between a three-month US$300 Google vanilla call and a three-month US$300 Google vanilla put. Depending on the value of Google stock on choice date (and on future perspectives or priorities), either the call or the put would be selected.

Chooser options allow the benefits of hedging against both price increases and decreases without having to purchase both a call and a put (ie, a straddle). This increased flexibility explains why choosers are more expensive than standard options. On the other hand, a chooser will always be cheaper than a straddle. Although buying a chooser option shares many similarities with buying a straddle (simultaneous purchase of put and call, bet on high volatility), after the choice is made the holder only owns one type of option whereas the holder of the straddle continues to have both up to maturity. At the same time, with the chooser the buyer runs the risk of "choosing wrongly", ie, selecting the option that eventually expires OTM (because the underlying moved against you between choice date and maturity date). In the case of a straddle (where both strike levels are identical), you are almost certainly guaranteed a payout irrespective of the final level of spot. Such relative superiority must obviously cost more.

The major potential for corporate use of chooser options is in hedging the following circumstances:

❑ conditions of extreme volatility in asset prices;
❑ when the direction of the exposure is unknown.

The use of chooser options to hedge against extreme volatility is reflected by the fact that these instruments first gained in popularity during the early-1991 Gulf conflict (although they seem to have been already in use prior to the Gulf War; apparently the first choosers were traded in 1990, all by Bankers Trust in London). During that period, both oil producers and purchasers utilised chooser structures to hedge against the extremely volatile conditions prevailing in the market for crude oil. Simply put, it wasn't exactly easy to predict whether oil prices would go up or down in the near future. This uncertainty set the perfect conditions for a choosers-friendly environment: a very popular underlying was suddenly exposed to a situation that promised very high volatility, but without pointing to any particular direction and with both outcomes (low prices/high prices) equally likely. At the time most people assumed a long and hard-fought war given the (assumed) might of Saddam Hussein's army and that the US did not have a lot of experience fighting in the desert. Hence, very high oil prices for a sustained period of time became a possibility. On the other hand, a fast US victory was of course always possible too. Under this scenario, oil prices would most likely quickly revert back to pre-war levels.

An oil purchaser, worried that the sharp jump in prices that took place right after Iraq's invasion of Kuwait in August 1990 may perpetuate itself in the face of a prolonged military showdown, would obviously want to buy upside protection. Let us analyse for instance the case of an airline. From the point of view of the airline, its concern was of course whether the price of oil would jump to the stratosphere as a result of the war. To hedge this risk it could buy an oil call. However, as we have already said, there was a very decent probability that the call might not be needed at all and that the (high) premium would have been entirely wasted. What if, for a little extra premium, the company could purchase the option to own a put in case oil prices eventually went down? The gain on the put could be then seen as a way to "pay" for the chooser (self-financing structure).

In brief, the chooser was an optimal strategy in a situation where the company was exposed to the risk of very high prices but with a high probability of such event not happening. Under these circumstances the probability that the pricey call premium would be wasted was quite high. A chooser option could correct for this by delivering a positive payoff in case the call option turned out not to be needed at all.

An example of a situation where the direction of the underlying exposure is unknown is a company that invests in a foreign location. The firm, when seeking to hedge its currency risk, must know the economic outcome of the venture; ie, whether it would be profitable or loss making (if there are profits then the company is long the currency, if there are losses it is short). Under these circumstances the company could use a chooser option on the currency as a hedge against changes in the value of the investment.

A third possible corporate application of chooser options is in those situations where a company has exposures to a particular underlying that go in both directions; ie, the company is both long and short the underlying. For instance, a corporate may export to a particular country from its home base, and at the same time could have manufacturing activities based in that same country. Its exporter status makes the firm long the foreign currency (the cheaper the base currency the more chances of enhanced business activity), while its manufacturer status makes it short the currency (so as to keep costs as low as possible). While the corporate would have calculated an amount of expected net exposure based on forecasted sales and production outsourced, as well as on the budget exchange rate, which allows it to claim a one-direction-only initial exposure (ie, either net long or net short), it is clear that such fore-casts may turn out to be wrong. Sales in a highly priced item may result much higher than previously imagined; sales in a lowly priced item much lower; the amount of outsourced production may be projected to be less significant than anticipated. These events might transform the company's net exposure to the foreign currency from short to long. That is, a put, not a call, would now be the most appropriate hedge. Having bought a chooser option at ini-tiation would allow the corporate to adjust its hedge by choice date according to the new prevailing realities.

COMPOUND OPTIONS

A compound option, also known as "mother and daughter" option, is an option on another option (or structure). Compound options give the holder the right, but not the obligation, to buy or to sell a call, a put or a structure (such as a risk reversal) at a predetermined price (compound strike) on a pre-determined future date (com-pound maturity). The holder pays for this right upfront and decides whether to exercise his right and pay the compound strike on the compound maturity date. The end-user can choose how much money they want to pay upfront for the compound option, and that will determine the size of the compound strike at com-pound maturity (this decision would most likely depend on how certain the user is regarding the potential need for the hedge; the less certain that need looks, the smaller the initial premium that the end-user would want to part with). This calculation is not symmet-rical: a decrease in the amount of upfront payment by x will have to be matched by an increase in the compound strike of more than x. The upfront compound premium plus the compound strike will always total more than the price of buying the vanilla option today. This is because the compound option gives more flexibility than the vanilla and the underlying is more sensitive to volatility.

Compound options are often used by people who don't know whether a hedge will be required in the future, and do not want to spend a lot of money until the necessity of the hedge has been con-firmed. That is, while in the case of chooser options the existence of an exposure is certain and only its direction is unknown, in the case of compounds the mere existence of an exposure is in doubt.

In order to clarify things, let us take a look at the following compound structure that was shown by bankers to corporate clients in late 2005:

❑ buy a three-month call on a €10,000,000 three-month € put/US$ call strike 1.26 compound strike US$250,000;
❑ initial premium US$145,000;
❑ pemium for €10,000,000 six-month € put/US$ call strike 1.26: US$320,000.

Here a treasurer could obtain the right, but not the obligation, to buy the euro put three months into the future. The treasurer has to pay US$145,000 upfront, which is far cheaper than the cost of the six-month put. If the treasurer eventually decides to buy the put (because his potential short euro exposure has materialised and, crucially, because the compound strike is lower than the market value of the put at expiration) they must put up an extra US$250,000. This would take the total cost of the strategy to US$395,000, more than the US$320,000 premium for the six-month vanilla. However, this extra real cost of US$75,000 might be worthy insurance against the possibility of having incurred opportunity costs of US$320,000 because the hedge turned out not to be needed after all.

Which are some typical corporate applications of compounds? Compound options are particularly common in M&A transactions, where a company has a certain exposure contingent on a deal being closed. The corporate wants some sort of protection now, but does not want to pay the full upfront cost for a vanilla option lest the contingent deal subsequently falls through.

Another straightforward application of compound options involves bidding contracts. This can be highlighted with the following example. A German construction company is bidding on a contract in the US and will only find out in six months whether it has received the contract or not. Should the company receive the contract, it will receive US$30 million 12 months from contract day for the completion of the contract. If the company does not hedge its possible dollar exposure, it leaves itself open to the possibility of a lower US$/€ rate. The company could hedge this risk by purchasing a call option on a dollar put option. This gives the company the right in six months to buy a 12-month dollar put for a pre-arranged premium.

If the German firm does get the contract and the dollar put has risen in value (for whatever reasons), then the compound call would be exercised and the company would become the proud owner of a US$30 million 12-month put. Alternatively, if the put has decreased in value, then the compound call would not be exercised and instead the company would go into the market and purchase the put at the new, lower premium.

If the German firm is not awarded the contract, it would obviously not need the hedge. However, it may still make sense to exercise the compound call and pay the compound strike in case that it expires ITM, since the 12-month put could then be profitably sold in the market.

Compound options can also add value to corporates involved in interest rate risk management. The raising of a significant amount of financing may depend on a certain event taking place in the near future, and the company might want to pre-hedge the potential interest rate exposure now. A commonly employed strategy for this type of situations is the purchase of a swaption (ie, an option to enter into a swap in the future, either as fixed rate payer or receiver). However, this contract requires full premium payment upfront, and this may be substantial. If the option expires OTM (if the agreed-upon swap has negative market value for the corporate), then the whole premium would be lost. Also, interest rate swaps may not be every treasurer's cup of tea when it comes to hedging. For those who look suspiciously at swaptions, a suitable alternative is available courtesy of the compound family. So-called "captions", or options on interest rate caps, allow corporate treasurers to guarantee the presence of a hedge in the contingency that one is eventually needed, in exchange for a small initial premium.

Imagine a corporate that has been promised a large syndicated loan provided that its external credit rating is enhanced to investment grade status. The decision by the major rating agencies is due in three months. The loan would have a maturity of five years. The company could simply purchase a five-year cap with start date three months from now. However, this would be expensive and in case the rating is finally not improved there would be no need for a hedge. The corporate would own a long-dated interest rate cap without having any underlying exposure. That is, the cap would no longer be a risk management tool (as initially intended) but a purely speculative position (a bet on short-term rates rising above the strike). Since it doesn't seem likely that any corporate would want to play that game, the cap would have to be sold into the market just three months after it was bought. The price obtained from such sale could very well be smaller than the premium originally paid.

Another alternative is for the company to wait until a decision has been reached by the agencies, and only buy the cap if the news is positive and the loan is disbursed. The problem with this approach is that, three months from now, caps may have drastically increased in value (due to a sharp steepening of the forward curve or a jump in volatility) making the hedge dangerously uneconomical.

A caption (call on a cap, in this case) would overcome all the obstacles described above. The initial disbursement would be modest. The extra payment would only be made if the hedge is needed. Crucially, because a cap is a collection of options, or caplets, the possibility that the compound would outperform the vanilla from a cost point of view is enhanced. In the caption, the payment of the agreed extra premium (the compound strike) would take place on each particular caplet (pro rata) only if that caplet expires ITM. In contrast, the vanilla cap is paid in full upfront, irrespective of how many individual caplets eventually end up ITM. What this means is that if not a lot of caplets expire in the red, the total final premium that would have been paid as part of the caption could very well result lower than the vanilla premium. Only if interest rates rise and all or most of the caplets are exercised would the compound strategy result be costlier.

A compound option can also be sold to raise premium for a hedging strategy. In this case, the underlying option of the compound is still considered to be an acceptable hedging level by the client, and they are, therefore, willing to risk being exercised. The attraction of selling compounds as opposed to selling vanilla options is that the company would receive premium money even if the counterparty does not exercise the compound option (ie, money with no risk strings attached). Also, if exercise does take place, the total premium money received would be larger than what would have been obtained from the sale of the vanilla (ie, more money for the same kind of risk).

Finally, a variation of the compound option structure is the instalment option (often referred as the deferred-premium or pay-as-you-go option). As the name suggests, this structure entails an option whose premiums are paid in instalments at regular intervals. If the end-user decides not to continue paying (for whatever reason), the contract will be cancelled. The advantage to the purchaser is that it facilitates a decision to abandon the option and cut the total premium cost at each instalment date. This contract could be used by a corporate involved in a multi-stage tender, or when hedging interest rate exposures that may have a shorter life than previously expected. Let us take a look at an example of the latter, drawing on a real-life structure from late 2005:

❑ buy a US$10,000,000 five-year instalment cap on three-month US Libor strike 5%;
❑ lock-out provision – one year (must keep the hedge on for at least one year);
❑ premium – US$13,750 per quarter, or 55 bps running (US$10,000,000 $\times$ 0.55% $\times$ 90/365);
❑ premium for equivalent vanilla cap – US$195,000.

This structure could be useful for a corporate that has just received a large floating-rate syndicated loan but that plans an IPO in the next 2–3 years, in which case part of the proceeds would be utilised to cancel the loan early. Under such scenario, the outstanding cap would no longer be necessary as there would no longer be a corresponding liability to cover. The long cap position, of course, could be immediately unwound following the debt repayment (ie, the cap could be sold in the market). However, this would be risky. The price to be received would most certainly be lower than the initial premium paid (if only because of foregone time value), and could be substantially so if the market has moved against the cap (either because of a flattened forward curve, plummeting volatility or both).

The instalment cap would allow the corporate to deal with this situation. If the IPO does go through and the loan is fully repaid the next scheduled payment will simply not be made, implying the termination of the hedge. The flip side is that if the IPO is cancelled and the cap is needed all the way till maturity, the final total premium under the instalment strategy (US$275,000) would be more expensive than if the company had opted for the vanilla cap from the start.

CONTINGENT-PREMIUM OPTIONS

A contingent-premium option (CPO) is an option transaction where the premium is not payable at commencement. The premium is only payable at maturity conditional on the option expiring ITM. If the option is not exercised no premium shall be payable. This structure is also known as cash-on-delivery option, money-back option and refundable-premium option. In a way, this option allows the end-user to "borrow" the premium for the vanilla contract from his future payout, whether it eventually exists or not.

The principal attraction of the CPO is that it enables the purchaser not to pay for the option in the case it expires OTM. However, the contingent nature of the premium payment dictates that a CPO is more expensive than a conventional option. The key dynamic that makes the CPO more expensive is the fact that the writer incurs the hedging costs while at the same time running the risk of never recovering those costs if the option is not exercised. This implies that the option has to expire deeper ITM to cover for the higher premium. Thus, the CPO is mostly appropriate for those wishing insurance against large one-way price movements at no initial cost.

The primary risk for the purchaser of a CPO is that the underlying asset price movement is such that the option expires slightly ITM but insufficiently to recover the high premium payable.

It is interesting to note that in the case of a CPO, the writer has an interest in the option expiring ITM (otherwise they won't collect any premium). Also interesting is the fact that an OTM option could be more expensive than an ITM option, reflecting the lower probability that the option writer will receive the premium.

What is the biggest appeal of a CPO for corporate treasurers? Plainly put, that they only have to pay if the option "works", if it delivers, if it is necessary, if it helps, if it's not a complete waste of time. In a slightly far-fetched simile, one could argue that while vanilla options resemble a bureaucrat (who gets paid independent of the quality of his work, if any), a CPO resembles a commissions-earning salesman (who gets paid only if they produces tangible results). In addition, as the salesman has the potential of making much more money than the bureaucrat, a CPO should be more expensive than their vanilla counterparts. Productivity is thus rewarded.

Corporates don't like paying for protection, and they definitely don't like wasting the spent cash in case protection was in the end not needed. A time-honoured tradition has been to fully finance the protection premium by selling an option (or combination of options) to the dealer. However, this creates several problems. The most obvious is that the corporate would be limiting the amount of possible gains in case that the underlying moves its way. In a typical example, a foreign exchange put is sold to finance the purchase of a currency call. If the sold put expires deep ITM, the company would have incurred very significant costs. This is as bad (if not worse) as having to pay upfront premium for protection.

The aims of CPO are truly revolutionary. The goal is to completely do away with those archaic traditions and to impose a new order. No more dangerous selling of havoc-wreaking options. No more nightmare-inducing collar structures. With a CPO the maximum loss is pre-set, and in any case will always be less than that because of the ITM cushion. So the advantages of CPO over traditional collars are clear-cut: same upside protection, no downside risk, and potential losses are capped and cushioned (maybe even into oblivion). The advantages of a CPO over single purchased vanillas can also be quite tempting: no upfront payment (ie, no need to have the cash on hand or spend it somewhere else), and pay only if the option is a winner.

BASKET OPTIONS

The payout of a basket option is similar to that of a vanilla option, except that it is based on the weighted sum of two or more assets or indexes rather than a single index or a single asset. The strike and settlement prices of the basket are given in terms of the net weighted sum of the assets. It follows, therefore, that the basket option earns a return based on how much the weighted sum basket spot level outperforms the weighted sum basket strike.

Basket options hedge a group of exposures from different assets or indexes in one option structure. This is simpler and easier to manage than buying the individual options.

The price of a basket option, by definition, cannot exceed the sum of the prices of the individual vanilla options. In addition, the payout of the basket can also not exceed the sum of the payouts of the individual vanillas.

In fact, basket options are cheaper than the sum of corresponding vanillas. In principle, this could be surprising as we have already seen that baskets have the added advantage of increased flexibility and ease of handling. The reason why baskets are cheaper is that the end-user might lose out on potential gains that they would have obtained had they chosen to opt for the group of vanillas. For example, imagine a US corporate that sells overseas and wants to hedge its euro, yen, and peso exposures. The corporate buys a basket put on the weighted sum of those three underlyings. Now suppose that, while the yen has tanked over the relevant period, the euro and the peso have actually appreciated. The payout to be received from the basket would be modest but in truth the firm would have incurred significant foreign exchange losses in its bottom line due to the adverse (and, in the end, quite unhedged) yen movements.

In other words, in the case of baskets when one or more of the underlyings moves in the company's favour, that is when the individual vanilla option would have ended out of the money, the end-user has to endure a negative payoff in the percentage of notional allocated to that particular underlying(s) (in the case of individual vanillas, the options would not have been exercised in the first place). These negative partial payoffs deduct from the possible partial positive payoffs incurred by those underlyings where the market has moved against the company (ie, the cases when the vanilla options would have ended in the money). The end result is that the company could end up with a hedge that is worse (maybe even much worse) than if he had opted for the group of vanillas.

Let us illustrate this key idea with an example: a US corporate wants to hedge flows in £, NZ$, and AU$ that it will receive in one year. At the insistence of his derivatives providers, the treasurer buys a Basket put/US$ call with the following parameters:

1. spot references – £/US$1.60, NZ$/US$0.50, AU$/US$0.60;
2. basket components – £62,500,000, NZ$200,000,000, AU$166,670, 000;
3. Basket/US$ spot rate – (62,500,000 × 1.60) + (200.00 × 0.50) + (166.76 × 0.60) = 300,000,000 (US$300,000,000 per "Basket unit");
4. strike – 300,000,000 (at the money spot).

At expiry of the option one year later:

1) spot references – £/US$1.70, NZ$/US$0.45, AU$/US$0.55;

2. Basket/US$ spot rate – $(62,500,000 \times 1.70) + (200.00 \times 0.45) + (166.76 \times 0.55) = 287,916,667$;
3. payoff: $(300,000,000 - 287,916,667) = 12,083,333$.

In contrast, the payout from the alternative strip of vanilla options would have been:

1. $62,500,000 \times 0 + 200,000,000 \times (0.50 - 0.45) + 166,760,000 \times (0.60 - 0.55) = 18,333,333$ as the £/US$ expires out of the money.

Thus, we clearly see how the payout of the basket can be inferior to the payout from the vanillas.

What all this implies is that correlation between the different underlyings becomes a key factor in determining the price of basket options and its cheapness in relation to a group of vanillas.

If the correlation between the individual components of the basket is low or negative, then the basket option can afford a hedger with an attractive way to buy a portfolio of hedges (the basket would have to be quite cheap to compensate for the fact that some underlyings would end up with a negative payoff while others end up with a positive payoff). If, on the other hand, the components of the basket are highly correlated the basket option will cost almost as much as the sum of individual vanillas.

We see that basket options offer two key advantages to corporate treasurers: the possibility of a much cheaper premium than the corresponding portfolio of vanillas, and the simplicity implied by not having to manage a large number of individual options.

With regards to the first point, typically deals are struck when a company can cut its premium paid by at least 20% *versus* the cost of buying a basket of options on each currency exposure. The trades, while relatively infrequent, are often huge, from US$100 million to US$1 billion, as treasurers take care of their entire hedging needs for the year in one stroke.

With regards to the second advantage of baskets, simplicity may be the most attractive feature for treasurers. The company essentially dumps its whole forex exposures on the dealer, and says, "You figure it out, and you take the risk".

Currency basket options used by corporates come in two principal types. Long-only or short-only basket options, which have been around for a decade, are used to cover a portfolio of 10 different currencies that are all long the dollar, or all short the dollar. A likely user of long-only baskets would be a pharmaceutical or petrochemical company that manufactures in one country and sells around the world.

The other type, long/short basket options or spread options, include both long and short positions. They may combine, for example, a long JP¥/US$ position and a short €/US$ position. Likely users of long/short baskets are automobile, consumer goods and computer companies that manufacture and sell all over the world. These basket options are a much more recent phenomenon, in good part because their complex analytics require enormous processing power.

In spite of the value that basket options can provide, it seems that their embracing by corporates has not been as widespread as might have been expected. Some companies find that they would not save much from buying basket options, because most of their exposures are long positions in highly correlated currencies. For others, basket options could provide exact matches on their exposures and decent premium savings, but they find that they are hard to mark-to-market. However, the most likely reason why corporates decide to opt out of basket territory is the possibility that the final cover would be ineffective and that large opportunity costs are incurred. We saw earlier how the final payout of the basket would be negatively affected if one or more of the underlying currencies goes the corporate's way. In those circumstances, the cheaper premium might not be enough to compensate for the payout gap with regards to the vanilla portfolio. In a sense, when a corporate enters into a basket option it is exposing itself to the same problem that those companies that hedge only with forwards: you are protected on the downside, but miss out when the currency moves in your favour. The reluctance to give up significant upside gains has prompted several corporates (among them Microsoft) to temporarily abandon the use of basket technology.

The paradox of basket options is that the very factor that makes them desirable (ie, the low or negative correlation among the basket components that produces an economical premium) could render the whole thing useless. For baskets to work, you need to find uncorrelated assets but must not believe that state of affairs to be true.

RAINBOW OPTIONS

Rainbow options belong to the family of multifactor options, whose main characteristic is that the payout is based on the relationship between several assets. This, of course, is in sharp contrast to standard options where all that matters is the performance of a single asset. While rainbows come in many flavours a particularly attractive type for corporate treasurers is the so-called "best of" option, which delivers the best performing (most favourable in terms of option payout) of all the underlying assets to which the company is exposed. These options can be useful to those corporates that are mostly concerned about the impact of the worst-behaving (in bottom line terms) underlying risk, and that don't care too much about the other, less-damaging, exposures. The best-of contract allows such firms to be covered against the most dangerous individual eventuality without having to pay for protection on the other, lesser-impact, eventualities that are deemed less relevant.

Let us try to clarify all this with an example. A UK-based manufacturing company has two main competitors, one in the US and the other in France. Its competitive position in this price-sensitive sector is determined by the £/US$ and £/€ exchange rates. If the pound strengthens against the dollar its competitiveness against the US company is hurt. If it strengthens against the euro, it becomes less competitive against the French company. However, while the company is exposed to a depreciation in both foreign currencies, in reality its concerns are disproportionately concentrated on the currency that depreciates the most, as this is what will truly determine its competitive position. The basic idea is that if the dollar has tanked more than the euro, then the US competitor can out price the UK company in the international markets more forcefully than the French competitor. Although it is unfortunate that French prices are now more competitive, this piece of bad news takes a back seat to the American threat that truly must be defended against. Buying a £ call/US$ put becomes the unavoidable priority. Once that is accomplished, also owning a euro put could be seen, frankly, as an expensive redundancy.

A best-of option that allows the UK manufacturer to buy pounds and sell either dollars or euros, whichever is cheaper, would provide a tailor-made, ideal and economical hedge for the company. The rainbow would generally cost much less than buying the two individual standard options separately. The reason for this is that if both individual vanillas expire ITM, the rainbow payout would be smaller (by an amount equal to the degree of moneyness experienced by the vanilla with the smallest payoff).

In our example, assume that the euro ends up appreciating while the dollar depreciates against the pound. The best-of option would pay the difference between the £/US$ strike level and the final £/US$ settlement rate. The gross payout would be equivalent to the scenario where the two vanilla options are purchased instead. The net payout would be much more favourable on account of the cheaper rainbow premium. These gains would offset potential losses in revenue deriving from the UK corporate's loss of competitiveness, which would be reflected in sales being lost to the American competitor.

4

Plain Vanilla Is Boring (II)

How exotic swaps can afford corporates value-enhancing opportunities

Think about it. You are a corporate treasurer who just successfully launched a new bond issue. Everything is rosy and you feel ecstatic. Now it's time to hedge the unavoidable interest rate liabilities. Your derivatives bankers come in the door. What would you prefer? A one-page presentation containing only the predictable vanilla swap or a much larger selection of goodies that includes some really fun-looking and adventurous alternative structures. Would you be content simply going through the straightforward process of closing the vanilla swap? Wouldn't you rather enjoy the excitement of deciding between several, ever more complex, ever more challenging tools? After all the hard work involved in launching the bond, wouldn't you be entitled to a little bit of fun?

In this chapter we are going to offer a window to non-vanilla swaps that corporates can use when designing their hedging strategies. It is likely that many readers would be familiar with some or all of the structures presented (especially, of course, if they have ever entered into them in the real world), but it is also possible that a significant number of them have not had such exposure in the past. For the latter group, this could be a good opportunity to appreciate the value (and, yes, new risks) that exotic swaps can offer to end-users. For the former, this could be a chance to revisit some old ideas and to appreciate how they have evolved with time.

Why should corporates consider exotic swaps? Simply put, if they want to obtain better results than they think would be possible through the vanilla channels. Some may call it greed. Some may call it excessive ambition on the part of treasurers. Perhaps even misplaced ego. Others, though, may call it intelligent decision-making. If a company can substantially reduce its net financing costs through the smart selection of swap structures that are a bit more daring than the usual medicine, why shouldn't they try? I know, I know. The more exotic solutions could bring with them unacceptable levels of risk, thus eventually proving to have been a deadly trap in disguise. There is no denying that exotic swaps endow end-users with the privilege of having to face new, previously non-existent risks. However, this fact, *per se*, is no reason to automatically dismiss the use of exotic options and to continue to rely only on no-fun vanilla swaps. After all, it is not like vanilla swaps are themselves devoid of any risks. They could have extremely harmful results to corporates if markets move the wrong way. This is explained, of course, by the most basic fact regarding hedging: it is not riskless.

Hedging is not about risk elimination, but about risk transformation. When hedging, whether this is done via simple or sophisticated tools, what the end-user is really doing is getting rid of the original exposure and substituting it by another, new exposure. When a corporate, say, swaps from fixed to floating it is eliminating the risk associated with paying fixed (ie, which is bad if rates go down), but taking on the new risk associated with paying floating (ie, which is bad if rates go up). The job of a corporate risk manager is essentially to decide what is the best risk-substitution strategy available. Are they more comfortable paying fixed or paying floating? Do they think rates will go up or down? What is their tolerance for losses if things don't go according to plan?

The honest truth is that, in some cases, the risk substitution proposed by exotic swaps can be very dangerous, because the maximum potential loss could be (under reasonable market movements) outrageously large. In other words, these would be transactions that have the potential to "blow up" the end-user (it can be argued that this what happened in the famous mid-1990s episodes of Procter & Gamble and Gibson Greetings involving the use of highly leveraged swaps). Clearly, such structures would most likely not be deemed appropriate for corporates, which simply cannot afford to blow up because of their use of derivatives. Corporates should use derivatives to prevent unaffordable losses, not to create them. When hedging, the mandate of a treasurer should not be taking blow-up calibre risks in exchange for possible impressive gains. Thus, when considering exotic swaps, it is advisable that treasurers use caution and always do the numbers to make sure that they would be comfortable with the maximum losses that could reasonably take place. It is important, though, that these words are properly understood: we are not saying that exotic swaps are dangerous *per se*; they are not. What we are saying is that some of them may be very dangerous, and inappropriately so for a non-financial company. However excessive caution could also be a negative force, by denying corporates the value-added that could derive from intelligently selected non-vanilla structures. The motto, then, should be the following: exotic stuff is good, not bad; too exotic stuff could be bad, not good.

In following paragraphs we will take a look at a real-life case study from a few years ago that helps shed some light into the possible benefits of using exotics over vanilla deals. That is, here we would be basically comparing exotic swaps to the vanilla benchmark (rather than analysing the use of tailor-made non-vanilla swaps for the purposes of hedging very particular exposures; so-called "roller-coaster swaps", for instance, would be an example of this type of instruments). We will also see, with the benefit of hindsight, how each proposed transaction would have fared, given subsequent market movements. Finally, we will analyse a couple of exotic swap strategies that have been shown to corporates in more recent times.

EXOTIC RESTRUCTURING

In 1996, a big company and a bigger bank entered into a high-notional euro-denominated hedging structure whereby the former sold a receiver swaption to the latter, under the following terms:

- ❏ expiry date of the option 13th July 2000;
- ❏ life of the swap 13th July 2000 to 13th July 2006;
- ❏ the company pays annually 9.17%;
- ❏ the bank pays semi-annually Euribor + 0.30%.

When the swaption's maturity date arrived on 13th July 2000, the company was obviously exercised into the six-year vanilla swap. Why? Well, rates had of course gone down since the good old mid-1990s and the corresponding swap rate was well below 9.17%. That is, the option was deep in-the-money for the bank.

This immediately created a big problem for the corporate. No one likes paying 9.17% when rates are much lower. The incurred negative carry could be a killer. This was not just a theoretical possibility; the company was actually experiencing it as it went through the first two payment dates before considering a restructuring. For the first payment (on 15th January 2001) the bank faced a level of Libor equal to 4.76%. For the second payment (on 13th July 2001), the bank faced a level of Libor equal to 4.70%. These two amounts put together were barely above half the amount of the first single payment that the company had to make on 13th July 2001, of course calculated using the fixed 9.17% rate. Thus, we can see that the negative carry was proving to be a drag on the firm's cash reserves. Restructuring was all but unavoidable. By early September 2001, the negative mark-to-market of the swap for the company was €46 million. With Libor getting lower by the minute (at 4.40% at that time, implying a negative carry of around 4.50%), escaping from the carry malaise became imperative. Bankers came knocking, peddling wonderful cures that would magically take away the pain. The key for the desperation-filled company was to decide which pill to swallow, depending on the savings in carry on offer (ie, the carrot) and the new future risks that would have to be faced.

Let us take a look at the restructuring trades that were proposed.

Plain vanilla swap
❑ The company pays six month Euribor + 4.45%.
❑ The bank pays 9.17% annually.
❑ The net position (original swap + plain vanilla swap) would now be:
  ❑ the company pays six months Euribor + 4.45%;
  ❑ the bank pays six month Euribor + 0.30%;
  ❑ that is, the company obtains an effective net position equal to paying 4.15% every six months.

This restructuring would basically transform the negative mark-to-market of the original swap into fixed annual payments on the part of the company. That is, the negative carry, or net cost for the corporate would be 4.15% for the duration. While there would be a significant reduction in negative carry initially with respect to the original position (of some 35 bps), the company would not be able to profit from possible future rises in Libor. On the other hand, were Libor to fall hard, being fixed at 4.15% may have seemed lovely in comparison to the alternative mayhem.

Structured swap

❑ The company pays six-month Euribor (with a floor struck at 4.00%) + 4.25%.
❑ The bank pays 9.17% annually.
❑ The net position (original swap + structured swap) would now be:
  ❑ the company pays six-month Euribor (with a floor struck at 4.00%) + 4.25%;
  ❑ the bank pays six-month Euribor + 0.30%;
  ❑ that is, the company obtains an effective net position equal to paying 3.95% + max (0, 4.00%–six-month Euribor) every six months.

We see that this structure is already a marked improvement over the vanilla swap, as the initial carry would 3.95% (20 bps less). This is due to the value embedded in the interest rate floor that the corporate would be selling to the bank. However, were Libor to be below 4%, the carry would increase. For this transaction to be attractive, the company should have the view that such an eventuality would not take place during the lifetime of the deal (or at least, not too often).

US$ quanto swap

❑ The company pays six-month US$ Libor + 4.10% in euros.
❑ The bank pays 9.17% annually.
❑ The net position (original swap + US$ quanto swap) would now be:
  ❑ the company pays six month US$ Libor + 4.10% in euros;
  ❑ the bank pays six-month Euribor + 0.30%;
  ❑ that is, the company obtains an effective net position equal to paying 3.80% + (six-month US$ Libor − six-month Euribor) in euros every six months

The carry would now be reduced to 2.84% (given the then lower level of US$ Libor with regards to Euribor). Quanto swaps are structures whereby one party generally pays a floating rate linked to a particular currency while the other party pays a flowing rate linked to another currency. What makes a quanto different from a regular cross-currency swap is that in the case of the former all payments are made in the same currency unit. Quanto swaps work when two factors are present at the same time: (1) one level of Libor (in this case US$) is significantly lower than the other (in this case, the euro) so that there are instant benefits to paying the lower rate; (2) the forward curve for the first currency (US$) is much steeper than for the other currency (euro) so that the party paying that first currency gets a better swap spread at initiation (so as to compensate for the higher Libor payments that the curves are "predicting"). These two factors were present at the time in the US$–€ pairing. This explains the 4.10% spread rather than the 4.45% for the plain vanilla swap. This structure profits/suffers from increases/decreases in the difference between six-month Euribor and six-month US$ Libor; that is, if US Libor goes to the roof hard and fast it could be really bad news.

US$ quanto swap in arrears

❑ The company pays six-month US$ Libor in arrears + 3.90% in euros.
❑ The bank pays 9.17% annually.
❑ The net position (original swap + US$ quanto swap in arrears) would now be:
  ❑ the company pays six-month US$ Libor iA + 3.90% in euros;
  ❑ the bank pays six-month Euribor + 0.30%;
  ❑ that is, the company obtains an effective net position equal to paying 3.60% + (six-month US$ Libor iA − six-month Euribor) in euros every six months.

The initial carry would now be just 2.58%. Why the reduction? Because by agreeing to pay "in arrears" the company saves some basis points. Paying in arrears simply means that the fixing of the Libor rate that applies in each payment date is postponed one period; that is, now the company would be paying the Libor rate quoting on the same day as the payment date, rather than the one quoting the period before (or "in advance", which is the way it is usually done). Under a steep forward curve (such as the one prevalent at the time), such willingness to postpone the fixing date is rewarded in the form of a lower swap spread. This structure increases the exposure to higher future US$ rates, and thus should be seen as riskier than the previous structure. However, we can already appreciate the wonders of financial engineering: the initial negative carry (actual monetary losses for the company) has been reduced by more than 150 basis points with regards to the original troublesome nightmare-inducing plain vanilla swap.

Structured US$ quanto swap
❏ The company pays six-month US$ Libor + 3.60% +
   ❏ 1.25% if US$ Libor > 7% in euros;
   ❏ 1.25% if US$ Libor > 8% in euros.
❏ The bank pays 9.17% annually.
❏ The net position (original swap + structured US$ quanto swap) would now be:
   ❏ the company pays six-month US$ Libor + 3.60% +
      ❏ 1.25% if US$ Libor > 7% in euros
      ❏ 1.25% if US$ Libor > 8% in euros;
   ❏ the bank pays six-month Euribor + 0.30%;
   ❏ that is, the company obtains an effective net position equal to paying 3.30% + (six-month US$ Libor– six-month Euribor) +:
      ❏ 1.25% if US$ Libor > 7% in euros;
      ❏ 1.25% if US$ Libor > 8% in euros every six months.

The initial carry now goes down to 2.34%. The reason for the pick-up is obvious. The company here would be selling two digital options to the bank, each posing potentially devastating threats: payments would experience a big jump precisely when Libor is very high. While the strikes of the digital were set at relatively comfortable levels, the steep forward curve assigned them a decent probability of being reached and thus made them valuable to sell. If the company believed that US$ rates could ever go that high, it shouldn't enter the trade regardless of how tasty the initial savings.

Extension swap 1
❏ The company pays six-month Euribor + 0.09% until 13th July 2011.
❏ The bank pays 9.17% annually until 13th July 2006.
❏ The net position (original swap + Extension swap 1) would now be as follows.
   ❏ The company pays six-month Euribor + 0.09% until 13th July 2011.
   ❏ The bank pays six-month Euribor + 0.30% until 13th July 2006.
   ❏ That is, the company obtains an effective net position equal to paying:

❑ −0.21% every six months until 13th July 2006;

❑ six-month Euribor + 0.09% until 13th July 2011.

The initial carry would be −0.21% (that is, positive carry for the company). Here we witness the complete turnaround afforded by exotic swaps: what was a hugely negative position has become positive. This is the extremely tempting value derived from entering into an extension swap. The problem is that the risks are also potentially impressive. Between 2006 and 2011 only the company would make payments, with no compensating payments emanating from the bank. This, of course, exposes the company to tremendous risks should Euribor stay high during that period. In essence, extension swaps allow end-users to "postpone" some of the negative mark-to-market of a position for the future ("delaying the pain", or "selling one's soul to the devil"). Usually, only companies in unavoidable need of relief jump into these structures. Sometimes, trading desks will refuse to do the deal (much to the annoyance of the sales-person) because they see them as financing in disguise.

Extension swap 2

❑ The company pays 5.27% until 13th July 2011.

❑ The bank pays 9.17% annually until 13th July 2006.

❑ The net position (original swap + Extension swap 2) would now be as follows.

    ❑ The company pays 5.27% until 13th July 2011.

    ❑ The bank pays six-month Euribor + 0.30% until 13th July 2006.

    ❑ That is, the company obtains an effective net position equal to paying:

        ❑ 4.97% − six-month Euribor until 13th July 2006;

        ❑ 5.27% until 13th July 2011.

The initial carry becomes 0.57% (back to negative for the company, though insignificantly so). Whether this strategy should be seen as preferable to the previous strategy depends on the company's view on Libor.

Extension swap 3

❑ The company pays six-month Euribor (with a cap at 6.5%) + 0.51% until 13th July 2011.

❑ The bank pays 9.17% annually until 13th July 2006.

❏ The net position (original swap + Extension swap 3) would now be as follows.
   ❏ The company pays six-month Euribor (with a cap at 6.5%) + 0.51% until 13th July 2011.
   ❏ The bank pays six-month Euribor + 0.30% until 13th July 2006.
   ❏ That is, the company obtains an effective net position equal to paying:
      ❏ min (0,6.5% − six-month Euribor) + 0.21% until 13th July 2006;
      ❏ six-month Euribor (with a cap at 6.5%) + 0.51% until 13th July 2011.

The initial carry would be 0.21%, 42 bps worse than the comparable Extension swap 1. This is due, of course, to the fact that here the company would be enjoying a cap on future Libor levels. That is, while the initial savings in carry are not as favourable, the level of potential pain in subsequent periods is limited. Thus, this would be preferable to Extension swap 1 if the corporate either feels that Libor will be above 6.50% or is not sure but wants to sleep peacefully anyway.

Extension swap 4
❏ The company pays six-month US$ Libor − 0.27% in euros until 13th July 2011.
❏ The bank pays 9.17% annually until 13th July 2006.
❏ The net position (original swap + Extension swap 4) would now be as follows.
   ❏ The company pays six-month US$ Libor − 0.27% in euros until 13th July 2011.
   ❏ The bank pays six-month Euribor + 0.30% until 13th July 2006.
   ❏ That is, the company obtains an effective net position equal to paying:
      ❏ (six-month US$ Libor − six-month Euribor) − 0.57% in euros until 13th July 2006;
      ❏ six-month US$ Libor − 0.27% in euros until 13th July 2011.

The carry for this structure would be −1.53% (positive for the company). This extraordinary result is due to the lower level of US$ Libor at the time. The company becomes exposed to very high rates in the US in the future.

Extension swap 5

❏ The company pays six-month US$ Libor (with a cap at 6.6%) + 0.45% in euros until 13th July 2011.

❏ The bank pays 9.17% annually until 13th July 2006.

❏ The net position (original swap + Extension swap 5) would now be as follows.

  ❏ The company pays six-month US$ Libor (with a cap at 6.6%) + 0.45% in euros until 13th July 2011.

  ❏ The bank pays six-month Euribor + 0.30% until 13th July 2006.

  ❏ That is, the company obtains an effective net position equal to paying:

    ❏ min (six-month US$ Libor − six-month Euribor, 6.6% − six-month Euribor) + 0.15% in euros until 13th July 2006;

    ❏ six-month US$ Libor (with a cap at 6.6%) + 0.45% in euros until 13th July 2011.

The carry gets reduced to −0.81% (still positive for the company). This is due to the high cost of the interest rate cap that the company is obtaining. The very steep US forward curve prevalent at the time made it very expensive to purchase upside protection that was relatively well struck. The good news is that the company's exposure to climbing US rates gets diminished.

To summarise:

Up to 13th July 2006

Plain vanilla Swap
Effective position: Company pays 4.15% fixed
Carry: 4.15%

Structured swap
Effective position: Company pays 3.95% + max (0, 4.00% − six-month Euribor)
Carry: 3.95%

US$ quanto swap
Effective position: Company pays 3.80% + (six-month US$ Libor − six-month Euribor) in €
Carry: 2.84%

US$ quanto swap in arrears
Effective position: Company pays 3.60% + (six-month US$ Libor iA − six-month Euribor) in €s
Carry: 2.58%

Structured US$ quanto swap
Effective position: Company pays 3.30% + (six-month US$ Libor − six-month Euribor) +:

1.25% if US$ Libor > 7% in €s
1.25% if US$ Libor > 8% in €s
Carry: 2.34%

Extension swaps

Idea 1
Effective position: Company pays −0.21% every six months until 13th July 2006 six-month Euribor + 0.09% until 13th July 2011
Carry: −0.21%

Idea 2
Effective position: Company pays 4.97% − six-month Euribor until 13th July 2006

5.27% until 13th July 2011
Carry: 0.57%

Idea 3
Effective position: Company pays min (0, 6.5% − six-month Euribor) + 0.21% until 13th July 2006

six-month Euribor (cap at 6.5%) + 0.51%
until 13th July 2011
Carry: 0.21%

Idea 4
Effective position: Company pays (six-month US$ Libor − six-month Euribor) − 0.57% in €s until 13th July 2006

six-month US$ Libor − 0.57% in €s until
13th July 2011
Carry: −1.53%

Idea 5
Effective position: Company pays min (six-month US$ Libor − six-month Euribor, 6.6% − six-month Euribor) + 0.15% in €s until 13th July 2006

six-month US$ Libor (cap at 6.6%) + 0.45%
in €s until 13th July 2011
Carry: −0.81%

We clearly see that the extension swaps have much better optics when it comes to providing a radical solution to the problem at hand. Overnight, they transform a massive downfall into a positive gain (or negligible setback). It may be irresistibly tempting to go for one of these. The downside, of course, is that in exchange for peace of mind up to July 2006 the company may be kick-starting the clock of a time bomb that could create considerable mayhem under very uncertain circumstances (who knows what the situation of the company may be more than four years into the future). However, would the outcome, unsettling as it could surely be, belong to the blowing-up category? Not really, as long as we consider reasonable market movements. None of the payment formulas up to 2011 is leveraged, and some of them are even capped.

Whatever the final choice between extension swaps and more conventional "one single maturity date" swaps, the analysis unquestionably shows the value to be found in exotic swaps. By including ever more imaginative twists to the structure, the amounts of immediate savings that can be obtained are ever increasing. Paying in arrears, selling floors, selling digitals or employing quanto technology constitute but a small sample of all the twists that the plain vanilla swap can be subject to in the quest for enhanced value.

What about the flip side? What about the risks involved in going exotic? If the original structure had been left untouched, the company's number one risk would have been defined by Euribor going down, as this would have increased the negative carry even more. By restructuring (or hedging a hedge) the company would have been able to transform such exposure, depending on the final choice of structure. For instance, in the case of the family of quanto swaps, the risk now becomes the eventuality that US$ Libor would shoot to the moon early in the trade. The company still wants Euribor to go up, but this in itself is not enough: what matters is the difference between both sets of Libor.

In the end, as we all know, monetary policies in both the € and US$ areas eased up considerably after the September 11th tragedy, particularly in the case of the latter. Short-term rates kept going down through the 2002–2003 period and remained at very low levels (1% in the US, 2% in the Eurozone) until mid-2004 when the Federal Reserve (Fed) began a measured tightening cycle. Today, of course, rates are not so low anymore, with the Fed's hawkish stance having pushed them into 4.75% (and still climbing) and even the usually shyer European Central Bank rising to 2.50%. What all this means is that the company would have been wise in restructuring its original poisonous position, as tanking Euribor was, as indicated before, the worst possible outcome. For instance, with six-month Euribor at 2.10% (more or less the average for 2004), the negative carry would have been almost 6.80%.

In comparison, the restructuring strategies (those expiring in 2006) would have worked quite well, at least for the first periods. The structured swap would have performed worse initially as rates almost instantly went down, thus taking the sold 4% floor into the money. The negative carry for this trade would have travelled the distance from around 4.50% to around 6% and then back to approximately 5.25%. High, but not as high as 6.80%.

The family of quantos would have delivered sensational results up to late 2004, when US$ Libor decisively overtook Euribor. Throughout 2002, US$ Libor was on average more than 150 bps below its Euribor cousin. This would have implied negative carry slightly above 2% for the simpler quanto versions and actually less than 2% for the quanto with digitals (which strikes, needless to say, weren't even perceived). During 2003, US$ Libor remained, on average, some 100–120 bps below Euribor, but still affording very attractive results. This state of affairs continued unaltered throughout the first part of 2004. After the Fed changed tact in June, things quickly changed and quanto users began to experience cold sweats late at night. By October, six-month US$ Libor reached and then surpassed six-month Euribor. Negative carry on the simpler quantos would have approached 4%. By late January 2005, US$ Libor was about 80 bps higher. With Alan Greenspan relentlessly tightening the screws (while the ECB stayed put), the gap was almost 100 bps by the summer. At year-end, the hole had reached 200 bps. Now, the negative carry on the quantos would have dangerously landed on the 5.50–6.00% range. It is possible that if the Fed, as expected, tightens rates a few more times this year then the negative carry on the simpler quantos could breach the 7% mark. Nevertheless, quanto swaps (as with any swap) must be analysed on a break-even basis: there might be unpleasant developments in the horizon, but this may be more than compensated for by the very substantial windfalls obtained during the first periods (which, of course, should be the most relevant to the company).

Most of the extension swaps would have worked really well up to July 2006, with those containing quanto technology delivering truly outstanding positive carry for a long time, and only modest negative carry at the end. Whether those gains would be later seen as justification enough for the pains of one-way payments until July 2011 is an entirely different matter.

MODERN EXOTICNESS

It is time now for us to take a look at a couple of exotic swap structures that have been presented to corporate clients a little bit more recently that those analysed above (which dated back to late 2001).

In December 2005, a company that had US-denominated floating interest rate liabilities, received the following sales pitch from a bank:

Putable swap with disaster cap

❑ five-year maturity;
❑ the company pays 4.77%;
❑ the bank pays three-month US$ Libor;
❑ the bank has a one-time option to cancel the swap after the first three years;
❑ the company owns a two-year cap on three-month Libor struck at 6.50% with an effective date of three years from trade date.

OK, what's going on here? What exactly is all this? Simple. As a way to lower the fixed rate paid on a swap, corporates sometimes agree to enter into so-called "putable swaps" or "cancellable swaps" whereby the bank has the one-time right to kill the swap at a pre-determined future exercise call date. In exchange for selling this option to the bank, the corporate enjoys a lower than market pay-fixed swap rate. That is, it obtains some savings on its new (fixed) net financing costs. Paying a few basis points less during the period prior to the call date may be tempting enough to convince treasurers to take on the risk of being left unhedged later on. This could be dangerous, particularly if protection has by then become extremely expensive due to moves in short-term rates or in the forward curve or both.

The structure described above provides some comfort in that respect. By embedding an interest rate cap it guarantees the company that it will never be left completely unhedged, even if the original swap is called by the dealer. In case the swap is killed and the company has to suddenly travel from the fixed dimension to the floating dimension, it knows that it won't have to suffer financing costs above 6.50%. Since such a strike was way out-of-the-money at the time (recall that by December 2005 the US$ curve was quite flat, thus assigning little probability to the high strike, more than 200 bps above Libor, being reached) it was deemed "disaster protection". In reality, however, 6.50% is not outrageously high by historical standards.

The key question, of course, is whether the reduction in the fixed rate on the swap afforded by making it cancellable would still be attractive once the cap has been included in the structure. The premium of the cap is basically amortized into the fixed rate. The more expensive the cap, the less attractive the pickup. This is why the trade really only works if the cap strike is set at "disaster-like" levels.

The fixed rate offered by the equivalent regular putable swap was 4.60% at the time. Thus, counting on cap protection for no upfront cash payment increases financing costs for the first three years (and maybe more) by 17 bps. Clearly, the company needs to have either a very strong view regarding the feasibility of Libor travelling above 6.50% in the distant future or it is obligated to be hedged at all times, perhaps due to the covenants of the loan. The extra 17 bps burden would otherwise be difficult to rationalise.

A good way to forget about that and to cheer oneself up is to recall that the five-year vanilla swap rate was 4.90%. Thus, the putable swap with disaster protection, while incurring an initial cost with regards to its cap-less sibling, affords the end-user a 13 bps pick-up over the tedious vanilla route. In addition, it shares the key characteristic of always providing cover. This is, then, just another example of how exotic toys can bring corporates that extra little bit of happiness.

In early 2005, a company that also had US-denominated floating interest rate liabilities asked for innovative hedging ideas and received the following pitch from his favourite derivatives dealer.

Periodic knock-in swap
❑ five-year maturity;
❑ the company pays a fixed rate subject to the knock-in provision;
❑ the bank pays three-month US$ Libor;

❏ knock-in provision: if Libor for a calculation period is less than the trigger rate, no effective swap rate; if Libor is equal or greater than the trigger rate, then the fixed swap becomes effective;
❏ trigger rate 1: 5.00%;
❏ fixed swap rate 1: 6.60%;
❏ trigger rate 2: 6.00%;
❏ fixed swap rate 2: 7.65%;

Admittedly, this is not a straightforward structure, at least at first glance.

The basic idea is that this exotic transaction, when compared to the plain vanilla swap, prevents corporates from suffering negative carry whenever Libor is below the swap rate (4.30% in this case). Given that three-month US$ Libor was quoting at 2.90%, the gap could be thought of as worryingly large. At the same time, the company would enjoy true disaster protection for free: if rates jumped to the stratosphere during the relevant period (ie, if they reached 8% or more) the corporate would not have to pay as much (only 7.65%).

Free disaster protection and the absence of negative carry when rates are low are obviously positive attributes. What gives? What exposures would the company have to face in return for such pleasantries? Yes, there is a catch. When Libor is above the swap rate, the company is clearly losing out. However, much more importantly, the exposure to high floating rates becomes leveraged at some point (ie, when the triggers are hit). When three-month US$ Libor on the relevant fixing date is in the range 6%<>=5%, then the company is entrapped into paying 6.60%. If Libor at 5% is bad enough when you are unhedged and when you know that you could be simply paying 4.30% had you not heeded the tempting calls emanating from "exoticland", the periodic knock-in adds salt to the wound by forcing the corporate to pay 6.60%, that is, a sudden jump of 160 bps in net financing costs.

Similarly, when three-month US$ Libor is equal to or greater than 6%, the end-user is entrapped into paying 7.65%, which is obviously only desirable if Libor is above that fixed rate (hence the true disaster protection benefits).

Under which circumstances should a treasurer enter into this transaction? The treasurer's views must be somewhat extreme.

They must expect short-term rates to remain low (or at least below 4.30%) for a long while, while at the same time envisaging the possibility that rates will drastically shoot up. They want to void the initial negative carry and would like free protection in case their darkest thoughts come true. Alternatively, they might not believe at all in very high rates down the road, but may have the mandate to be hedged from blow-up scenarios and don't want to (or can't) spend upfront premium on a regular cap. The leveraged effects embedded in the periodic knock-in swap may be an acceptable price to be (especially if you don't believe that the triggers stand a decent chance).

The main drawback from this exotic transaction lies in the possibility that Libor goes up fast and overtakes the vanilla swap rate earlier than expected (thus limiting the positive carry honeymoon), only to continue escalating (thus unleashing the negative carry nightmare) and breaching the first, then the second triggers (thus kicking-in the leverage malaise) but never actually hitting disaster-calibre figures (like 7.50% or above, thus making the protective power of the structure totally inefficient).

Guess what path US$ Libor has taken since early 2005? Exactly. It surpassed the 4.30% level in the first days of November and it never looked back, cheered by the relentless tightening spirit present at the Fed since mid-2004. At the time of writing, it quotes above 4.90%, seriously toying with the idea of reaching the first trigger barrier and jumping periodic knock-in's, end-users into big trouble. Taking into account that the Fed is not done yet, it is extremely likely that such eventuality will take place.

The conclusion is inescapable. This particular exotic swap would not have delivered particularly good value to corporates. There would have been some welcome avoidance of negative carry at the beginning but it would have been short-lived and progressively decreased over time. Definitely not enough to compensate for the deep sense of regret for not having locked-in at 4.30%, especially when one is about to be propelled from 5% financing costs to 6.60%. Looking back, perhaps the best thing in early 2005, with a tightening cycle in full motion and with no end in sight, was not to bet heavily on the Fed suddenly and surprisingly stopping on its tracks.

Section 3

21st Century Developments

5

An Inverted Era

*The new century has already produced two periods of inverted yield curves;
how much should corporates hedging strategies be redefined in the
face of abnormal curves?*

So far the 21st century has undoubtedly proven to be a wild ride for
interest rate risk managers. Not only were central bankers forced to
deliver super-easy monetary policies in a dramatic fashion and for
much longer than generally anticipated but also the yield curve
more often than not adopted funny-looking shapes that did not
correspond with most people's expectations, sending confusing
messages to market players. A dollar-indebted treasurer that had,
for example, entered into a pay fixed-receive floating swap in
August 2001 as a hedge for his US Libor liabilities in the belief
(widely shared at the time) that the Federal Reserve was about to
bring the then-prevalent easing cycle to an end, would have been
caught up in the downward spiral in rates that derived from the
nasty combination of 9/11, Enron and WorldCom. Being locked at
a rate of 5.25% or thereabouts (the five-year swap just prior to the
terrorist attack on New York) when short-rates are diving from 3.50
to 3.00%, 2.50%, 2.00% all the way to 1.00% in June 2003, is clearly
not a desirable scenario. Similarly, any treasurer designing a hedging strategy in 2002 and 2003 was confronted by a US yield curve
that was much steeper than perhaps would be expected given the
economic circumstances. The market seemed to be pricing a very
quick recovery, with some analysts predicting short-term rates in
excess of 4% by mid-2002. The surprisingly steep curve made
swaps (and interest rate options such as caps) very expensive, and

thus significantly complicated matters for hedgers. Should they trust the "recession is over" optimistic crowd and fix their financing costs at levels in the 4.50–5.50% range (for five-year swaps in the first half of 2002), or should they continue to pay floating and hope that the monetary authorities do not go into tightening mood too soon and too eagerly? Of course, armed with the benefit of hindsight, we now know that any hedging structure that did not allow corporates to enjoy at least a substantial part of the easing spiral that lasted until mid-2004 would have incurred significant costs and would have most likely been deemed a failure. However, back then, in the thick of things, the decision-making process for treasurers was made extremely challenging by the lethal combination of a very uncertain policy path and a very weird yield curve.

Nowadays, while future policy actions seem clearer (not only in the US but also in the Euro area and in the UK), the shape of the curve continues to be a problem, for the complete opposite reasons than in the 2002–2003 period. Lately in the US and for a long time in the UK, the yield curve has adopted an inverted figure. Shorter-term rates (ie, two-year) are hovering above their longer-term counterparts (five-year in the US, all of them in the UK). Analysing the possible factors behind such abnormality is indeed an interesting and useful exercise. However, in this chapter we will rather focus on how hedging decisions by corporates could be affected by the new curves and, crucially, on trying to offer some (hopefully useful) advice. Given that the curve only recently began to invert there and that everybody's attention is being captured by such phenomenon, we will devote most of the analysis to the US market (this is also more relevant as, of course, dollar-denominated products account for a very significant proportion of all over-the-counter interest rate derivatives traded worldwide).

DEALING WITH TEMPTATION

With three-month US Libor at nearly 5% and five-year swaps at around 5.20%, and with a tightening cycle in place, it is most definitely tempting for corporate treasurers to fix their net financing costs at what appears to be a relatively very favourable level. With the Fed likely to keep raising rates a while longer in the face of resilient economic growth, persistently high energy prices, a never-ending housing boom and a desire on the part of newly-appointed chairman Ben Bernanke to establish strong inflation-fighting credentials, entering now into a swap would offer the promise of positive carry for what could be a long time (as it is foreseeable that the Fed would wait before reverting back to a new easing cycle). Let us assume, as some analysts do, that short-term rates reach 5.50% by mid-2006 from the current 4.75% level. By taking advantage of the strange-looking yield curve (which delivers low swap rates) a treasurer could spend at least the next, say, couple of years paying 50–75 bps below Libor. That is, it would be as if the last stage of the tightening period had not happened at all (and possibly even better, as many competing firms may at the same time be fully suffering the higher Libor rates). Here there would be a fantastic chance for treasurers to deliver plenty of value to their employers and to perhaps become heroes and obtain a much-desired promotion. In this sense, the temptation to enter into swaps now could be hard to resist.

The same would be true in the case of an options-based hedging strategy. The inverted curve results in low premiums for caps with very attractive strikes relative to Libor (ie, strikes close enough to make the protection look very effective) as the forward rates would be indicating that very few of the caplets (if any) would expire in-the-money (obviously, were interest rate volatility to jump the option would become pricier). As we all know, the advantages of a cap over a swap is that in the case of the former the end-user can enjoy the benefits of Libor rates below the strike (ie, why they cost money).

In case the corporate will not (or cannot) pay premium for protection, the current yield curve also favours zero-cost strategies such as collars. Because under an inverted curve one can sell floors at attractive strike levels relative to Libor (strikes that are not in the red for the corporate) and still obtain significant economic value. The main drawback of entering into collars, of course, is the possibility of being forced to enter into floors with strikes that are so high that would immediately be in-the-money were monetary policy to be quickly (and unexpectedly) reversed.

The options-friendly aspect of the current environment is in sharp contrast to the extremely options-hostile environment of the

2001–2003 period. The very steep curve made it very expensive to enter into options strategies that offered decent trade optics. Buying caps with attractive strikes relative to Libor (ie, not so far above that makes protection look unnecessary) was very expensive. And collars were no help, given that floors with attractive strikes relative to Libor were impossibly cheap (since the forward curve was indicating that very few of the floorlets would be exercised). For example, in late January 2002 (with five-year swaps at around 5%), a corporate could choose between the following zero-cost collar structures:

❑ trade dates: 30th January, 2002–30th January, 2007;
❑ cap 5.50% – floor 4.60%;
❑ cap 6.00% – floor 4.20%;
❑ cap 8.00% – floor 3.00%.

With three-month US Libor at approximately 1.85%, it is clear that zero-cost collars were unfeasible as the end-user would start already deep in the red since the floor strike would be way above the market rate (and as we now know this was to remain so for a long time). Under the steep curve, the sold floors were simply too cheap and the bought caps were simply too costly.

For those treasurers who were at the time pushed into swaps for lack of an options-based alternative (though it must be said that more exotic structures could have delivered better opportunities) this could be the time for revenge. No more sleepless nights thinking about the larger-than-life negative carry being incurred, no more embarrassing moments at the office having to explain why your financing costs are 4% higher than your competitors, no more wise cracks from your banker reminding you how the more exotic options would have worked wonders. This time there is no need to entrap yourself into a fixed rate. You can simply put up the limited premium money upfront in return for a nice-looking cap, or save even that modest sum by entering into collars with floors that seem very unlikely to be reached. If Libor goes above the cap strike you are protected, if it stays below you enjoy it.

In sum, the key differences between the current interest rate hedging environment and that of a few years back is that under the scenario of very low Libor rates and very steep forward curve, a corporate could not purchase attractively-struck caps without either parting with a lot of cash or having to sell deep-in-the-money floors, nor could it fix its financing costs through a vanilla swap without incurring vast negative carry. In contrast, the current scenario of higher Libor and an inverted curve allows for the economical purchase of attractive caps without the need to sell nastily-struck floors, and for the fixing of floating liabilities with minor negative carry (if at all) which could easily become positive very soon.

As can be seen, temptation is all around interest rate risk managers these days. Option strategies are feasible and swaps are cheap. Should corporate treasurers "just do it" or is there a possible dark side to the tasty possibilities afforded by the yield curve?

The truth is that the tempting swap, cap and collar quotes being currently shown by bankers could end up being the financial equivalent of The Odyssey's beautiful island sirens, whose irresistibly charming songs drove sailors into madness and eventual self-destruction. No matter how pre-warned one was as to the potential dangers, no one could resist the temptation of the songs. The only way to avoid the dreadful fate was to have your ears filled with wax as your ship passed by the sirens' island (or, like Odysseus, by tying yourself to the mast). Today's interest rate derivatives look so irresistible that it would appear as if a corporate treasurer would have to be mute, blind and deaf to decline to transact. However, over-eagerness could lead, *à la* The Odyssey, to misery.

No matter how low swap rates may seem, how economical cap strikes are or how attractive the levels of zero-cost collars might be, companies would still be exposed to short-term rates not going up or, especially, going down. If Bernanke's Fed decided to stay put and call the tightening game quits earlier than most people expect, Libor would not exceed the swap rate and thus there would be no positive carry for fixed payers. Not having hedged would have delivered a lower net financing cost. What is worse, were policy to start being eased soon (perhaps due to a dramatic bursting of the housing bubble) the negative carry implied by being locked into the swap could become truly worrisome. Far from being hailed a hero and assigned a corner office, the treasurer may become the subject of disdain and scorn.

Had the corporate purchased a cap instead, the amount of regret would be reduced to the cash spent, as it would have been possible to fully benefit from the lower rates. Given that, again, under the inverted curve the cap would have been economical, not too many tears would be shed. However, when compared to the free-of-charge alternative of not having hedged, the cap premium would be seen as an inefficient use of highly valuable cash. Collars would attenuate the whining as no money would have been wasted but would expose the corporate to negative carry if rates go below the floor's strike (although the inverted curve, by allowing the company to obtain good economic value from the sale of low strikes, would have made this possibility less likely).

Thus, before blindly jumping into the derivatives sea charmed by the quotes emanating from bank's presentations, treasurers would be well advised to thoroughly analyse the possible drawbacks of the structures. For those treasurers who believe that a renewed easing cycle is on the cards for the near future, the apparently irresistible hedging opportunities being dangled before their eyes may look like dangerous traps in disguise. Next time a Wall Street derivatives banker shows up at the door, he may find that such clients have waxed their ears and cannot be charmed away.

Recent history would seem to justify a certain scepticism on the part of treasurers. In February 2000 the US yield curve inverted and remained in abnormal mode for the rest of the year. This coincided with tightening policy moves that saw Fed funds go from 5.50% at the end of 1999 to 6.50% at the end of 2000. By December 2000, a corporate could enter into a five-year swap paying around 6% when three-month Libor was quoting at 6.50%. Views on future policy moves at the time mostly pointed towards a waiting period before Greenspan reversed gear (there had been a tightening cycle in place since mid-1999), given that so far concerns had overwhelmingly been placed on the possibility of an overheating economy and accelerating inflation. Some experts were even betting that the Fed was not done tightening. A September 2000 roundtable of very senior derivatives professionals from leading investment banks organised by *Risk* magazine concluded that US short rates still had some room to climb and/or that there was no scope for easing in the medium term. And while economic data was disappointing in several fronts, it must be pointed out that no big shocking event had afflicted the US (this was before 9/11 and prior to Enron's and WorldCom's bankruptcies). Under this scenario, it is understandable that more than a few corporates may have been tempted to fix their financing costs at the below-Libor levels offered by the first inverted curve of the new millennium. The risk of such strategy, just as now, was that the Fed would declare an abrupt end to the prevalent policy cycle and reverse course in no time.

In a totally unexpected move, Greenspan cut rates by 50 bps on 2nd January 2001 as a result of an unscheduled policy meeting and signalled that its bias had switched from inflation fighting to recession preventing. The decision, dubbed by some as one of the more surprising moves the Fed had done in a long time and as puzzling by others, immediately took Libor below 5.80%, not only erasing any positive carry implied by swaps but actually forcing negative carry upon fixed payers. After less than a few weeks, the decision to be tempted into swaps would have already become regrettable. As a new easing cycle gathered strength and rates dived, swap-embracing treasurers would have switched from regret to full-blown panic.

Is this a useful lesson for today's environment? Should the 2000 experience automatically discourage corporates from giving in to yield curve temptation? Will the siren songs being whispered from the swap market spell doom for treasurers this time around too? Not necessarily. It can be argued that the current situation presents several key dissimilarities with that of December 2000. The only way through which swap payers would end up suffering is if the economy slows down, perhaps pronouncedly, and the Fed is forced to ease policy. If there is something that has characterised the modern-day Fed (and that is poised to continue unabated under the new Bernanke regime) is its ruthless determination to lower rates whenever things threaten to go sour. Were demand to slow or the housing bubble to burst, it is almost a certainty that rates would go down as hard as needed. Those paying fixed in a swap would have to go into hiding, at least temporarily.

So the real question is, will the inverted curve pre-date an economic slowdown, even a recession? Depending on the answer, those tempting swap rates, cap premiums and collar levels would appear more or less attractive.

Economists and analysts usually take it as an article of faith that an inverted yield curve is always an indication of trouble in the horizon. First, the argument goes, this is simply what has regularly happened. In fact, the last two US recessions (1990 and 2001) were preceded by abnormal curves. Second, and somewhat more rigorously, inverted curves can wreak havoc on financial institutions that make a living borrowing at short rates and lending at long rates. If the non-normal period is long enough and the degree of inversion deep enough, then banks may be forced to restrict the supply of credit. In the last two cases of recession-preceding inversion, which saw bank lending growth become negative, the anomaly lasted for about nine months and the gap between two-year and 10-year yields reached 50 bps. Third, and this applies directly to the current environment, inverted curves may be the result of central bankers over-tightening policy, that is, being unnecessarily restrictive and perhaps reaching levels that could begin to hurt the economy, triggering a recession and leading to interest rate cuts (which the market is supposed to be pricing in at the medium and long end, thus adding fuel to the inversion phenomenon). For instance, several analysts thought at the time that the last tightening move in 2000, which saw the Fed funds rate go from 6% to a nine-year high of 6.50%, was probably a step too far.

Nowadays, however, lots of people doubt that an inverted curve would lead to economic malaise (and to the lowering of rates that would ensue). This time, lots of people say, long rates are low for a good reason. The so-called "yield conundrum" (ie, the puzzling reluctance of long rates to go up in spite of a prolonged tightening cycle; in fact, they have gone down since Greenspan changed tact in mid-2004) is explained by several factors other than the market pricing a nearby slowdown. For one, foreign investors have become big buyers of US government bonds (as they search for higher yields and as governments try to prevent their currencies from strengthening) and that increased demand is depressing yields on the back end. There is also a growing need by pension funds for increased investments in longer-term bonds as baby boomers near retirement. At the same time, the success by the Fed in proactively fighting inflation may have reduced the market's risk premium on long-dated securities. In this sense, then, this inversion would be a false indicator of an upcoming recession. Alan Greenspan himself seems to belong to this school of thought.

A possible problem with this argument is that, back in 2000, people were saying the same things. The inverted curve was believed not to be reflecting forecasted doom but rather scarcity value at the long end having to do with Treasury buybacks (recall that the 30-year bond was discontinued), as well as doubts over the credit status of government-sponsored agencies such as Fannie Mae and Freddie Mac that drove benchmark-seeking investors away from those securities and into the arms of long-dated bonds issued by the real government itself.

Several analysts go beyond saying that an inverted curve is not necessarily a description of the market's economic pessimism, and even express doubts about the real danger that inversion can cause. These people debate whether the last two recessions were in fact induced by the abnormal shape of the curve (where the degree of inversion was mild, at least in comparison with the previous episodes of the 1980–1982 period when short-term rates stood more than 100 bps above long-term rates). For instance, many attribute the 1990–1991 recession to external factors such as the phased removal of key tax breaks for commercial real estate that began in 1986 and that resulted in the collapse of that market negatively impacting banks' balance sheets, and severe cuts in defence spending that made previously recession-free communities vulnerable. As for the 2001 recession, well, we had that big dot-com bubble bursting, didn't we?

In the end, whether one believes that the last recessions were directly caused by the inverted curve, the undeniable fact is that, just as it has happened since 1960, those downturns were preceded by inversion, thus adding statistical ammunition to the "inversion is doom" crowd. Will it really be different this time, as some point out? Two things must be highlighted in this respect. First, while there are indeed good reasons behind the yield conundrum at the long end (ie, the market may not be indicating a slowdown likely) and while the US economy is undoubtedly in good shape (the envy of Europe) it is undeniable that the foundations are not rock-solid and that there is considerable exposure to potentially destabilising risks. The chief concern, of course, is the housing bubble that has sustained private consumption for the last few years. Were the bubble to burst, severe mayhem may ensue. Second, it seems that financial institutions are already feeling the pain of an inverted curve. Recent newspaper articles under headings such as "Interest rates curb US bank profits" report how large regional institutions are struggling with the yield curve, which crimps profit by limiting their ability to lend at high long-term rates and pay deposits at low short-term rates. While credit quality remains at historically high levels, some banks are starting to show flat or declining profits, which is in large part attributable to the inverted curve.

The conclusion must be that there are plenty of valid arguments from both sides of the debate. The "the end is nigh" crowd has history on its side; the "this time's different" crowd, for its part, presents convincing arguments and has Greenspan on its side (and also, mind you, a bit of historical backing as technically not every recent curve inversion has led to recession, as was the case in 1998).

Of course, this lack of consensus is not good news for corporate treasurers, who would much prefer a clearer future path for the economy that would make it easier for them to decide whether to take advantage of the tempting interest rate hedging opportunities made available by the inverted curve. The inversions of 1989 and 2000 were followed by aggressive easing cycles. Those who had just previously entered into swaps as fixed payers would have incurred heavy losses. Those who had purchased caps would have wasted their money. The danger for today's treasurers is that the same fate may await them. If this time turns out not to be different after all, rates could begin to be cut only a few months after they reached their peak. In this sense, seduced corporates would be fully caught up in the paradox implied by inverted yield curves; they offer very tempting hedging opportunities but at the same time may indicate drastic rate cuts in the near future that would render such opportunities inefficient and costly. Inverted curves have been called many things, from anomalies to crystal balls, but for many treasurers who cannot resist temptation they may forever be known as deadly traps.

EXOTIC WORLD

So far, our discussion has focused on vanilla products. As we have said, for regular swaps and options the shape of the yield curve can deliver contradictory messages. When the curve is steep (like it was from 2001–2003) the market seems to be indicating a quick economic recovery and rate rises in the horizon from which you should protect yourself. However, this protection is prohibitively expensive on account of that very steepness. When the curve is inverted, the market seems to be indicating an imminent recession and rate cuts, so you might not need any protection. However, it is precisely under such scenario that protection might be too cheap to forgo.

The use of exotic, non-vanilla hedging strategies can allow treasurers to escape such annoying contradictions and obtain extra value by taking advantage of the yield curve in intelligent ways. Under a steep curve, exotic structures can be devised that, while still delivering acceptable protection from rising rates, can at the same time allow the end-user to benefit in case the curve is "lying" and rates remain low. Under an inverted curve, exotic solutions could offer upside protection in case the curve is wrong while reducing the costs of eventually not having needed the protection.

Clearly, a steep curve is a wonderful time for exotic options to be transacted as vanilla collars do not work, regular caps are very expensive and swap rates are way too high (thus requiring an alternative). Since selling floors that are deep in the red from the start, paying tons of premium for a cap struck far above Libor, and incurring huge negative carry are clearly not attractive prospects, it is only normal that hedgers would demand alternative structures. Flat or inverted curves, on the other hand, are in principle less conducive to exotic alternatives since collars work well and caps and swaps are cheap. Having said this, exotic structures could be a good hedge for those treasurers who believe that "this time is not different" and that an easing cycle is around the corner.

Here we are going to analyse which exotic tools would work best under an inverted regime, and whether exotic structures that worked under the previous steep curve universe would work today and why or why not. In order to clarify things as much as possible, we will use a real-life structure presented to corporate clients in early 2002, when steepness in the US curve was extreme.

In January 2002, a corporate that had five-year US-denominated interest rate liabilities and that wanted to obtain protection was visited by his favourite derivatives bankers. With Libor at 1.90%, the swap rate of 5.10% seemed too much of an opportunity cost. Vanilla caps were out of the question. Vanilla collars, as we saw earlier, were unworkable as the sold floors would start deep in the red. As the client wanted to be able to enjoy the low short-rates prevalent, it asked its bankers to be inventive and find a way to come up with cap-like protection at an affordable price. They returned with the following zero-cost exotic structure.

❑ A client buys a knock-out cap strike 4.95% barrier 7.50%.
❑ The client buys knock-in cap strike 8.75% barrier 7.50%.
❑ The client sells a string of floors with strikes:
  ❑ 1.50% for the first year;
  ❑ 3.00% for the next four years;
  ❑ 2.50% for the next 10 years.
❑ The client sells a 5 × 10 receiver swaption strike 3.75%.

What would the customer accomplish? What new risks would it become exposed to? The basic rationale for this structure is that, in order to obtain (free of charge) cap protection at attractive levels under such a steep curve, the client has to sell several options to the bank so that the premiums obtained are used to finance the bought cap. The chosen cap strike would be 4.95%. The client would sell a knock-out, a string of long-dated floors and a swaption. There would have been just enough premium left to purchase a knock-in cap with a very high strike so that the corporate would never be left unhedged. The corporate would have obtained protection from Libor going above 4.95% as long as it did not reach 7.50%, in which case the 4.95% cap would disappear and the new cap struck at 8.75% would emerge. Losses would only be incurred when Libor is in the 7.50–8.75% range. Potentially more damaging outcomes could derive from the sold floors, given their very long maturities. Were interest rates to be very low for a prolonged period (perhaps Japanese-style low), the opportunity costs could be prohibitive. Finally, the swaption further enhanced the exposure to low future rates, as both the swap and the floor could be in the red for the corporate at the same time for the last 10 years of the trade (ie, were Libor to quote at 2.00% the client's negative carry would be 2.25%).

Because the 4.95% cap was impossibly expensive, the corporate had to add a knock-out barrier. The good news is that, given the steep curve, a high barrier level was still worth a lot, as the forward curve was assigning a high probability to the apparently safe 7.50% barrier being reached. The bad news is that because of the steep curve floors were not worth much unless the selected strikes were high (in relation to the then current Libor rate) or very long-dated or both. The same applied to the swaption. A final, though less influential, piece of bad news is that the cost of the knock-in cap, even having been struck at a really high level, would not be negligible as even 8.75% was assigned some probability by the curve.

What about today? Would such structure be feasible under an inverted curve? We see that back in the steep-curve period corporates could obtain lots of value from selling knock-outs with very attractive barrier levels relative to Libor (the barrier being so much higher that it could be reasonably deemed unreachable). That was obviously a good thing, and probably a smart way to finance the purchase of a cap. Under an inverted curve, this may no longer be the case, as the knock-out barrier would now have to be much closer to Libor, perhaps too close for comfort. Corporates may understandably be much more reticent to sell knock-outs under an inverted curve than under a steep curve (we are assuming similar volatility levels in both instances, so that the differences in premium are due entirely to the relative shapes of the curves). This practically rules out not just knock-out caps but also knock-out swaps, a very popular trade a few years ago (whereby the corporate enjoys a below-market swap rate for the first periods at the risk of being switched into floating were Libor to hit a pre-defined high barrier). Another key component of treasurers' hedging toolkits in the 2001–2003 period that doesn't work nowadays are so-called in-arrears swaps, that offered substantial initial savings (ie, smaller spread over Libor) in return for leveraging the end-user's exposure to higher future rates by postponing Libor resetting by one period. A steep curve clearly rewards those willing to undertake such risk. Finally, the selling of digital options with very high strikes relative to Libor (7–8% in the 2001–2003 period, thus reasonably unreachable) that offers corporates inmediate significant reductions in net financing costs at the risk of future large increases is also currently less feasible.

Nevertheless, today's corporates may not care much about not being able to use some of the exotic tricks that were fashionable only a few years ago. The cheapness of attractive protection made possible by the inverted curve dictates that selling floors and swaptions might suffice, with the tremendous advantage that they don't have to be struck at dangerous levels. And certain exotic tools could still be profitably used to add value. An attractively struck cap that protects from higher rates could be financed by the sale of a knock-in floor with a barrier level below the floor strike of the corresponding vanilla collar (so as to be able to benefit more from lower rates, were a recession to follow curve inversion) and with the strike at the same level as the cap. At the same time, and taking advantage of the inverted curve, a long-dated receiver swaption would be sold at a strike that both delivers good economic value and that makes sense from a risk point of view (ie, the strike would be set at a level that, even if exercised, would not kill the company; this is usually a long-term financing cost that the company can comfortably live with). Depending on market timing, a structure could be arranged whereby the cap and the floor strikes are set at the same level (or even lower) as the vanilla swap for that maturity so that the worst thing that could happen to the corporate is to be locked at levels similar to the vanilla swap for some periods, while enjoying the possibility of lower rates in those periods when the knock-in barrier is not reached. In the long term, the worst thing that could happen is to be locked at the swaption strike, but in principle this should be set at an acceptable level for the company (an affordable trade-off for the free attractive protection achieved in the short term). Such structure would obviously be superior to a vanilla swap, and could be superior to a regular cap and collar too. It does not cost anything and as long as the (presumably quite low) knock-in barrier is not reached, it would outperform the vanilla collar.

In sum, while a steep curve is a good time to finance the purchase of protection (caps) or the enhancement of available protection levels (swaps, collars) by taking exposures to interest rate levels above the desired level of protection (selling knock-outs, selling digitals, doing the resetting in-arrears), an inverted curve is a good time to do the opposite: get attractive and free protection by taking exposures to interest rate levels below the desired level of protection. Selling floors (both vanilla and exotic) and swaptions can offer substantial value at attractive risk levels (ie, comfortable strikes relative to Libor).

Under a low Libor-steep curve scenario, exposures to much higher rates have significant worth since the curve indicates a decent probability of those levels being reached in the future; if one believes that the curve is showing unrealistic levels (as many did back in the 2001–2003 period) and that it is highly unlikely that Libor would eventually be so high during the life of the transaction, then selling 7.50%-struck knock-outs or 8%-struck digitals when Libor is quoting below 2% can be a fantastic way of financing valuable protection at minimum risks. In other words, a very steep curve allows great value to be obtained in exchange for taking on what seems like little real risk. Under an inverted curve, in order to obtain significant worth from exposures to higher rates the strikes have to be much closer to Libor, as the forward curve is assigning very little chance to the possibility that rates way above Libor would quote in the future. In this case, great value can only be obtained in exchange for taking on very substantial amounts of risk. As this arrangement would most likely be undesirable to many corporate treasurers, different strategies must be followed if one wants to continue using exotic solutions. The good news is that, as we know, the inverted environment reverses the risk-reward profile of selling floors and swaptions: if under the steep environment good value could only be obtained from selling high-strikes floors (ie, in-the-money), now low-strikes floors (ie, out-of-the-money) can do the trick; similarly, long-dated swaptions struck at low levels (relative to Libor) can now be worth a lot. This is why it is possible to significantly improve the terms of vanilla-style protection by selling knock-in floors with attractive barrier levels and receiver swaptions with attractive strikes.

We see then that corporates these days could find costless strategies that would not only hedge their exposure to higher interest rates but also take care of the risk that, once again, an inverted curve accurately forecasts a recession and easy monetary policy. These strategies would be a suitable alternative to blindly sucumbing to the tempting vanilla offerings. As long as the economic slowdown, if it finally were to take place, is not too pronounced and does not warrant severe rate cuts on the part of the Fed, treasurers would have successfully sailed through very treacherous hedging waters.

ACCOUNTING INCENTIVES

All the above arguments and recommendations assume that treasurers are constraint-free when it comes to selecting a hedging strategy. Beyond the normal company policies ("too much exoticism is not allowed", "can't face interest rates higher than 6%") and market realities (shape of the curve, volatility levels, liquidity) this has traditionally been the case. When the time came to deal with interest rate exposures, a treasurer could just call his favourite dealers and select from the menu of available (and allowed) structures.

Nowadays, of course, that paradise of freedom has been shattered by the introduction of the new derivatives accounting rules that, as it is widely known, force corporates to record their derivatives holdings on the balance sheet. Unless certain stringent conditions are met, changes in the market value of a derivative will impact earnings every reporting period. As such value can swing wildly, derivatives that do not qualify for so-called hedge accounting become *de facto* income-volatility time bombs. Given the animosity of corporate bigwigs towards earnings surprises, it is expected that many of them would prohibit entering into hedges that are not deemed efficient. This is, therefore, the new and powerful constraint faced by formerly free treasurers.

Why is this important in the context of this chapter? Because of the bias that the standards have chosen to show in favour of some structures and against others. With somewhat different degrees of intensity, both the FAS 133 (for US-listed companies) and the IAS 39 (for Europe and Asia) share the commonality of treating vanilla interest rate swaps better than any other derivative. The treatment afforded to options (particularly single purchased and sold options) can be nightmare inducing. The treatment afforded to exotics can be depression inducing.

Under the new rules, swaps can easily be considered perfectly (or almost perfectly) effective. Their mark-to-market would not introduce any extra volatility whatsoever into the income statement. Options and exotics, in contrast, can prove to be devastatingly destabilising. Guess which type of hedge stability-seeking CEOs would rather opt for? If it begins with an "s" you guessed it right. What this means in the current yield curve environment is that treasurers, on top of the hard-to-resist temptation of low swap rates, may have a mandate from on high to get into vanilla swaps as soon as the dealer is back from lunch and to avoid everything else like the plague. As we know, such a strategy could turn out to be economically disastrous (even if trouble free from an accounting point of view) in case this time is not different and 2006 joins the long list of years when an inverted curve preceded economic malaise. In this sense, the incentives emanating from the accounting regulators would have turned out to be of the havoc-wreaking variety. By trying to avoid accounting troubles, the company would have got real trouble in the form of higher (perhaps much higher) net financing costs than the market's rate.

Paradoxically, the company may even end up regretting not having any earnings exposure to the swap's changing market value. Just as it happened in the past, the yield curve is widely expected to steepen significantly once the abnormality of inversion ends. This implies a large improvement in the mark-to-market of swaps entered into at low fixed rates. However, none of these gains would be recorded in the income statement, on account of the hedge's perfect effectiveness. Had the corporate purchased a cap instead, it could have enjoyed the earnings improvements.

6

Hedging Is Not Riskless

What the headline-grabbing currency losses at South African Airways
of a few years ago teach about the essence of risk management

It has been dubbed "the big bet on the Rand that went horribly wrong". Not too long after the turn of the century, South African Airways (SAA), the government-owned flagship carrier and Africa's leading airline, decided to enter into long-term plain vanilla currency forwards to hedge its exposure to the US dollar, derived from future purchases of fuel and the acquisition of 40-odd planes from Airbus, where both factors would become costlier were the greenback to strengthen. The belief of SAA's strategic risk committee, backed by a commissioned study from a bank, in a strong dollar (weak rand) and its desire to lock its costs at an acceptable rate that would allow the company to plan long-term was the rationale behind the selection of that particular hedging strategy. The achievement of cost certainty at the lowest possible cost seems to have also been a key driving factor. Unfortunately for SAA, the dollar suddenly reversed its previously unchallenged dominant position in 2002 and entered into a pronounced weak phase that is still ongoing. As a result, the string of forwards (from which the company profited if the dollar went up) went into the red. In the 2002–2003 financial year, the company posted an unrealised hedging loss of around R6 billion (some US$850 million), as the local currency strengthened by almost 30% in 2003. The airline went temporarily insolvent, and the South African government had to step up and provide guarantees so as to keep the carrier operating. SAA's CEO, CFO and a host of other senior staff were let go. As the dollar hit record lows in early 2004, losses for 2003–2004 approached R9 billion (US$1.4 billion). That year the hedging book was finally closed and sold to banks at a substantial cost.

What are the main lessons to emerge from the SAA debacle? Simply put, that hedging is not devoid of risks. Even the simplest strategies can present a dark side. In fact, if something comes out of the SAA episode it is that the simplest instruments can be the most dangerous. Instead of using options, the company decided to go for the plainest of vanilla derivatives, the currency forward. As we all know, a forward does not impose any upfront premium and guarantees a fixed, certain exchange rate for a particular future transaction (in this case, the future purchase of dollar-denominated assets). However, by entering into the forward, the company would be exposing itself to a substantial risk: if the underlying rate moves in your favour, you will not be able to enjoy any of the benefits and will be irremediably locked into an unfriendly rate (ie, losses) for what could be a long time. The elimination of this type of contingency is precisely the reason that makes options carry an initial premium. While a forward can kill you, an option never will.

It is not only in the case of forwards that risks may be underestimated. In general, there seems to be a misconception as to what hedging really entails. Hedging never eliminates all risks. A hedged position is not a riskless position. Hedging is merely a risk-switching strategy whereby the hedger gets rid of one risk in return for shouldering a new risk. Many people would argue that a forward does eliminate all risk, since it eliminates all uncertainty (deviation from a fixed level). However, non-certainty and no risk are not, of course, the same thing. In fact, the very factor that makes a forward such a risky strategy is precisely its uncertainty-eliminating characteristic. SAA provides a very clear example of these ideas.

The third main lesson to draw from the SAA cataclysm relates to the (controversial) new derivatives accounting rules and the ways in which they can influence treasurers hedging decisions. There is a danger that in some instances corporates would be geared towards certain derivatives strategies over others, and that the former may end up causing very substantial losses (accounting and/or economic). Forwards, that have received a friendly treatment by the new standards relative to alternative hedging tools, decisively drive this crucial point home.

HEDGING 101

For years, corporates have been accused of not understanding how derivatives work and of having recklessly embraced the use of exotic structures in the name of financial risk management. The scandals surrounding firms such as Procter & Gamble, Gibson Greetings, Ashanti Gold or Poste Italiane at different points in the past decade or so have given plenty of ammunition to the vast army of derivatives critics out there. How, they ask, could products purportedly used for hedging purposes expose corporates so dangerously? Wasn't the point precisely to isolate companies from risk? Surely, such headline-grabbing losses must be the result of some obscure speculative activity going on inside treasury departments. In fact, it is widely assumed that the new derivatives accounting standards introduced in the past few years are an attempt on the part of regulators to tame the "derivatives beast" and to make sure that corporates use derivatives to control risk, ie, to hedge and not speculate.

However, the case can be made that the critics and the standards are the ones suffering from a profound misconception regarding the nature of derivatives and what they *really* do for their users. To put it bluntly, hedging is a widely misunderstood term. While many people assume that by hedging your existing risks you are effectively left out with no exposures, nothing could be further from the truth. Hedging is not about risk elimination, but rather about risk transformation. Thus, every derivative structure entered into by a corporate involves switching from the existing risk profile into a new profile, according to the views of the treasurer and the finance director (and, arguably, the selling abilities of the bankers). While the original risk is most certainly eliminated, the company's new net position is not riskless. All that has happened is that a new risk has taken the place of the old. And, of course, the new risk could very well turn out to be more risky that the previous risk that it is replacing. When corporates suffer large losses (some of them simply of an accounting nature) this is exactly what has taken place: market movements render the risk-switching strategy (ie, the hedging decision) hugely unfavourable. It is not necessarily that derivatives were being employed for speculative purposes. They were being used as hedging tools, and as such they never stopped being risky.

The SAA episode highlights this key idea better than most other derivatives-related scandals. After the losses were announced, many commentators, in predictable fashion, proceeded to voice alarmist concerns and pass misinformed judgement on the company's derivatives forays. The word speculation was used. The treasury team was accused of not adopting a judicious and informed risk management strategy. Bigwigs were slammed for alleged lack of expertise. The hedge portfolio was dubbed "a massive investment". Lack of accountability was mentioned. And yes, the name Enron showed up too.

What these outsiders do not understand is that derivatives losses do not necessarily imply that reckless, unchecked, amateurish and even downright fraudulent speculation was taking place inside the hallowed confines of a company's treasury department. Losses, are one of the possible, natural and perfectly normal outcomes of any derivative transaction. Even the most mild-mannered, conservative, law-abiding, decent and knowledgeable treasurer is subjecting himself to the possibility of losses when entering into a hedging position. Such possibility derives from the new risk that the corporate has chosen to assume in exchange for saying good-bye to the previous, bothersome, nightmares-inducing risk. In the case of SAA, CFO Richard Forson and his team decided to eliminate the risk that the airline would face, on average, a dollar stronger than R10.80 over a period of 10 years (as detailed in the next section). This was consistent with the length of the dollar-denominated obligations on the Airbus deliveries, locked-in the cost of those obligations in rands at what one assumes to have been an internally-considered acceptable level, allowed the company to plan long-term with certainty, and was done in a way that minimised accounting earnings volatility when compared to other alternative tools. In return for achieving all this, at zero cost no less, Forson chose to expose SAA to a new risk: huge losses should the dollar tank below R10.80. And tank it did. And the consequent losses materialised. However, this does not mean that Forson's strategy was irresponsible or ill conceived. The same thing would have happened to anybody who had entered into a long-dollar forward position.

To suffer losses when using derivatives does not require speculative activity to take place. Positions intended purely as hedges (ie, risk-swapping devices) can, and do everyday, inflict pain. The new risk simply turned out to be too much to bear. Yes, the hedger made the wrong bet, but that does not mean that his main intention was to bet. His main goal was to get rid of the original risk. The new risk is simply the unavoidable price tag for a valuable service. The job of a treasurer, and the measure by which he should be judged, is to wisely and professionally select the most appropriate price tag possible. However, there are neither guaranteed results nor refunds. Forson and others at SAA strongly felt that the dollar was going to show resilience. In light of this, and the stated prime objective of achieving certainty of costs at the lowest possible cost, the forward was a reasonable proposition. Not everyone's cup of tea (lots of folks do not want the pressure of a potential disaster), but definitely not a reckless, irresponsible, Enron-like decision. After all, we are talking about the simplest, easiest-to-understand and most popular currency derivative.

So, to recap: hedging does not equal an absence of negative outcomes, all it means is that a company has turned the causality of those outcomes upside down. For SAA, the possible negative outcome went from a very high dollar to a very high rand. Had it used options (another non-riskless hedge), the new possible negative events would have been, among many, the loss of the (perhaps substantial) initial premium in the case of vanilla options, the sharp appreciation of the rand in the case of collars, and the reaching or not of a certain spot level in the case of barrier options. The only sure way to avoid hedging-related surprises is, plainly, not to hedge at all. Is this what the derivatives nay-Sayers and Monday-morning quarterbacks would rather have companies do?

FORWARDS VERSUS OPTIONS

When it comes to using derivatives with the purpose of hedging currency exposures, the two basic available tools for corporates are forwards and options. The job of derivatives bankers is to, first, try to convince companies to hedge their forex risks (not all firms do, and many academics do not even think they should) and second, to try to convince them to use options instead of forwards (as the former provide fatter margins). The motivation behind this counsel is not simply the cynical pursuit of profits on the part of bonus-hungry bankers, but also the desire (and professional obligation) to offer value-added services that can critically assist corporate treasurers in a key area. The practical validity of covering oneself from the wild swings of the unpredictable and untameable currency markets is a very subjective (and controversial) issue on which we will not dwell here. Much more clear-cut, however, are the distinctions between forwards and options. As any treasurer who has ever been visited by derivatives professionals knows, the pros and cons of each type of product can be delineated as follows:

Forwards	Options (single)	Options (collars)
Zero cost	Positive cost	Zero cost possible
Full certainty regarding future exchange rate	Uncertainty regarding future exchange rate	Reduced uncertainty regarding future exchange rate
Full downside protection	Full downside protection (net of premium paid)	Full downside protection (net of premium paid)
No participation in upside gains	Full participation in upside gains (net of premium paid)	Limited participation in upside gains (net of premium paid)
Potential liquidity and credit concerns	No credit concerns	Limited credit concerns
Requires credit lines	Does not require credit lines	Requires credit lines
Hedge accounting friendly	Potential earnings volatility	Limited earnings volatility

As can be deducted from the above box, the potential for losses is greater under a forward than under an option-driven strategy (some exotic products, such as barrier options, may prove to be an exception). While the maximum economic loss of a purchased option is defined by the premium paid, in the case of a forward the maximum loss is virtually unlimited. Some may argue that corporate treasurers do not care about losses on the forward because they are matched by gains in the underlying exposure. If the forward is hedging, say, an appreciation of the euro with respect to the dollar above US$1.30, and the dollar strengthens all the way to US$1.18, all the treasurer is giving up, the argument would be, are opportunity costs. The real threat (a dollar below US$1.30) is fully covered. The trouble with this line of thinking is that such opportunity costs are more dangerous than they appear at first. For one, the corporate (perhaps a US importer of Italian products) would be entrapped at a rate of US$1.30 when all his competitors are enjoying the much more beneficial US$1.18. The company may thus be priced out of the market. Its reported results could show relatively disappointing earnings, which may prompt analysts to point their fingers at the firm's negative exceptionalism. Investments undertaken by competitors (afforded by the cheaper cost of imports) might not be afforded by the company, which would effectively be left behind. If the forward strategy is for the long-term (*à la* SAA) then real mark-to-market damage may ensue. In the previous example, assume that the US importer, for whatever reason, has entered into a strip of forwards extending for the next five years. That is, the importer is hedged for a period of five years at a fixed, unchangeable rate of US$1.30. After the dollar experiences a sudden and pronounced bump-up, the strip of forwards would suffer mark-to-market losses as the new forward curve would be indicating that future spot levels would be below US$1.30. In other words, the curve would be saying that large negative cash settlements await the company in each of the forward contracts entered into. While obviously eventual future spot levels may very well be at or above US$1.30 (forward curves "lie" all the time), the point is that today the corporate would own a hedging strategy that has a negative market worth and that creates a large negative liability (ie, an unrealised loss). Such accounting setbacks could have serious implications for the credit standing of the company, perhaps even affecting its cost of capital. And there might be human casualties (just ask those departed personnel formerly employed at SAA).

These potentially dire consequences of using forwards (facing a devastating price war, earning the wrath of analysts and investors, severe valuation malaise, dismissed staff, etc) contrast with the more benign dark side of options. The only area in which options could truly prove to be more harmful than forwards is their accounting treatment, as options usage may result in unwelcome income statement volatility (more on this below). However, even in this case, the mark-to-market figures should not be destructive (as the net total-income effect would not be higher than the option's premium) and, crucially, they do not carry credit implications as purchased options do not imply any future payment obligation on the part of the end-user.

In light of all this, it may seem paradoxical that forward contracts are usually labelled as simple, conservative tools; risk-free. The very first strategy shown to corporate clients in a banker's presentation. Nothing like those mischievous and strange-sounding exotic options. Knock-outs? Knock-ins? Lookbacks? Double-average rate? Who needs them when you can use, free of charge, the easy-to-understand forward. Especially when so many of the other treasurers are also going with it. The problem is, of course, that in real life the exotic structures can end up being much less risky than the vanilla forward. The simpler tool may produce the most damage.

The risk of a derivative instrument should not be defined by the complexity of its payout or the advanced mathematical techniques involved in its pricing. It should be defined by the worst possible outcome that can derive from the new position into which the end-user has voluntarily entered. As was said earlier, when a hedge is contracted, a shifting of exposures takes place. In the case of SAA, the corporate effectively eliminated its previously existent exposure (a rising dollar). However, because of the forward position, a new risk had emerged: if the dollar went down significantly, the company would suffer large losses (in the form of real opportunity costs, unrealised accounting setbacks and liquidity and credit concerns). Notice that what was a blessing before the forwards (a strong rand) has now, almost magically, been transformed into a threat. Under the new scenario, the worst possible outcome would indeed be bad as the company would be exposed in a limitless way to a dollar crash. Contrast this with the much-limited exposure of a purchased option where the only downside is the (known) premium paid (granted, knock-out options could die and knock-in options may never come into existence, but even in these cases the barrier can be set in such a way that limits potential danger).

Having said this, with the introduction of the new derivatives accounting rules in the past few years (FAS 133 for US-listed companies and IAS 39 for everybody else) the use of options has become potentially disturbing as in many instances corporate end-users would have to record changes in the market value of the contracts in current earnings, thus giving rise to unwelcome income volatility. Forwards, in contrast, get a more favourable accounting treatment as changes in fair value are "stored" in shareholders' equity and are reclassified into earnings only at the time that the underlying transaction takes place (it should be noted, though, that this is not devoid of problems, as will be demonstrated in the analysis at the final section of this chapter). That is, with forwards the income statement would not be subjected to wild mark-to-market swings. In this sense, it can be argued that the new standards incentivise the use of forwards over options (more on this crucial point later).

Accounting and other considerations may prevent companies from using options and throw them into the arms of forwards by default. The two other important factors that can make forwards more attractive for treasurers are, on the one hand, the existence of very specific risk-management goals, and on the other, a reluctance to pay for protection. For some corporates, absolute certainty may be exactly what they want (this seems to have been the case with SAA). In this scenario, a forward would be the most appropriate instrument and would deliver the desired "perfect hedge". Similarly, and perhaps surprisingly, many corporates often show a reluctance to part with their cash when the time comes to obtain protection from financial risks (as opposed to paying for regular insurance). This may be explained by several factors, such as spending restrictions, an underestimation of risk that may make the premium appear relatively expensive and a fear of financial engineering in general. The never-ending design by banks of innovative cheaper structures, including zero-cost, does not appear to have dramatically impulsed the use of options and altered treasurers' love affair with forwards. To this day, after more than a decade of breathless technical innovation, many corporates still do not use anything but forwards when hedging their currency exposures. According to the Bank of America's 2004 FX Survey, for the US-based companies sampled, when it came to hedging forecasted transactions 75% was done using forwards as opposed to just 20% using options. Similarly, 65% of the translation exposure hedged was done with forwards and only 30% with options. In the case of balance sheet exposures (transaction exposures), the figures were 88% and 8%, respectively. In other words, by far the most widely used corporate forex risk-management instrument is the old, boring forward. As the SAA saga shows, by making such a choice, treasurers may be taking a path where the ultimate destination could very well be insolvency.

SAA entered into forward contracts that yielded an average price of R10.80 per dollar over 10 years. That is, for the company not to suffer losses on the hedge the rand should not, on average, strengthen below that level. Clearly, by the time the rand hit a four-year high of R6.09 in early December 2003 things were not going SAA's way. For the rest of the 2003–2004 fiscal year, the currency hovered around the R6.50 level. Had SAA purchased options (dollar calls/rand puts) instead, the airline would have been able to enjoy the wonderful developments taking place in the forex market. Both the purchase of fuel and the payments on the Airbus fleet would have seemed quite economical in rand terms. And while the premium on long-dated forex option structures can be very expensive, SAA may have been able to avoid paying anything at all or at least incur just a small cost had it been willing to employ other strategies, such as collars or more exotic structures (Asian options, barrier options, etc). The bottom line is that SAA provides a very clear and dramatic example of how a company can go berserk as a consequence of having used forwards, and how the use of options could have avoided all the mayhem. Even more important, the South African carrier is not the only high-profile case of forwards-induced misery and regrettable options-neglect. It is not even the only high-profile airline. Germany's Lufthansa went through the same hell in the mid-1980s, as a direct consequence of (you guessed it) an unexpectedly declining dollar.

At a time of unusually pronounced dollar strength, Lufthansa placed an order with Boeing for delivery of planes approximately one year later. As with SAA, the German carrier became thus exposed to a strong greenback. When it came to making hedging-related decisions, it basically faced three alternatives: (1) buy dollars forward, (2) buy an option strategy, (3) do nothing and hope that the dollar would be weaker when the planes are due for delivery. Given the princely state of the dollar, fixing the whole purchase price at the then-prevalent (high) forward rate seemed unattractive. In view of this, and added to the company's apparent belief in a strong future deutschmark, Lufthansa decided to opt for a fourth strategy: buy just half the required dollars forward, and roll the dice in the forex markets for the other half.

Did the forex roulette go the company's way? Yes, as the dollar dived. This was good news for the portion that was left unhedged, but disastrous news for the half that was hedged with a high-price forward. Mayhem struck when the company reported separately the planes purchase (at a very favourable spot exchange rate) and the forward dollars purchase (at a very unfavourable rate). This way, the sizeable currency loss derived from the forward position was recorded uncoupled from the money-saving spot transaction, for everyone to see. As a result, those inside Lufthansa responsible for the strategy lost their jobs amid what nearly became a national scandal. Imagine what would have happened if the company had decided to hedge the entire exposure with forwards.

ACCOUNTING TRAP

It was mentioned earlier that the new derivatives accounting standards afford forwards better treatment than options. By "better" we mean less potential for continuous income-statement volatility. When it comes to hedging the type of exposure faced by SAA (a so-called cashflow hedge, whereby the company covers the risk of anticipated variable future purchases), the currency forward would be deemed perfectly effective (ie, changes in the derivative are a perfect offset to changes in the underlying exposure). As such, fluctuations in the fair value of the forward (gains or losses) would be recorded every reporting period not under earnings, but under equity, where they would accumulate until the hedged forecasted transaction hits earnings (ie, at maturity). At that point, the accumulated figure would be reclassified into earnings too.

In contrast, purchased options (such as a dollar call/rand put) can become volatility time bombs. This is, it must be said, less so in FAS 133-land than in IAS 39-territory after US regulators introduced new guidance for options accounting a few months after the initial implementation date of January 2001. However, given the voluntary, non obligatory, nature of such an amendment and the fact that its drawbacks may make some corporates opt out and revert to the original methodology, it is safe to argue that options remain a bigger threat to earnings stability than forwards. Under the original FAS 133-IAS 39 treatment for purchased options, only intrinsic value can be deemed effective with changes in time value (an entity that can swing wildly) hitting reported income right away. The potential for destabilising (and analysts-despised) earning volatility is thus significant.

What is the point of all this? The point is, quite simply, that for those corporates that care about avoiding nasty surprises in their reported results the new rules represent an incentive not to get into options and to choose forwards instead (it must be said that a zero-cost collar would receive friendly accounting treatment). For those treasurers that act on such incentive, the new rules may deliver an entrapment with dire consequences (both economic and, yes, accounting). As the SAA and Lufthansa episodes show, forwards can be bad for the health of corporate treasurers. It can be very unpleasant from a bottom line perspective to have to face a sinking dollar when your forward was entered into at a time of dollar strength. And the supposedly accounting-friendly aspect of forwards can quickly turn into a Trojan horse that has as much potential for wreaking havoc as those wild-eyed options. Recall that the main selling point of forwards in this new accounting era is that their mark-to-market will not touch income until maturity, when it is offset by the underlying transaction. In other words, they should not, in principle, create much accounting mischief. However, accumulating value changes in shareholders' equity is not devoid of potential nastiness. To understand why this could be the case, let us take a look at a real-life example courtesy of Fitch Ratings.

As part of a comprehensive survey on derivatives accounting and reporting by corporates conducted in late 2004, Fitch disclosed the illuminating case of Amarada Hess, which uses commodity forwards to hedge future cashflows. On 31st December 2003, the company had shareholders' equity of US$5.34 billion. However, accumulated other comprehensive income (AOCI) from cashflow hedges showed a loss of US$357 million, or 7% of total equity. In other words, the company's forward hedges were experiencing large mark-to-market losses (ie, the forwards were deep out-of-the-money). This made Amerada appear as a much more leveraged enterprise than it really was. Given a total debt figure of US$3.94 billion, the company's debt-to-equity ratio was 0.74. If one excluded the negative effects of hedge accounting (ie, equity increases), the number became a sunnier 0.69. The paradox is, of course, that while the company was prudently hedging its financial risks it was being painted as a riskier firm (more geared) by the accounting rules. In fact, the new artificial risk was created by the very actions aimed at limiting real risk.

The conclusion must be that while forwards accounting effectively neutralises income statement volatility, it causes equity (balance sheet) volatility that, although likely to be less of a concern than earnings volatility, can still create considerable damage. When deciding between the use of options and forwards, corporates must decide which type of volatility they care more about. For those situations where options receive somewhat similar treatment than forwards (collars and, possibly, purchased options under FAS 133) it is vital to point out that options have a clear advantage over forwards in relation to changes in AOCI, as the maximum net decrease in equity resulting from the fair valuation of the option is the option premium (if any), while forward hedging can result in very significant reductions (and volatility) in equity.

As we can see, the trap set up by the new standards (which may intimidate treasurers towards forwards through the earnings volatility threat) can end up delivering a nasty double-whammy: real economic losses and accounting losses. Of course, the latter should only be significant if the hedging strategy is long-term. For forward hedges of one year or less (the usual maturities in the forex world) the accounting malaise should be limited. The nastiness, however, can be headline grabbing for hedges of longer maturities. A 10-year horizon (the risk hedged by SAA) would clearly belong to that category.

7

DARO-Loving Chicagoans

*How medical equipment manufacturer Dade Behring has recently
highlighted the practical relevance of the "undiscovered
jewel" of the currency-hedging world*

Despite having been used to hedge the currency risks derived from
the sales of such mainstream items as PowerPoint and the Big Mac,
so-called double average rate options (DAROs) remain a pretty much
undiscovered, seldom used and highly exotic risk management tool
for multinational companies. A member of the Asian options family, a
DARO is in fact akin to a combination of its two, better known, rela-
tives: the average rate option (ARO) and the average strike option
(ASO). Simply put, what this implies is that the DARO is a product
that hedges the difference between two averages of the prices of the
underlying asset, with each average corresponding to a different
sample period. As neither average is known when the contract is
entered into, the DARO is an option that effectively has no strike at
initiation. The main reason for using DAROs is to protect a corporate's earnings-per-share from the vagaries of the currency markets.
By using this exotic product, a company can report revenue on a
"constant currency basis", thus providing a more meaningful analysis of the underlying activity since it eliminates the effect of changing
foreign exchange rates when comparing the results of a given quarter
with those of its equivalent in the previous year (the relevance of such
reporting is of course explained by analysts' focus on year-on-year
earnings in the company's functional currency).

By eliminating the potentially highly destabilising translation
exposure faced by multinational corporates that must consolidate

the income earned abroad at the average exchange rate every quarter, it is clear that DAROs perform a valuable service. No wonder, then, that Microsoft and McDonalds were eager early users when DAROs started showing up around 1999. As both giants sell vast amounts of their products around the world, they cannot afford being complacent when it comes to their accounting (never mind economic) exposure to currency fluctuations. The international commercial success of a new project could be decisively hampered by a decline in value of the local currencies, which depresses their US$ worth when the accounting translation takes place. No matter how many new burgers McDonalds sells overseas, if the dollar has strengthened significantly then reported earnings may look weak when compared to the previous, commercially less brilliant, year. The stock price may dive as a result, the viability of the new product strategy might be put in question and heads could roll. Wouldn't it be nice if a bank would sell me a financial product that takes care of all such worries? Well, these days many financial institutions can structure a DARO and the price would likely be quite economical too.

This makes it all the more puzzling that not many other corporates seem to have followed Microsoft's and McDonald's lead. Dealers unequivocally report very slight interest in DAROs. Why? This apathy is most likely due to a series of factors. One could be lack of awareness as to what the product can do for the end-user. While it must be expected that sophisticated dealers have shown DARO strategies to their corporate clients, the truth is that it is quite difficult to find information on these options (none of the major derivatives textbooks even mention the name). Another factor could be that many companies may already be hedging their quarterly net revenue exposure with strips of plain vanilla ARO options that effectively guarantee that the average exchange rate for the quarter does not deviate from a given, pre-selected strike level. While this strategy would not hedge the year-on-year translation risk, it might make the additional use of DAROs appear unnecessary (not to mention an extra cost burden). Finally, and possibly the biggest reason behind the modest use of DAROs, the treatment afforded by the new derivatives accounting standards is quite unfriendly, essentially forcing end-users to subject their reported earnings to the potential volatility brought about by changes in the mark-to-market of the option.

In this context, it must indeed be considered good news (at least for those who root for the extensive, but responsible, usage of financial engineering tools) to hear that Chicago-based Dade Behring started implementing DARO-based currency hedging strategies in 2004. As the world's largest company in its field (clinical diagnostics equipment manufacturing), its endorsement clearly highlights the practical relevance of the product. If such an important corporate is using DAROs, perhaps other companies should dust off those forgotten, nicely-binded presentations from derivatives bankers that were previously discarded and take a second look at the structures. For those treasurers that were unaware of the existence of such risk management tools, Dade's example may incite them to demand some information next time they get a visit from the Wall Street crowd. In other words, the well-publicised use of DAROs by a leading member of corporate America (which was awarded the prestigious Alexander Hamilton Gold Award for excellence in financial risk management in late 2005, precisely in recognition of its adoption of such innovative currency hedging strategies) may provide a much-needed push to the corporate use of an exotic derivative that, while offering highly valuable assistance in the critical area of translation exposure, has so far been mostly ignored.

DARO LAND

As mentioned before, a DARO option is a combination of an ARO and an ASO. Alternatively, a DARO may be considered as a combination of the characteristic (ie, exotic) features of both options. That is, the strike of a DARO is an average (ASO influence) and the settlement price is also an average (ARO influence). Both averages are calculated using different, pre-defined sampling periods. As also pointed out earlier, and though there are other possible applications, DAROs are mostly used to hedge the translation risks incurred by multinational companies by providing a cash compensation in case of an unfavourable exchange rate during the current reporting quarter in comparison with the rate prevalent during the same quarter in the previous year. This way, a corporate's earnings will be fully protected from unpredictable currency swings that may make today's results look bad when compared to last year's, even though the underlying real activity could very well have performed much better. In this sense, a DARO protects a corporate from earnings-obsessed analysts who do not have the time or patience to discriminate between real results and forex-induced results (which, of course, are beyond the company's control).

To understand how translation risk can affect a multinational, let us briefly analyse the case of McDonald's. At the end of every quarter, the foreign currency-denominated income earned by its many international subsidiaries is consolidated to reflect the company's global total results. In accordance with accounting rules, these figures are converted to US Dollars (McDonald's functional currency) at the average daily exchange rate for the quarter. This, of course, is why Asian options are useful when dealing with this kind of risk (this would be the ARO part of the DARO). McDonald's quarterly earnings releases report its performance in the current quarter compared to the previous year's quarter, where the foreign component was consolidated at the then-prevailing average daily exchange rates. The difference between both dollar-based results represents, in part (a large part in the case of McDonald's, which earns more than half its income outside of the US), a translation gain or loss. If the foreign currencies strengthen on average from one period to the other, then (assuming more or less constant international sales levels) more dollars would be reported in the current period, yielding a translation gain (good news). A translation loss (bad news) would result from the opposite scenario whereby weakened average currencies represent fewer reported dollars. McDonald's treasury professionals obviously wish to minimise or eliminate such possible translation losses (which may not only be disastrous, but unfair as the company may be forced to report disappointed overall results in spite of having sold lots more Big Macs and Chicken McNuggets to their European, Chinese or Australian customers than in the same quarter 12 months before). In this light, the target exchange rates for a given quarter become the average daily rates of that quarter in the previous year (this would be the ASO component of the DARO). By hedging at this target rate, the company ensures no translation loss on the selected notional amount.

DARO options were tailor-made to take care of such hedging needs. Assume a US multinational that wants to ensure that currency movements will not make Q2-2007 results look poor when compared to Q2-2006. The company could purchase a DARO with a strike level based on the average rate for the three months of Q2-2006 that will settle based on the average rate for the three months of Q2-2007. Thus, earnings would be reported on an equal currency basis regardless of fluctuations in the foreign exchange market. Obviously, the option is transacted prior to the end of Q2-2006 (but not necessarily before the beginning), otherwise the corporate could just wait and later buy a regular ARO with the Q2-2006 known average rate as the fixed strike level. This key characteristic can make the DARO cheaper than an ARO and explains the rationale for the product.

As the risk being hedged is the depreciation of a specific foreign currency (or a basket of foreign currencies) against the company's base currency, an end-user would need to purchase a DARO call on its functional currency (a DARO put on the foreign currency). For instance, a US multinational that exports heavily to Holland would buy a DARO dollar call/Euro put that will deliver a positive pay-out if the average quarterly exchange rate for the "settlement quarter" has gone down with respect to the average quarterly rate for the "strike quarter" (ie, if the dollar has increased in value). Assuming an average exchange rate of US$1.25 for Q2-2006, the DARO would pay out only if the eventual average rate for Q2-2007 is below US$1.25. This way, the corporate's reported earnings would be protected from a relative quarter-on-quarter depreciation of the Euro that implies translation losses. In case that the settlement average is above US$1.25 then the option would be out-of-the-money and the corporate would be more than happy nakedly translating its Q2-2007 Euro-denominated income into dollars at the new, stronger exchange rate.

This last scenario is exactly what happened to Dade Behring in Q2-2005. As the dollar had been significantly weaker during that period than during Q2-2004 (trading in the US$1.25–1.30 range against the Euro for the April–May 2005 period, while barely touching US$1.20 the year before), the relevant DARO did expire worthless as protection was eventually not needed. According to its released results, revenue grew year-on-year by 9% (from US$388 million to US$423 million). However, the "constant currency basis" results showed an increase of just 6.5%. In other words, if we applied the current year's exchange rate to both sets of figures

(Dade's preferred method for comparison purposes) the translated number for the previous year would end up higher than if translated at its own average rate (thus the smaller difference between both reported revenue sums). What this obviously implies is that the dollar was on average higher during Q2-2004 than during Q2-2005. For Dade's DAROs to expire in-the-money, the constant currency-basis revenue growth should be higher, not lower, than that reported (ie, the current year's average rate would have translated into less dollars if prevalent during the previous year).

In previous paragraphs we mentioned that DAROs can be cheaper than AROs and that this very fact represented the key rationale for corporate use in the first place. Let us now try to elaborate this point. When trying to hedge the year-on-year translation risk, a company can use a DARO, as we know, but could also use the simpler ARO. Why not wait until, say, the average Dollar/Yen rate for Q2-2006 is known with certainty and then enter into a regular ARO with the strike price set at that fixed level and the settlement price being the daily average of the exchange rate for Q2-2007? Recall that in the case of the DARO we would not wait. We would have to sign on the contract before the average for Q2-2006 is known. Could this uncertainty be worth it in terms of cheaper premium? Well, by allowing the end-user some waiting time the DARO affords more chances of obtaining a cheap price than the later-entered-into ARO. In a sense, the DARO could be seen as an ARO "in advance", in contrast to the regular "deferred" ARO. This time advance may allow the right market conditions to present themselves and guarantee a very economical price for the desired hedge. If the corporate chose to give up such opportunity it would be running the risk of having to pay more for the regular ARO later on, once the average strike is known.

Under which circumstances would a DARO be cheap? It would depend on the shape of the forward curve. In the case of a dollar call, if the dollar is at a discount *versus* the foreign currency the "expected" average strike (defined by the shape of the curve) will be higher than the average forward rate for the rate-averaging period, making the price of the DARO clearly cheap. On the other hand, if the dollar was at a premium then the expected average strike would be lower than the settlement average rate, resulting in an expensive DARO. If just prior to the start of Q2-2006 the dollar traded at a significant discount a US multinational could purchase the desired protection from translation exposure in an economical way. However, perhaps, for whatever reason, the company may wish to postpone the purchase of the hedge until after the end of Q2-2006, when an ARO with the now-known strike price would be bought. The problem is that by then the forward curve may indicate an expected settlement rate for Q2-2007 way above the fixed strike level, thus making the ARO very expensive and rendering the prior decision to forgo the DARO a very costly one. The main idea is that both the ARO and the DARO will naturally end up having the same strike (ie, the daily average exchange rate for Q2-2006), but the exact time when the option is entered into will produce different option premiums. It is up to the end-user to decide whether the premium for the DARO is low enough to avoid incurring large opportunity costs later on.

ACCOUNTING OBSTACLES

The real key question is, why haven't more corporates embraced the use of DARO options? Any CEO or CFO is concerned about year-on-year reported results and would like to tightly control every element that could impact those numbers. For multinationals, foreign exchange is clearly a major source of concern, especially when a particular base currency is going through a prolonged period of strength (such as, for instance, was the case of the dollar in the 2000–2002 period or the case of the Euro ever since) that could severely limit the otherwise positive effects of a successful overseas operation. In the case of a company such as Dade Behring, that obtains half its revenues from overseas (it sells into more than 100 countries in more than 20 different currencies), leaving reported earnings to the vagaries of the foreign exchange markets could spell doom and critically endanger the firm's relationships with its creditors and investors.

As we have seen, DAROs can be a highly effective and possibly an economical way of managing the dreaded year-on-year translation risk. They come with the seal of approval not only from giants Microsoft and McDonald's but also the relatively less-known Dade, three companies with highly sophisticated and derivatives savvy treasury departments. For any public company with international subsidiaries that cares about earnings-per-share (who doesn't?),

DARO options should, in principle, be part of the mainstream hedging toolkit.

However, sadly for bankers, this does not seem to be the case. According to Dade's treasurer Mark Moran, none of the top forex dealers has more than a dozen corporate clients using DAROs and most have fewer than 10 DARO users. When these figures are viewed in the wider context of the thousands of existing US multi-national companies (let alone non-US firms), we are undoubtedly talking about a very small market. In previous paragraphs, we made an early attempt at trying to figure out why this could be the case. It was pointed out that perhaps not too many potential end-users are aware of the existence of DAROs and what they can do for them. Even in the case of Microsoft, it apparently took the company a long while to realise that it had the type of period-on-period translation exposure that DAROs can hedge and that it could be substantial. For those corporates that are fully familiar with the product, perhaps some of its inherent characteristics may discourage usage. Treasurers might find them too complex and exotic, and could dislike the fact that the modelling involved in the pricing of the option would be quite challenging, as many corporates do not enter into derivatives that cannot be priced internally (prior to entering into its first DARO contract in mid-1999, Microsoft had some in-house mathematicians build a pricing model so as to validate the quotes obtained from bankers; clearly, few other companies can afford such sophisticated treasury operations).

Another key possible technical drawback is the fact that the option has not known strike at inception. This may be unacceptable to some corporates, and not simply due to the uncertainty involved in not knowing exactly which risk you are hedging against. The main concern regarding the strike-less feature of DAROs is that it does not allow the end-user to ascertain the chances that the option will expire in-the-money (ie, that the spent premium would not have been wasted). With a more conventional option (such as a regular ARO), the strike reference is known in advance and this helps develop a view as to whether the settlement price at maturity would be above (for a call) or below (for a put). Without the possibility of developing such a view, many treasurers may walk away from the option (would you pay upfront for a bet that delivers a payoff in case the underlying is above or below a certain parameter if such parameter is not known in advance?). The argument could be made that, for the kind of risk hedged with DAROs, it is not necessary to know the precise strike level before transacting. All we care about is that we get compensated if there is a translation loss when comparing the current period's consolidated earnings with last year's. We don't need to know the precise figure for the latter, as it is only the difference that bothers us. However, there is a possible flaw in this line of reasoning. Imagine a US multinational that has lots of operations in Mexico and that wants to cover its year-on-year translation exposure. It purchases a DARO prior to the beginning of Q2-2006, only to witness a rapid depreciation of the Peso (maybe due to temporary jitters regarding political developments in Latin America) that results in an average exchange rate (the option's strike) of 15 Pesos per dollar. Now, at that strike level, the company considers the chances of the option expiring in-the-money at the end of Q2-2007 to be negligible. It does not believe that the dollar will be trading above 15 Pesos by then, as it considers the current market turmoil a short-term irrational reaction by investors to the spread of populist, anti-American governments in the region. Mexico, the treasury people would argue, is a reliable country that will continue to pursue sound economic policies. Once the temporary panic subsides, investors will surely learn to calmly discriminate between a modern nation such as Mexico and its troublesome southern neighbours and the Peso would go back up to normal levels. Under this scenario, there would be no year-on-year translation risk as the dollar could not possibly trade above 15 Pesos on average during the settlement quarter. In the eyes of the corporate, the premium spent on the DARO would have been effectively wasted (another way to explain this is by arguing that after Q2-2006 the company would not have purchased an ARO expiring at the end of Q2-2007 with a strike of 15).

A third possible obstacle to corporate use of DAROs is that companies that are already using AROs to hedge the absolute translation risks of each individual period may find it redundant to hedge the relative period-on-period exposures, and would especially be reluctant to spend yet more premium money on currency hedges. To understand how a corporate may use AROs to hedge its net foreign revenue we can take a look at the case of Microsoft. This is an exposure for which no real money has moved (as opposed to the cashflow hedging programme that manages very short-term foreign receivables), ie, the exposure is of an accounting nature (a "paper" exposure). As we know, the revenue that is going to be booked (consolidated) depends on the average foreign exchange rate for the period. If the foreign currencies weaken, then this revenue will be translated into fewer dollars. If they strengthen, the opposite will take place. Microsoft would like to purchase a hedging instrument that covers the difference between the average settlement rates and the chosen strike (usually, the budgeted currency rate for that year), so that the money made on the derivative if it expires in-the-money gets booked as revenue offsetting any decline in the foreign currencies. In order to achieve this goal, Microsoft was an early user of ARO options in 1994. After using strips of AROs on a basket of currencies, the company later resorted to individual AROs for each regional risk area. In general, Microsoft attempts to hedge the entire budgeted revenue in a given quarter. The goal is to be fully hedged for the next 12 months at the time when the fiscal year's budgeting cycle provides Microsoft's treasury with a revenue forecast (ie, with the amounts to hedge and the relevant strike rate of the option).

To see how the ARO can help Microsoft, consider the following hypothetical example: the company buys a dollar call/Euro put ARO on a notional of €200 million at a fixed strike of US$1.20. If the dollar averages US$1.15 in that period (ie, the call expires in-the-money), Microsoft's net revenue translation is US$230 million. If the company is paid US$10 million from the option's counterparty, less US$2 million in premium, the final net revenue becomes US$238 million. Microsoft would thus have achieved a better effective exchange rate of US$1.19. This is the value-added offered by the ARO. It clearly allows corporates to take care of the translation risk of any particular reporting period, with regards to the specific chosen budgeted rate. However, it doesn't allow them to hedge the year-on-year reported results from the vagaries of the currency markets. The ARO covering, say, Q2-2006 would cover the gap between the average settlement rate and the budgeted rate for 2006; similarly the ARO covering Q2-2007 would cover the gap between that average settlement rate and the budgeted rate for 2007. What is needed is an option that covers the gap between both average settlement rates. Some corporates may be unwilling or unable to pay the extra premium represented by the DARO, in effect deciding that they can only afford the strip of AROs (which they may deem more important) and not both strategies at the same time.

However, most probably the biggest factor that explains why DAROs have remained relatively unpopular is their accounting treatment. The new accounting standards for derivatives (both FAS 133 and IAS 39) prohibit hedge accounting status for derivatives that manage the translation exposure on subsidiary profit and loss account balances. In other words, hedging earnings translation is a risk that cannot be designated as a hedged item under FAS 133 or IAS 39. Thus, an instrument such as a DARO would have to be marked-to-market with changes in fair value flowing through the income statement, which companies are very reluctant to see happen. The changing value of a DARO would hit income every reporting period from initiation, with the corporate only experiencing a compensating payout (if at all) at maturity. Even while finding the economic value of the option very attractive, a stability-seeking corporate treasurer would likely find the potential accounting malaise (in the form of extra, and unwarranted, continuous income volatility) simply unacceptable and decide that, regrettably, they have no other alternative but to forgo the use of DAROs. Such reaction would result in the following paradox: in order to avoid possible accounting trouble, the treasurer would be discarding the use of a product that protects against accounting trouble. When it comes to other derivative structures that hedge actual transactions and cashflows (such as interest rate swaps or vanilla options) the dilemma faced by corporates is between the potential earnings volatility derived from using products that do not qualify for hedge accounting (or that present a high degree of ineffectiveness) and the potential real economic losses derived from not using such products. It essentially comes down to a choice between accounting malaise and economic malaise. In the case of DAROs, the decision not to use the option could very well result in enhanced, not diminished, accounting nastiness.

IF BILL GATES IS DOING IT...

It is clear that DAROs present a perfect example of the conflict brought about by the new accounting rules between strategic priorities and accounting priorities when selecting a hedging strategy. They provide valuable strategic benefits to corporate end-users but at the cost of potential continuous mark-to-market malaise. As much as treasurers would like to hedge the year-on-year translation exposure they face, they would rather not subject the income statement to the swings of the option's market value. Alternatively, perhaps treasurers would not mind switching one type of earnings volatility for another, but they are simply not allowed to enter into derivatives that do not qualify for hedge accounting. Given the complexity of the new standards, the lack of consensus among auditors and the many high-profile cases of restatements and dismissals (think Fannie Mae), corporate heads may be reluctant to enter into any but the most vanilla and accounting friendly hedges. In this light, trying to explain the intricacies and valuation issues of DAROs to his CEO or CFO might understandably appear like an unappealing and fruitless (never mind career-threatening) prospect to the average treasurer. If the answer to the most likely, and veto-carrying, first question (does this thing qualify for 100% hedge accounting?) is already known (no), then there surely is no point in wasting time putting together a nice presentation explaining how a strike-less super-exotic option that few competitors use can bring substantial value to the company.

In fact, one could argue that translation hedges may be the most important victim of the new accounting standards. Few things are more critical for corporate heads than reported earnings and the year-on-year change that drives analysts and investors perception of the company's health. By threatening the viability of DAROs, the new rules may deprive corporates of a very efficient and economical method of protecting their hallowed earnings-per-share figures. In this sense, the destruction of the market for DAROs could turn out to be one of the most dreaded legacies of the new rules.

This, of course, would be bad news. Not just for profit-hungry bankers or financial engineering fanatics but, mostly, for corporates. As was pointed out in previous paragraphs, not using a DARO could result in very significant accounting malaise, precisely the ill that the company was trying to get away from by discarding the non-efficient option. For a company such as Dade Behring, which depends on overseas results for more than 50% of it total consolidated net earnings, not being protected from a prolonged and sharp dollar rally could mean the difference between looking good and looking horrible. Having emerged from bankruptcy protection only in 2003, the Chicagoans surely know what it feels like when your reported results don't look good. The last thing they want to do is risk going back to the dark days simply because international investors suddenly fall passionately in love with the dollar (perhaps coinciding with a period of flattening overseas activity due to recession in, say, Europe). A sustained 25% rise in the greenback (a common sight in the forex world) would wipe out one-quarter of the dollar value of the company's consolidated overseas operations. Talk about accounting malaise! And while Dade's released reports would be telling outsiders that the large drop in revenue is mostly due to uncontrollable events in the wild currency markets, chances are that more than a few analysts wouldn't pay much attention to that "constant currency basis" line, wouldn't understand it, or, worse, would ruthlessly question the wisdom of such critical dependence on foreign business. Soon, lenders may be toying with the idea of raising financing costs and lowering internal credit ratings.

It is mainly to avoid such nightmarish scenarios that a few multinationals have decided to embrace DAROs for the past five years or so. Others could do worse than follow their lead. And not just on account of the year-on-year accounting chaos that they would be hedging themselves from. Equally important as a sales-pitch is the fact that the accounting excuse not to use DAROs is probably pretty powerless. Simply put, the income impact of marking-to-market the option every period should be limited. And certainly, should be expected to be much tamer than the impact caused by a naked translation of net foreign earnings. Crucially, there are even instances when DAROs would get the hedge accounting treatment. If the product is used to hedge anticipated currency exposures (so-called unrecognised firm commitments, as opposed to recognised monetary assets and liabilities) then hedge accounting would be possible. Although DAROs are best used for hedging earnings translation, some corporates may also find them useful to protect future real transactions.

Apparently, Dade is one of those corporates. It views the DARO as a good alternative to the vanilla strategy of simply purchasing a regular put on the foreign currency that guarantees a rate at which to sell that currency into dollars at the end of the relevant period. Buying a conventional put option is an event. What you pay reflects the market at the time of that event. In a volatile market, there is always a chance that you could buy on a bad day (ie, a day when the dollar spiked abnormally high) and thus incur a very high premium cost for the desired strike. That was a risk Dade did not want to take, so it went with the DARO instead. The strike would be determined by an average yet to be known, rather than a fixed pre-set level, and the settlement rate would also not be made dependent of a single spot level, thus providing an antidote to daily volatility (and a cheaper premium). The key idea is that the company would be selling the foreign currency (buying dollars) at a relevant rate (the volatility-independent average) that is at least as good as that prevalent a year ago. This way, Dade's treasury people can boast of severely limiting the firm's exposure to the vagaries of the forex markets: they sell at an average rate that is no worse than last year's.

The conclusion must be that the main excuse for the general absence of corporates from the world of DAROs, namely their accounting treatment, is most likely a toothless one, especially when the potential drawbacks of not using the product (really significant translation-related accounting malaise, costlier premiums) are taken into consideration. Dade Behring's recent publicised use of DAROs has brought the product back into the limelight and has rekindled memories of the pioneering efforts of giants Microsoft and McDonald's. Perhaps the time has come for other companies to have a go at it, and to finally take this exotic instrument into the mainstream of corporate financial risk management.

A Practitioner's View: Stéphane Knauf Structured Solutions To Year-On-Year Earnings Hedging

Stéphane Knauf is a Director and Global Head of the Structuring Group. Mr. Knauf is responsible for directing the delivery of structured solutions across our business segments. He was previously advising US corporations on FX risk management related issues out of New York. He has contributed, among other things, to the conception of risk management tools such as the Corporate Risk Optimizer and various econometric models. Stéphane has pursued a 10-year international career at Citigroup as an Investor & Corporate Strategist in Tokyo, an FX Structurer & Corporate Strategist in London, and as an FX Salesperson in Paris. Previous to Citigroup, Mr. Knauf worked for Société Générale's Options Division in Frankfurt and Paris.

INTRODUCTION

Many multinationals run hedging programmes for earnings translation and anticipated cash flows. Both programmes share a lot in common. They aim at mitigating the impact of FX on consolidated earnings. Their durations are generally similar. In practice, earnings translation issues are even often handled as part of anticipated cash flow hedging by centralised treasuries in order to obtain favourable hedge accounting treatment.

Most existing programmes use horizons of 12–15 months and a quarterly approach. The rationale is to reduce or eliminate the fluctuation in currency rates between the equivalent quarters of two consecutive fiscal years. Year-on-year (YoY) hedging cycles don't allow reducing earnings volatility *per se*, as currency effects are simply postponed by one year. In that respect, layered hedging techniques over multiple years are more efficient.[1] It is however very consistent with how analysts look at a company's performance, as the last quarterly results are usually compared to the earnings produced one year before.

The purpose of this section is to explore structured solutions that enable replicating quarterly translation rates in a cost effective way. As earnings volatility finds its source in the differences between accounting and settlement or hedging rates, the question of reproducing accounting rates in hedging programmes is an important one. Forward hedges may achieve this objective but only at the cost of numerous and time-consuming transactions. We here introduce two classes of products that can greatly simplify the task: average rate and basket options.

In the following examples, we will assume the case of a US multinational with earnings in EUR, JP¥ and CAD for equivalent amounts. The earnings translation rate is defined as the average of daily fixings over a given quarter. While this definition might change from one company to another, it is the most commonly met.

For reference, the price for 15-month (start of a quarter to end of the equivalent quarter, one year later) ATM Forward currency puts are the following:

Currency	Strike	Premium (% US$)
EUR/US$	1.2275	3.93
US$/JP¥	112.00	3.63
US$/CAD	1.1335	3.39

This corresponds to a weighted average premium of 3.60% US$.

AVERAGE RATE PRODUCTS
We can distinguish between two types of options based on averages: average rate options and average strike options.

AVERAGE RATE OPTIONS
An average rate option (ARO) is an option with a fixed strike paying out against an average of pre-set fixings instead of an at-expiry spot rate. Taking the EUR/US$ example, we can define (as above) a EUR Put struck ATM Forward (1.2275) and paying out against the average of daily EUR/US$ fixings over Q1 2007 (ie, the EUR translation rate for that quarter). Over a YoY horizon, such an option allows protecting a desired level (the strike) against a future translation rate.

A usual advantage of such options is their relative cheapness. This can be intuitively explained by the fact that the option's payout is a function of an average rather than a spot rate and that this average is bound to be less volatile than spot by definition. It can alternatively be explained by the option's payout itself, as an ARO will have a lower payout than an equivalent strip of plain vanilla options. To demonstrate this, let's consider the case of a US corporation looking to hedge a EUR long position made of four end-of-quarter cash flows of EUR 10 Mio over the coming year. The treasurer could buy a strip of four EUR Puts maturing at the end of each quarter or invest into a single average rate option paying out against the average of the corresponding four quarter-end fixings. If strikes are equal, both strategies will guarantee the same weighted average protection level. This application of AROs is quite different from translation risk hedging, but it is actually this way AROs have first been used by corporations: cover the average value of small recurring cash flows in one single transaction. Let's pretend that the initial EUR/US$ spot rate is 1.20 and that the strikes are set on that level at inception. We could have following outcome:

Fixings		Payout vanilla put	Payout ARO
Q1	1.18	+0.02	–
Q2	1.22	0	–
Q3	1.18	+0.02	–
Q4	1.22	0	–
Average	1.20	+0.01	0

Over the year, two of the vanilla options would have ended in the money (Q1 and Q3) and produced a positive payout, while the ARO finished worthless.

Reverting to the YoY earnings hedging, premium savings are however bound to be limited as the averaging process only starts after around twelve months and lasts for three. The option's payout is a function of spot volatility for the longest period of time giving it a profile of a vanilla option. In this case, AROs have to be retained for their flexibility and ability to replicate any accounting rate (including one fixing "averages"). To get a sense of the savings achieved we give an indication of 15-month average rate currency puts (paying against the average of fixings in month 13 to 15) in the table below:

Currency	Strike	Premium (% US$)
EUR/US$	1.2275	3.71
US$/JP¥	112.00	3.60
US$/CAD	1.1335	3.16

This corresponds to a weighted average premium of 3.49% or a 3% saving against the equivalent strip of vanilla options.

AVERAGE STRIKE OPTIONS

An average strike option (ASO), as a vanilla option, will have its final value determined against a spot rate. Its strike is however not known at inception and defined as an average of future fixings (for example, the daily fixings over Q1 2006). It can therefore be defined at a beginning of any given quarter as its future translation rate. Again, the tool's flexibility allows accommodating for any accounting rate definition. This type of option enables therefore to get perfect protection against any type of translation rate. Assuming we find ourselves at the start of a quarter, price levels for 15M average strike options are given below:

Currency	Strike	Premium (% US$)
EUR/US$	Avg. of upcoming quarter	2.78
US$/JP¥	Avg. of upcoming quarter	1.53
US$/CAD	Avg. of upcoming quarter	2.80

Straight comparison to the premium of ATM Forward vanilla options wouldn't be fair, as the ASOs strike won't capture the full extent of the 15-month carry. Because the strike's averaging process starts from inception, the ASOs strike is bound to be closer to current spot rate than the 15M forward outright in theory. As our three currencies have lower yields than the US$, one would expect the ASOs to be out-of-the money once the strike is determined (as the

ATM spot strike would be). In any case, the weighted average premium is of 2.37%. This is indeed very close to the price of a strip of 15M ATM Spot currency puts: EUR (2.89%), JP¥ (1.44%), CAD (2.90%) for an average of 2.41% US$.

DOUBLE AVERAGE RATE OPTIONS

Ideally, one would like to combine both options into one in order to get protection *versus* a given translation rate (eg, Q1 2006) and a payout consistent with a targeted accounting rate in the future (or Q1 2007). This is possible using double average rate options (DARO). As the name may hint to, the first average of fixings determines the strike, while the second one defines its payout. It is an ideal tool to hedge against the change in accounting rates from one period to another. The price for such options is given next:

Currency	Strike	Premium (%)
EUR/US$	Avg. of upcoming quarter	2.57
US$/JP¥	Avg. of upcoming quarter	1.42
US$/CAD	Avg. of upcoming quarter	2.56

The weighted average premium is of 2.18% US$.

A number of multinationals are using that type of tool to hedge their future net revenues. If "optionality" is not needed, hedges can be structured as synthetic forwards also know as "double average rate forwards" (DARF). This type of structure will compensate accurately for any variation in translation rates for a relatively small upfront premium (received or paid). Divergence from 0-cost will depend on both yield curves and, to a lesser extent, the currency pair's volatility curve. To replicate such a hedge using forwards, one would have to enter a one-year hedge every day over any given quarter or a total of 60+ transactions. The advantages of DAROs and DARFs in terms of time efficiency are obvious to say the least.

The following graph illustrates the mechanism of a double average rate US$ Call JP¥ Put implemented at the start of Q4 2004 and maturing at the end of Q4 2005:

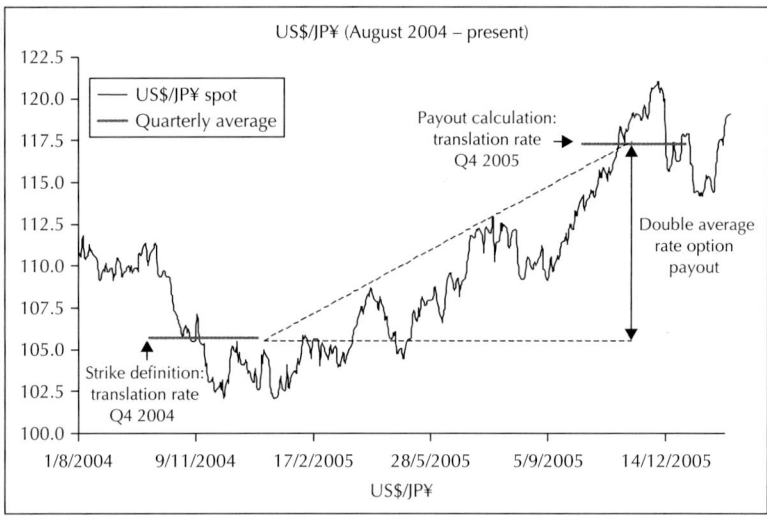

ACCOUNTING

The accounting for average rate products and strategies under DIG G20 guidelines is usually favourable. Many multinationals benefit from cash flow hedge accounting using this type of product. They can either be designated as hedging multiple cash flows that are similar in nature and/or be proven consistent with accounting rates and thus efficient on that basis.

While IAS interpretation differs from FASB for option hedges and may require distinguishing between intrinsic and time value of an option, synthetic forwards may pass the test and be considered fully efficient.

BASKET OPTIONS

In summary, the first advantage of a basket option is that it allows hedging an aggregate (eg, the US$ value of currency denominated revenues). This is convenient for corporations, as they tend to think in these terms. The second advantage is obviously diversification. A basket of currencies, similarly to any equity index or basket of equities (S&P 500, FTSE 100, DJ STOXX 50 etc...), is less volatile than the weighted average of its components. This is due to port-folio diversification, which in turn depends on the way currencies correlate against one another. The more diversified a portfolio, the less risky or volatile it will be. The less volatile, the less costly options will be to cover it or, in other words, the more savings will be obtained compared to an equivalent strip of individual options.

Basket option mechanisms

In our example, assuming equal weights for the different currencies, one could hedge the whole portfolio of exposures via a 15-month basket put option:

Maturity: 15 months;
Buy US$ Call Basket Put;
Basket composition: 1/3 EUR, 1/3 JP¥, 1/3 CAD;
Strike: US$ Value of currency flow translated at the 15M Forward Rate;
Premium: 2.95%;
Savings *versus* equivalent vanilla options: 18%.

The 18% savings make baskets cost efficient tools, especially for a longer-term hedging programme. These savings usually translate into substantial amounts in absolute cash terms.

Basket options are generally cash settled at expiry. The basket option basically guarantees a certain minimum US$ value (the basket's strike) for the currency cash flows it covers. We here assume a notional of US$ 100 Mio for simplification. The ATM Forward strike of the basket sets amount of currencies, which will be used to determine whether the option is in the money at expiry and whether a cash settlement will consequently occur. The basket option basically guarantees a US$ amount (the notional, ie, US$ 100 Mio) for EUR 27.2 Mio (or US$ 33.3 Mio at the forward rate of 1.2275), JP¥ 3.73 Bio (US$ 33.3 Mio at the forward rate 112.00) and CAD 37.8 Mio (US$ 33.3 Mio at the forward rate of 1.1335)

The basket can be seen as the right to sell the currency cash flows at expiry and receive no less than US$ 100 Mio. To determine whether the option is in the money at expiry, all that needs to be done is to translate the currency amounts as defined in the option contract back into dollars using the spot rates at that time. If the total translates into less than US$ 100 Mio, the holder of the option is compensated for the difference.

At expiry profiles

We present at-expiry profiles in terms of P/L or hedging performance for a notional amount of US$ 100 Mio.

DOUBLE AVERAGE RATE BASKETS

Basket options can integrate all the features of the different types of average rate products while capturing the benefits of portfolio diversification. It is, for example, possible to structure a basket option so that its strike (a US$ amount) is defined as the US$ value of currency cash flows translated at an average rate over a given period. Similarly, one could structure a basket option with fixed strike and a payout defined against the US$ value of the currency cash flows using an average rate rather than at-maturity spot levels. A Double Average

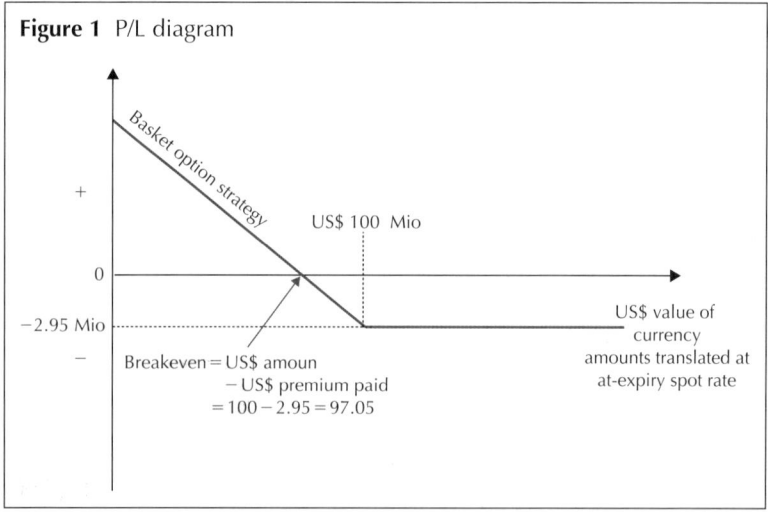

Figure 1 P/L diagram

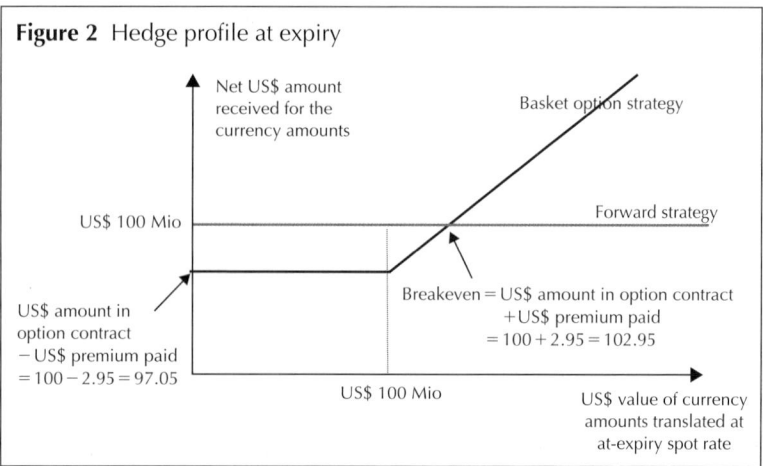

Figure 2 Hedge profile at expiry

Rate Basket (DARB) would basically combine both of these features. For the purpose of YoY hedging, a DARB could be structured in following way (assuming today is the first day in a new quarter):

Maturity: 15 months;
Buy US$ Call Basket Put;
Basket composition: 1/3 EUR, 1/3 JP¥, 1/3 CAD;
Strike: US$ Value of currency flows translated at the average of daily fixings over the three first months (accounting rate for the inception quarter);
Payout: Max (0; Strike – US$ Value of currency flows translated using final average rate);
Final Average Rate: average of daily fixings over the three last months for the various currencies;
Premium: 1.85%;
Savings *versus* equivalent DAROs: 15%.

If the underlying exposure is net revenues in these currencies, the DARB basically protects the overall US$ value of net FC revenues due one year from now against changes in translation rates, taking current accounting rates as reference. It can be therefore interpreted as the ultimate macro-hedge.

ACCOUNTING

To benefit from cash flow hedge accounting under a FAS framework, we recommend splitting basket options into a strip of plain vanilla or average rate options and a "correlation option". The correlation option is somewhat an abstract concept and defined as the diversification benefit embedded in the basket option. Basically, it would be valued as the price difference between the basket option and the equivalent strip of vanilla options or average rate options.

While the latter may be DIG G20 compliant, the correlation option would have to be marked to market via Income. The volatility added to earnings will depend on the composition of the basket itself. Empirically, we have found that it is usually limited and worth the cash savings obtained by reducing premium spending. It is also worth noting that the value of correlation options is decaying in time. As the holder of the basket option is long plain vanilla options and short the correlation option (you "receive" premium savings), the expected change in value and consequently the expected impact on earnings is therefore positive, all other things being equal.

CONCLUSION

The table below summarises each strategy's ability to replicate accounting rates at inception or at maturity and highlights the strategy's cost. While the various strategies below don't provide the holder with the same rights, they enable treasury centres to hedge their specific benchmarks in a cost- and time-effective way. If "optionality" is needed (because of forecasting errors or other criteria), DARBs will guarantee minimum or no slippage against accounting references at the lowest cost.

Strategy	Deviation *versus* initial translation rates	Deviation *versus* final translation rates	Overall cost (% US$)
DARB	No	No	1.85
Strip of DARO	No	No	2.18
Strip of ASO	No	Yes	2.37
Strip of ATMS Vanillas	Yes	Yes	2.41
Basket Option	Yes	Yes	2.95
Strip of ARO	Yes	No	3.49
Strip of ATMF Vanillas	Yes	Yes	3.60

1 Joakim Lidbark, "Minimizing year-on-year currency impact on earnings: A layered hedging approach", *Currency Advisor*, January 2006 edition.

8

2001: A Quanto Odyssey

The dramatic steepness experienced by the US yield curve at the beginning of the new century provided excellent interest rate quanto swaps opportunities, both for hedgers and investors. Here we analyse, with the benefit of hindsight, some of the trades shown by banks

An interest rate quanto swap (also known as a "differential swap") is an agreement between two parties where one makes payments referenced to a particular floating rate (eg, US$ Libor) against receiving payments referenced to another floating rate. The important factor that differentiates the quanto swap from a plain vanilla cross-currency swap is that in the quanto both parties make payments in the same currency. That is, the quanto is a pure play on international interest rate differentials since it does not involve any foreign exchange risk.

Developments in the US fixed income market during 2001 made it the "Year of the Quanto". The very dramatic steepness experienced by the US yield curve offered tremendous opportunities for those willing to bet that US$ Libor would stay below the Libor rate of other currencies (in particular, the Euro) for a while, and that once it overtook its foreign counterpart it would not do so in a dramatic fashion. In other words, the bet for anybody entering into, say, a US$–€ interest rate quanto swap in the early 2000s was that Greenspan was going to wait before raising rates and that once US$ rates started to climb up they would not overshoot drastically above € rate. Given the fact that for maturities beyond around the 1.5 year level the US$ forward curve started to rise well above the € forward curve, those paying US$ Libor as part of a quanto swap

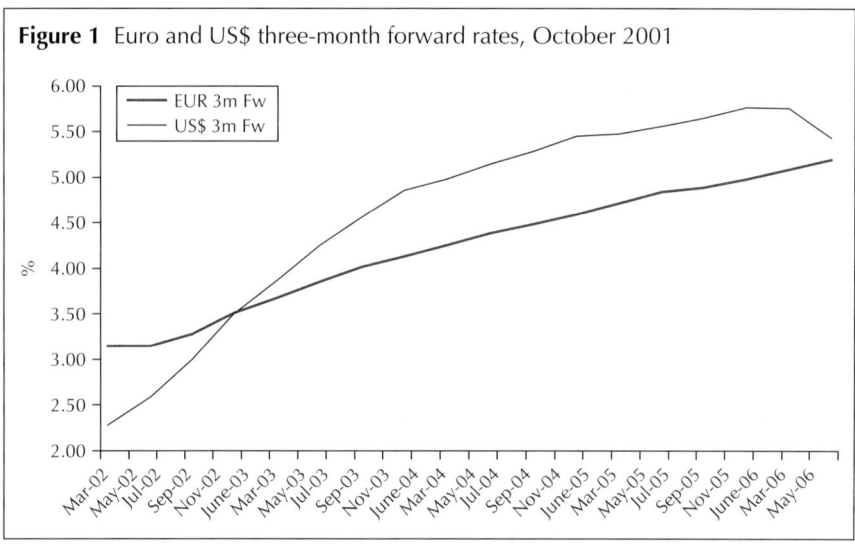

Figure 1 Euro and US$ three-month forward rates, October 2001

could enjoy substantial negative spreads on their floating payments (since the forward curves were "saying" that US$ Libor was going to be so much higher than € Libor the party paying the former would have to be initially compensated). At the same time, the short rate in US$ was much lower than the short rate in Euro: depending on which month of 2001 the trade was priced this differential could be as high as 150 basis points (bps). These two factors (super-steep US$ forward curve, short-rates gap) contributed to a positive carry for the US$ leg payer that could be higher than 200 bps (again, depending on pricing date, maturity and payment frequency). No wonder, then, that so many people found these trades impossible to say no to. For corporate hedgers here was a way to lower your funding costs by more than 200 bps! For savvy investors here was a trade in which they started receiving significant net income from the beginning, without having to put up any capital, and which could continue to provide cash if the investor's view on interest rate differentials proved to be correct.

The relative forward curves shown in Figure 1 (dating from early October 2001 and pricing a structure that would start in early 2002) are an example of the ideal conditions for a quanto to work.

A big advantage of the quanto swap trade is that it has to be analysed on a break-even basis. That is, even if US$ rates were to start climbing sooner than expected the US$ leg payer is compensated by the fact that he received very large net payments during the first periods. In the end, the US$ leg payer might find that overall there was no advantage in paying US$ Libor as opposed to, say, € Libor because the initial net income received would have been wiped out by large net payments made in future periods as US$ rates shoot over € rates. In that situation the US$ leg payer roughly breaks even, meaning that overall he was no better off paying US$ Libor rather than € Libor. However, crucially, under the quanto swap nobody can take away from you the fact that you did receive substantial net payments during the initial periods of the trade. In other words, even if US$ rates reach the break-even level or higher the quanto can still be a great strategy for those wishing or needing large infusions of cash at the beginning. For example, a heavily indebted company that needs to lower its financing costs as much as possible for the next months so as not to harm the viability of its business plan.

Of course, both hedgers and investors would have been facing very large risks if Greenspan had gone wild and started to raise rates like there was no tomorrow. However, as will be analysed in more detail later, economic realities and historical evidence pointed towards the opposite scenario, especially as the year progressed.

The key point is that during 2001 the ideal conditions for a US$ interest rate quanto swap took place (especially against the € curve): US$ short-rates were well below short-rates in other countries + US$ forward rates were soon overtaking the foreign curve + a super-steep US$ forward curve afterwards + reasonable expectations that the market was wrongly pricing the too aggressive rate-hikes by the Federal Reserve (Fed) and that future US$ Libor rates would not end up being as high as the forward curve implied.

In the following pages we analyse some of the US$–€ quanto structures that derivatives desks at major investment banks were showing to their clients. We will pay particular attention to the marketing side of the products, ie, under what circumstances the trade made sense for a client and why he should have considered it. With the benefit of hindsight we will crucially also be able to follow the behaviour of the structures so far. In particular, we will aim to answer the following key question: did those players who chose to enter into a quanto swap in the early 2000s end up as winners or as losers?

ECONOMIC BACKGROUND: SHOULD THE FORWARD CURVE BE TRUSTED?

As was already mentioned, in 2001 "the stars aligned themselves in the right way" for quanto swaps to be workable, as the forward curves combined perfectly to yield the numbers that could make corporate treasurers eagerly throw themselves into quanto territory. While the year 2000 ended with the US$ curve clearly above the € curve for maturities of less than 15 years (thus making the quanto swap not viable for corporate hedgers), as soon as January 2001 came to life the relatively flat US$ curve quickly transformed into a steep figure beyond the two-year maturity. The main drivers behind the shifting curve were an unanticipated rate cut signalling the start of an easing cycle together with a perception that the economic slowdown detected in late 2000 would be of relatively short duration (more on this later). By the end of the month the US$ curve had developed a shape similar to its € counterpart (clearly not flat, but only modestly upwardly steep), with rates about 50 bps higher across all maturities. As the year progressed, both curves became gradually steeper, with most of the steepening reflecting declines in short-term rates rather than increases in the long end. This increased steepness was again motivated by the easing cycle together with market confidence that the slowdown would be short-lived. Since the Fed had lowered rates many more times than the European Central Bank (ECB), short-term US$ yields were well below their € cousins by late June. At the same time, the US$ curve clearly overtook its € counterpart after the two-year point and from there opened a gap that reached about 50 bps at the 10-year point. In other words, by mid-2001 the markets were in "quanto heaven". This state of affairs was going to remain more or less unchanged during the summer, with the relative forward curves showing little modification. The consecutive rate cuts following the tragedy of 11th September resulted in a further steepening of both curves, with the US$ swap rates falling around 110 bps between mid-June and mid-October, and short rates falling 170 bps. It is interesting to note that while the short-term gap between US$ and € rates had widened (the Fed was naturally more aggressive than the ECB), in the long end the gap actually closed a little initially, most likely due to the US Treasury's decision to suspend the issuance of 30-year bonds. In the last two

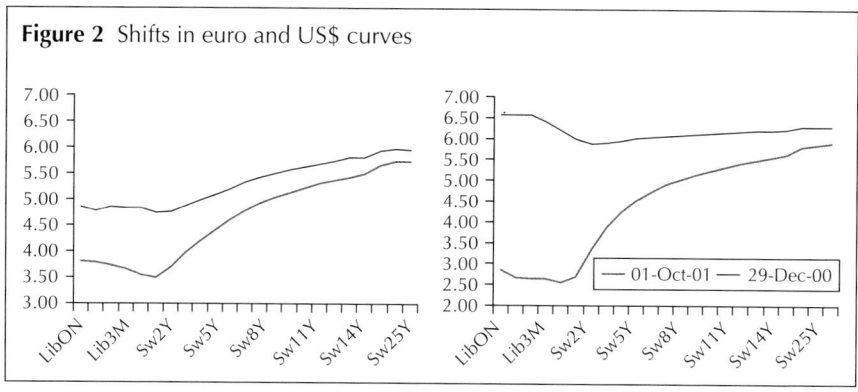

Figure 2 Shifts in euro and US$ curves

months of 2001 the appearance of positive economic indicators together with military victories by the US army brought back confidence to the market that the recovery would be swift and relatively fast, bringing yields at two years and above back to pre 11th September. In other words, the US$ curve experienced truly dramatic steepness in that last part of the year, with the gap between 10-year and three-month yields reaching the highest levels since 1994. In essence, both the short-end and the long-end gaps between the US$ and the € curves increased, further enhancing the terms of quanto swaps and making the optics of the trade truly attractive to potential end-users.

Figure 2 clearly shows how the curves experienced dramatic shifts in 2001 with respect to the shapes they had in late 2000, and how they aligned themselves to quanto perfection. The left-hand graph corresponds to the € curves, while the right-hand graph shows US$ curves.

But as we also know, entering into a quanto can be suicide if US$ Libor takes off like a rocket early in the trade. Thus, the numbers offered by the structure are not enough of a carrot to commit to a quanto. Future interest rates perspectives are also crucial. That is, while the right forward curves allow bankers to show quanto ideas to clients, interest rates forecasts will determine whether the deal is closed or not. If corporate treasurers believe that the Fed is about to start tightening aggressively, they will most likely not enter into a quanto.

The plain fact is that interest rate perspectives were extremely quanto-friendly in 2001. The case could easily be made that the easing cycle, which had started in January (after a tightening cycle that took rates to 6.5% by mid-2000), was not going to be reversed any time soon, and in fact it could (should) actually be further strengthened with more rate cuts.

Not only was the US economy in pretty bad shape and full of large disequilibria (namely, historically huge debt burdens on consumers and companies and an ever-growing current account deficit), the world economy was also suffering from lacklustre performance and we were in a period of disinflationary pressures. Substantial shortfalls in corporate sales and earnings, eroding consumer confidence and rising energy prices had slowed the pace of economic activity by late 2000, prompting the Fed to switch off its focus on inflation and instead alter its assessment of the risks to the economy as being slanted toward slowing growth or even a recession. This led to the 50 bps unexpected interest rates cut of 3rd January 2001 which kick-started the new easing cycle. With Greenspan declaring economic growth to be "very close to zero", rates reached 5.5% by the end of the month in a move defined as a hedge against the possibility of a recession. With the stock market in free fall, the Fed cut another 50 bps on 20th March. Another surprise move in mid-April ("in-between-meetings") took rates to 4.5%, with the Fed expressing deep concern for the severe slowdown in corporate capital spending. Continuous evidence of economic sluggishness forced Greenspan to keep cutting all the way to 3.5% by late August, with the easing bias still in place. However, at this juncture perspectives on the economy were beginning to change, with many people believing that the corner had been turned and that essentially the Fed's work had been done. A Reuters poll of primary dealers (major banks that deal with the Fed in the fixed-income markets) taken around that time showed that less than half expected a further rate cut. Positive showings of the leading economic indicators, continuing strength in the housing market, a possible recovery in the labour market and signs that companies were working off their inventories led some economists to declare that "The Fed is anxious to bring the current easing cycle to an end". In summation, the consensus at the time among the analysts was that rates were going to stabilise at the 3.5% floor with the cycle reversal taking place about a year later.

Of course, this scenario was dramatically altered by, first, the tragic events of 11th September, and then by the string of high pro-file corporate bankruptcies and accounting scandals that plagued the US economy in the final months of the year. Both developments struck a heavy blow to consumers, companies and investors confi-dence and made a recession all but inevitable. As a response, the Fed returned to an aggressively loose policy of 50 bps cuts (the pre-vious cuts had been for a milder 25 bps) starting on 17th September that took rates to a 40-year low of 1.75% by mid-December, with Greenspan's commitment to an easing bias firmly stated, especially taking into account the facts that third quarter GDP had shrunk and that the unemployment rate had hit a six-year high in November.

All this, obviously, made entering into a quanto swap a much more favourable proposition than before 11th September. Not only had US$ short rates fallen dramatically in relation to other rates (such as € Libor), but the economic environment prevalent at the time was certainly not the ideal landscape for dangerously fast and aggressive rate hikes from the Fed. Moreover, even in the highly unlikely case that Greenspan decided to start reversing the mone-tary policy cycle by, say, the second quarter of 2002 (earlier than expected by even the most bullish analysts), past performance by the Fed gave very encouraging signs to anybody willing to enter into quanto structures. During the last economic recession of 1991–92 the Fed lowered rates actively until they reached a level of 3% in September 1992. After that, Greenspan waited until February 1994 to start the hiking cycle. That is, it took him 17 months to begin to raise rates. Especially relevant for those contemplating quantos is the fact that the maximum that the Fed raised was 300 bps, when the repo rate reached 6% in February 1995, 29 months after rates had reached their trough.

The 1991–92 experience is very interesting because it shares com-mon characteristics with the recession of late 2001. In both cases the Fed continued lowering rates even though the market was dis-counting an immediate recovery and a drastic change in policy cycle. Even after declaring itself to be in a "neutral" position in May 1992 the Fed still cut a further 50 bps. In late 2001 the Fed was still keeping a "lowering bias". That is, not only rates were going to take a while to go up, but also there was a chance they could even go lower; and let us not forget that the late 2001 recession presented far greater disequilibria and on a much more global scale than the 1991–92 period, thus in theory warranting an even more cautious approach to rate hikes.

In conclusion, we can see that as 2001 proceeded it become clearer and clearer that the very steep US$ forward curve was not "telling the truth", as it was essentially discounting a very rapid economic recovery with the accompanying tightening cycle. That is in essence the challenge that corporate treasurers were facing in 2001 (notably in the second half of the year, and especially after 11th September): do we trust the forward curve and thus become reluctant to enter into quanto swaps? Or do we fearlessly consider the curve to be a big liar and fully embrace the tremendous gains offered by quantos? This chapter will later analyse who was right in the end, the fearful (prudent?) or the fearless (reckless?).

MONETARY POLICY: WHAT EVENTUALLY HAPPENED TO INTEREST RATES?

In the end, the US economy did not recover quickly. Contrary to many economists' and analysts' forecasts, not only did rates not go up but in fact continued going down as the risk of deflation became the Fed's major concern. On 6th November 2002 Greenspan lowered rates by 50 bps to 1.25%, worried by a combination of falling stock prices, more corporate scandals, soft jobs data, lacklustre business spending and fears regarding the possible war in Iraq. On 25th June 2003 rates were cut a further 25 bps, taking them to a 45-year low of 1%. The Fed expressed the worry that the economy was still not strong enough to fight deflation and thus needed a little extra help to get out of the quagmire.

With the economy not being able to reverse its soft performance and inflation moribund, the Fed ended 2003 without modifying its highly accommodative interest rate policy, and started 2004 stating its intention to be patient before switching to a tightening cycle. The change in tone finally came about in early May after the data had shown a pick-up in inflation and the job market, with Greenspan dropping the patient stance and replacing it with a commitment to a measured removal of the loose-policy strategy. The first step of the new cycle took place on 29th June, with a 25 bps

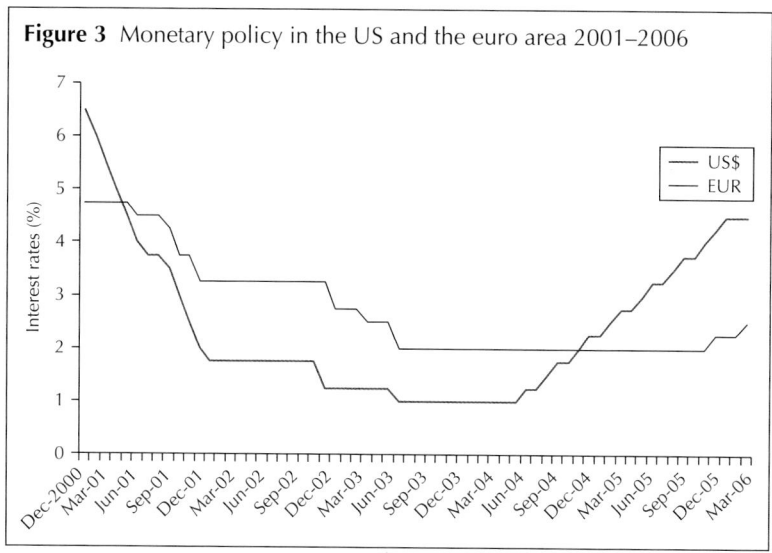

Figure 3 Monetary policy in the US and the euro area 2001–2006

increase (see figure 3). The Fed indicated that a measured pace of rate increases was appropriate because, even though it was clear that the economy had turned the corner, its health was still far from perfect, as indicated by the Fed's own modest forecasts for GDP and unemployment. Subsequent quarter-point raises took US$ rates to 4.50% by early 2006.

What are the prospects for the near future? Will the measured-pace approach continue to reign supreme at the Fed, will it shift gear considerably and proceed in a faster manner, or will the US central bank declare itself done? Ben Bernanke, Alan Greenspan's recently appointed successor, has indicated on several ocassions that he intends to continue on the policy path that he has inherited, at least for a while. With energy prices stubbornly high and with the economy on an upbeat mood, there seems to be plenty of scope for further rate hikes. The market certainly seems to believe so, with most people expecting two or more extra rate rises in the near future. Whether the tightening effort culminates at 5%, 5.50%, or maybe even higher, rates will depend on several factors, most prominently among them, of course, inflationary pressures and economic activity. But perhaps in the end Bernanke's desire to be seen as a tough inflation-fighter that is fully capable of filling

Greenspan's oversized shoes will be the most determinant factor when setting monetary policy.

PRODUCTS: RATIONALE AND CHRONOLOGICAL EVOLUTION

Now we proceed to analyse some of the quanto products that banks were offering their clients in 2001, mostly as hedging tools. With the benefit of hindsight we will use real-life data to see the evolution of these structures through time, thereby answering the key question of whether end-users made the right decision by becoming a party to the quanto swaps.

Case study no. 1

In July 2001 a corporate client that had floating € interest rate liabilities, and did not want to pay a premium for protection, was shown the following levels for a *plain vanilla quanto swap*:

❑ effective date 30th September 2001;
❑ maturity date 30the December 2004;
❑ bank pays 3 month € Libor;
❑ client pays 3 month US$ Libor – 0.87% in euros.

Given that the prevailing short rates were 4.4 and 3.8% respectively in € and US$, the trade represented a positive carry (cost savings with respect to paying € Libor flat) of 147 bps for the client. That is, by entering into this swap the company could obtain instant savings of almost 1.50% on its debt liabilities. Obviously, such a result would be very pleasing for any company, in particular one that wishes (or needs) to significantly reduce its interest rate liabilities in the short term. The risk, of course, is that the Fed would raise rates quickly and by a lot. However, given that the alternative plain vanilla € swap would fix the company at 4.73%, US$ Libor would have to quickly reach and then surpass 5.60% in order for the quanto swap to deliver worse results than the plain vanilla swap. Even in mid-2001 (before 11th September, Enron and WorldCom) the case could be made that the chances of Greenspan raising rates fast and furiously were pretty slim. Thus, the client could start enjoying the large immediate benefits afforded by the quanto, comfortable with the thought that US rates would take a while to increase by 1.8% (the difference between Libor rates in July 2001 and the 5.60% break-even level with respect to the vanilla swap).

Table 1 Case study 1 – plain vanilla quanto swap

Effective date	€ 3 month Libor	US$ 3 month Libor	US$ 3 month Libor – 0.87	Savings with respect to € 3 month Libor
30-Sep-01	3.65263	2.59000	1.72000	1.93263
30-Dec-01	3.30000	1.88125	1.01125	2.28875
30-Mar-02	3.45000	2.03000	1.16000	2.29000
30-Jun-02	3.44000	1.86000	0.99000	2.45000
30-Sep-02	3.29213	1.79000	0.92000	2.37213
30-Dec-02	2.86125	1.38000	0.51000	2.35125
30-Mar-03	2.52000	1.27875	0.40875	2.11125
30-Jun-03	2.14275	1.11625	0.24625	1.89650
30-Sep-03	2.12663	1.16000	0.29000	1.83663
30-Dec-03	2.12300	1.15188	0.28188	1.84112
30-Mar-04	1.96000	1.11000	0.24000	1.72000
30-Jun-04	2.12000	1.61000	0.74000	1.38000
30-Sep-04	2.14625	2.02000	1.15000	0.99625

Table 1 shows how a hypothetical corporate that had shown the courage to enter into this quanto swap would have fared.

Without a doubt, the final results would have been nothing short of spectacular. The corporate treasurer would have ended up a hero, perhaps with a promotion to boot. The quanto swap would have allowed the company to dramatically reduce its financing costs, both with respect to having been unhedged (ie, paying 3 month Libor) and with respect to having entered into a plain vanilla swap (ie, paying 4.73% fixed). As can be seen from the table, during many quarters the effective interest rate paid would have been well below 1% (note, however, that this analysis does not take into account the possible spreads paid over Libor and due to the company's creditworthiness). In fact, the average rate paid would have been a paltry 0.74%, due to an average US$ Libor of 1.61%. The resulting average savings with regards to € Libor would have been a tremendous 1.95%.

An interesting way to see this quanto in perspective is to see it as a close proxy to an interest rate cap with an extremely low strike level, in the sense that just as in the case of the low strike cap this quanto swap would have basically eliminated all exposure to floating rates. Since US monetary policy remained quite loose during the life of the transaction, the effective variable rate paid by the corporate turned out to be almost zero. The difference, of course, is that while the low strike cap would have been prohibitively expensive, the quanto required no upfront premium. All in all, not a bad trade for those visionary enough (or gutsy enough) to take the bet in mid-2001 that Greenspan was not going to become a killjoy (ie, reverse the policy cycle) any time soon for the next three and a half years. As was explained earlier in this paper, the conventional wisdom at the time was that while the US economy was certainly nothing to write home about, the situation was expected to improve soon and rates were widely forecasted to experience one last reduction before Greenspan reversed the policy cycle around mid-2002. Of course, 11th September, Enron and Worldcom changed all of that, but in July 2001 who could have foreseen such tragic events?

One client who took a look at the above quanto structure voiced concerns that, while the trade offered sensational short-term cost savings, it did not offer upside protection in case US$ Libor shot to the moon. The most obvious solution was to provide the client with a US$ quanto cap, accounting for the premium by reducing the negative spread on the US$ leg. The steep forward curve and high volatility made interest rate options very expensive, even for deep out-of-the-money strikes. Thus, adding the US$ quanto cap to the swap worsened the spread on the US$ leg by quite a lot. Additionally, given that the client was uncertain as to whether it would have any outstanding Euro-denominated debt after 2004 (because it was planning an IPO by then), it wanted to have the optionality of being able to protect itself from high € rates in the future. The solution presented by the bank was to add a long-dated € payer swaption to the trade. Amortising the premium of this option further reduced the spread on the swap, even though it was struck out-of-the-money. The following zero-cost structure was presented:

Quanto swap + cap
❏ effective date 30th September 2001;
❏ maturity date 30th December 2004;
❏ bank pays 3 month € Libor;
❏ client pays 3 month US$ Libor in euros, subject to a 6.2% cap.

Table 2 Case study 1 – quanto swap + cap + swaption

Effective date	€ 3 month Libor	US$ 3 month Libor	Savings with respect to € 3 month Libor
30-Sep-01	3.65263	2.59000	1.06263
30-Dec-01	3.30000	1.88125	1.41875
30-Mar-02	3.45000	2.03000	1.42000
30-Jun-02	3.44000	1.86000	1.58000
30-Sep-02	3.29213	1.79000	1.50213
30-Dec-02	2.86125	1.38000	1.48125
30-Mar-03	2.52000	1.27875	1.24125
30-Jun-03	2.14275	1.11625	1.02650
30-Sep-03	2.12663	1.16000	0.96663
30-Dec-03	2.12300	1.15188	0.97112
30-Mar-04	1.96000	1.11000	0.85000
30-Jun-04	2.12000	1.61000	0.51000
30-Sep-04	2.14625	2.02000	0.12625

Payer swaption
❑ effective date 30th September 2004;
❑ maturity date 30th December 2009;
❑ bank pays 3 month € Libor;
❑ client pays 6.2% fixed.

In the end, the client was still able to enjoy a positive initial carry of 60 bps (the difference between both Libor rates), and it had satisfied its goals of having capped exposure to US$ Libor plus long-dated optionality on a € Libor hedge. The key point here is that despite very stringent conditions on the part of the customer, the quanto swap still worked reasonably well. That is, this structure is a testament to the dramatic resilience of the quanto as a value-adding product when the ideal conditions (ie, relative forward curves) present themselves.

Table 2 shows the results that a hypothetical end-user would have enjoyed had he entered into this structure.

In this case, the final results would also have been satisfactory, though not as spectacular as in the vanilla-quanto swap (the one analysed first, without adding the cap and the swaption). The average floating rate paid by the client would have been 1.61%, with an average saving over € Libor of 1.09%. Of course, the quanto structure would still be far superior to having gone fixed in a plain vanilla swap.

It is worth noting that the very scenario that made the quanto swap such a success also makes the cap unnecessary: US$ Libor was never remotely close to the 6.2% strike. At the same time, the payer swaption obtained by the company would eventually not have been exercised as the flatter yield curve made it out-of-the-money. Thus, the client would have given up substantial gains in the quanto because of its desire to have a cap and a swaption attached to it, but at the same time one needs to understand that without such sweeteners the deal would not have been entered into in the first place (in fact, it could be argued that the quanto part may have been used precisely to be able to afford the zero-cost purchase of the cap and the swaption in the first place; ie, it was perhaps not so much large debt cost savings that was the main goal, but rather the acquisition of free interest rate protection, using the then highly valuable quanto currency to that end).

In late September 2001, the bank went back to the client with fresh levels on the quanto swap + cap + payer swaption structure, and it offered a slight modification. Of course, short rates had changed dramatically since July, with levels now at 3.6% in € and 2.5% in US$. The refreshed levels were:

Quanto swap + cap
❑ effective date 30th September 2001;
❑ maturity date 30th December 2004;
❑ bank pays 3 month € Libor;
❑ client pays 3 month US$ Libor + 0.03% in euros, subject to a 6.2% cap.

Payer swaption
❑ effective date 30th December 2004;
❑ maturity date 30th December 2009;
❑ bank pays 3 month € Libor;
❑ client pays 6.2% fixed.

While the spread on the US$ leg of the swap had barely changed, because the gap in short rates had widened quite a lot the structure now offered an initial positive carry of 107 bps.

The slightly modified structure involved the client making payments "in arrears", ie, with the resetting period being the same as the payment period (as opposed to the previous levels, which were "in advance", with the resetting period being one period before the payment period). The very steep US$ forward curve rewarded those willing to postpone the resetting date, as can be seen by the levels shown by the bank:

Quanto swap in arrears + cap
❑ effective date 30th September 2001;
❑ maturity date 30th December 2004;
❑ bank pays 3 month € Libor;
❑ client pays 3 month US$ Libor in arrears – 0.18% in euros, subject to a 6.2% cap.

Payer swaption
❑ effective date 30th September 2004;
❑ maturity date 30th December 2009;
❑ bank pays 3 month € Libor;
❑ client pays 6.2% fixed.

Now the positive carry that could be enjoyed by the company was 128 bps. The flip side is that by doing the trade in arrears the client was increasing its exposure to very high US$ rates in the future, see Table 3.

The average floating rate paid would have been 1.43%, implying average savings of 1.27% over € Libor. It is clear that the end-user would have been rewarded by his decision to leverage his bet against US rates going up soon and fast.

Case study no. 2
In early October 2001, another corporate client was shown the following liability structures:

Quanto swap plain vanilla
❑ effective date 10th October 2001;
❑ maturity date 10th October 2005;
❑ bank pays 6 month € Libor;
❑ client pays 6 month US$ Libor – 0.05% in euros.

Table 3 Case study 1 – quanto swap in arrears + cap + swaption

Effective date	€ 3 month Libor	US$ 3 month Libor in arrears	US$ 3 month Libor in arrears – 0.18	Savings with respect to € 3 month Libor
30-Dec-01	3.65263	1.88125	1.70125	1.95138
30-Mar-02	3.30000	2.03000	1.85000	1.45000
30-Jun-02	3.45000	1.86000	1.68000	1.77000
30-Sep-02	3.44000	1.79000	1.61000	1.83000
30-Dec-02	3.29213	1.38000	1.20000	2.09213
30-Mar-03	2.86125	1.27875	1.09875	1.76250
30-Jun-03	2.52000	1.11625	0.93625	1.58375
30-Sep-03	2.14275	1.16000	0.98000	1.16275
30-Dec-03	2.12663	1.15188	0.97188	1.15475
30-Mar-04	2.12300	1.11000	0.93000	1.19300
30-Jun-04	1.96000	1.61000	1.43000	0.53000
30-Sep-04	2.12000	2.02000	1.84000	0.28000
30-Dec-04	2.14625	2.56438	2.38438	−0.23813

Quanto swap in arrears
❏ effective date 10th October 2001;
❏ maturity date 10th October 2005;
❏ bank pays 6 month € Libor;
❏ client pays 6 month US$ Libor in arrears – 0.48% in euros.

Quanto swap in arrears with digitals
❏ effective date 10th October 2001;
❏ maturity date 10th October 2005;
❏ bank pays 6 month € Libor;
❏ client pays 6 month US$ Libor in arrears – 0.64% in euros +
    ❏ 1% if 6 month US$ Libor ⩾ 7.50%;
    ❏ 1% if 6 month US$ Libor ⩾ 8.00%.

Here the client would be selling digital options ("bets") to the bank and amortising the premium as a wider negative spread on the US$ leg. With 6 month € Libor at 3.55% and 6 month US$ Libor at 2.44%, the customer would be enjoying 175 bps of positive carry. This is 16 bps above the 159 bps it would enjoy under the plain quanto in arrears. Of course, this is a tremendous result. The flip side is the amount of risk the company would be facing if the bets went against it. In the extreme scenario, the client could end up paying 6 month US$ Libor + 136 bps precisely at the time when US$ rates are very high.

However, the strikes on the digitals suggested that if one had to sell bets on US$ Libor, it could do much worse then sell them at 7.50 and 8.00%, for 6 month US$ Libor has not touched 7.50% since January 1991, and 8.00% since December 1990. In other words, for a company whose priority is to lower short-term financing cost as much as possible, selling these digitals could be a reasonable proposition.

This structure is an example of a practice that was widely used in 2001: customers selling options in order to improve the terms of the quanto swap. We will see more complex examples in the following pages.

Table 4 shows how this structure would have worked.

That is, the end-user of the quanto structure would have faced an average floating rate of 1.54%, representing an average carry of 1.10%. It is clear that the last two payment dates would have seriously hampered the overall performance of the structure, as Greenspan's relentless tightening spirit began to cause real trouble. In this sense, the risks implied by the "in arrears" factor would have in the end materialised themselves. Nevertheless, given the very substantial gains obtained in the earlier periods (when the Fed was still lowering rates), the corporate would have had a big enough cushion to eventually enjoy decent net final cost savings.

Table 4 Case study 2 – quanto swap in arrears + digital options

Effective date	€ 6 month Libor	US$ 6 month Libor in arrears	US$ 6 month Libor in arrears – 0.64	Savings with respect to € 6 month Libor
10-Apr-02	3.48763	2.22125	1.58125	1.90638
10-Oct-02	3.54463	1.68875	1.04875	2.49588
10-Apr-03	3.11200	1.23375	0.59375	2.51825
10-Oct-03	2.43075	1.18000	0.54000	1.89075
10-Apr-04	2.15438	1.22500	0.58500	1.56938
10-Oct-04	2.03688	2.24000	1.60000	0.43688
10-Apr-05	2.20000	3.38375	2.74375	−0.54375
10-Oct-05	2.19194	4.3025	3.66250	−1.47056

Needless to say, the digital options were not even close to reaching an in-the-money situation. US$ Libor and the 7.50% and 8% strikes have been as far away as they could be. For the digitals to negatively affect the end-user, the interest rate cycle in the US would need to have been reversed quickly and dramatically. Of course, not only did this not happen, but in fact rates were lowered further and the loosening regime maintained much longer than anybody would probably have expected in late 2001.

Case study no. 3
In late December, a corporate with € debt liabilities that imports heavily from the US was shown the following trades:

Quanto swap + vanilla cap + FX option
❑ effective date 30th January 2002;
❑ maturity date 30th January 2007;
❑ bank pays 6 month € Libor;
❑ client pays 6 month US$ Libor – 0.55% in euros subject to:
  ❑ cap on 6 month US$ Libor strike 5.00%.
❑ client sells the following FX option:
  ❑ maturity 30th January 2007;
  ❑ € call/US$ put;
  ❑ strike: 0.95.

Quanto swap + KOKI cap + FX option
❑ effective date 30th January 2002;
❑ maturity date 30th January 2007;
❑ bank pays 6 month € Libor;
❑ client pays 6 month US$ Libor – 0.79% in euros subject to:
  ❑ knock-out cap on 6 month US$ Libor with strike 4.90% and barrier 7.50%;
  ❑ knock-in cap on 6 month US$ Libor strike 8.75% and barrier 7.50%.
❑ client sells the following FX option:
  ❑ maturity date 30th January 2007;
  ❑ € call/US$ put;
  ❑ strike: 0.95.

Both structures involve the company selling a € call/US$ put. This makes sense for this particular client since its bottom line profits from a stronger Euro/weaker US$. In other words, if the FX option expired in-the-money this contingency would have a natural hedge in that the company's bottom line would have improved. As long as the company is willing to let go some of this improvement in the future in exchange for obtaining cheaper financing in the short term, the structure would make sense.

Is the positive carry obtained worth the potential giving up of bottom line gains due to FX movements? Well, the short-term savings in financing costs do look very impressive. With 6 month € Libor at 3.41% and 6 month US$ Libor at 2.02%, the client would be getting an initial positive carry of 194 bps (plain vanilla cap structure) and 218 bps (KOKI structure). The difference in positive carry (24 bps) is due to the fact that the KO was worth a great deal, because of the very steep forward curve and volatility in US$ rates.

It should be emphasised that under both structures the interest rate that the client would pay is capped. In the plain vanilla structure the company would never pay more than 4.44%, while under the KOKI trade it would never pay more than 4.11% if the barrier is not touched and 7.96% otherwise.

Thus, here we have two structures with extremely attractive positive carry and a maximum interest rate that is set at quite a low level, especially if the barrier level is not reached (again, 6 month US$ Libor has not reached 7.50% since January 1991). The client can be offered such good conditions because of the very high value of the FX option it sells (which, once more, has a natural hedge in the company's bottom line).

Let us analyse the evolution of the second structure in Table 5.

We see that so far the structure has produced pretty good results for the hypothetical corporate client, which has been able to pay a variable rate of just 1.55% (including two payment periods with a level below 0.5%) and enjoy debt cost savings of just below 1%. However, there is still one more payment date to go and with almost all certainty it will signify negative carry for the end-user, which will further eat away at the average positive carry accumulated. The key question, of course, is by how much will US$ Libor have climbed come 30th July. Assuming a worst case scenario of two more rate hikes by the Fed that takes the discount rate to 5% by mid-2006, the effective financing cost faced by the corporate would

Table 5 Case study 3 – quanto swap + KOKI cap + FX option

Effective date	€ 6 month Libor	US$ 6 month Libor	US$ 6 month Libor – 0.79	Savings with respect to € 6 month Libor
30-Jan-02	3.38363	1.98875	1.19875	2.18488
30-Jul-02	3.43063	1.86125	1.07125	2.35938
30-Jan-03	2.72063	1.35000	0.56000	2.16063
30-Jul-03	2.10781	1.15000	0.36000	1.74781
30-Jan-04	2.13400	1.21375	0.42375	1.71025
30-Jul-04	2.19875	1.98000	1.19000	1.00875
30-Jan-05	2.17913	2.96000	2.17000	0.00913
30-Jul-05	2.14888	3.92375	3.13375	−0.98487
30-Jan-06	2.70000	4.70000	3.91000	−1.21000
30-Jul-06				

have been above 1.80% with a positive carry over Eurlibor of barely 70 bps (assuming that the ECB stays put).

In any case, what is undeniable is that the positive carry presented by the trade so far will be eventually reduced. In that sense, one could conclude that the structure would have already delivered all of its magic by mid-2005, and that it was downhill from then on. But, as we already know, quanto swaps (just like swaps in general) must be analysed on a break-even basis and even if the overall carry deteriorated vastly the end-user could still walk out a winner because the initial very positive outcomes helped him exactly when he needed help.

As far as the cap is concerned, the 4.90% strike would have proven to be highly effective protection as it was breached in February 2006. It is forseeable that by the following July (the last setting date, or last caplet period) the cap will still be in-the-money and thus the free protection obtained by the client would have proven to be quite useful indeed. The breaching of the 7.50% knock-out barrier, on the other hand, looks totally implausible.

Finally, what about that long-dated currency option? What is the situation with that? Well, when the trade was structured and shown to the client the US$ was strong and the euro was weak. As we all know the tide was soon reversed, with the US$ entering into a sustained slump. This implies three things: as of late March 2006 the option would have been deep in-the-money against the client, the chances of the option eventually expiring in-the-money could be seen as large given the prevailing view that we have embarked on a "dollar-crisis" era, and the chances of the option eventually expiring in-the-money could be seen as low given the fact that the next phase of the US$–€ rollercoaster saga could soon take place this time implying a strong US$ again. The good news is that, as has already been stated, the company has a natural hedge in case it has to face option-related liabilities in January 2007: if the US$ is weak that hurts the company's short option position, but it benefits its bottom line.

Case study no. 4: should corporates enter into leveraged quanto swaps? pros and cons. Leveraged swaps are those where the exposure to a particular floating rate is magnified by a certain parameter, usually a multiplier. Obviously this can dramatically increase the potential risks of the transaction, and that is why the party willing to face such risks has to be compensated in the form of a much wider negative spread. In the early 2000s the extremely steep US$ curve made leverage quanto swaps an extremely daring proposition, thus demanding an equally sizable compensation. In other words, the carrot to enter into the trade was undeniably attractive and the temptations to close the deal for a corporate hedger resembled those faced by Faust when he pledged his soul to Mephistopheles: the fulfilment of your wildest dreams and ambitions, if only for the short-term. And unlike the inevitability of Mephistopheles return to demand Faust's soul in the story, in the case of leveraged swaps it may well be the case that the end-user escapes his tragic destiny and exits the transaction intact, perhaps even a winner.

In summary, leveraged swaps are not for the faint-hearted and offer sensational immediate gains that could either extend themselves for the rest of the trade, be gradually reduced or eventually result in unsustainably large losses. They are the financial markets' equivalent of "selling one's soul to the devil" and are especially sensitive in the corporate hedging arena, as it was leveraged swaps that ultimately caused the now legendary derivatives scandals at Procter & Gamble and Gibson & Greetings in the mid-1990s.

Let us now see how the example analysed in the previous case study would look like once a leverage factor was introduced into the structure:

Leveraged quanto swap + KOKI cap + FX option
❑ effective date 30th January 2002;
❑ maturity date 30th January 2007;
❑ bank pays six-month € Libor;
❑ client pays 2 ∗ six-month US$ Libor – 5.096% in euros subject to:
  ❑ knock-out cap on six-month US$ Libor with strike 4.90% and barrier 7.50%;
  ❑ knock-in cap on six-month US$ Libor strike 8.75% and barrier 7.50%.
❑ client sells the following FX option:
  ❑ maturity date 30th January 2007;
  ❑ € call/US$ put;
  ❑ strike: 0.95.

As we can see, in this case six-month US$ Libor is multiplied by a leverage factor of two. As compensation, the negative spread goes from –0.79 to –5.096%. Thus, the corporate would end up facing a *negative* net financing cost, at least for the earliest periods. Hence the unavoidable temptation of this trade, especially for cash-strapped firms. The other side of the coin was that were Greenspan to start raising rates quickly, such moves would be magnified through the leverage factor and the company could face very large net financing costs. For instance, if six-month US$ Libor reached 7% the corporate would be paying almost 9% interest, while under the unleveraged version of the structure it would only be paying slightly above 6%.

Let us analyse how things would have turned out for the hypothetical end-user, see Table 6.

The numbers tell us that the corporate would have faced an average financing cost of –0.40%, implying an average carry of 2.95%. These are, clearly, results of the jaw-dropping variety. One can only imagine the treasurer happily uncorking a bottle of expensive champagne in celebration of his promotion and substantial salary raise.

But, of course, things are not over yet. There is still one final payment date pending, precisely at a time when almost everyone

Table 6 Case study 4 – leveraged quanto swap + KOKI cap + swaption

Effective date	€ 6 month Libor	US$ 6 month Libor	2 * US$ 6 month Libor – 5.096	Savings with respect to € 6 month Libor
30-Jan-02	3.38363	1.98875	−1.11850	4.50213
30-Jul-02	3.43063	1.86125	−1.37350	4.80413
30-Jan-03	2.72063	1.35000	−2.39600	5.11663
30-Jul-03	2.10781	1.15000	−2.79600	4.90381
30-Jan-04	2.13400	1.21375	−2.66850	4.80250
30-Jul-04	2.19875	1.98000	−1.13600	3.33475
30-Jan-05	2.17913	2.96000	0.82400	1.35513
30-Jul-05	2.14888	3.92375	2.75150	−0.60262
30-Jan-06	2.70000	4.70000	4.30400	−1.60400
30-Jul-06				

expects the Fed to continue its relentless tightening phase. It seems unlikely that in the end the average financing cost would remain at a negative level, but final cost savings could very well remain above 2%. Effectively, then, Mephistopheles would not have returned to demand Faust's compliance with his side of the bargain.

CONCLUDING REMARKS: TO THE BRAVE GO THE SPOILS, BUT DON'T POINT THE FINGER AT THE OTHER GUYS

This chapter has analysed, with the benefit of hindsight, how different quanto swap structures presented in 2001 would have performed given the changing interest rate environment in the US. The inescapable conclusion is that thanks to the Fed's lengthy period with an accommodative stance, those who would have dared to enter into quanto trades would have performed admirably well. Those corporates who entered into relatively short-term transactions ending before the advent of 2005 would have come out as clear winners, with sensational reductions in their net financing costs. Even for those structures with several payment dates still pending the change in the rates cycle that has taken place since mid-2004 should not entirely erase the very substantial gains obtained up to that point.

So, have all those who refused to enter into quanto swaps in the early 2000s (either due to conservatism, ignorance or access to other alternatives) been proven to be a bunch of fools? Should they be reprimanded, perhaps even be fired for gross incompetence? Not really. While in our opinion the lacklustre state of the US economy prior to 11th September, Enron and WorldCom combined with those watershed events created an ideal environment to enter into the quanto swap opportunities afforded by the forward curves, in fact a "once in a lifetime" chance to lower financing costs by a wide margin, it is undeniable that things could have gone the other way and the economy might have proven extremely resilient and the Fed might have started to change tack before 2003. After all, a lot of renowned economists and analysts were predicting a very quick economic recovery, with people talking about 4% rates in the US by mid-2002. No one could blame a corporate treasurer (especially non-US) for becoming quanto-allergic after reading such reports.

Recognising and capitalising on the tremendous and unique opportunities offered by quantos in 2001 required some thinking outside the box, plenty of information on the historical behaviour of the US$ curve and lots of guts. These are positive attributes that may, however, not be shared by all, or even a majority, of corporate treasurers. But that does not make those treasurers bad treasurers. After all, a Swedish or Italian treasurer should not be required to be an expert in the US fixed income market. They should be expected to perform their regular duties in a satisfactory way, not be brilliant visionaries who know a unique opportunity when they see one. Thus, no blame should be assigned to those who decided not to enter into quanto swaps as they had good reasons for it. No blame, but no glory either.

9

Regulatory Incentives

What Sarbanes–Oxley means for corporate hedgers

It is hard to deny that the 21st century has begun with a bang. While still very much in its infancy, the new millennium has already delivered a large number of high-impact events the consequences of which will reverberate for years to come and the analysis will surely become part of the history books. Some of these events are of a political nature (September 11th, the Iraq War), others of an economic nature (the bursting of the Nasdaq bubble, the Enron and WorldCom bankruptcies), and yet others of a scientific nature (the death of Dolly the sheep, robot-guided images from Mars). For corporate users of derivatives, the new century has also brought sensational developments, even if perhaps not capable of capturing the general public's imagination in the same way as the previous episodes. While neither the new accounting rules (FAS 133/IAS 39) nor the new corporate governance regulations (Sarbanes–Oxley) have the power to ignite a global war, kick-start an economic recession or clone human beings, their relevance for treasurers and finance directors is of a similarly paramount nature. Just like two planes crushing into a tower gave way to a war on terror with very uncertain ramifications, the implementation of the new rules and regulations in 2001 (FAS 133), 2002 (Sarbanes–Oxley) and 2005 (IAS 39) signalled the beginning of a new era for corporate derivatives, equally plagued by uncertainty as to its final outcomes.

Nevertheless, it must be said that when it comes to influencing the use of derivatives by non-financial companies there are big differences between the accounting regulations and those of corporate governance. Plainly stated, while the former can do a lot of damage the latter should do a lot of good. At its core, all the new accounting standards really do is gear corporates towards certain derivatives products over others by penalising the use of those structures that it doesn't favour (the penalty coming in the shape of enhanced earnings volatility that derives from the new mark-to-market regime, in itself highly inappropriate for non-trading corporate treasurers). As the actual economic performance of the hedges promoted by the standard-setters could very well turn out to be much inferior than that of the accounting-unfriendly alternatives, both FAS 133 and IAS 39 may in the end not only not improve corporates' risk management practices but actually entrap them into loss-making positions. Not a pretty picture indeed.

Sarbanes–Oxley, on the other hand, should be viewed as positive news. The new regulation offers corporates an incentive (in the form of a stick, rather than a carrot) to apply a best practices framework to their hedging policies. The end result should be a more articulate and well-defined derivatives strategy, an improved understanding of risk, the design of hedging objectives that are consistent with business objectives and heightened communication with senior management. The key issue is that such approach offers a better chance of a successful hedging policy than the out-of-control, unaccountable, badly designed and undisclosed risk management strategies that Sarbanes–Oxley attempts to eliminate.

Crucially, Sarbanes–Oxley does not incentivise one type of derivatives structure over another. There is nothing in the best practices that says that using a swap is better than using an option. What this means is that the new corporate governance regulations would not, by themselves, intimidate corporates into economically inferior hedges. In other words, the benefits for companies of complying with the best practices framework are twofold: the design of well-controlled and appropriate risk management processes, and no regulatory meddling in the product selection exercise. Contrast this with the new accounting rules, where meddling is rampant and the potential malaise (whether accounting or economic) so disturbing that it forces treasurers to contemplate exiting the derivatives arena for good.

In summary, while FAS 133/IAS 39 hurt more than help the corporate derivatives business, Sarbanes–Oxley should prove to be a beneficial influence. By limiting the damage caused by unauthorised and ineffective derivatives transactions, the new regulatory environment may drastically reduce the number of financial engineering-related corporate scandals, thus freeing the D-word of its sometimes soiled reputation. In this sense, adoption of the risk management best practices endorsed by Sarbanes–Oxley could very well lead to an increase, not a reduction, in the use of derivatives by corporates.

THE MARYLAND–OHIO COALITION

The Sarbanes–Oxley Act of 2002, sponsored by US Senator Paul Sarbanes from Maryland and US Congressman Michael Oxley from Ohio in the wake of the Enron and WorldCom scandals, is the most far-reaching legislation affecting financial reporting, disclosure and internal controls for companies operating in the US since the Securities Act of 1933. For the first time Chief Executive Officers (CEOs) and Chief Financial Officers (CFOs) are required to certify in writing that not only are their financial disclosures complete and accurate, but that they have enacted disclosure controls and procedures to ensure reporting of material information affecting the company. The number one goal of the Act is to rein in corporate malfeasance and restore faith in financial reporting.

Sarbanes–Oxley is a complex act with many provisions. The two sections most relevant to public corporations are Sections 302 and 404. Section 302 pertains to disclosure controls and procedures. Section 404 pertains to internal controls and procedures for financial reporting. Section 302 mandates that CEOs and CFOs personally certify financial statements and filings, as well as affirm that they are responsible for establishing and enforcing disclosure controls and procedures at all levels of their corporation. With each quarterly filing, they must certify that they have evaluated the effectiveness of these controls. In addition, they must disclose to their audit committee all significant deficiencies, material weaknesses and acts of fraud.

Section 404 requires an annual evaluation of internal controls and procedures for financial reporting. Under this section, a corporation must document its existing controls that have a bearing on financial reporting, test them for effectiveness and report on gaps and deficiencies. Furthermore, the company's independent auditor must issue a report, to be included in the company's annual report, that attests to management's assertion on the effectiveness of internal controls.

For CEOs and CFOs, complying with these new strict standards is not a matter of choice; it is the cost of doing business in the new compliance age. For the first time, failure to comply carries the prospect of personal criminal liability. And, for the first time, the definition of corporate governance is extending from the boardroom to outsiders, to every investor, taxpayer, customer and employee. Companies will find that auditors will now take a firm stand on doing everything "by the book" because their livelihood is very much at stake.

What is the link between Sarbanes–Oxley and corporate use of derivatives? Why can the new corporate governance regulations affect hedging practices? By placing a strong focus on internal control, Sarbanes–Oxley encourages the adoption of risk management best practices. In particular, it encourages the adoption of the Committee of Sponsoring Organisations of the Treadway Commission (COSO) enterprise risk management framework.

In the autumn of 2004, COSO released its Enterprise Risk Management – Integrated Framework, which was authored by auditing firm PricewaterhouseCoopers (PwC). This principles-based framework provides direction and criteria for improving an organisation's ability to manage risk. The enterprise risk management framework is fully aligned with the also PwC-authored COSO Internal Control – Integrated Framework, which is used by most organisations as the basis for their reporting under Section 404 of Sarbanes–Oxley. This enables organisations to build on their investment in internal control as they make improvements in risk management.

Improved risk management clearly improves financial reporting and transparency (thus the derivatives-regulation link). The new COSO framework requires that organisations establish a risk appetite, measure actions and decisions against that risk appetite and communicate results. Communication of enterprise risk management to users of financial information obviously enhances transparency. Essentially, under Sarbanes–Oxley, corporate heads must now be informed of everything and must inform of everything, so it is crucial that everything is done as rightly as possible. This includes risk management, and the COSO guidelines seem to be the most appropriate to follow.

COSO-LAND

COSO is a voluntary private sector organisation dedicated to improving the quality of financial reporting through business ethics, effective internal controls and corporate governance. Since its founding in 1985, COSO has issued recommendations to public companies and their independent auditors, for the SEC and other regulators and for educational institutions. The complicated sounding name derives from the fact that COSO was originally formed to sponsor the National Commission on Fraudulent Financial Reporting, the chairman at the time being James C. Treadway, Jr, Executive Vice President and General Counsel of Paine Webber and a former commissioner of the Securities and Exchange Commission (SEC). The National Commission was jointly sponsored by five major professional associations in the US, and contained representatives from industry, public accounting, investment firms and the New York Stock Exchange.

More than a decade ago, COSO issued the "Internal Control-Integrated Framework" to help businesses assess and enhance their internal control systems. This framework has since been incorporated into policy, rule and regulation and used by thousands of enterprises to better control their activities in moving towards their business objectives.

Recent years have witnessed heightened concern and focus on risk management, and it became increasingly clear that a need existed for a robust framework to effectively identify, assess and manage risk. In this light, in 2001 COSO initiated a project, with the participation of PwC, to develop such a framework with the ultimate goal of allowing management to evaluate and improve their organisations' enterprise risk management.

The period of the framework's development was marked by a series of high-profile business scandals where investors, employees and other stakeholders suffered huge losses. The need for an enterprise risk management framework, providing key principles and concepts, and clear direction and guidance, a common language, became even more compelling. COSO's "Enterprise Risk

Management-Integrated Framework" is supposed to fill this need, and it is expected to be widely accepted by all interested parties.

Of course, those very same episodes gave rise to the Sarbanes–Oxley Act in the US, with similar legislation having been enacted or being considered in other countries. "Internal Control-Integrated Framework", which continues to stand the test of time, serves as the broadly accepted standard for satisfying the new reporting requirements. "Enterprise Risk Management-Integrated Framework" expands on internal control, providing a more robust and extensive focus on the broader subject of enterprise risk management. While it is not intended to replace the internal control framework, companies may look to this enterprise risk management framework both to satisfy their internal control needs and to move towards a fuller risk management process.

How does COSO define enterprise risk management? It says that it deals with risks and opportunities affecting stakeholders value creation or preservation, defined as follows:

> "Enterprise risk management is a process, effected by an entity's board of directors, management and other personnel, applied in strategic settings and across the enterprise, designed to identify potential events that may affect the entity, and manage risk to be within its risk appetite, to provide reasonable assurance regarding the achievement of entity objectives."

The definition reflects certain fundamental concepts. Enterprise risk management is:

❑ a process, ongoing and flowing through an entity;
❑ effected by people at every level in the organisation;
❑ applied in strategy setting;
❑ applied across the enterprise, at every level and unit, and includes taking an entity-level portfolio view of risk;
❑ designed to identify potential events that, if they occur, will affect the entity and to manage risk within its risk appetite;
❑ able to provide reasonable assurance to an entity's management and board of directors;
❑ geared towards the achievement of business objectives in one or more separate but overlapping categories.

This definition is purposefully broad. It captures key concepts fundamental to how companies and other organisations manage risk, providing a basis for application across organisations. It focuses directly on the achievement of objectives established by a particular entity and provides a basis for defining enterprise risk management effectiveness.

An entity's objectives towards which achievement enterprise risk management is geared are in turn defined as:

❑ strategic: high-level goals, aligned with and supporting its mission;
❑ operations: effective and efficient use of its resources;
❑ reporting: reliability of reporting;
❑ compliance: compliance with applicable laws and regulations.

Because objectives relating to the reliability of reporting and compliance are within the entity's direct control, enterprise risk management can be expected to provide reasonable assurance of achieving those objectives. The achievement of strategic and operational objectives, however, is subjected to external events not always within the entity's control; accordingly, for these objectives, enterprise risk management can provide reasonable assurance that management and the board are made aware, in a timely fashion, of the extent to which the entity is moving toward achievement of the objectives.

In order to achieve the above-mentioned objectives, a number of enterprise risk management components are needed. COSO enumerates eight interrelated components.

❑ Internal environment: encompasses the tone of an organisation, and sets the basis for how risk is viewed and addressed by an entity, including risk management philosophy and risk appetite. In other words, it establishes the entity's risk culture.
❑ Objective setting: objectives must exit before management can identify potential events affecting their achievement. Enterprise risk management ensures that management has in place a process to set objectives and that the chosen objectives support and align with the entity's mission and are consistent with its risk appetite. That is, this component forms the company's risk appetite: how much risk the board and management are willing to accept, and which type of objectives can be set in this light.

❑ Event identification: involves identifying those events, both external and internal, that could affect strategy and achievement of objectives, distinguishing between risks (events with a negative impact) and opportunities (positive impact).

❑ Risk assessment: allows an entity to understand the extent to which potential events may impact objectives. Risks are assessed from two perspectives (likelihood and impact) and both qualitative and quantitative techniques are employed.

❑ Risk response: management selects risk responses (avoiding, accepting, reducing or sharing risk) developing a set of actions to align risks with the entity's risk tolerance and risk appetite.

❑ Control activities: policies and procedures are established and implemented to help ensure that the risk responses are effectively carried out.

❑ Information and communication: relevant information is identified, captured and communicated in a form and timeframe that enable people to carry out their responsibilities. Communication occurs in a broader sense, flowing down, across and up the entity.

❑ Monitoring: the entirety of enterprise risk management is monitored and modifications made as necessary. Monitoring is accomplished through ongoing management activities, separate evaluations, or both.

We have now completed the so-called "enterprise risk management cube" (see Figure 1) depicting the four objectives categories, the eight components needed to achieve them and an entity's units. This depiction portrays the ability to focus on the entirety of an entity's enterprise risk management, or by objectives category, component, entity unit or any subset thereof.

An entity's enterprise risk management is deemed effective if the eight components are present and functioning properly. For this to be the case, there can be no material weaknesses and risk needs to have been brought within the entity's risk appetite.

When enterprise risk management is determined to be effective in each of the four categories of objectives, the board and management have reasonable assurance that they understand the extent to which the entity's strategic and operational objectives are being achieved, and that the entity's reporting is reliable and applicable laws and regulations are being complied with.

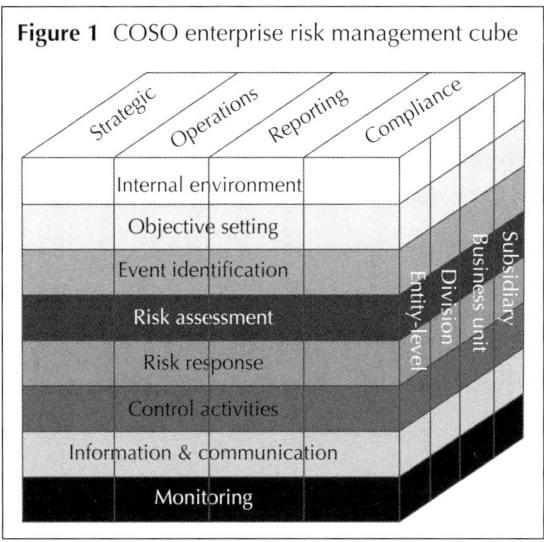

Figure 1 COSO enterprise risk management cube

BEST MEANS BETTER

The main message of this chapter is that adopting COSO best practices, on top of helping satisfy the Sarbanes–Oxley requirements, should result in better risk management. What justifies this assertion? Why would a risk management programme designed around these principles lead to better results?

Quite simply, COSO principles embrace what may be considered as "the holy trinity" of risk management, especially in the current control-obsessed environment: thorough involvement of both the board and management, design of risk management objectives in accordance to an entity's business objectives, and a fully supervised treatment of risk.

This type of approach is more important than ever for companies. While only a few years ago it might have been acceptable to avoid sharing with senior management and board members "too many details that they might not understand", such lack of internal control and disclosure is much less acceptable in the brave new world of Sarbanes–Oxley. Now, managers (and auditors) will have to examine internal controls at a level of detail not previously imagined. One could say that personal liability has a dramatic effect on attention. Corporate decision makers need to dig in more because their signatures are on it. Sarbanes–Oxley creates for them a very direct interest in knowing everything about the structure of the derivative, the risks it's hedging, the model being used for its mark-to-market, the management and procedural controls between the front and back offices and the conformance with trading policies and limits.

Clearly, all this senior involvement can only strengthen the quality of the risk management process. Without it, the company's risk policy may be left entirely to the whims of uncontrolled treasury officials, who could pursue strategies that are at odds with management's and the board's wishes. By following COSO guidelines, the scope for unauthorised and inappropriate derivatives transactions that may end up wreaking havoc is greatly reduced. For instance, if the company's established risk culture is conservative, then the CEO and CFO should not have to wake up one morning to the news that the firm is in big trouble because someone at the treasury had entered into non-compliant super exotic structures. A similar example would be an unsupervised treasurer that trades beyond previously set limits. The point of emphasising internal controls and continuous management involvement is to precisely avoid such situations.

Making sure that the goals of the risk management strategy are fully aligned with the company's overall business objectives should also be seen as positive guidance from the COSO. Derivatives should not be used in a vacuum, or at random. They should serve a very specific purpose, fully related to management's aims. This principle could be seen as a safeguard against the use of derivatives for speculation purposes by non-speculating corporates.

Finally, a comprehensive and all-encompassing treatment of risk should also be considered as part of a good hedging philosophy. The COSO approach offers such treatment, by centring on the identification of risk, the measurement of risk, the setting of specific levels of risk tolerance and the monitoring of risk to ensure that it is always within acceptable limits. In other words, under the COSO guidelines derivatives would hedge the appropriate (relevant) type of risk, in the exact amounts needed, and in a flexible (constantly adapting) way.

The conclusion must be that companies have much to gain from adopting the COSO framework as they try to comply with the strict requirements of Sarbanes–Oxley. Whatever the specific risk management approach of a firm (conservative, sophisticated, accounting-focused, economics-focused, etc), articulate and well-defined policies, improved understanding of risk, hedging objectives consistent with business objectives and heightened communication with senior management offer a better chance of success than the alternatives. The plain truth is that poor policies, poor controls and poor risk management decisions often go hand-in-hand.

What kind of problematic hedging policies would be avoided by following and enforcing the COSO guidelines? If we want to peddle the COSO approach it makes sense to highlight the malaise that such approach can prevent. Leading investment banking practitioners who deal with corporate risk management have recently described some problematic situations that they have encountered when dealing with corporate clients in the real world. The two common themes to all these episodes are, on one hand, the frequent existence of a discrepancy between what senior management expects and what the hedging programme actually delivers, and on the other hand, that risk management strategies are being established without the company having a deep understanding as to the risks that are supposedly being hedged. These are, of course, exactly the types of communication, disclosure, awareness and risk supervision failures that the COSO framework is designed to combat. Herein lies the key issue: had the companies involved been following a set of risk management best practices they would not have incurred the described poor hedging decisions. These misguided decisions could have serious real economic consequences. By incentivising (in a forceful manner) the adoption of best practice guidelines, Sarbanes–Oxley may be decisively contributing to confining to the dustbin ineffective and damaging risk management approaches such as those highlighted by practitioners:

❑ a company's policy states that its risk management objectives are to reduce earnings volatility from the effects of swings in the underlying exposure, but it has not identified how much potential volatility exists, to what extent volatility has been reduced, or whether the hedging programme actually produces the intended results;
❑ a hedge objective of bearing a budget rate creates an incentive for a company to hedge less risk (or no risk) when current market

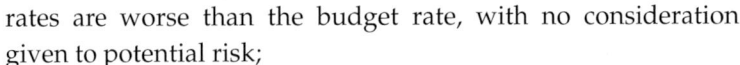

rates are worse than the budget rate, with no consideration given to potential risk;

❑ risk managers are given a mandate to use market timing to improve hedging performance. Their performance is not benchmarked, senior management does not know to what extent these efforts have been successful, does not understand what value has been added from these activities, or how much risk is being taken to achieve the result;

❑ a company's risk management policy only allows for zero-cost option structures as a way to control hedging costs, but there are no other controls around other types of risks when designing the hedges;

❑ the CFO states that "we are a conservative company and we consider hedging to be too risky", but the company has no mechanism in place to identify and quantify the risk of the unhedged exposures and this information is not reported to senior management or the board on a regular basis.

By gearing companies towards more controlled and efficient hedging policies, it is logical to assume that a side effect of the widespread adoption of the COSO principles would be a sharp reduction in the number of derivatives-related corporate scandals. This should spell good news for derivatives bankers. Companies that are using derivatives would tend to continue using them in the absence of risk management disasters, while newcomers would be encouraged by a climate that lacks negative publicity regarding the use of financial engineering tools. In fact, companies that have traditionally not been hedging may now be pushed by Sarbanes–Oxley into the arms of dealers. Since in today's regulatory environment not hedging is no excuse for failing to identify risks and report them to senior management and the board, there is no absence of workload advantage in not using derivatives. Given that the investment needed to quantify, monitor and report exposures must be in place anyway, you might as well do some real hedging while you are at it. This is once more in contrast to the effects that the new accounting rules are expected to have (and have had) on the corporate derivatives business: here, the extra workload required by the regulations acts very much as a deterrent, not an incentive, for the use of derivatives.

APPENDIX: SELF-ASSESSMENT GRID

The following evaluation "grid" can be used by corporates for purposes of self-assessment against industry best practices related to risk management activities. It must be said that this is just a sample of the type of processes that constitute a best practices approach and by no means constitutes a complete list.

Best practice	Yes?	No?

1. Oversight of Risk Management Activities

The Board of Directors oversees all aspects of the risk
  management programme and receives periodic updates on results
Senior management formulates, implements and delegates
  approved policy, and is responsible for monitoring
  day-to-day operations
There is a risk management function that quantifies and
  reports risk to senior management, enforces risk limits,
  manages exceptions, approves counterparties and proposes
  changes to policies
The Risk Management function approves specific hedging
  strategies within policy guidelines
The Audit Committee understands the scope of internal and
  external audit testing of compliance with risk management
  policies, procedures and limits and FAS 133 requirements
Controller establishes accounting policies

2. Strategies and Objectives

Risk management objectives are tied to business objectives
Business objectives are clearly communicated to risk
  management personnel
Senior management and the Board of Directors have determined
  and communicated their risk tolerance on a qualified basis
Senior management and the Board of Directors have set
  and communicated the benchmarks for the evaluation
  of the hedge performance

3. Organisation and Human Resources

There are adequate people resources to carry out the risk
  management objectives
Responsibility for hedge performance versus benchmarks is clear
Compensation policies are structured to discourage
  excessive risk taking
A programme is established to provide for training,
  improving skill sets and documenting collective
  knowledge – including members of senior management
Ethics standards have been established

APPENDIX: SELF-ASSESSMENT GRID (continued)

Best practice	Yes?	No?

4. Policies and Controls

Types of exposures and risks are defined in the policy
There are risk limits based on quantifiable data that lead
  to hedging actions to reduce risk to acceptable limits
Approved hedging instruments, approved counterparties
  and hedging instruments are outlined in policy document
Exceeded risk limits are reported to management and
  resolved in a timely basis
Segregation of duties is maintained
Risk management terms are fully defined and the policy
  builds expectations of what the risk management programme
  will and will not achieve

5. Front, Middle and Back Office Functions

Risk managers are aware of risk management policies
  and execute transactions consistent with approved policies
Transaction execution and data capture is authorised,
  accurate and complete
Market risk is quantified, monitored and reported
  to senior management
Risk-based limits are determined and monitored independent
  of the executors of transactions
The performance of risk management activities against
  benchmarks is evaluated periodically and reported
  to senior management
Credit, operational and legal risks have been fully evaluated
  and monitored ongoing
Trade verification and confirmation are performed by
  back office personnel to insure that transactions are valid
  and complete and the segregation of duties is maintained

6. Reporting

Key reports are generated and provided to senior management
  on a regular basis, information should include: performance
  against benchmark, total risk, exceptions to policy, risk against
  limits, mark-to-market values, credit risks, accounting impacts,
  changes to underlying exposures, etc

Section 4

Accounting

10

Accounting Headlines

How the new accounting rules have taken derivatives back to the front pages and, just as in the mid-1990s, not exactly for good reasons

Similarly to the 1993–95 period, when a group of well-known companies and public entities suffered large and widely publicised losses, derivatives-related troubles are back in the headlines. For the past few years there has been a relatively regular stream of news stories describing how corporates and financial institutions from both the US and Europe have suffered setbacks due to their derivatives positions. The now legendary mid-1990s episodes of Procter & Gamble, Gibson Greetings, Orange County, Metallgesellschaft and Barings Bank that guaranteed derivatives a place in popular culture (even if one filled with negative connotations) are finding their 21st century match in the likes of Fannie Mae, Freddie Mac, Poste Italiane, General Electric (GE), Sears Roebuck and many more. While it is not likely that the latter group would ever achieve the same iconic status as the former, it is clear that after a lengthy absence the "wild beast of finance" is back. Derivatives and bad news are once again being associated, and the current environment risks a descent into the same unrelenting derivatives-bashing that took place some ten years ago. For those who consider the advances of financial engineering as highly value-enhancing ways to improve the management and distribution of risk in the economy these must surely be worrying times.

There is, however, a key difference between the events of the mid-1990s and those that have unfolded in more recent times. While Procter & Gamble, Orange County, Barings and the others suffered real economic pain caused by trades where payouts had gone drastically against them due to market movements, the troubles of the last few years have for the most part been of an accounting nature. That is, it wasn't necessarily the case that the companies involved were incurring unsustainable real costs (in the shape, for instance, of very high net financing costs). Rather, they became front-page items because of the way that they were affected by the new derivatives accounting rules, or because of the way that they reacted to such rules.

Prior to the introduction of the new standards in early 2001 (FAS 133 for US-listed firms) and early 2005 (IAS 39 for Europe and Asia-listed firms), derivatives were off-balance sheet instruments. Nowadays, they must show up on companies' accounts with their mark-to-market value immediately hitting earnings (unless certain stringent conditions are met). As that value can swing wildly, given its sensitivity to highly fluctuating variables such as volatility or forward curves, the potential for accounting malaise caused by derivatives positions is clear. Plainly stated, under the new rules derivatives can become volatility time bombs that heavily distort the income statements of end-users.

Marking-to-market of derivatives used for speculative purposes makes a lot of sense since those involved in the buying and selling of derivatives in search of a profit or a return (ie, traders, investors, asset managers, etc) should be exposed to the changing market value of the securities, as this indicates how much their positions are worth at any one time. On the other hand, subjecting those who use derivatives purely for hedging purposes (such as non-financial companies or public lending institutions) to the tyranny of the mark-to-market regime does not make sense, as they would be treated as if they were traders when in reality they enter into derivatives transactions to keep them until maturity (when the underlying risk materialises) and not to trade in and out of them in order to make some money. By forcing, say, corporate hedgers to mark-to-market their derivatives positions the new rules are effectively exposing them to new risks (such as movements in volatility or forward curves) that did not exist before and that have nothing to do with how those companies make a living.

It is the unexpected and unwarranted enhanced earnings volatility (perhaps accompanied by large accounting losses) that results from the new mark-to-market regime that has placed some companies and their derivatives activities in the headlines in recent years. In the US there has been among others, the well-publicised cases of GE (US$ 500 million reported loss in net income at the beginning of 2001), Verizon (US$180 million hit against income also in early 2001) and mortgage giant Fannie Mae (52% fall in profits in January 2003 despite a surge in business). Europe has more recently witnessed the cases of state-owned Poste Italiane (€104 million loss in early 2004) and also-Italian media group L'Espresso (€16 million in late 2003).

However, it is not only through earnings volatility that the new accounting rules can spell trouble for companies. Given the complexity involved in the actual implementation of the rules there is plenty of scope for reporting entities to "get it wrong" and to be later on forced by auditors and regulators to restate results, a potentially disruptive process that, as recent history shows, can get really messy. Fannie Mae shows up again here, together with its mortgage twin Freddie Mac. In late 2004, Fannie was forced by regulators to restate earnings by recording US$9 billion of derivatives mark-to-market losses, thus erasing 38% of the profit that the government-sponsored company had claimed since the beginning of 2001. The US Securities and Exchange Commission charged that Fannie had inappropriately used its internally-developed methodology to account for derivatives, and that its positions did not qualify for so-called hedge accounting, therefore making mark-to-market into earnings unavoidable. Fannie Mae's politically powerful chairman had to resign in response to the widely covered crisis. Freddie Mac, for its part, tried to implement a transition strategy in order to prevent a large derivatives mark-to-market gain (more than US$4 billion) from being reported all at once. The semi-public mortgage lender feared that analysts and investors wouldn't understand the one-time gain. They might see those billions and prop up the stock. If the stock went up because of this windfall, it could then fall precipitously when the derivatives profits evaporated later on. This would go dramatically against the favoured internal practice of stable earnings known as "Steady Freddie" and thus had to be prevented. While apparently the chosen strategy (which involved the use of very complex tools) was approved by Freddie's auditors as following the letter of the accounting standards, the board nonetheless initiated an investigation whose results were disclosed in June 2003. A major conclusion was that management intentionally tried to "transact FAS 133 around" because they considered that it did not reflect the economic fundamentals of the lender's business. As a result of the ensuing scandal, the CEO, the CFO and the President had to leave. Thus, we see that the new standards can also create considerable mayhem for institutions that are experiencing large accounting gains, not losses, on their derivatives portfolio. A more recent, and hopefully less troublesome, case is that of GE that in May of last year was ordered to positively restate earnings for the 2001–2004 period for an amount of almost US$400 million after internal auditors discovered errors related to how it accounted for derivatives.

In the following pages we will provide an extended analysis of some of the modern-day highest profile derivatives accounting-related episodes to have made the headlines. Given the nature of this book, the focus will be on non-financial corporations, paying particular attention to the more recent cases of Poste Italiane and L'Espresso, which share the key characteristic of having claimed human casualties. We will consider examples of what is probably the most devastating burden that the new accounting standards can impose on reporting entities, namely the forced restatement of prior results.

GENESIS: 2001

With FAS 133 becoming mandatory in January 2001, the first headline-grabbing news regarding accounting-driven earnings volatility and/or losses began to emerge early in that year. Table 1 contains the initial FAS 133 disclosures for a sample of leading US corporates as reported in regulatory filings. It can be seen that for about half of the entities, the impact was deemed immaterial. For the other half, some significant effects were detected. Income statement impacts ranged from a US$500 million loss (GE) to a US$30 million gain (Lucent). Equity effects were more dramatic, with GE posting a US$1 billion loss (2% of the company's then US$50 billion in shareholders' equity).

Rating agency Moody's stated then that these results should be thought of as one-time impacts from the initial transition to the new accounting regime and that they should not be considered as being representative of expected future volatility, at least not of the same magnitude.

Table 1 Initial FAS 133 disclosures for a group of leading US companies

Company	Filing source	Expected impact
Albertson's Inc.	10-K 1st February 2001	Not material
The Boeing Company	10-K 31st December 2000	At initial adoption: US$1 million after tax gain in net income; US$9 million after tax gain in other comprehensive income
Compaq Computer Corporation	10-K 31st December 2000	Not material
Enron Corporation	10-K 31st December 2000	At initial adoption: US$5 million after tax loss in net income; US$22 million after tax gain in other comprehensive income
Exxon Mobil Corporation	10-K 31st December 2000	Not material
Ford Motor Company	10-K 31st December 2000	At initial adoption: US$70 million after tax loss in net income; US$550 million after tax loss in other comprehensive income
GE Company	10-K 31st December 2000	At initial adoption: US$500 million after tax loss in net income; US$1 billion after tax loss in other comprehensive income
General Motors Corporation	10-K 31st December 2000	At initial adoption: US$6 million after tax loss in net income; US$77 million after tax loss in other comprehensive income
Hewlett-Packard Company	10-K 31st October 2000	Not material
International Business Machines Corporation	10-K 31st December 2000	At initial adoption: US$6 million after tax loss in net income; US$219 million after tax gain in other comprehensive income
The Kroger Company	10-K 3rd February 2001	Not material

Table 1 (continued)

Company	Filing source	Expected impact
Lucent Technologies Inc.	10-Q 31st December 2000	At initial adoption: US$30 million after tax gain in net income; US$11 million after tax gain in other comprehensive income
Merck & Co, Inc.	10-K 31st December 2000	At initial adoption: insignificant impact on net income; US$46 million after tax gain in other comprehensive income
Motorola, Inc.	10-30th September 2000	Not material
J.C. Penney Company, Inc.	10-K 27th January 2001	Not material
Sears, Roebuck and Company	10-K 30th December 2000	At initial adoption: US$270 million after tax loss in other comprehensive income
Target Corporation	10-Q 28th October 2000	Not material
Texaco Inc.	10-K 31st December 2000	Not material
Verizon Communications Inc.	10-K 31st December 2000	At initial adoption: US$180 million after tax loss in net income
Wal-Mart Stores, Inc.	10-K 31st January 2001	Not material

While even these initial results seemed to have a relatively non-tragic impact (with earnings losses representing 4% of total net income for GE, 2% for Ford, 1.5% for Verizon and 0.1% for IBM and GM), the debut of FAS 133 was greeted by the media with headlines such as "New derivatives accounting rule spurs bumpy corporate earnings", or "How many more companies will get nailed by the new derivatives accounting rule?". Hear the tune? Derivatives. Bumpy earnings. People getting nailed. How mid-1990s it all sounds.

THE FALL OF ROME

Italian companies have a well-established reputation as some of the most daring when it comes to using derivatives, never shying away from the most complex and sophisticated structures. In this sense, it shouldn't be too surprising that the two best-known cases so far of derivatives accounting trouble in Europe involve Rome-based firms.

In mid-2003, media company Gruppo Editoriale L'Espresso and state-owned postal and retail financial services giant Poste Italiane both suffered large mark-to-market accounting losses deriving from certain interest rate hedging structures. The cause of both disasters was the same, namely the large-scale sell-off experienced by US Treasury bonds that July, with the consequent steepening of the US forward curve. Given that L'Espresso and Poste had entered into derivatives whose value went against them in case of increasing dollar yields, the bond market meltdown instantly produced hair-raising accounting malaise. Big headline-grabbing scandals ensued with senior staff being dismissed. The irony of it all is that in both cases the structures were most likely delivering positive economic results.

Before we proceed to analyse these cases in more detail, it is worth addressing first a point that the alert reader may have already noticed. If IAS 39 did not become mandatory for Euro countries until January 2005, why was mark-to-market valuation a concern in the summer of 2003? More to the point, why would a non-listed public entity such as Poste even care about the market value of its derivatives positions? These are important questions, as many private corporates (IAS 39, and also FAS 133, only applies to listed firms) continue to struggle with whether to report like the "big boys" or not. Many non-listed companies may want to comply with IAS 39/FAS 133 so that they can position themselves on the same playing field as listed firms, which presumably are larger and more influential. It is not surprising that private companies would want to speak to outsiders in the same language as their public counterparts. Otherwise, investors, lenders, suppliers or regulators might have a hard time understanding them in the new era of mark-to-market accounting. Crucially, the implementation of the new standards would be less well policed in the case of non-listed entities, so that adopting the rules could deliver all the positives without necessarily suffering all the negatives.

Generally, the most important reason that would prompt private companies to comply with IAS 39 or FAS 133 is the intention to sell shares to the public in the future. This was the case with Poste Italiane. Senior management had apparently asked newly appointed auditor PriceWaterhouseCoopers (PwC) to apply IAS 39 hedge accounting rules in order to prepare the company for future privatisation. It was the consequent audit carried out by PwC in February 2004 that uncovered the €104 million mark-to-market hole that made the headlines and created mayhem for Poste's staff and its bankers.

In the case of L'Espresso, the losses did not seem to derive directly from an intention to comply with the new derivatives rules, but rather from the margin call that its banking counterpart (JP Morgan, curiously also Poste's derivatives dealer) is understood to have made as a result of the deteriorating mark-to-market of the company's hedging position (L'Espresso was apparently subject to a collateral agreement). That is, for the media company the 16 million Euros losses, though prompted by accounting trouble, were very much real (ie, cash).

So, what kind of structures did Poste and L'Espresso enter into, why did the summer 2003 bond sell-off hurt them, what were the ramifications of the scandals and what are the lessons to be drawn from these stories? While the details are somewhat blurry, it looks as if both companies undertook exposures to US interest rates (though none had dollar-denominated debt) in order to lower their Euro-denominated net financing costs. In other words, they both chose to take advantage of the very attractive opportunities afforded by the family of derivatives known as "quantos". Provided that the US forward curve and the Euro forward curve are aligned the right way relative to each other, quanto technology can allow very significant reductions in net financing costs, at least for the first periods and possibly for the others too, depending on the evolution of US monetary policy. In exchange for such pleasantries, the end-user becomes highly exposed to two types of contingencies (which may or may not take place at the same time): from an economic point of view, the possibility that short-term interest rates in the US go up very soon, very fast, thus significantly increasing the company's financing cost; from an accounting point of view, the possibility that the US forward curve would steepen with regards to the Euro curve thus causing mark-to-market malaise.

In the case of Poste, the amount of publicly available information is more extensive and it is therefore easier to dissect what they got themselves into. In early July 2003, Massimo Catasta, Poste's then finance director, entered into a so-called "knock-in quanto swap" with JP Morgan. The notional amount was very substantial (especially for such an exotic trade), at €250 million. The carrot of the structure seems to be that it guaranteed Poste a fixed net financing cost much lower than would have been obtainable through the plain vanilla swap market. Such significant cost savings would have continued unaltered until at least the end of 2006. After that, the company was exposed to US Libor reaching a barrier (set at a high level of 7%), in which case it would be switched to a quanto swap with a maturity date of 2013. As per the quanto swap, Poste's net financing cost would now be referenced to US Libor but expressed in Euros. In other words, the stick of the trade is that Poste would be facing the possibility of being switched into paying US Libor precisely when US Libor was quite high.

Clearly, the dramatic steepening experienced by the US curve following the bond market sell-off in July and August 2003 must have resulted in massive negative mark-to-market for Poste as the curve was "saying" that the 7% barrier would in fact be breached in the future and the company would be knocked-in into a quanto swap whereby it would pay US Libor and receive Euro Libor (with both payments denominated in Euros). The market value of such a swap would be determined by the gap between both curves, especially at the medium and long ends. Were the US curve to steepen with regards to the Euro curve after, say, the two-year maturity, the quanto would go into the red for the corporate because the curves would be "indicating" that future payment dates would involve larger net cashflows from the corporate to the bank than previously assumed. As during the summer of 2003, the long-end of the US curve steepened by more than 70 basis points (bps) over its Euro counterpart, those treasurers holding quanto positions would have been devastated by the accounting bogeyman. Of course, it is crucial to point out here that if quanto swaps qualified for so-called hedge accounting then its mark-to-market would not hit a company's income statement and thus bad news would be avoided. The real problem is that unless a corporate has foreign currency revenues or debt, quantos would be treated as speculative, not hedging, positions.

At the end of 2003, the mark-to-market losses of Poste's knock-in quanto position reached €44 million, out of the €104 million of total derivatives accounting-related losses revealed by the PwC audit. Massimo Catasta was let go. Public prosecutors initiated an investigation and even the Italian parliament became involved. In June 2004, Poste decided to sue JP Morgan to the tune of €40 million.

What about L'Espresso? What structure did they enter into? Here, unfortunately, the amount of available information is not as satisfactory as in the Poste situation. We know that the publisher of La Reppublica had in 2000 issued a €200 million fixed-coupon bond, and that it wanted to hedge its exposure by swapping to a floating rate liability. Up until the beginning of 2003 this strategy seemed to be working wonderfully, given the sharp reduction in short-term rates witnessed in 2001 and 2002. According to the company's 2002 annual report, at the end of that year average interest expense amounted to 3.9%, well below the 6.5% bond coupon. In the second quarter of 2003, L'Espresso apparently entered into a leveraged swap transaction with JP Morgan for a notional of €200 million (the total amount of its outstanding debt). As with Poste Italiane, the trade could go sour were the US curve to steepen (ie, were US swap rates to go up). Throughout the summer 2003 massacre, with five-year US swaps going from 2.30% at the beginning of July to 3.50% at the end of August, the mark-to-market deteriorated wildly. Towards the end of July, with the swap already heavily underwater, JP Morgan is understood to have made the margin call that was mentioned earlier. An agreement was made to limit the payment due to a sum substantially inferior to the original margin call, and on 24th July CFO Raffaele Vanni resigned. According to a regulatory filing made by L'Espresso the following September, the firm's losses incurred through "financial operations on interest rates" in the first half of 2003 totalled €15.87 million, a substantial part of which was made up of the money paid to JP Morgan.

The tales of Poste and L'Espresso surely contain the ingredients for a drama. Cutting-edge investment bankers peddling highly complex financial engineering devices that could blow up in the users' faces in case a foreign interest rate market were to go ballistic. Daring corporate professionals willing to accept the high risk-reward stakes. Media-covered scandals when the losses materialised, including the sacking of high-profile staff and the involvement of prosecutors. Secret negotiations between bankers and their clients to determine the size of the paycheck. Lawsuits.

Intriguing though all this surely is, for the purposes of this chapter the issue surrounding these Roman stories that should interest us more is perhaps the least glamorous of all, namely the effects on corporate hedging activities of the new derivatives accounting rules.

In this respect, one thing seems clear: it is unlikely that either Poste or L'Espresso will be entering into quanto structures any time soon (and not only because these transactions no longer work, given the tightening monetary cycle and inverted yield curve in the US). This, frankly, is in itself a great loss. For the truth is that quanto swaps, in general, have delivered sensational economic value to those treasurers that decided to embrace them in the 2001–2003 period. Given the very aggressive easing cycle pursued by Alan Greenspan all the way to mid-2004, corporates that paid US Libor experienced extremely low net financing costs (in some cases, negative figures). In fact, from what it is known about the knock-in quanto, it is reasonable to assume that Poste had been enjoying large economic gains from the hedge by the time disaster struck in the bond markets in July 2003. In other words, Massimo Catasta may have been transformed from hero to villain by the new accounting standards (though it must be said it later emerged that Catasta had exceeded his mandate to hedge against interest rate fluctuations using contracts with notionals not above €50 million; however, it seems obvious that this violation would not have caused great concern had the mark-to-market not been so detrimental). While it is clear that Poste faced the risk of having to pay US Libor precisely at a time when it was high, the truth is that this was simply a possibility that may or may not happen. However, the large economic gains that the structure was purportedly delivering and would continue to deliver for at least three more years by the time Catasta was let go were very much real. That is, in Catasta we have a finance director that was most likely saving his employer millions in financing costs thanks to his vision and initiative to enter into an exotic structure rather than a plain vanilla one, and who was terminated on account of forward curves movements that did not affect the real financing costs of the company at all and that were caused by forces completely out of Catasta's radar screen (while finance directors should be expected to be able to make reasonable forecasts of the future levels of Libor, it is totally unreasonable to expect them to predict future forward curves movements).

The risk is that many corporate treasurers and risk officers would take a look at episodes such as Poste's or L'Espresso's and conclude that the personal liabilities of entering into derivatives structures that have the slightest chance of going sour from an accounting point of view are just too high. Unacceptably high. The temptation to stick with accounting-friendly plain vanilla trades would prove too much to resist. By doing so, they may be doing a disservice to the company where it should matter most, namely the bottom line, since nothing guarantees that the simplest hedges would deliver the best economics (in fact, they could very well end up being rather economically inferior to the exotic alternatives). Had Massimo Catasta or Raffaele Vanni kicked out the quanto-peddling JP Morgan bankers from their offices and instead entered into vanilla swaps their employers would most likely have suffered higher financing costs.

The Poste and L'Espresso case studies are important not only because they are (to a degree) entertaining stories, but because they clearly highlight the dark side of the new derivatives accounting rules: they can conspire to eliminate structures and professionals that are delivering stellar economic results. Perhaps the worst consequence to come out of the implementation of the new accounting rules will be the substitution of value-enhancing strategies for economically inferior alternatives, and the replacement of sophisticated forward-thinking corporate finance staff by sub par conservative replacements.

RESTATEMENT BLUES

In the previous pages we have analysed several cases of corporates that suffered large mark-to-market losses on their derivatives positions. All these episodes highlight the power of the new accounting standards to enhance earnings volatility and produce large paper losses. Both of these effects are highly unfair as hedging structures entered into with the purpose of keeping them until maturity (such as corporate treasurers generally do) should not be treated as speculative positions. This unfair character is compounded in those situations when the economics of the derivative are performing admirably.

Needless to say, it is not only non-financial companies that hedge their risks. Financial entities also need to protect themselves from interest rate movements. As such, they too become vulnerable to being treated unfairly by the accounting rules. Mortgage lending giants Freddie Mac and Fannie Mae can attest to that. Given their outsized exposures to interest rate swings, these institutions routinely enter into hundreds of swaps and other interest rate derivatives in order to obtain a protective shell. Marking-to-market these portfolios into earnings clearly has the potential of causing accounting mayhem of biblical proportions. Especially when a stated golden goal of both Fannie and Freddie has always been the deliverance of steady surprise-free results. It is no wonder, then, that the introduction of FAS 133 in January 2001 made these agency lenders a bit uncomfortable, to say the least. Of course, as we now know, those suspicions became fully justified as only a few years later each of them was immersed in widely publicised scandals centring on derivatives accounting. The biggest heads rolled. The stock prices of these former Wall Street darlings plunged. The press had a field day dragging the D word through the mud.

The Fannie and Freddie episodes are important for the corporate community because they are the best-known and highest-profile examples of entities being forced to restate their reported earnings as a result of mistakes (whether wilful or accidental) regarding the actual implementation of the new derivatives accounting standards, and they very forcefully point to the highly destabilising consequences that such restatements can bring about. Due to different reasons (more "fraudulent" in the case of Freddie, more "technical" in the case of Fannie), both lending agencies had to restate reported results dating back several years to the tune of billions of dollars. In late 2003 it was Freddie Mac's turn, positively restating earnings by US$4.5 billion (ie, gains). In late 2004, it was Fannie Mae that negatively restated earnings by US$9 billion (ie, losses), or more than one third of its profits since 2001. It is crucial to note that while Fannie was obviously very upset about having to admit such huge downfall all at once (much lower profits being a no-no), Freddie wasn't chipper about having to declare the large windfall all at once (earnings volatility being a big no-no). Substantial income statement hits can be chaotic irrespective of whether they represent losses or gains. In this sense, the new accounting rules have managed to turn even apparently positive news into very bad news.

Non-financial companies have also been involved in derivatives accounting-induced restatements, though not as sensational as those of the Washington DC mortgage siblings. The most widely publicised cases have been those of energy company El Paso, storage company Shurgard Inc, drilling contractor Pride International and, as mentioned in previous paragraphs, GE.

The case of GE provides a good example of what seems to have been the most dominant type of implementation error (again, whether intentional or not) on the part of reporting entities (mostly financial institutions, but also a few corporates), namely the application of the so-called "short-cut method" for interest rate swaps. The short-cut method is a wonderful thing if you can get it, because it allows you to assume perfect hedge effectiveness from the start. This means not just that the income statement will not be affected whatsoever by any possible mark-to-market volatility, but, crucially, that there is no need for any ongoing effectiveness tests during the life of the transaction. Hedges that are deemed perfectly effective but that are not entitled to short-cut treatment must, in contrast, prove their effectiveness every reporting period. Clearly, qualifying for the short-cut method would significantly reduce the workload involved in using derivatives. In brief, the short-cut gift may be the only truly good piece of news for treasurers regarding the new accounting standards.

So, what type of instruments would be deemed suitable for the short-cut? Simply put, only plain vanilla interest rate swaps would qualify, provided that they satisfy certain stringent conditions. Paragraph 68 of FAS 133 provides specific guidelines as to when an interest rate swap can be assumed to be perfectly effective, and has become one of the best-known paragraphs. The swap would qualify for the short-cut method if:

- ❏ the notional amount of the swap matches the principal amount of the interest bearing asset or liability;
- ❏ the fair value of the swap at inception of the hedging relationship is zero;
- ❏ the formula for computing net settlements under the swap is the same for each net settlements (ie, the fixed rate is the same throughout the term, and the variable rate is based on the same index);
- ❏ the payment and reset dates are the same for the swap and for the underlying being hedged;
- ❏ the interest bearing asset or liability is not prepayable;
- ❏ the index on which the variable leg of the swap is based matches the benchmark interest rate designated as the interest rate risk being hedged;
- ❏ there can be no floor or cap on the variable interest rate of the swap (unless, if applicable, the variable-rate asset or liability has a floor or a cap);
- ❏ any other terms in the interest-bearing instrument and swap are typical of those instruments (ie, no "atypical" features).

GE's implementation error had to do with the second point. The company essentially treated a swap with a non-zero initial value as a member of the short-cut family. On 5th May 2005, GE announced that an internal audit, part of a regularly scheduled exercise, identified the mistake and as a consequence it duly restated financial statements for 2004, 2003, and 2002, and financial information for 2001. This resulted in an increase in non-cash earnings of almost US$400 million from 2001 through Q1 2005.

The company described the misguided application of the short-cut method in the following terms:

"The first errors were in accounting for interest rate and currency swaps at GECC that included fees paid or received at inception. These swaps related to about 14% of our overall borrowings at January 1, 2001, and about 6% of our overall borrowings at December 31, 2004. Our initial accounting viewed these fees as immaterial. KPMG LLP, our registered public accounting firm, reviewed this initial accounting in connection with their 2001 audit. In 2003, we discontinued use of such swaps, except for one immaterial transaction, but continued the previous accounting for those already in place. Because of the swap fees, however, the fair value of the swaps was not

zero at inception as required by SFAS 133 and, accordingly, we were required to, but did not, test periodically for effectiveness"

While the restatement had a very limited relative impact (representing less than 1% of profits for the affected period), it nonetheless made the headlines in force. To the untrained eye (or to the impatient observer who has little time for details), it seemed as if GE had gotten itself into some kind of attention-grabbing trouble because of some derivatives-related mishap. Such a view was reinforced the following October, when the SEC initiated a formal probe on GE's derivatives accounting practices.

The main point is that, of course, had the new accounting rules not been imposed on corporates, none of these restatements would have taken place. Let us repeat a central theme of this book: it does not make sense to force non-financial companies that use derivatives for hedging purposes to be exposed to the changing market value of those derivatives. It just does not make sense to treat Joe the treasurer as if he were Frank the trader (if at least the standard-setters would pay Joe as much money as Frank makes...). While a trader lives and dies by the mark-to-market of his book (ie, how much he would make by unwinding his positions and how different that is from the original levels at which the position was entered into), the same is not (should not) be true in the case of a corporate treasurer who is not mandated to trade in and out of his derivatives depending on market valuations. If you are a speculator then the market value of your position is paramount because that tells you (and your backers) how profitable (or not) your strategy is. A profitable position (ie, one where value has gone up) is the ultimate measure of success for a trader, and what determines his payroll. For Joe and his peers what really matters is whether the derivative has achieved its risk management goal or not. This means, of course, whether the derivative has delivered a cashflow that matches (perfectly or partially) the detrimental effects of unfavourable movements in the underlying exposure. So, the relevance of a derivative as a hedging tool lies exclusively on the possibility of those cashflows, in other words, on the economic performance of the derivative. A treasurer that buys an interest rate cap to hedge their Libor liabilities derived from a bond issue does so because they want to get cash compensation for those fixing periods when Libor quotes above the cap strike.

That's all they want. They would not be interested in taking a view on the future shape of the forward curve or in changes in volatility. Their company's financing costs are not affected in any way whatsoever by those two variables. They are only affected by changes in Libor, and that is why the corporate risk manager only cares about hedging changes in Libor and not in the curve or volatility.

What the accounting rules are basically telling treasurers is that, no matter what reality dictates, they should care about changes in factors such as the forward curve, and that they should be judged accordingly. Nowadays, it is not enough that a treasurer delivers, say, low financing costs through his judicious use of derivatives. His choice of derivatives tools must also bring stable mark-to-market effects. Do these effects directly alter the company's bottom line in any way? Of course not. Nothing real happens to a car manufacturer, a milk producer or a telecom firm when the forward curve steepens or when interest rate volatility goes crazy. Nothing real happens to competing companies either. Nevertheless, the regulators decided that these irrelevant variables should from now on become highly relevant, through the accounting conduit. As if by magic, the standards have suddenly created new exposures that can induce nightmares on corporate bigwigs who run away from earnings volatility like the plague. If facing Libor (or foreign exchange or equity) volatility wasn't problematic enough already, thanks to the new standards' new risks (again, irrelevant in hard cash terms) show up. A treasurer that has been doing a great job at what really matters (reducing financing costs, limiting currency exposures, etc) may be disciplined because of mark-to-market malaise. The new rules are basically a way through which success can be punished, and mediocrity rewarded (as a treasurer that is using accounting-friendly, but economically inefficient, tools would shine in comparison). Why this should be so is something that the regulators have not dared explain.

However, as we know after reading this section of the chapter, this is not all. It can get even worse. Not only can the new rules wreak havoc because of what they are (ie, because they force corporates into the tyranny of the mark-to-market regime), but also because of how they are implemented. The philosophy behind both FAS 133 and IAS 39 is not only irremediably flawed when it comes to corporate hedgers, their mechanics are insurmountably complex (the standards have been repeatedly deemed the most complicated ever). It is easy to make mistakes when tying to comply with FAS 133/IAS 39 and to be subject to subsequent potentially destabilising earnings restatements. While the spirit of the rules can harm treasurers, the implementation mechanisms can devastate them.

This (deeply unfair) double whammy is akin to forcing a non-traffic-exposed pedestrian who doesn't need to drive to get to work into a high-cylinder motorcycle and then punishing him for not using the machine in the proper way. The pedestrian would now be exposed to an unwarranted new risk that he didn't face before (heavy traffic), achieving his objective (getting to work on time) would have not necessarily been made easier, and he could suffer large fines for misusing the technically challenging bike. Likewise, the new accounting rules absurdly expose corporates to new risks, hedging practices are not necessarily improved and the end result may be big painful restatements.

A RETURN TO DERIVATIVES PHOBIA?

In the current environment, as opposed to the realities of a decade ago, it is not necessary for a company's derivatives positions to be heavily underwater from an economic point of view for it to be the subject of bad press. Accounting troubles would suffice (in fact, and this is a particularly acute drawback of the new standards, it is entirely possible for a company to face serious accounting setbacks while enjoying sensational economic gains from the derivative: this, for example, seems to have been clearly the case in the Poste Italiane affair). That is, nowadays companies are exposed to obtaining negative publicity for two kinds of derivatives-related trouble: real, and accounting. Clearly, what this directly implies is that the potential number of bad news stories reaching the headlines becomes much larger than in the days of Procter & Gamble and Metallgesellschaft. In this sense, the public reputation of derivatives could take a hit at least as spectacular as that experienced in the mid-1990s. Just as in the old days, the troublesome news is not devoid of a human face as the number of high-profile staff that have been sacked as a result is by no means insignificant. Obviously, such developments inevitably tend to draw even more public attention towards the events and, consequently, towards the "damaging" effects of derivatives. When the CEOs of Fannie Mae and Freddie Mac, the Finance Director of Poste Italiane and the CFO of L'Espresso suddenly lose their jobs, outside attention as to the causes of such abrupt dismissals is guaranteed and, just as it happened a decade ago, a link between disastrous corporate news and derivatives use gets unavoidably embedded in the public psyche.

Whether the troubles are simply of an accounting, not economic, nature probably won't make much of a difference when it comes to the popularity levels of derivatives. Outside parties are not expected to fully understand the implications of the new accounting standards and how they dramatically alter the playing field for corporate hedgers. This applies not just to shareholders, investors, the general public or even the journalists who report on such developments. Crucially, it also applies to analysts covering the affected companies. For instance, in a well-known episode, Swiss food group Nestlé was recently subjected to intense scrutiny by analysts who couldn't understand the more than US$6 billion in derivatives trading (ie, speculative) positions reported in its 2004 annual accounts. What had simply happened is that these particular derivatives structures (which the company states have a hedging purpose) did not, for whatever reasons, qualify for hedge accounting and as such had to be recorded as trading instruments using the new rules, with their mark-to-market immediately hitting earnings. Even after Nestlé explained this at length, some analysts still concluded that the company was taking too much risk trading derivatives and, perhaps worse, that it did not seem to be hedging a proportion of its market risks. This case helps us visualise not only another possible conduit through which the new standards can create trouble for corporates, but essentially their highly unfair character.

The new accounting rules, which some people see as regulation in disguise, were put in place as a way to guarantee that the scandals of the past could not be repeated. The belief is that the new standards improve disclosure and derivatives use to such an extent that a company would never again be willing or able to expose itself to events such as the level of the five-year US Treasury yield multiplied by a factor of seventeen (*a là* Procter & Gamble) or to the level of Libor squared (*a là* Gibson Greetings). In this way, the new standards were supposed to put an end to derivatives-related trouble. Wouldn't it be ironic then that as a result of the new rules a wave of scandals and bad news afflicted the derivatives industry once again? Wouldn't it also be sinister if the reasons behind the trouble were of a purely accounting, not real, nature?

11

The Four Horsemen of the (Accounting) Apocalypse

Four non-obvious ways in which the new derivatives accounting standards can inflict serious harm to reporting companies

Few issues have raised as much controversy in the financial markets in the last few years as the new accounting standards for derivatives. Since the introduction of FAS 133 in the US approximately five years ago and IAS 39 in Europe beginning January 2005, rivers of ink have been used to describe the pros and cons of the new rules (with arguably more having been written on the cons). The debate has been particularly tense when it comes to the corporate side of the derivatives business. While the new standards also affect financial institutions in a big way, as was witnessed, for example, by the very strong resistance to the full implementation of IAS 39 by French banks, most of the focus has been on how the derivatives activities of non-financial companies have been and will continue to be affected as a consequence of the accounting sea change. Some people initially feared that corporates would simply stop using derivatives at all. Many derivatives bankers probably started circulating their résumés around in response to such negativity. Other observers and market players assumed that firms would continue using derivatives but in a much simpler way, favouring vanilla products over exotic structures. Only a small minority ventured that the new rules would change nothing in terms of how treasurers go about hedging their risks.

Why the controversy? What is it about the new standards that is so contentious? Why the worry about how corporates would react? The main aspect of both FAS 133 and IAS 39 that has dominated the discussion and has prompted the responses by both corporate end-users and the bankers that cater to them (and whose livelihood is at stake) has been the fact that, plainly speaking, the new rules have the potential to dramatically enhance income statement volatility, not to mention creating large accounting losses. Under the new regime corporates have to mark-to-market all their derivatives positions in the balance sheet. As derivatives values can swing wildly, unless they can qualify for so-called "hedge accounting" they would introduce unwelcome volatility into companies' earnings. In order to prevent this undesirable result, corporate executives would find it essential to only enter into derivatives that have a high chance of being deemed effective. In many cases, this entails that accounting considerations become more important than economic considerations when it comes to selecting a hedging strategy. Thus causing the distortions that the new rules can bring to the corporate derivatives market, and the accompanying controversy.

The new standards were introduced with the goal of increasing the level of transparency and disclosure on the part of end-users. Regulators, fed up with large derivatives-related losses and assorted scandals, pushed for a definite way to tame the "derivatives beast" and to make sure that corporates use derivatives to control risk, that is, to hedge and not speculate. The belief is that by mandating companies to show the value of their derivatives on the balance sheet it would be possible to remove the secrecy veil surrounding derivatives use by corporations and guarantee that shareholders and investors can at all times be aware of what those people at the treasury are doing. While these two main goals of the standards, namely making sure that corporates use derivatives for hedging rather than speculation and that external parties are not kept in the dark, are surely noble objectives, and while few would doubt the importance of achieving them, the problem is that, plainly stated, the new accounting regime goes about it in the wrong way. In doing so, it may be entrapping reporting corporates into highly detrimental situations with potentially large negative economic, and not just accounting, outcomes.

TREASURERS ARE NOT TRADERS

By subjecting corporates to the tyranny of the mark-to-market regime the new rules are not solving a problem, but rather creating one. For the purposes of hedging, corporates enter into derivatives contracts with the intention of keeping them until maturity, not to trade in and out of them, as speculators would do. What matter to the corporates are the payoffs of the derivative, not the market movements in the interim. Yet, the new standards do it the other way around by treating treasurers as if they were traders. Instead of being rewarded or penalised for the wisdom of their choice of a hedging strategy and the attached economic results (did the London interbank offered rate (Libor) go up or down? Did the dollar rise against the yen?), treasurers are now being judged for their trading abilities and the variables that affect them (did the forward curve flatten? Did volatility spike?).

Clearly, mark-to-market of derivatives used for hedging is highly inappropriate as it exposes companies to new risks that did not exist before and that have nothing to do with how they make a living. Movements in forward curves (which can have a dramatic effect on the market value of a derivative), for instance, now become key determinants in whether a company's earnings go up or down. Obviously, in reality corporates have no forward curve exposures (as opposed to interest rates or currency exchange exposures), as the shape of the curve *per se* does not directly affect its bottom line. The same would be true of volatility, another crucial component of a derivative's market value. The key idea here is that in the name of disclosure, the new rules force companies to disclose the wrong kind of information: changes in the value of a derivative held by a corporate for hedging purposes are irrelevant, as they do not affect in any way the motivation behind the strategy or the final payoff to which the corporate is truly exposed. Thus, disclosure does not improve, but rather worsens as the standards subject corporate accounts to wild-swinging factors to which the company is in no way exposed from an economic and operational point of view.

What is worse is that by treating corporate treasurers as if they were traders, the new accounting standards provide powerful incentives to take decisions that could yield significantly negative results for the company. As the possibility of enhanced income volatility is obviously an unwelcome prospect for stability-obsessed corporate bigwigs, they would predictably try to do as much as possible in order to prevent such an outcome. By trying to escape the perceived number one evil side of the rules, namely accounting volatility and losses, companies force themselves into a menacing landscape populated by what in this chapter will be deemed as "The Four Horsemen of the Accounting Apocalypse" brought about by the new standards. Just as the more familiar foursome of war, famine, pestilence and death can have devastating real effects on those affected by its presence, the accounting foursome can have devastating economic and strategic (as opposed to simply account-ing) effects on those corporates caught up in its blazing trail. And here lies the truly troublesome character of the new standards: by threatening accounting malaise they leave corporates little option other than to face very negative, real consequences.

The four accounting horsemen can be summed up as Annihilation (the possibility that value-enhancing, highly-performing, economi-cally-winning derivatives structures would be eliminated from the corporate lexicon because of the potentially negative accounting effects), Dismissal (the possibility that sophisticated, performing treasurers or finance directors may be dismissed due to temporary accounting setbacks and replaced by conservative, low performing staff), Discrimination (the possibility that accounting fears may prev-ent companies with inferior credit ratings from hedging their risks at all) and Intimidation (the possibility that corporates would be intim-ated into the derivatives structures deemed more desirable by regu-lators, which could very well turn out to be economically inferior).

In following paragraphs we will thoroughly describe each of these elements and how they can create pain for corporates, but before that, it is essential to point out that while the standards set up the scenario for the emergence of the accounting horsemen through its mark-to-market paradigm, it is only because of the sub-sequent actions taken by corporates themselves that the devastating effects of annihilation, dismissal, discrimination and intimidation are allowed to take place. In this sense, the wounds would be very much self-inflicted. If corporates did not assign so much impor-tance to the accounting results of using derivatives, nor let outside parties do so, they would then not have to subject themselves to the ruthlessness of the four horsemen.

ANNIHILATION

As was mentioned before, under the new standards if a derivative structure does not qualify for so-called hedge accounting its market value would hit a corporate's income statement immediately. Undue earnings volatility and losses may follow as a result. If these are large enough (perhaps to reach the newspapers) then stability-loving bosses who may end up regretting in a big way having entered into the structure in the first place, would most likely unwind the transaction, and might possibly swear never to make the same mistake again, committing them to never letting their treasurers enter into non-effective hedges.

The problem with this line of thought is that corporates may be shooting themselves in the foot by restricting their access to potentially economically superior structures. There are many derivatives trades that would not qualify for hedge accounting, but still prove to be better hedges than those that do qualify. Yes, the latter would not induce income volatility-related nightmares on the part of CEOs and CFOs, but would end up hurting the company's bottom line (ie, would end up costing cold hard cash). As long as corporate executives are prey to the accounting tyranny, they run the risk of incurring significant real economic costs. And while outside parties (analysts, investors and shareholders) may only notice the much-more publicised accounting results, they need to understand that derivatives that do not bring any volatility into the balance sheet may be precisely those that yield sub-par economic results, for example in the form of higher net financing costs.

We are going to analyse how superior hedging structures could be annihilated by the new accounting rules through an example involving the swaps market. In practice, plain vanilla swaps enjoy very favourable accounting treatment, generally being considered highly effective and in many cases getting hedge accounting treatment from the get-go. However, from an economic point of view, sometimes companies might be much better off entering into other, more exotic swaps. Unfortunately, those structures would most likely not be deemed to be effective. This could not only prevent treasurers from entering into such transactions in the first place (and thus deprive the company's shareholders of economically superior risk management) but, much worse, could force treasurers to unwind or close-down economically profitable positions simply because of temporarily detrimental mark-to-market numbers.

One such type of exotic swap is the so-called quanto swap. Quantos (or "differential swaps") are agreements whereby two parties exchange cashflows referenced to two different floating rates (for instance, one party pays US Libor while the other pays Euro Libor) with both streams being paid in the same currency (for instance, euros). Quanto swaps can be very attractive to those corporates who would like to switch the interest rate curve under which their net financing costs are referenced (for example, going from a Euro curve to a US curve) but without changing the currency denomination of their debt. If the relative forward curves are aligned in the correct way, quanto swaps can help corporates enjoy very substantial financing cost savings, at least in the short run. The early 2000s became such a perfect time to enter into quanto swaps, as by mid-2001 the US curve had become much steeper than the Euro curve, with short-end rates much lower and with long-end rates much higher. Thus, those willing to pay US Libor and receive Euro Libor started out with a significant positive carry (ie, financing cost savings). Such gains would remain intact (or perhaps even expand) as long as the Federal Reserve (Fed) did not raise rates fast and hard in the near future. One example of a quanto structure that was shown at the time to corporate clients with floating euro liabilities was the following:

❑ effective date 30/9/2001;
❑ maturity date 30/12/2004;
❑ bank pays 3 month Euro Libor;
❑ client pays 3 month US Libor – 0.87% in euros.

Given that the prevailing short rates were 4.4 and 3.8% respectively in Euro and US, the trade represented a positive carry (cost savings with respect to paying Euro Libor flat) of 147 basis points (bps) for the client. That is, by entering into this swap the company could obtain instant savings of almost 1.50% on its debt liabilities.

The accounting treatment of quantos is likely to be unfriendly. A company that does not have foreign currency revenues or foreign debt must treat quanto swaps as speculative positions from an accounting point of view, as the corporate's net derivatives position would be an exposure to US Libor, while it does not have any underlying US Libor (or US) risk. In other words, they must be irrevocably marked-to-market and thus become clear sources of income volatility. It is obvious that many European companies, for example, do not have dollar revenues or dollar debt (national railroad operators, local cell phone companies, local construction firms, etc).

The mark-to-market of quanto swaps is heavily dependent on the relative shape of the forward curves. In our example, if the gap between the US curve and the Euro curve at the long end widened, then the mark-to-market of the trade would move against the company (since it is paying US dollar Libor and the curves are now "saying" that it would have to pay more over Euro Libor than when the transaction was initiated). On the other hand, if the gap between the Euro curve and the US dollar curve at the short-end widened (perhaps because of rate cuts by the Fed, while the European Central Bank, ECB, stayed put) then the mark-to-market would move in the company's favour. Thus, we could say that a company that entered into a quanto would be mostly exposed to the possibility that long-dated US dollar rates would go up over its Euro counterparts. If those differences proved to be significant, then the accounting losses could be of the headline grabbing variety. Such an event took place in the summer of 2003, when US Treasuries sold off. The sell-off (due to a combination of factors, such as renewed economic optimism, changed perceptions regarding the Fed's intentions to act in the open markets in order to keep long rates low, and the dumping of foreign securities by Japanese banks) was the largest since the 1994 bond market crash. Long rates, naturally, shot up. From a low of 3.11% on 13th June, 10-year Treasury yields jumped above 4.40% by the end of July. Since the equivalent increase in German Bund yields was only of 70 bps, it is clear that in those summer months the gap between both curves widened dramatically at the long end. In other words, the mark-to-market of quanto swaps greatly deteriorated and many end users surely experienced large negative accounting losses.

Paradoxically, at the time of the bond sell-off quanto users were, in general, experiencing quite large economic benefits given that the Federal Reserve had lowered rates much more dramatically than the ECB after the tragedy of 11th September. That is, not only had the initial positive carry of the trade been preserved but also in fact it had become even larger. By mid-2003 the quanto structure from our previous example had been delivering financing cost savings in excess of 2% on average. And yet, the accounting losses derived from the new shape of the forward curves could have been so large that treasurers, finance directors and even CEOs might have been tempted or pressured to close down the position. The real issue is that in doing so they would have forsaken further significant savings, as the Fed did not begin to tighten monetary policy until mid-2004. This is real money that the company would have given away if its decision-makers had succumbed to the accounting pressure and annihilated their quanto swaps positions.

This shows the unfair character of derivatives accounting. Negative accounting numbers can suddenly cloud the status of structures that had been delivering outstanding economic results (and would continue to do so). By succumbing to the mark-to-market pressure and killing the structures, corporates in effect would be allowing the annihilation horseman to reign supreme and to spread economic misery all over the company's accounts.

DISMISSAL

Forcing treasurers and finance directors to annihilate economically profitable hedging structures is a bad enough possible outcome of the new mark-to-market accounting regime. However, this could be merely child's play compared with a related and much more daunting prospect: namely, that the treasurers and finance directors, that is, the structures' sponsors, get themselves annihilated (ie, fired from their posts) as a result of the temporary accounting malaise. In other words, the new accounting standards may end up having dramatic effects on how companies organise their finance departments, with potentially negative ramifications that go beyond the simple choice of derivatives tools. In the extreme scenario, under the mark-to-market paradigm a successful and sophisticated treasurer or finance director might lose his job due to derivatives valuation issues (even though the structure he put in place had been delivering substantially positive economic results) only to be replaced by a much more conservative and backward-looking candidate. This development could harm the company not just through its consequences pertaining to the financial risk management area, but also through its consequences on the other crucial responsibilities of a finance unit such as capital markets, credit management or control. There can be no denying the potentially disastrous (and hugely unjust) effects of the dismissal horseman.

Going back to the quanto swap example analysed in the previous section, the bond market meltdown (with the consequent steepening of the US curve with regards to the Euro curve) could have claimed the heads of those directly responsible for entering into the transaction in the first place, as the hair-raising accounting losses might have forced the hand of their terrified superiors. In this sense, the dismissal horseman brought about by the new standards would turn winners (people who were saving the company more than 2% in financing costs, the result of achieving a net cost under 1%) into losers.

What about another treasurer that would have chosen to enter into the much more accounting-friendly plain vanilla swap rather than a highly exotic one? How would he have fared, both from an accounting and an economic point of view? Would his job have also been in jeopardy? The euro plain vanilla swap rate for the relevant period (30 September, 2001–30 December, 2004) was 4.73% at the time. Thus, during the entire three years the corporate would have experienced a net financing cost of 4.73%. You do not need a PhD in maths to know that an average cost of less than 1% is economically preferable to 4.73%. And yet, the new accounting rules clearly would have protected the vanilla treasurer. The plain vanilla swap position would not only not have suffered adversely on a mark-to-market basis from the summer 2003 bond sell-off but it would have actually benefited as the company would be receiving Euro Libor against a fixed parameter and as such it enjoyed the new steeper curve that was indicating higher future floating cashflows in its favour. In this sense, the magic wand of the new standards would have transformed the underperformer into the winner and made the treasurer paying almost 400 bps extra in financing costs look like an angel when compared to his rogue counterpart that was creating so much havoc with those strange-sounding exotic swaps.

In sum, we see that a hero (eg, someone who entered into a quanto swap in 2001 expiring in, say, 2005 and that would have achieved an average financing cost below 1% for his company) could have been made a villain by the new rules. People who had done an outstanding job at what really matters, such as obtaining extremely cheap financing for the company, could be punished for the unfair weight that the accounting rules place on valuation issues (factors that in the end do not determine the firm's actual financing cost).

Which brings us to the very real case of Massimo Catasta, Poste Italiane's former finance director who was dismissed in early 2004 due to large accounting losses coming from, curiously, a quanto swap position. Catasta was a casualty of the summer 2003 bond market meltdown, and stands to date as the highest-profile example from the corporate sector of the highly damaging effects of the dismissal horseman (while it must be noted that Catasta apparently exceeded the maximum notional amounts that he was mandated to hedge, it is reasonable to assume that it was the substantial accounting losses, uncovered by a new auditor, and not this breach of authority which ultimately caused his downfall).

The structure that Catasta entered into with JP Morgan in July 2003 guaranteed Poste a fixed net financing cost much lower than what would have been obtainable through the plain vanilla swap market. Such significant cost savings would have continued unaltered until at least the end of 2006. After that, the company was exposed to US Libor reaching a barrier (set at a high level of 7%), in which case it would be switched to a quanto swap with a maturity date of 2013. Clearly, the dramatic steepening experienced by the US curve in July and August resulted in massive negative mark-to-market for Poste as the curve was "saying" that the 7% barrier would in fact be breached in the future.

While it is clear that Poste faced the risk of having to pay US Libor precisely at a time when it was high, the truth is that this was simply a possibility, which could or could not happen. However, the large economic gains that the structure was delivering and would continue to deliver for at least three more years by the time Catasta was let go were very much real. That is, in Catasta we have a finance director who was saving his employer millions of hard cash in financing costs thanks to his vision and initiative to enter into an exotic structure rather than a plain vanilla one, and who was terminated because of a temporary accounting malaise induced by forward curves movements that did not affect the real financing costs of the company at all, and that were caused by forces completely out of Catasta's control (or that of any other finance director for that matter).

DISCRIMINATION

As every corporate that has experience dealing with derivatives knows, when it comes to selecting a hedging strategy there are two basic alternatives: either purchase an option or enter into a forward/swap type of structure. The corporate's wishes, needs and views regarding future market movements all play key roles in determining the final choice of hedging tool.

Since the introduction of the new accounting standards, a new deciding factor has appeared that threatens to generate significant bias in the options–swaps debate. Swaps can, in general, enjoy a friendly accounting treatment (more so in the US than in Europe). Options, on the other hand, have not been afforded the same preferential treatment, being treated from the beginning in such a way that guaranteed substantial earnings impact. Clearly, this suddenly made options extremely unattractive to corporate end-users, and swaps more attractive by default (this may apply less to FAS 133 since the introduction in mid-2001 of amendments that afford total effectiveness to certain option contracts).

The envisaged outcome of all this would be for corporates to forsake the use of options and instead replace them with an increased use of forwards and swaps. But another outcome is also possible. Corporates who are forced to stop dialling the numbers of banks' options desks and instead call the swaps desks, might encounter an unwelcoming voice at the end of the line, and a refusal to deal.

The reason for such unpleasantness lies in one of the holy grails of the derivatives market, namely credit lines. A purchased option does not require any credit checks on the part of the bank nor does it eat into any of the existing approved lines, as all it requires is an upfront payment from the customer who from that point on does not face any further disbursements. Thus, the corporate's creditworthiness would be a complete non-issue. Any firm with the necessary cash to pay the initial premium can purchase an option from a bank, no questions asked. In the case of swaps, however, things are of course not so simple. As swaps require many future payments on the part of the customer, a healthy credit rating is a must before the deal is agreed to. Any corporate that does not qualify in the eyes of the bank's credit officers will simply be refused as a client (the same would apply to healthier credits that nonetheless have their existing lines filled to capacity). In the end, then, such corporates would be left with no alternative but to remain unhedged: unwilling to expose themselves to the volatility monster brought about by options, unable to enter into swaps.

The inevitable conclusion, then, is that the new accounting standards (or to be exact, the European version at least) put those companies with the lowest credit ratings in a very tight spot. If they absolutely cannot afford the potential extra volatility into their income statement (as their credit standing might go even lower as a result, perhaps causing a complete drying-up of new financing and a run for the exits from investors), then they are only left with the prospect of rolling the dice in the markets and getting ready to spend countless sleepless nights worrying about the risks derived from being completely unhedged. Clearly, if these corporates absolutely could not afford to incur, say, high financing costs in the short term, aggressive tightening policies by Greenspan and similar could then spell total and unmitigated disaster. At the same time, they know that while they must wander the business landscape unprotected from the several financial risks out there, their creditworthy competitors can count on a large arsenal of hedging tools. By forcing lesser credits out of the options market, IAS 39 would thus have effectively handed down a potentially significant competitive advantage to those corporates with healthier credits that are more than welcomed by the swaps desks.

In this sense, the new accounting standards could work against the "democratisation" of the corporate derivatives market, by favouring the rich and powerful over the deprived and needy. Such would be the sinister effect of the discrimination horseman.

INTIMIDATION

To put it bluntly, hedging is a widely misunderstood term. While many people assume that by hedging your existing risks you are effectively left with no exposures, nothing could be further from the truth. Hedging is not about risk elimination, but rather about risk transformation. Thus, every derivative structure entered into by a corporate involves switching from the existing risk profile into a new profile. While the original risk is most certainly eliminated, the company's new net position is not risk-free. All that has happened is that a new risk profile has taken the place of the old. Of course, the new risk could very well turn out to be more risky that the previous one that it is replacing.

The job of a corporate treasurer has traditionally been to decide which available alternative risk profiles are preferable to the current existing one (depending on market conditions and future outlook). Skilful, or lucky, treasurers manage to steer the company into a risk environment that yields better economic results than would have been possible under the prior scenario. Incompetent, or unlucky, treasurers manage to do exactly the opposite. The introduction of the new accounting rules heavily distorts this traditional landscape, since it clearly provides an incentive to use certain strategies over others. By forcing companies into so-called effective hedges, the regulators' argument goes, the new rules guarantee that derivatives are used in a sensible way and that the goal of risk control is achieved. In practice, what this means is that corporates are being geared towards the risk profile that the standard setters deem more appropriate. In fact, "intimidated" might be a more suitable term than geared, with the threat of potential income volatility being used as the intimidatory weapon of choice.

Under the new world of FAS 133 and IAS 39, corporates may be forced into a new risk regime that they would not have chosen had the new standards not been in place. Corporates may also be forbidden from entering into the risk regime that they would have chosen had the new standards not been in place. In effect, treasurers are no longer entirely free to decide which risk switching strategy is more appropriate for the company. In a big way, regulators are now doing the job for them. Plain vanilla interest rate swaps, for instance, can railroad their exotic counterparts aided by the income volatility threat. The former are essentially guaranteed hedge accounting and thus promise very little or no income volatility whatsoever, while those corporates that choose to stick with the latter do so at their accounting peril, as most probably they would be deemed ineffective. In a way, then, accounting authorities and regulators are behaving like "treasurers wannabes" and deciding which hedging structures are more appropriate and which alternatives should not be considered.

However, who is to say that regulators are better at picking hedging strategies than treasurers or finance directors? More to the point, what entitles regulators to consider themselves apt players at the complex game of risk profiles selection? Why should a plain vanilla swap as a matter of principle be considered a better risk exposure than an exotic swap? Are corporate finance professionals not better equipped at making those decisions? After all, they do it for a living.

Table 1 Comparision of alternative structures

	Swap vanilla	Swap KO	Quanto	Quanto KO
Starting date	30 September, 2001	30 September, 2001	30 September, 2001	30 September, 2001
Maturity date	30 December, 2004	30 December, 2004	30 December, 2004	30 December, 2004
Corporate receives	Euro three-month Libor	Euro three-month Libor	Euro three-month Libor	Euro three-month Libor
Corporate pays	4.73%	4.43% if Euro three-month Libor <5.40%	US dollar three-month Libor −0.87% in euros	3.98% if US dollar three-month Libor <6.50% in euros
		Euro three-month Libor otherwise		US dollar three-month Libor in euros otherwise

Let us analyse the potentially negative consequences derived from choosing the risk profile deemed more appropriate by the standards setters. We draw from several derivatives structures shown to a real corporate client by an investment bank. As these transactions would have already matured, we can clearly see which one resulted in superior economic results. The four structures presented in mid-2001 to a European company that had interest rate liabilities linked to a three-month euro Libor are given in Table 1.

Here we have a menu composed of one plain vanilla derivative (the 4.73% swap), one relatively exotic derivative (the Swap KO) and two very exotic derivatives (the quanto family members). As we already know, only the first one would get beneficial accounting treatment. The quanto structures will not qualify for hedge accounting as the corporate would be left facing a net financing cost referenced to a Libor rate different from the one at which the underlying hedged borrowing is referenced (this could change if the corporate has US dollar debt or revenues). The swap KO would also not be deemed to be an effective cover as the hedge can literally disappear depending on market movements.

All structures can be categorised as "hedges", because they all eliminate the original risk faced by the corporate. Under any of the four the company receives three-month euro Libor, which it duly passes along to the original lenders, thus synthetically erasing that liability. But at the same time it is clear that none of the four eliminates risk completely. Each of them offers a new risk profile, and they must be compared before making a decision. The vanilla swap is exposed to the possibility of a continuing period of low (perhaps even declining) floating rates that would render its fixed rate as comparatively too high. The corporate may find itself paying several hundred basis points above its competitors in financing costs for a long time, a potentially disastrous outcome. The KO swap can leave the company unhedged precisely at a time of high (and presumably rising) floating rates. The quanto swaps expose the end-user to the possibility that US dollar rates rise fast and far with respect to euro rates.

Prior to FAS 133 and IAS 39 a treasurer would simply have had to analyse which risk profile looked more attractive and risk-free, based on interest rate perspectives. Certainly, many decisions would be influenced by other factors such as the level of conservatism prevalent at the firm or the liquidity of the product, but generally speaking corporate finance staff were free to choose the strategy considered more desirable. Once the new accounting rules are in place, though, such a constraint-free environment no longer exists. The very real threat of income statement volatility must now be taken into consideration, becoming perhaps the most decisive factor. In our example, the treasurer may have been willing to try one of the quanto swaps given his conviction that dollar rates would take a while to go up as the economic situation in the US was not healthy enough for Greenspan to reverse the then prevalent easing cycle any time soon. But the unpleasant accounting treatment of such a strategy might have made it impossible for him to take that course. Instead, he may have been forced to be content entering into the plain vanilla swap.

By following the path delineated by the accounting authorities the corporate would have incurred very large economic losses, as can be seen from Table 2, which describes the net financing costs resulting from each of the four structures. As monetary policy became very accommodative in both the US and the euro zone (due to several factors, including 11th September and corporate accounting scandals), being stuck paying a high fixed rate became a very unwise choice. On the other hand, corporates were more than happy facing floating payments, especially those that came accompanied by substantial negative spreads. Needless to say, none of

Table 2 Net financing cost implied by each structure

Effective date	Euro 3 month Libor	US dollar 3 month Libor	Swap vanilla	Swap KO	Quanto	Quanto KO
30 September, 2001	3.65263	2.59000	4.73	4.43	1.72000	3.98
30 December, 2001	3.30000	1.88125	4.73	4.43	1.01125	3.98
30 March, 2002	3.45000	2.03000	4.73	4.43	1.16000	3.98
30 June, 2002	3.44000	1.86000	4.73	4.43	0.99000	3.98
30 September, 2002	3.29213	1.79000	4.73	4.43	0.92000	3.98
30 December, 2002	2.86125	1.38000	4.73	4.43	0.51000	3.98
30 March, 2003	2.52000	1.27875	4.73	4.43	0.40875	3.98
30 June, 2003	2.14275	1.11625	4.73	4.43	0.24625	3.98
30 September, 2003	2.12663	1.16000	4.73	4.43	0.29000	3.98
30 December, 2003	2.12300	1.15188	4.73	4.43	0.28188	3.98
30 March, 2004	1.96000	1.11000	4.73	4.43	0.24000	3.98
30 June, 2004	2.12000	1.61000	4.73	4.43	0.74000	3.98
30 September, 2004	2.14625	2.02000	4.73	4.43	1.15000	3.98
30 December, 2004	2.15438	2.56438	4.73	4.43	1.69438	3.98

the KO barriers were even approached. The inevitable conclusion is that, at least in this case, the regulators would have done quite a lousy job at playing treasurers. Those real treasurers gutsy enough to sideline accounting considerations and who would have entered into any of the more exotic transactions would have come away as economic winners. Their more conservative counterparts, by trying to escape the consequences of mark-to-market valuation, would have allowed the intimidation horseman to entrap them into losing positions.

While the effects of the three other accounting horsemen are clearly destructive, it can be safely argued that the intimidation horseman is potentially the most devastating of all. The reason for this assertion lies in the fact that the latter could create systemic problems, given its wider reach. While the annihilation horseman can indeed create harm, the extent of it will be determined on a case by case basis and will be different for each corporate depending on the particular exotic structure that would apply. While the dismissal horseman can result in the termination of otherwise successful treasurers or finance directors, it is highly unlikely that this would affect the whole corporate spectrum. While the discrimination horseman can introduce unfair competitive advantages and maybe force troubled companies into bankruptcy, this would only apply to a small segment of the corporate sector. In contrast to all these limited-reach effects, the mark-to-market paradigm potentially intimidates all corporates into the same hedging structures at the same time. In the previous example, if all (or a very substantial proportion) of the corporate sector would have been intimidated into a plain vanilla swap hedge then the resulting economic losses would have had a systemic dimension. The corporate sector as a whole would have been stuck facing net financing costs several hundred basis points above prevalent floating rates. In other words, corporate treasurers would not have been able to participate in one of recent history's most drastic (and lengthiest) easing cycles. In this sense, then, the new accounting rules could have rendered the intended monetary policy expansionary stimulus totally useless, at least when it comes to corporates' financing costs.

ACCOUNTING APOCALYPSE OR REAL APOCALYPSE?

We see that the new accounting standards present a less-than-stellar score sheet. The new rules not only do not eliminate risk or even necessarily reduce it (as any hedging strategy only implies a transformation of risk, not its elimination, and as the strategies favoured by the standards can be the riskiest), but they do present obvious negative effects; potential income volatility and the disclosure of the wrong kind of information are only the more visible of those. The annihilation of profitable hedging structures, the dismissal of highly performing staff, the discrimination against lower-credit corporates and the intimidation into certain strategies are the less obvious, but much more damaging, unfavourable outcomes.

It must be concluded that under the new standards neither corporate hedging practices nor derivatives activity disclosures are necessarily improved. All the rules really do in uncertain terms is place a threat to corporates: gear your derivatives strategies towards those favoured by the regulators or expose yourself to mark-to-market volatility. And whatever the reaction to that threat, corporates would face negative outcomes. If they decide not to yield and continue hedging as usual they may preserve economically winning structures but at the cost of facing accounting malaise and being exposed to newly-created risks. If they decide to yield to the threat and always seek a hedge accounting treatment, then they would be preventing accounting unpleasantness, but this would be at the risk of facing the wrath of the four horsemen (ie, this could incur significant real economic costs).

Therefore, we see that the trade-off that the accounting standards are proposing is undoubtedly frightening. They give corporates the dubious privilege of choosing between turbulent accounting results and the possible economic and strategic devastation caused by the horsemen. In other words, it is a choice between accounting troubles or real troubles. When facing such a disjunctive, corporates would have to decide what kind of pain they could live with. Are unstable earnings due to unpredictable, uncontrollable and largely irrelevant market factors more worrying than the possibility of incurring large economic losses from inefficient hedges? More worrying than the possibility of losing star employees? More worrying than the possibility of being unable to hedge your risks at all?

Of course, there is a third possible scenario. Uncomfortable with any of the two choices, corporates may just withdraw from the derivatives game completely. Facing market risks totally unprotected might seem like a walk in the park compared to the alternatives. There are already reports that a proportion of corporates have lowered their derivatives activity as a result of the new rules. Perhaps as more treasurers and finance directors come face to face with the accounting horsemen and suffer their wrath, the corporate derivatives market will dry up significantly, thus drastically reversing more than two decades of progress. In this sense, the effects of the new accounting standards would be nothing short of, well, apocalyptic.

ROOTING FOR AN ECONOMIC-VALUE PARADIGM

Given these ugly aspects of the new accounting paradigm, should something not be done about it? The philosophy behind the rules is, it must be said, highly valid. Corporates should be very upfront as to whether they are using derivatives for hedging or for speculation. If they choose to become traders (ie, if they choose to speculate on market conditions through the use of derivatives that are not directly related to their underlying risks) then they should be afforded the same accounting treatment as traders. Corporates should also be more generous when it comes to disclosing their derivatives hedging activities and how they are performing.

Financial risk management is nowadays such an important corporate function that shareholders and investors have every right to know whether a particular firm is hedging at all and how wise it has been in selecting a strategy.

The proposal here is the preservation of these two desirable aims, while at the same time doing away with the unpleasant parts of the new rules. First, divide all corporate derivatives use into either hedging or speculation. Hedging should be defined as the elimination of the original risk profile and its consequent substitution by another, to be carefully chosen by treasurers and finance directors based on their views about the future. Any derivative structure that now achieves that goal would be qualified as speculative and marked-to-market into earnings from the start. Structures used for hedging should be considered perfectly efficient from the outset and thus leave the income statement alone.

For really useful disclosure purposes, an economic-value paradigm should be enforced whereby corporates clearly detail the economic results derived from their hedges and compare them with the non-hedging alternative as well as with the plainest vanilla solution. This way, outside parties could instantly analyse whether a company is hedging its financial risks and how good a job it is doing at it.

For instance, going back to our example in the previous sections, a corporate that had decided to enter into the quanto swap in mid-2001 would have reported the economic numbers, given in Table 3, by say 30th June 2003.

The picture would be one of a company that indeed hedges its interest rate liabilities and that seems to have excelled at that function. Shareholders and investors would be happy and would probably recommend that the treasurer and finance director be congratulated for their skilful selection of hedging tools. What is even more important, if the company had opted for the plain vanilla swap instead of the exotic alternative, that is, in the case where the hedge was delivering negative economics rather than positive ones, there would be no hiding those (real) losses from outside parties who could then exhort pressure to have the situation remedied.

The conclusion is that by getting rid of the mark-to-market paradigm and replacing it with an economic-value regime, hedges

Table 3 Reporting of economic perfomance of hedge

Average net financial cost implied by interest rate hedging strategy	0.87078%
Average net financial cost implied by not having hedged	3.08235%
Average net financial cost implied by plain vanilla hedge (interest rate swap)	4.73000%

would be maintained or eliminated for the right reasons (economic results), rather than for the wrong reasons (accounting results). Disclosure and good practices would be assured, without the need to intimidate treasurers into any particular risk profile. In other words, corporates would have been effectively freed from exposure to the apocalyptic horsemen.

12

The Anti-Greenspan

How the new derivatives accounting rules can conspire to
make monetary policy ineffective

Plenty has been written on the many possible effects of the new derivatives accounting standards. Given that the rules have been in place for some time now, in at least some parts of the world (FAS 133 was introduced in the US more than four years ago), several of those effects have already been felt in real life by market participants. Enhanced income statement volatility, the reduction of derivatives activity and the partial abandonment of exotic structures are the most talked about and familiar consequences of the new accounting regime. With the introduction early in 2005 of IAS 39 in Europe, renewed attention has been directed towards these issues and undoubtedly derivatives accounting has consolidated itself as one of the most controversial and hottest themes in the financial markets.

To recap, the new rules force reporting entities to record the market value of their derivatives positions on the balance sheet. Depending on whether or not so-called hedge accounting treatment is attained, changes in the mark-to-market value would affect the income statement straight away. This explains the possibility of excess earnings volatility. It also explains why several non-financial corporates (for which the notion of mark-to-market exposures is more foreign and more worrying) have decided to forgo the use of derivatives or at least to reduce (and simplify) it.

Curiously, the long arm of the new accounting standards could extend beyond the realm of those directly affected by them (ie, the reporting entities and their shareholders and investors) and into the unseemly arena of public policy. Strange as it may seem, it is not difficult to conceive scenarios whereby the actions taken by market participants in response to the new rules may render some monetary policy initiatives ineffective. Plainly speaking, the new rules could force a significant proportion of market players, with deep impacts on the economy's performance, to face high interest rates at a time when policy is being loosened as part of an expansionary strategy. Similarly, those same players could be enjoying low rates during a tightening cycle designed to bring down inflationary pressures.

In other words, the new standards could very well turn out to be a thorn in the side of the likes of Ben Bernanke (who recently took over the reigns at the Federal Reserve (Fed) from the legendary chairman Alan Greenspan), by pushing in the opposite direction to their policy moves. Some reporting entities (be it banks or corporates) have already blamed derivatives accounting for unexpected results. Could we see the day when central bankers use the same excuse to justify the ineffectiveness of their decisions?

PUSHED INTO SWAPS

The possible counter-policy effects of the new rules derive from the way in which they alter the traditional corporate interest rate risk management landscape. When deciding how to hedge their exposure to rising interest rates (which, of course, entails higher financing costs), corporates have traditionally had to choose between two basic tools: swaps and options (ie, interest rate caps). Depending on market realities, future perspectives, available structures and company policies a treasurer or finance director would choose one tool or another. For instance, if the view were that rates were going to go down then switching to a fixed rate under a swap agreement would not make much sense, as this would lock the company's financing costs at an above-market rate for what could be a long time. On the other hand, if option premiums were expensive then perhaps the swap would become the only affordable alternative. The new accounting regime drastically distorts this decision-making process since it is clearly an incentive to use plain vanilla swaps while affording options a less friendly treatment. It is important to note, though, that big differences exist between FAS 133 and IAS 39 in these respects: in general, both swaps and options receive much better accounting treatment under US rules, thus decisively giving incentives to use vanilla swaps, but at the same time making options a viable tool; under IAS 39 options can have devastatingly volatile effects on the income statement.

In fact, it would not be unreasonable to say that the biggest (or most important) difference between both sets of rules is precisely the accounting treatment of swaps and options. When it comes to the former, FAS 133 allowed the so-called "short cut method" from the start, which assumes 100% hedge effectiveness for plain vanilla swaps that exactly match the terms of the underlying item. This guarantees not only that the derivative position will not have any income statement effect whatsoever, but also that the end-user does not have to continuously implement the bothersome tests needed to obtain hedge accounting status. IAS 39, on the other hand, does not afford reporting companies anything similar to the short-cut method. When accounting for a plain vanilla swap, effectiveness must be demonstrated every reporting period, with any ineffective portion affecting earnings straight away. Although the final income effect should not be significant, corporates would not be able to escape the heavy workload required to pass those tests.

More significant differences between FAS 133 and IAS 39 arise in the case of options accounting. The methodology favoured by the latter mirrors that originally embraced by the former: only the intrinsic value is considered effective with changes in time value hitting income immediately. Clearly, the potential for continuous earnings volatility is tremendous. No wonder that the US witnessed an initial drop in options activity by corporates and that signs of the same virus are being detected in Europe. However, in mid-2001 (only a few months after FAS 133 was first introduced) US regulators changed their tactics and decided to shape a more options-friendly standard. With the introduction of the so-called Issue G20, end-users could now have the whole value of an option (both the intrinsic value and the time value) deemed to be effective under certain conditions and thus guarantee that changes in fair value affect earnings only at maturity, and not during the interim. The positive impact on option usage by corporates has been significant, as documented by several surveys and anecdotal market evidence. This kind of news, however, has so far not provided enough ammunition for those who would like to see something like Issue G20 amended into IAS 39. The big guns at the International Accounting Standards Board (IASB) have so far not heeded the relentless calls by prominent voices, such us the Association of Corporate Treasurers, for instance, to put an end to the current volatility-enhancing treatment of options (although, crucially, certain European corporates have apparently been able to obtain full hedge accounting for options, and at least one major audit firm has announced that they do think that G20 treatment is appropriate under IAS 39).

However, it is critical to understand that Issue G20 is no panacea. While it is certainly a considerable improvement over the previous situation, it still does not entirely devoid option users of possible accounting discomfort (which the short-cut method truly does for vanilla swaps). Crucially for the purposes of this chapter, this assertion holds especially true in the case of interest rate caps.

The main reason why some corporates may find the G20 treatment unattractive is that, while continuous income volatility due to changing market factors is avoided, they would be subjected to a large one-time hit in their accounts as under the new amendment the option premium would be entirely expensed to profit and loss at maturity (offset by intrinsic value, if any). The recognition of the whole premium expense in a single period may present G20 as a less desirable feature than the alternatives. Pre-FAS 133 corporates were generally amortising the option premium over the life of the option in a linear fashion. For instance, assume a one year plain vanilla US dollar call/euro put used for hedging US dollar purchases one year from now that has an initial fair value (ie, premium cost) of US$1 million. Each quarter the company would report US$250,000. This was the world of so-called "historical cost accounting" and it obviously rules out market-driven earnings volatility. Post-FAS 133 (pre-G20) corporates have to amortise the option in a market-driven fashion, depending on the changes in its time value from initiation until maturity. In our example, because of changes in the underlying spot rate, forward curves, time to expiration and volatility, the time value of the call may end up being worth US$195,000 less after one quarter, US$225,000 less after two quarters, US$180,000 less after three quarters and US$400,000 less after four quarters (note that at maturity the time value of an option obviously becomes zero, so that the accounting impact in the last quarter could be quite large by default if the option got to that point whilst still enjoying considerable time value). These numbers would negatively impact the income statement on each respective quarter. One can clearly see how volatile this is with regards to linear amortisation.

Under G20, the entire US$1 million would be recognised as part of the fourth quarter's results, as the change in total fair value from trading date until maturity is obviously the entire option premium (this negative hit may be offset by any possible intrinsic value at expiry; time value is of course zero at maturity). It is not too difficult to understand why the possibility of this sudden hit would upset some corporate bigwigs, especially for those companies who value revenue growth above all. These people may very well decide that they are better off opting out of G20 treatment and reverting to the (highly undesirable in itself) original FAS 133 world of continuous time value volatility.

This inconvenience of G20 is magnified in the case of interest rate caps (or floors) for the simple reason that they are in essence a collection of several options (caplets or floorlets), each with its own maturity date. In other words, in the case of a cap the unique upfront premium will not affect a corporate's accounts at once in the final period, but rather would have to be sliced among the several expiry dates that the option as a whole entails. What this means is that the purchaser of a cap would now be exposed to several income statement hits (one per caplet maturity date) rather than a single big one. The real issue is that these smaller hits would not be uniform, as they would depend on the fair value at initiation of the individual caplets. Just like the initial fair value of the currency option analysed previously was accounted for at the one-year maturity date (when it is reclassified from equity into earnings, as befits any hedge deemed to be effective), the initial value of each caplet must be accounted for at their respective maturity dates. As the value of each caplet would be different from the others, depending on the shape of the forward curve and the term structure of interest rates volatility, the end-user would experience income statement volatility (eg, a two-year cap with four semi-annual caplets where the initial total premium of US$150,000 is made up of the following individual caplet values: US$27,000,

33,000, 37,500 and 52,500). That is, while in general the volatility in earnings is somewhat diminished under G20 when compared to the original FAS 133 (which would have taken into account the changing market values of the caplets), it is not eliminated, and the goal of achieving a smooth recognition of time value is unlikely to be fulfilled.

Also, and again crucially for revenue growth-oriented firms, given the fact that caplets tend to have higher values the longer their maturity (just like options in general), the amortisation of the initial premium would be done in an increasing fashion, as we saw in the example above. That is, under G20, the expensing of a cap would be back-weighted to later periods, with the biggest hit taking place at maturity (this is in contrast to the linear amortisation that ruled supreme in the pre-FAS 133 world). In our US$150,000 cap, when the option is priced at the initiation of the two-year trade the longer-dated caplets would naturally be more expensive, resulting in the back-weighted amortisation under G20 (it is important to note that these conclusions are valid only under a normal, not inverted, yield curve; if the curve was inverted the opposite would hold true). The conclusion is that when G20 is applied to interest rate options, corporates can be penalised both in terms of enhanced earnings volatility and in terms of hampered revenue growth.

Such a "double whammy" would not necessarily derive from a non-G20 approach: by subjecting the premium amortisation to the evolving market value of the caplets throughout the life of the option the corporate may avoid ever-increasing earnings impacts. The value of the cap may change in varying amounts, sometimes large, sometimes small, thus impacting earnings in an irregular pattern (rather than in an ever-increasing way). For instance, after one quarter the time value of the cap might have gone down to US$102,000 and the corporate would get a hit of US$48,000 in income. By the end of the second quarter time value could be worth US$68,000, implying an accounting hit of US$34,000 (which is obviously lower than the previous entry of US$48,000). In the last two quarters the cap's time value may have been US$37,000 and US$0. In this case, then, the premium amortisation experienced by the corporate would have been US$48,000, 34,000, 31,000 and 37,000. This schedule may look more attractive to a treasurer, focused on revenue growth, than the G20 alternative (although it is more volatile, as expected). As was mentioned before, such scenarios could prompt corporates to opt out and revert to the original pre-G20 treatment.

The main message from all these analyses must be that accounting for interest rate options can create significant inconveniences for corporate end-users, not only in the options-unfriendly IAS 39 environment but also in supposedly friendlier FAS 133-G20 territory. They face potentially high income volatility if the derivative does not qualify for G20 (or if they choose to opt out), just as in the case of equity or currency options, but here the relief brought about by G20 is less valuable as earnings volatility would still be present (even if somewhat reduced) and it would coexist with the revenue growth-unfriendly characteristic.

It is thus reasonable to assume that one result of the new standards would be to throw corporates into the arms of the swaps market, which as was stated earlier affords much more favourable accounting treatment. Instead of buying caps to protect themselves from the risk of rising floating rates, stability-seeking corporates would enter into plain vanilla swaps as fixed-rate payers. By doing so, treasurers and finance directors would mostly avoid the dreadful mark-to-market effects on their reported results.

VICTIMS OF THE FORWARD CURVE

The move from options into swaps would, of course, leave corporates at the mercy of the main determinant of swap rates, namely forward curves. If the curve is steep then the swap rate (which can be seen as the average of the forward rates along the curve, all the way to the desired maturity date) will be high at a time when short-term rates (which is what the company actually pays in financing costs) are comparatively low. Under a steep curve, then, a corporate that wants to hedge its floating rate liabilities resulting from a loan or a bond issue would have to incur higher costs than if it had not hedged or if it had hedged with an option (such as an interest rate cap), at least for the first periods. If short-term rates were to remain low or even go down as a result of a central bank's loosening policies, then the corporate would be entrapped into a seriously unfavourable proposition.

Such a situation took place in the 2001–2004 period. Due to a combination of factors, both the US dollar and the euro curves steepened dramatically (especially in the first case) while both markets experienced substantially eased monetary policies (again, especially in the US). What this meant is that the difference between the swap rates and the short-term rates became higher as the latter became lower and lower. Those corporates entering into, say, five-year swaps would have been entrapped into a situation whereby they were paying 4–5% interest on their debt when the relevant short rate could be as low as 1% (the 45-year low that the Fed funds rate reached by late June 2003). That is, they would not have been able to enjoy the extremely generous easing cycle undertaken by Greenspan's Fed and, less so, the European Central Bank (ECB). In fact, for these companies it would have been as if a tightening, not a loosening, policy had been in place as they would have ended up suffering net financing costs higher than the interest rates prevailing at the time the swap was initiated. Obviously, under such a scenario the strategic decisions afforded by decreasing financing costs (the undertaking of new investment projects, the hiring of new employees, the replenishment of stocks), which all have expansionary effects on the economy (as desired by the monetary authorities), cannot be put in place. The things that could be done under 1% rates cannot be done under 5% rates.

HAMPERING THE MAESTRO'S LEGACY

We clearly see, then, how under certain market conditions a rush to the swaps market by corporates trying to escape the potential income statement volatility brought about by the new accounting standards could derail the policy intentions of central bankers. Lowering interest rates could end up being an inefficient expansionary tool if some of the bigger economic players are locked into paying much higher rates. Or, touching on the current US environment of flat or inverted curves (and thus, low swap rates) and the hawkish monetary stance by the Fed (ongoing since Greenspan reversed the policy cycle in mid-2004), raising interest rates could end up having a limited effect when it comes to taming the inflationary expectations if those big players are, presumably happily, entrapped into paying lower rates. With five-year swap rates at around 5.15% and short-term rates at 4.75% (three month US$ Libor at 5.00%) it would only take a few more tightening moves and/or some renewed inversion of the curve for swap payers to face lower financing costs than the market.

The latest inversion of the US curve began at the end of November 2005, when five-year yields traded at lower levels than those of two-year yields for the first time since the curve last inverted ahead of the 2001 recession. The Treasury 2/10 slope has been at the flattest level in more than four years, having precipitously decreased since 2004. The inversion may have been exacerbated by traders and speculators putting on so-called "flattening trades", whereby shorter-dated securities are shortened while longer-dated securities are purchased, thus attempting to profit from the inverted curve (ie, a curve under which front-end yields rise and back-end yields fall). In a sense, then, these trades are potentially self-fulfilling: by believing in a future inversion of the curve, they help that belief come true.

But what justifies such expectations? Why did the curve invert in the first place, even if by a limited amount? One popular explanation is that the market now expects the Fed to continue raising rates for longer than previously assumed, perhaps reaching levels that start to damage economic activity and trigger a slowdown, if not an outright recession, which would warrant an early return to loose monetary policies. According to this line of thought, the possibility of lower rates in the medium run is what is prompting the inversion. Another, non-excluding, explanation is that of course the current flat curve can be perfectly explained by the combination of an enduring tightening cycle at the Fed with the persistent "yield conundrum" that has seen the long-end stubbornly (and somewhat puzzlingly) refusing to go up even as Greenspan relentlessly tightened the screws. While the Fed funds rate has been raised by almost 400 basis points (bps) since mid-2004, 10-year Treasury yields have traded in an exceptionally narrow range of 3.75–4.75% during the same period. Obviously, higher and higher rates at the front-end plus a calm stability at the back-end must, by force, result in a flatter curve.

Whatever the final factor (or combination of factors) behind the inversion, the key question must be by how much would the curve invert. This is akin to wondering how far the Fed will go until it has finished tightening and whether or not the investors love affair with the medium and long end (the rationale behind the yield conundrum) will continue unabated. It is not irrational to assume that there is still some way to go before US monetary authorities quit the hawkish game, as after finishing unwinding an unnecessarily accommodative stance they are likely to focus on forestalling incipient inflation pressures in the face of resilient economic growth, persistently high energy prices and a never-ending housing boom. Bernanke is also likely to want to establish strong inflation-fighting credentials by continuing to raise rates ("I am another Greenspan"), even at the risk of erring on the upside. As to the back-end of the curve, it seems similarly reasonable to make the case for a continuation of low yields, as the number of factors that would support strong demand for Treasuries continues to be large: much higher returns than most of the alternative markets, the desire of foreign central banks to prevent the US dollar from collapsing, the global savings glut, reform of the pension system and the recent takeover of responsibility for the pension funds of a number of high-profile companies by a bonds-friendly public agency, and, perhaps most importantly, a sure-fire conviction by the market that the Greenspan-inspired Fed will keep inflation in check and thus erase or limit the need for a risk premium for longer maturities. In light of all of this, some analysts expect curve inversion to continue and to possibly be pronounced, as the Fed takes short-term rates to 5% and higher. Since it should take a long while for policymakers to change course and start a new easing cycle (barring some high-impact catastrophe), the non-normal look of the curve may reign supreme for quite some time.

Under the above scenario, swap rates in the three–five year range may quote 50–75 bps below Libor (during the last inversion episode in late 2000, five-year swaps quoted as low as 5.75% while Libor was at its 6.50% peak). This would entail that, effectively, swaps-embracing corporates who run away from accounting troublesome caps would experience a loosening, not a tightening, of monetary conditions. Clearly, these companies would have fewer incentives to undertake conservative, self-restraining measures (as expected by the hawkish monetary authorities), as there would be no penalty in the form of higher financial costs. Thus, expansionary (and inflationary) practices such as investing in new projects or hiring extra staff may continue unabated, potentially derailing the carefully crafted plans of central bankers to cool off the economy.

It would indeed be ironic if Alan Greenspan, who just retired and who has signified himself during the years for his endorsement of derivatives, would have his last main policy initiative railroaded by the side-effects of the new derivatives accounting rules.

13

Exotic Solutions

Some possible ways to preserve the use of exotic options by
corporates in the face of unfriendly accounting rules

Non-financial corporations have been using exotic options as hedging instruments for many years. Since the so-called exotic revolution began in earnest some 15 years ago the size and liquidity of the market has grown spectacularly, affording corporations ever more flexible, ever more economic risk management tools. Possibly the two most widely used exotic products by corporates (both currently and historically) are barrier options and Asian options. The first comprised of the familiar knock-out and knock-in versions, allows treasurers to save some premium money by taking a precise view as to the future levels of the underlying asset. The second adds substantial value to those corporates exposed to the average, rather than the final, level of the underlying over the life of the trade. It is no exaggeration to say that both instruments have revolutionised the hedging strategies of hundreds of corporations all over the world.

However, nowadays barrier and Asian options (just like exotic, and even vanilla, options in general) face what is perhaps the biggest threat to their popularity and ongoing intensity of use since their presence became widespread in the early 1990s. While exotics went through a perilous phase in the 1994–95 period due to the heavily-publicised high-profile losses by corporate users (Procter & Gamble amongst others) and big-impact turbulence in the underlying markets allegedly caused by the actions of exotic traders (the mayhem in the US dollar/deutschmark and US dollar/yen markets that prompted George Soros to ask for the banning of barrier options), the current menace is arguably much more worrying and potentially much more damaging. We are talking, of course, about the new accounting standards for derivatives introduced just a few years ago.

In the new world of FAS 133 (for US-listed firms) and IAS 39 (for Europe and Asia) derivatives positions must always be shown on the balance sheet. This is supposed to enhance disclosure and allow outside parties to be aware at all times of what a particular entity is doing when it comes to those dangerous derivatives. The real issue surrounding the new rules is that unless the derivative qualifies for so-called "hedge accounting" its market value will impact reported earnings straight away. As changes in the mark-to-market of a derivative can swing wildly, the concern is that unless the derivative is deemed to be highly effective it will introduce undue volatility into an entity's income statement. Since corporate bigwigs tend to dislike accounting surprises, unless hedge accounting can be achieved the derivative may not be entered into in the first place.

The problem when it comes to options is that, as opposed to plain vanilla swaps, they have not received very favourable treatment by the standard setters. While the situation has been somewhat reversed in the case of FAS 133, IAS 39 continues to back the methodology originally embraced by its American cousin: only intrinsic value is considered effective with changes in time value hitting income immediately. Clearly, the potential for continuous earnings volatility is tremendous. No wonder that the US witnessed an initial drop in options activity by corporates and that signs of the same virus are being detected in Europe, where several treasurers have been lobbying regulators aggressively to adopt the same amendment incorporated into FAS 133 in mid-2001, when standard setters changed tactic and decided to shape a more options-friendly standard. With the introduction of so-called Issue G20, end-users could now have the whole value of an option (both the intrinsic value and the time value) deemed to be completely effective under certain conditions and thus guarantee that changes in fair value affects earnings only at maturity, and not during the interim. In other words, under G20 (which is optional, and not an imposition) the scope for options-induced earnings volatility is greatly reduced. Stability-seeking corporates that would like to continue using options for hedging purposes have obviously found its introduction quite a blessing (it is important to note, though, that some corporates may decide to opt out of G20 as they would dislike the large one-time hit in their accounts implied by the option premium being entirely expensed to profit and loss at maturity).

The most important thing to understand about G20 is that while it applies perfectly to European-style plain vanilla options, its applicability to exotics is much less straightforward. In many instances, the final verdict will depend on the interpretations of a particular auditor. Unless the characteristics of the exotic option clearly fall under the G20 specifications or the corporate helps to convince its auditors that the hedge should qualify, changes in time value will hit earnings. The bottom line is that unless G20 treatment can be achieved it is likely that many corporates would forgo the use of exotic products, thus putting a stop to almost two decades of innovation.

In this chapter we will analyse whether Asian and barrier options would qualify for G20 treatment, and thus allow corporates to keep using them without concerns about the accounting malaise that they could bring about. Crucially, we will try to offer possible, more accounting-friendly alternatives that may help treasurers continue to enjoy the benefits afforded by these exotic products in the case where the auditors eventually declare them to be ineffective hedges. The analysis will apply both to FAS 133 and to G20-less IAS 39, given that apparently certain European corporates have been able to obtain full hedge accounting treatment for options (although at least one major audit firm has announced that they do not think that G20 is appropriate under IAS 39).

A BARRIER TO ASIANS

Issue G20 literally states that for an option that is used as a cash-flow hedge (where the exposure being hedged is the variability in expected future cashflows), the hedging relationship may be considered to be perfectly effective (resulting in recognising no ineffectiveness into earnings) if the following conditions are met.

1. The critical terms of the hedging instrument (such as its notional amount, underlying and maturity date, etc) completely match the related terms of the hedged forecasted transaction (such as the

notional amount, the variable that determines the variability in cashflows and the expected date of the hedged transaction, etc).

2. The strike price of the hedging option matches the specified level beyond which the entity's exposure is being hedged.

3. The hedging instrument's inflows (outflows) at its maturity date completely offset the change in the hedged transaction's cashflows for the risk that is being hedged.

4. The hedging instrument can be exercised only on a single date (its contractual maturity date).

In other words, the option's market value will not bring volatility into the income statement as long as it is a European-style contract that perfectly offsets the changes in the underlying exposure beyond the strike level and that matures at exactly the same time as the underlying.

After reading these lines, it is easy to understand why some prospective users of Asian options have had lots of trouble trying to obtain favourable accounting treatment for such products. This is true for both major types of Asian options, namely average-rate options (ARO) and average-strike options (ASO). In the first case, as is widely known, the strike rate is pre-set and the final settlement level equals the average price of the underlying during the life of the trade; in the second case, the strike rate will now equal the average price and the final settlement level will be the price of the underlying at maturity. Neither FAS 133 nor IAS 39 make an explicit reference to Asian options, so their accounting treatment is left entirely to the discretion of the auditors (especially in the case of IAS 39, where again no G20-like firm guidance exists). In this sense, at least one of the big auditors has openly ruled out hedge accounting for ASOs. The explanation is that it would be impossible at the inception of the hedge to define the hedged risk, because the strike level beyond which the option provides protection is not yet fixed.

The treatment of AROs is less clear-cut, and it would depend on the exact type of underlying exposure the company is facing. If the risk is based on an average price (say, a corporate that has a supply contract where the purchase price is determined by the average price during a future period of time) then the ARO would usually qualify for G20-type accounting (ie, full effectiveness) as the final payoff of the option would perfectly offset the change in the expected cashflows of the hedged item beyond the strike level. At maturity, if the average price turns out to be above the strike the ARO would pay the corporate an amount equal to that difference, thus effectively allowing the corporate to make the purchase at the desired pre-specified price.

Things become more complicated if the underlying risk entails multiple exposures taking place at several known future intervals (possibly the main reason for using AROs). For instance, a corporate may be exposed to monthly purchases of an asset (commodity, foreign currency) for the next year. Its risk is that the average of all future month-end spot asset prices will be above a predefined strike level. An ARO with monthly fixings and the same strike price will make for a perfect offset. Or would it? While the hedge would be perfectly efficient from an economic point of view (the final payoff from the option would exactly match the difference between the average spot level and the strike, if any), the same cannot be said when it comes to accounting effectiveness. The problem is that the ARO would make its single payout on the final maturity date at year-end, but the payouts involved in each purchase of the underlying would impact the company's accounts every interim quarter.

For example, when the corporate reports its first quarter's results, its earnings would have been impacted by the purchases of the first three months, but the hedging instrument (the ARO) would not have paid out anything yet. Clearly, the hedge is not providing offsetting cashflows that compensate for changes in the hedged risk. By the time the ARO delivers a payout, the underlying exposure would have already impacted the income statement three times. In other words, against the stream of purchases there is no stream of potential settlements of the ARO. The maturity date of the hedging instrument simply does not match the maturity dates of the hedged forecasted transactions. Thus, a G20-type treatment would not be possible, and the changes in the time value of the ARO would have to be immediately recorded on a mark-to-market basis in the income statement (as the ARO has substantially smaller exposure to volatility, time to maturity, and the level of the underlying than a vanilla option the swings in market value should be tamer in any case). Most accountants seem to have agreed on this point.

Does this mean that for corporate use of ARO options the end is nigh? While the products have more than proven their worth for the past years, many corporate executives simply cannot tolerate the possibility of enhanced earnings volatility, especially when the new standards have already claimed their first human victims in the form of high-profile dismissals of finance directors at a few well-known companies that went through a period of derivatives-induced accounting malaise. Moreover, in the case of AROs, the reluctance to use them may be compounded by the fact that they have a ready substitute that would be G20-compliant. As any derivatives expert knows, a strip of vanilla options (calls if the underlying transaction is a purchase, puts if it is a sale) makes for an easy substitute for an ARO as a hedging strategy. As the strip of vanillas will deliver at least the same economic payout as the ARO (and potentially a better one depending on how the underlying market behaves during the life of the trade), its initial premium will cost more and this is why many corporates would rather opt for the ARO. However, the unfriendly accounting treatment of the latter may now bias corporates' choices towards the vanilla strip, which would be deemed effective as each European option would mature at exactly the same time as each of the scheduled purchases/sales takes place.

In order to avert the extinction of AROs, some companies have apparently suggested reclassifying some portion of the ARO's value in the first quarter, and in subsequent quarters until maturity. The problem with this is that, of course, it is entirely possible for the ARO to have value in the initial averaging periods (say, because the underlying quickly and consistently rose above the strike level) but expire worthless (due to, say, a reversal in the trend that lowers the average level at maturity below the strike) and thus never provide a positive payoff. In this situations, the gains booked in the earlier periods would not be eventually backed-up by an actual, real gain on the option (ie, the accounting "advance" of intrinsic value would not have been returned). No wonder, than, that auditors do not seem to have endorsed the suggested approach.

WALKING DOWN THE STRIP

A better solution might be to use a strip of AROs, each maturing at the end of each reporting quarter. This way, the payout from the

AROs would coincide with the accounting impact of the underlying exposure (say, three yen-denominated purchases, one for each month in the quarter). A strip of four AROs with monthly fixings each maturing three months after the other would make for a perfect accounting offset to an underlying exposure consisting of twelve monthly future forecasted transactions. In principle, it seems reasonable to assume that such a strategy would have a pretty good chance of qualifying for G20 treatment: the underlying risk (the average future spot level) continues to be economically hedged and the hedging instrument provides a perfect accounting offset. The only issue is that a strip of AROs would be more expensive than a single ARO (as some individual AROs may end up in-the-money, while the single longer-maturity contract expires out-of-the-money), but still cheaper than a strip of vanillas.

When deciding between a strip of AROs and a strip of vanillas (assuming that both get hedge accounting), the corporate end-user must take into account the same factors that would make him decide between a single ARO and a vanilla strip, only that now the arguments in favour of using the latter would lose some weight. If the treasurer believes that the underlying asset would move in such a way that all the vanilla options expire either out-of-the-money or in-the-money then, from an economic point of view, going with the single ARO would have been the wisest choice, as its gross payout would exactly equal that of the family of vanillas, while its initial cost was inferior (perhaps by a wide margin). Alternatively, if the view is that the market would experience volatile swings that make some vanilla options expire in-the-money and others expire out-of-the-money (preferably deeply so) and that deliver an average spot level at maturity that is only slightly in-the-money (if at all), then the gross payout of the strip could outperform that of the ARO (which may well be zero) by a margin large enough to cover for the initial difference in premium. If we are talking about a strip of AROs rather than a single one, then obviously the strip of vanillas would benefit relatively less from a turbulent market, as some of those effects may be incorporated into the payouts of the individual AROs. For instance, the first individual AROs could profit from an early rally that helps them deliver a positive payout (even if lower than that experienced by their vanilla counterparts); in contrast, the single longer-maturity

ARO may not have been able to obtain such benefits as a posterior market decline would have flattened the final average price.

We can analyse this through the example of an American company that needs to buy €20 million every month to pay for scheduled imports; the company determines its related currency risk as the contingency that €1 > US$1.25. We consider Scenarios 1 and 2 of possible paths for the currency rate.

The conclusion is that a strip of AROs has more chances of delivering economic gains to its user than a single ARO. Consequently, the potential economic advantages of using a strip of vanillas become diminished. For a vanilla strip to deliver a substantially better gross overall payout the underlying market would have to experience wild movements, with the spot price dancing up and down the strike level in a jagged fashion (such process of the underlying could render all quarterly averages out-of-the-money, while a few individual vanillas would deliver a payout). Unless such nerve-wrecking outcome takes place, it is likely that the ARO strip's gross payoff would closely mirror that of the vanilla's under most market scenarios, even trend-reversing ones. It should not be too hard, then,

Scenario 1 All vanilla options expire in-the-money

	EUR/US$ at end of each monthly interval	Quarterly averages	Payoff from single vanilla options (US$)	Quarterly earnings from vanilla strip (US$)	Payoff from each ARO strip (US$)
January	1.26		200,000		
February	1.27		400,000		
March	1.27	1.27	400,000	1,000,000	1,000,000
April	1.28		600,000		
May	1.30		1,000,000		
June	1.31	1.30	1,200,000	2,800,000	2,800,000
July	1.30		1,000,000		
August	1.26		200,000		
September	1.27	1.28	400,000	1,600,000	1,600,000
October	1.29		800,000		
November	1.28		600,000		
December	1.32	1.30	1,400,000	2,800,000	2,800,000
Final average	1.28	Sum	8,200,000	Sum	8,200,000
Payoff from single ARO	US$8,200,000				

Scenario 2 The underlying spot market follows a jagged path

	EUR/US$ at end of each monthly interval	Quarterly averages	Payoff from single vanilla options (US$)	Quarterly earnings from vanilla strip (US$)	Payoff from each ARO strip (US$)
January	1.22		0		
February	1.29		800,000		
March	1.24	1.25	0	800,000	0
April	1.25		0		
May	1.30		1,000,000		
June	1.22	1.26	0	1,000,000	400,000
July	1.27		400,000		
August	1.20		0		
September	1.22	1.23	0	400,000	0
October	1.29		800,000		
November	1.24		0		
December	1.22	1.25	0	800,000	0
Final average	1.25	Sum	3,000,000	Sum	400,000
Payoff from single ARO	US$0				

for dealers to convince corporate clients to use accounting-friendly ARO strips. Perhaps the end result of the introduction of the new accounting rules will be not only the preservation of AROs as hedging tools, but in fact an increase in the number of contracts traded.

REGULATORY KNOCK-OUT

Just as in the case of Asian options, prospective users of barrier options should expect trouble trying to obtain favourable, G20-like, accounting treatment. This is true for both major types of barrier options, namely knock-ins (KI) and knock-outs (KO). In the first case, as is widely known, the option initially does not exist and must reach the predetermined barrier level in order for it to be alive; in the second case, the option is active from initiation but could disappear should the barrier be breached. Although, as will be seen later, FAS 133 makes an explicit reference to one kind of barrier option (IAS 39 makes none), the accounting treatment for these products is not clear-cut and, in general, the way they are reported is left entirely to the discretion of the auditors. As a result of this, different companies and auditors have reached very different conclusions on the matter.

The simple reason that makes the KI and KO options G20-unfriendly is the fact that, plainly, a product cannot claim to offer a perfect offset (both accounting and economic) to an underlying hedged transaction if there is the likelihood that it could disappear or never exist. This reasoning is easy to understand. In the case of barrier options, there is just no way to guarantee that the hedging instrument's cashflows at maturity completely offset the change in the hedged transaction's cashflows. At maturity there may simply not be any hedging instrument, thus leaving the corporate totally exposed (ie, unhedged). How can something that could very well leave the end-user unhedged be deemed to be a hedge?

Well, it just may be. While it is clear that barrier options would not by themselves comply with a strict interpretation of G20, the standard setters included a "second-chance" feature when they put together the amendment. If the four conditions described before are not met, the reporting entity can determine whether ineffectiveness must be recognised in earnings by comparing the change in fair value of the actual hedging instrument with the change in fair value of a "perfectly effective" hypothetical hedging instrument that meets the four conditions listed above (which usually means the vanilla equivalent). So, if it can be shown that the swings in value of a KO or a KI option closely mirror those of the corresponding vanilla option, the corporate would be able to claim 100% effectiveness for his exotic structure. The reason why prospective users of barrier options should not sit back and relax fully confident that the second-chance feature would allow them to use their favourite exotic derivative without unpleasant accounting consequences is that, of course, the market value of some members of the barrier family can react to changing market conditions very differently from that of vanilla options. In options parlance, the "Greeks" of barrier options can be very different from those of vanilla options. When one or more of the variables that affect the market value of an option (eg, time to maturity, volatility, moves in the underlying) changes, the consequent change in the option's value (measured by the relevant Greek parameter, such as delta or vega) can differ greatly depending on whether the contract is a vanilla or a KI/KO.

In particular, some barrier options can present so-called discontinuous Greeks that change sign. Vanilla Greeks, in contrast, never change sign. For instance, vega (the sensitivity of the option's value to changes in volatility) could go from positive (an increase in volatility causing an increase in the market value of the option) to negative (more volatility resulting in a reduction in value) in the case of KOs. The vega of a vanilla is always positive. Thus, one could have a situation where the vanilla is going up in value, while the KO is going down in value. No perfect offset here, to be sure. The hypothetical option test would not have been passed. Other barrier options could show much smaller or much larger Greeks than their vanilla counterparts. For example, in the case of KIs delta (the sensitivity of the option's value to changes in the underlying asset) could go from being much smaller than in the vanilla option to being much larger. While in both cases delta could be positive (ie, the value of both options goes up when spot price goes up), they would not closely track each other. Again, the chances are that the hypothetical test would have been failed.

If neither the strict interpretation of G20 nor its second-chance feature seem to unequivocally apply to barrier options, is this the end of the road for KOs and KIs when it comes to corporate users?

No, as the standards provide yet another try. More precisely, hidden inside FAS 133 lies the only known direct reference to barrier options, namely Issue G22 (just like some auditors believe that a G20 approach should be appropriate for inhabitants of IAS 39-land, it may be expected that the same conclusion would be reached with respect to G22; in this sense, the following analysis would again apply to both standards). The main message from G22 is, simply stated, that a KO option cannot in principle be considered a highly effective cashflow hedge. In regulatory language, "*Generally, it would be unlikely that a company could conclude that the KO option is expected to be highly effective in achieving offsetting cashflows if it is reasonably possible that the cash inflows from the derivative will knock-out*". No big surprise here. Issue G22 simply ratifies what we have been saying all along: the very nature of barrier options (ie, the fact that they can die or never be born at all) indisputably precludes them from strict G20-compliance. However, if one looks more closely at the above statement there is a word that might cause a bit of puzzlement and that may open a window of hope for would-be corporate users. The term we are referring to is, of course, the initial "generally". What could the standard setters mean by this apparent allowance for exceptions to the rule? Well, let us clarify it in their own words: "*In the **unlikely*** *event that the company was able to conclude that the relationship was expected to be highly effective (because the complex option was expected to be highly effective for all changes in the underlying beyond the contractually specified rate due to the **remoteness** that the knock-out barrier would be breached over the contractual life of the debt), the complex option could be used as the hedging derivative"*. In other words, if it can be shown that the probability of reaching the barrier is negligible then the rules would allow for effectiveness and the option's market value would not introduce unwelcome volatility into the income statement. Obviously, if we can disregard the barrier as a non-event then the option would be akin to an accounting friendly vanilla.

WE LOVE PARIS

While the window provided by Issue G22 (introduced by US regulators in September 2001, a few months after G20) is a value-adding rule for those corporates desperate to ride the barrier options bandwagon, its practical applicability is doubtful at best. KO options are usually designed with barrier levels that have some likelihood of being hit. In fact, and paradoxically, it is in the interest of the corporate client that the barrier level chosen has a significant mathematical probability of being breached, since otherwise the premium would be higher, perhaps very close to that of the vanilla, thus erasing the rationale for entering into the KO contract in the first place. In this sense, the economic interests of the corporate would clash with its accounting interests. The simple conclusion is that in the case of regular KO options, corporates do not have many incentives to take advantage of the window of opportunity afforded by G22 (the following unpleasant scenario may take place: a corporate purchases a KO option with the barrier level extremely far from the current spot level, which somehow qualifies for perfect effectiveness due to the assumed remoteness of hitting the barrier; the premium is only at a slight discount to the vanilla since the pricing model assigns an insignificant probability to knocking-out; eventually, and unexpectedly, the market swings violently and the barrier is reached; the corporate would have spent a lot of money for protection that eventually disappeared).

If G22 would not work for regular KOs, how useful is it? Well, it could be useful for more exotic types of KO. In particular, it could be quite useful in the case of so-called "soft options". These are members of the barrier options family that while still affording the customer more tailor-made and economic protection than the plain vanilla alternative, also provide less exposure to sudden large moves in the underlying than regular KO options. Two main types of soft contracts are so-called Parisian and Parasian options. Parisian KOs are options that die only if the underlying hits the designated barrier a predetermined number of times, and must do so consecutively (ie, in a row). In the case of Parasian KOs the number of times the barrier is hit does not need to be consecutive (ie, in total is fine). Clearly, both Parisians and Parasians are much more resilient than regular KOs. They are much harder to kill (and thus more expensive, though still cheaper than the vanilla alternative). Of the two, the Parasian would be less applicable for the purposes of this discussion since clearly the chances of knocking-out are higher, thus making G22-compliance more difficult. For corporates that want to make sure that the hedge can qualify as effective, the Parisian would, in principle, be more attractive (though somewhat costlier, see Examples 1 and 2). A Parisian euro call/US$ put, say, struck at US$1.20 that knocks-out only if the US$1.10 barrier is hit ten times in a row in the next twelve months should be easier to present as unlikely to go away than the regular KO where US$1.10 has to be reached only once (ie, no persistent market trend is required for the option to die, a simple sudden spike would suffice).

In sum, Parisian options may be considered highly effective due to their apparent compliance with the window offered by Issue G22. Their "seven-lives" characteristic may be enough to convince auditors of the remoteness that the option would disappear. The chances that the underlying hedged transaction would not be perfectly offset are thus greatly diminished in Parisian territory. In this light, Parisian options could prove to be highly valuable to those corporates who dislike the probable accounting trouble and confusion brought about by regular KOs, but who wish to continue saving premium money. Paradoxically then, the new standards (which have been accused of posing an unbearable threat to the use of exotic derivatives) might encourage the use of a product that pre-eminently symbolises the wonders of financial engineering.

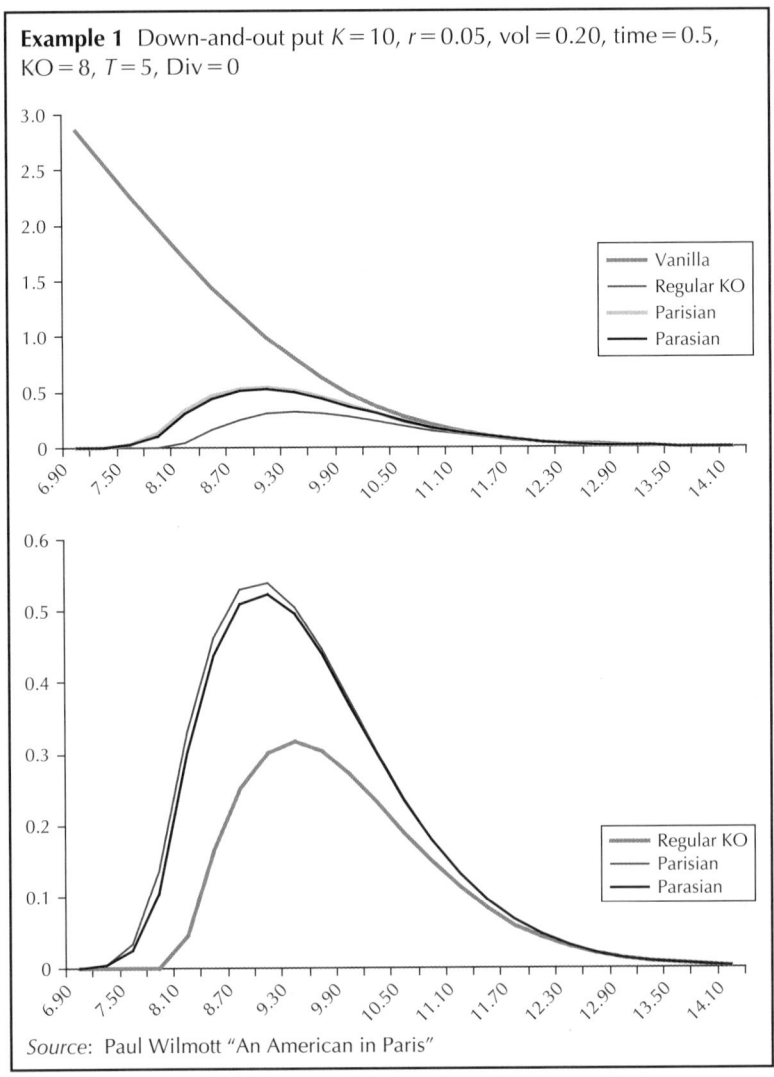

Example 1 Down-and-out put $K = 10$, $r = 0.05$, vol $= 0.20$, time $= 0.5$, KO $= 8$, $T = 5$, Div $= 0$

Source: Paul Wilmott "An American in Paris"

EXOTICISM: FROM AFFORDABLE TO EXPENSIVE LUXURY?

A very attractive feature of exotic options in general, and Asian and barriers in particular, is their cheaper cost when compared to the vanilla alternative. As both Asian and barrier contracts rapidly gained in popularity they became ever more liquid and economical. For years, they have equipped sophisticated corporate

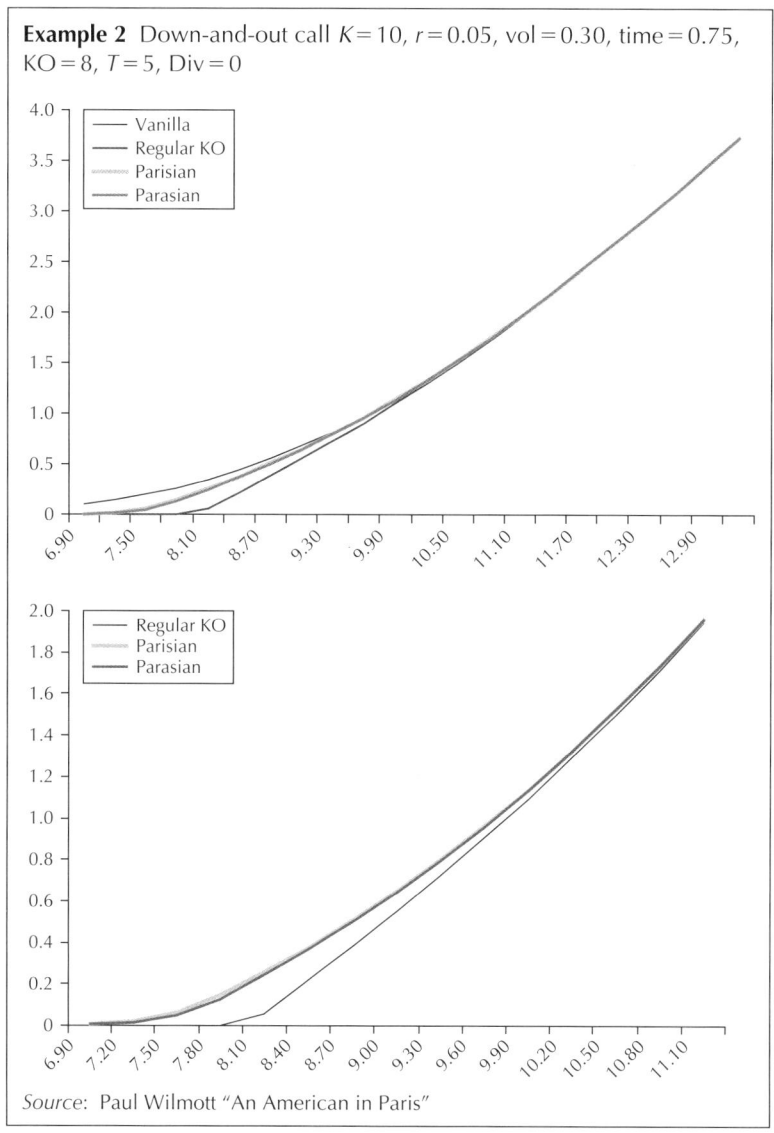

Example 2 Down-and-out call $K = 10$, $r = 0.05$, vol $= 0.30$, time $= 0.75$, KO $= 8$, $T = 5$, Div $= 0$

Source: Paul Wilmott "An American in Paris"

treasurers with tailor-made, highly effective, affordable protection from havoc-wreaking markets. As has been repeatedly emphasised in the previous paragraphs, the new accounting rules threaten the continuation of this cosy state of affairs.

The main conclusion of this paper is that, in spite of the strictly unfavourable treatment of exotic options by IAS 39 and (much less so) FAS 133, Asian options and KO options may still be used in an accounting-friendly way, but only if corporates are willing to use modified versions of the standard products. These new strategies would involve a higher cost than the regular, more familiar ones. A strip of Asians is more expensive than a single Asian. A soft KO is more expensive than a regular KO (a soft KI would be cheaper than a regular KI, but its compliance with G22 would be even tougher, as the possibility that the option would ever come alive would be much lower). So the tentative window of opportunity provided by the new standards comes at a price, which could be unacceptably high to many corporates.

Having said this, it has to be noted that the more complex and pricier strategies that may be forced upon corporates by accounting pressure would probably be economically superior. As was analysed before, the strip of AROs is more expensive than the single ARO precisely because some individual AROs may deliver a pay-off, while the single longer-maturity one expires out-of-the-money. It is quite probable that the final gross payout from the strip strategy would be sufficiently larger than that of the single ARO to cover the differences in the initial premium. Thus, the corporate would receive a larger windfall that better matches the losses caused by those individual underlying transactions that suffered a spot price worse than the strike level. Similarly, in the case of the Parisian KO, by making it much harder for the option to die, the strategy makes it much likelier that the end-user would receive a payout at maturity.

In the end, then, not only may the derided accounting standards allow two of the most popular exotics among corporates to qualify as effective hedges, but they could in fact gear treasurers towards hedges that prove to be much more efficient risk management tools than the usual choice. The extra money spent on the premium might turn out to be a wise, even if somewhat forced, investment.

14

The Pollock Doctrine

*Why corporate treasurers and other executives should listen to the
gospel of this unabashed critic of the derivatives accounting rules*

The new derivatives accounting rules have been deemed the most complicated for non-financial corporations ever to be introduced. As many treasurers, finance directors, Chief Financial Officers (CFOs), and even Chief Executive Officers (CEOs) can surely attest such definition is more than appropriate. It is not only that the new standards blackmail companies into certain hedging strategies that may well be economically inferior. It is not only that the penalty for not yielding to those demands would be deeply undesirable reported income volatility. The new rules are also extremely challenging from an implementation point of view. They are cumbersome to implement, and the potential for making technical mistakes is vast. The not insignificant number of troubling earnings restatements that have taken place in the last few years as a result of improper derivatives accounting testify to that.

In this light, then, it would be expected that anyone who dares stand up to the standard setters would be considered a hero by fed-up corporates. A brave voice that speaks up for all those disaffected executives. A valiant defender of downtrodden treasurers. A defiant knight facing up to the accounting dragon.

Well, it seems that we have such a hero among us. And he is not shy about it. He has loudly proclaimed that "FAS 133 has to go". That it is so deeply flawed that it should be scrapped altogether and re-thought from scratch. That all the effort and enormous sums of money to comply produce distorted, misleading and opaque financial statements. That it is apparent that a rule no one, including the public accounting firms, can get clear is a bad rule. That it diverts organisational effort from risk management to complicated book-keeping exercises. That it creates a strong and perverse incentive not to hedge. That it makes accounting risk a bigger problem than real risk and thus tends to increase real risk. That seldom has a rule adopted with the goal of clarifying a situation so failed in its purpose and instead spread confusion.

All this, of course, is music to the ears of long-suffering reporting entities. So, whom should they thank and worship for such pearls of (timely) wisdom?

His name is Alex J. Pollock, and he works in Washington DC for those CFOs who would like to send a congratulatory message. A former high-profile banker, he is now a guru at a respected think-tank (more bio details are offered later in the chapter, when some of the latest pieces by Mr Pollock are introduced in his own words). His animosity towards the new accounting rules originated in force with mortgage-related issues, leading to the Freddie Mac and Fannie Mae scandals, two prime examples of the potentially devastating effects of FAS 133, but his conclusions can of course be easily extended to the corporate arena. It is important for company bigwigs to listen to what he has to say, if only because many (all?) would surely welcome such an agreeable opinion.

SIR GALAHAD IS NICE, BUT NOT REALISTIC

The essence of Alex Pollock's view concerning the new derivatives accounting rules can be easily summarised: they make financial statements less clear, less transparent, less understandable, and less useful. They ought to be destroyed.

While this author, for one, wouldn't mind if Mr Pollock stopped mincing words and clearly said what he really thinks, it is obvious that, as stated earlier, his views are widely shared by many and particularly those who have experienced the dark side of the accounting rules firsthand. By now, the corporate treasurers reading this must be full converts to the "Pollock doctrine", eagerly awaiting ideas from their newly found guru. For no other player is treated more unfairly by the standards (Freddie Mac's and Fannie Mae's former CFOs, of course, may beg to differ). The new rules essentially treat treasurers as if they were traders, by forcing them to mark-to-market their derivatives positions even though companies enter into hedging structures with the purpose of keeping them until maturity, not to trade in and out of them as speculators would do. Treasurers now become exposed to new risks that have nothing to do with the way a company makes a living and that have no effect whatsoever on the real economic bottom line (risks such as changes in volatility or in forward curves, factors that dramatically impact the market value of a derivative). This is highly unfair. In addition, it can produce very unfair, and negative, results. First, stability-seeking treasurers who fear the potential reported income volatility derived from marking-to-market may be forced into those hedges that the standards favour, thus giving away their independence as risk managers. Those hedges may perform much worse economically than the alternatives. Second, it is entirely possible that hedging strategies that are affording sensational economic results may at the same time be creating an accounting malaise due to the treatment that the new rules impose upon them. Nothing can make financial statements less useful than a rule that has the potential to paint a very black picture of something that is really going very well. The key point that the standard setters forgot is that, when it comes to corporate hedgers, the market value of a derivative can say absolutely nothing about the only thing that matters concerning that derivative, namely its economic performance. Talk about lack of transparency.

Complaining about the shortcomings of the accounting rules is justified (and quite liberating), but in itself will lead companies nowhere. The rules are, for now, here to stay and they must be fully taken into account when thinking about financial reporting. In other words, the key question is not "Does anyone know when FAS 133 will be scrapped?" but "How should I practically cope with such a bad standard?" That is, if the standard setters have imposed a perverse rule, how should financial disclosure deal with it?

Mr Pollock comes to the rescue here, proving to be not just a complainer but also a practical problem-fixer (or at least, an adviser to those executives who, between whining sessions, wish to find the best possible way to deal with the effects of derivatives accounting).

According to him, the inevitable tension between economics and accounting under the new standards leaves six possible choices.

❑ Publish only Generally Accepted Accounting Principles (GAAP) financial statements and confuse stockholders, creditors and anybody else with no access to inside economic information. Not the ideal case.

❑ Reduce hedging and actual risk management in order to escape from the anomalies and vagaries, not to mention the overhead expenses, of the new rules. A bad idea, but tempting.

❑ Engage in dubious accounting-oriented transactions to adjust accounting results: the former Freddie Mac approach. Another bad idea.

❑ The Sir Galahad approach, relying on purity of heart – do what is right economically and let the accounting chips fall where they may, with the success of the hedging strategy demonstrated in the long run. This approach may not last beyond the first quarter in which the GAAP financial statements show a loss resulting from hedging. Whatever the company's internal knowledge of its real economic position, published financial statements take on a reality of their own and management may not survive while waiting for the long run. To paraphrase an old financial market saying: "The accounting can stay irrational longer than you can stay employed".

❑ Discover the domain in which economically correct hedging and the rules overlap, so that doing the right thing and having acceptable accounting results are consistent. This seems to be the superior strategy. Unfortunately, it results in seriously reducing the hedging alternatives available for risk management to those that easily qualify for so-called "hedge accounting" and thus do not impact earnings on a continuous basis. As the portfolio or activity being managed grows larger, this approach becomes less and less attractive or practicable.

❑ Finally, publish two sets of financial statements, one the audited statements prepared in strict accordance with GAAP and the other being the one the company thinks is the most accurate representation of the results.

We see that the first five alternatives all present serious drawbacks. Not surprisingly, then, Pollock believes that the "two books" alternative is the best of those available because it provides the most information. More to the point, it provides the "right" information.

Once more, let us repeat the key motto when it comes to corporate use of derivatives for hedging purposes: all that matters is whether the derivative will provide a monetary payout or not. In other words, all that matters is the economic performance of the hedge. Why? Because those payouts are what compensates for the losses on the underlying exposure that the derivative is intended to cover in the first place. The fluctuating market values of the derivative don't matter because they do not provide any cover against the underlying exposure (or worse; as said before, they senselessly expose reporting entities to new risks). Thus, if GAAP results, afflicted with the mark-to-market disease, would not provide the correct picture of a corporate's derivatives activities, a different set of results is needed that highlights the true real value of those activities. The new accounting rules make GAAP results totally unreliable as to the true character of a company's hedging strategies, and can unfairly create considerable mayhem. In the interest of clarity, transparency, understanding and usefulness a second book must be prepared, this time detailing the economic performance of the hedges.

Let us illustrate this with an example. A corporate treasurer that has just issued a fixed rate bond would like to switch its financing costs into a floating rate (perhaps because it believes that future rates will be lower), and thus enters into an interest rate swap with a bank. Immediately after the deal has been struck, two critical things happen. First, the central bank proceeds to kick-start a loose monetary policy cycle. Second, the forward curve steepens, with medium and long-end rates shifting upwards. This twin development affects the corporate significantly, both economically and accounting-wise. Its floating payments on the swap will now be lower than expected (the rate that it pays, Libor, closely tracking the central bank's set rate), thus generating a welcomed economic gain (ie, the difference between the fixed rate that it receives from the bank and the increasingly lower floating rate that it pays). However, from an accounting point of view, mark-to-market malaise would set in. The upward shift in the curve "indicates" that future Libor payments will be higher than originally thought, in essence rendering the originally agreed fixed swap rate too low to compensate for such future floating rates. Thus, the market value of the swap would have moved against the corporate.

Depending on the intensity of the curve shift and on the swap's maturity the bad accounting news could be quite worrisome.

In a post-FAS 133 world, such accounting chaos (here, of course, we are assuming for illustrative purposes that the swap would not be deemed effective, and that hedge accounting would not apply) could portray an image of failure that would not correspond at all with the real economic success of the hedging strategy. Outsiders would not be aware of the good news; they would only see the enhanced accounting instability and conclude that something is amiss inside the company. Embarrassing questions from analysts may follow. The stock price may dive. Heads may roll. And all this because of a hedging strategy that allows the company to significantly reduce its net financing costs.

The "two books" reporting approach would have gone a long way towards preventing such outcomes. By allowing people to realise how well the hedge is actually performing (and how much good it is doing to the corporate) it would put the accounting troubles in the proper context. After all, who would dare attack a treasurer or a finance director that is performing admirably where it truly matters because of the effects of accounting rules that are obviously inappropriate for corporate hedgers.

As Mr Pollock indicates, the "two books" approach was adopted by the old management of Fannie Mae and it appeared to be very successful in convincing the markets that "core earnings" were more relevant than the reported results under FAS 133. However, having won the conceptual battle, they threw their victory away by then failing to implement FAS 133 correctly. This points to what is perhaps the most troublesome aspect of the new derivatives accounting rules: the insurmountable technical difficulties related to their implementation. Even when a company manages to convince the markets to discount the FAS 133 accounting effects (a difficult feat in itself), it can still fall prey to the innate complexity of the rules. In addition, as the Fannie episode also shows, having obtained prior consent from your auditors won't help matters.

It is tempting to ask: is there any way at all in which the new standards cannot cause damage? Yes, there is one sure way to end the nightmare. As Alex Pollock would say, just dump them.

A Practitioner's View: Alex J. Pollock

Alex J. Pollock has been a resident fellow at the American Enterprise Institute (AEI) in Washington DC since July 2004, focusing on financial policy issues, including government-sponsored enterprises, Social Security reform, accounting standards, and the issues raised by the Sarbanes–Oxley Act. Previously he spent 35 years in banking, including 12 years as president and chief executive officer of the Federal Home Loan Bank of Chicago, while also writing numerous articles on financial systems and management. He is a director of Allied Capital Corporation, the Chicago Mercantile Exchange, the Great Lakes Higher Education Corporation, the International Union for Housing Finance, and the Great Books Foundation. Mr Pollock holds degrees from Princeton University, the University of Chicago, and Williams College.

FASB admits FAS 133 is a loser

The Bank of America is the latest victim of the conceptual incoherence and labyrinthine demands of FAS 133, the US accounting standard for derivatives. In 2005, at least 40 companies had to restate financials, according to the Wall Street Journal, from being unable to cope with this byzantine accounting rule.

An accounting rule that no one can follow is a bad rule.

Now the Financial Accounting Standards Board (FASB) is proposing an alternative to the existing FAS 133 – one radically different in concept and form. This proposal implicitly admits that FAS 133 is a failure.

It took the FASB a decade to create this failure, a mass of convoluted micro-rules and required procedures that no single mind, let alone the average accounting engagement partner, can understand. Various groups of accountants have laboured mightily to produce conflicting interpretations.

Meanwhile, FAS 133 has imposed vast, non-productive expenses on US companies, just as its original opponents predicted, in order to obscure financial performance and confuse creditors and investors. As usual, these expenses have gone to enrich the accounting firms, whose billings have correspondingly risen.

It has taken the FASB half a decade to recognise its failure. Better late than never. However, the real need is not just an alternative, but to scrap FAS 133 altogether and start over.

A notable case to ponder is Fannie Mae's disastrous meeting with FAS 133. The Rudman Report has now concluded that Fannie's implementation of FAS 133 "deviated from the standard's clear requirements in numerous and important respects".

Of course Fannie should have followed the GAAP standard to the best of its ability, however silly and flawed it may be: that is the requirement for being a public company. However, consider, from an economic welfare and public policy perspective, the expense to shareholders (which is also a wealth transfer to accounting firms) of having 2,000 consultants at Fannie costing hundreds of millions of dollars re-doing the books, largely to implement with precision an accounting rule that is conceptual nonsense.

New financial statements will be produced at immense cost – but what will they be worth? Since FAS 133 distorts the real economics, not much. How ironic to spend a fortune to produce misleading and opaque "corrected" statements.

The new FASB proposal is to allow the use of market prices or calculated "fair values" – also known as "mark-to-model" – on a wider variety of balance sheet items. This is so their movements in value will offset movements in the value of derivatives that are hedging the company's cash flow relationships. The same approach already appears in required fair value disclosures. This approach is better than FAS 133, but hardly a panacea.

The new approach takes as a governing model for accounting for all companies that of a trading book or investment company. Such a model is perfect for Wall Street, but problematic when applied to the rest of the world.

It relies on projections of possible future scenarios, mathematically reduced to changes in present values using constantly fluctuating guesses about discount rates that represent risks and probabilities of future events.

This author believes that one of the great problems of the accounting fashion of our time is the mistaken belief that financial statements should predict future market prices. It would be much wiser for accountants to stick to recording the past, trying to keep guesses and estimates about the future to as small a role as possible.

Even though it is true that you cannot completely get away from making such guesses and estimates, in essence accounting is and should be about recording the past – just as finance is about estimating the future.

When accounting tries to be finance, it produces failures like FAS 133.

FAS 133 gets a D–

Financial Accounting Standard 133 was contentious from the outset, and still is. Everybody always knew it would be complex and costly, but it has had much more impressive and unexpected results – notably bringing down the management of both Freddie Mac and Fannie Mae.

What has it meant for the rest of us, especially for those engaged in the hedging-intensive mortgage business? After four years of experience with FAS 133 as a required rule, now is a good time to consider the judgement of the market of financial professionals as to whether it is a success or not.

How does the market rate the effects of FAS 133? Has it made GAAP financial statements more or less useful? Is it worth what it costs? How does the market rate the performance of the FASB in producing the more than 800 pages of this rule and its copious interpretations? Should FAS 133 be kept or replaced?

To answer these questions in a clear way, National Mortgage News Online ran a short and straightforward questionnaire on the topic, which could be answered (of course) online and that was also sent by e-mail to informed mortgage and financial professionals. The respondents included mortgage bankers, investment bankers, investment and hedging officers, accountants and financial consultants. There were 36 total responses, not a huge number, but the judgements were so nearly uniform that the message is utterly clear.

In sum: FAS 133 gets a D–.

Answers to the specific questions were as follows:

1. Has FAS 133 made financial statements more or less clear?
   Less clear: 86%
   More clear: 11%
   No change: 3%

2. How do the benefits and costs of FAS 133 compare?
   Costs greater than benefits: 89%
   Benefits greater than costs: 11%

3. Are FAS 133 rules too complex or not?
   Too complex: 97%
   Just right: 3%

4. What should be done with FAS 133 going forward?
   Should be withdrawn or replaced: 63%
   Needs major revisions: 31%
   Continue as is: 6%

5. What letter grade would you give the FASB for FAS 133 from A (excellent) to E (fail)?
   The average grade, as stated, was D-. This was broken down as follows:
   A: 0%
   B: 0%
   C: 9%
   D: 41%
   E: 50%

   Quite a report card!
   Respondents were also given the chance to make open-ended comments or suggestions. Some of the more pointed of these were:
   "FAS 133 has made annual reports cryptic."
   "FAS 133 creates an incentive not to hedge."
   "Firms that are traditionally risk averse are not hedging risks they should be hedging. FAS 133 has made financial institutions more risky."
   "The requirement to mark only one side of a hedged position is simply wrongheaded."
   "The intricate and process-oriented tests for hedge effectiveness need to be scrapped."
   "The propensity under FAS 133 rules is to throw out effective hedges."

"The rule has created obfuscation at best, but probably misrepresentation is a better term."

"FASB wants to look at hedging as strictly a micro-hedge concept, whereas most financial firms hedge at the enterprise level. This is a major disconnect between the FASB perspective and reality."

"Our smaller clients are terrified of FAS 133 and our larger clients should be."

"If a transaction is indeed a hedge, then hedge accounting should be required."

"Under FAS 133, conservative accounting means misleading accounting."

"Grade: E. Only an imbecile would answer otherwise."

"FAS 133 is a disaster."

"Disband FASB soon."

It seems clear that after four years these financial professionals are not resigned to FAS 133. It is a notable historical irony that such a hopelessly flawed accounting rule became the "soft underbelly" of political vulnerability of Fannie and Freddie, long viewed as virtually unassailable founts of the US homeownership dream. The disasters at Fannie and Freddie resulting from their meeting with FAS 133 represent a highly interesting collision of two major government-sponsored efforts. These are leveraged mortgage finance, on one hand, and the elaboration of detailed top-down accounting rules, on the other.

It may seem unfamiliar to think of the FASB as another government-sponsored entity, but it is. The use of its products, however generally opposed they may be, is mandated by the government. Since Sarbanes–Oxley, its funding derives from a statutory assessment, in effect, a tax.

So far the force of the government-sponsored accounting idea is prevailing over the government-sponsored mortgage finance idea – an outcome worth pondering.

For example, the chief accountant of the US Securities and Exchange Commission (SEC) is reported to have said to Franklin Raines, "Sir, hedge accounting is a privilege, not a right." "Privilege?" "Right?" This is political language, not measurement language. The relevant question is measurement: how to convey through the highly imperfect medium of financial statements a reasonable approximation of the cash reality.

Does FAS 133 succeed in doing this? Our survey is unambiguous that in the judgement of financial professionals it does not. The consensus is that it is time at a minimum for major revisions, if not for FAS 133 to be scrapped altogether and replaced. This is an issue of the highest importance to the mortgage business.

Section 5

Credit Derivatives

15

Addressing Concerns

The perceived corporate unfriendliness of credit derivatives
may be widely exaggerated

Ralf Lierow must sometimes feel like a very lonely man. As perhaps the best-known corporate user of credit derivatives, the Siemens Financial Services (SFS) portfolio manager has been repeatedly portrayed as the exception that confirms the rule. Simply put, not many other non-financial companies seem to have become keen users of the otherwise fast growing credit derivatives market. This is a bit puzzling, as bankers have always had high hopes for this customer segment, given the many benefits that the products can offer to corporate treasurers and finance directors. It is no secret that corporates all over the world face huge amounts of credit exposure. Examples are many and varied: trade receivables, vendor financing loans, lines of credit, derivatives counterparties, financial leases, sovereign risk, etc. And while other kinds of corporate exposure, such as interest rates or currency risk, draw both more attention and more risk-management resources there is no doubt that credit exposures can have devastating effects on the financial health of a company. Not so distant examples such as the Kmart and the Enron bankruptcies, or the telecom equipment vendor financing fiasco highlight the critical importance of sound credit risk management practices.

Corporate credit risk management did not, of course, begin with the advent of the credit derivatives market. Other tools have been available since time immemorial. So credit derivatives did not revolutionise the scene in terms of offering risk management services that were not available before. Their value rather lies in the fact that they offer the possibility of obtaining such services in a cheaper, more flexible and more efficient way.

For credit risk management purposes, corporates have traditionally used credit insurance, factoring services, surety bonds, discount programmes or securitisation. All of these strategies present serious drawbacks that can be corrected by credit derivatives, thus allowing this new tool to present itself as a viable alternative. For example, insurers demand the evidence of loss before they produce any compensation payment, while credit derivatives do not. With insurance, the corporate usually retains some of the credit risk (first loss position), while in the case of credit derivatives the transfer of risk is complete. Insurers frequently have the right to revoke coverage or cut down the line in the event of a rating agency downgrade, while credit derivatives do not. Insurance coverage is typically guaranteed for no longer than one year, which does little to protect corporates with long-term exposures; credit derivatives, in contrast, can have maturities of 10 years or longer. To top it all, credit insurance is a heavily cyclical product, meaning that insurers can and do shy away from offering affordable protection, if any at all, during times of economic turbulence. The conclusion must be that insurance is only suitable for corporates with many small exposures, as its many drawbacks could have very negative effects in the case of large concentrated risks.

Factoring, while guaranteeing a large payment upfront and thus often seen as easily obtainable funding, can in the end be quite expensive for the corporate. At the same time, as most factoring companies are relatively small this strategy would also not work well for very large or highly concentrated risks.

In the case of surety bonds, they are conditional obligations where the insurer has the right to reject the claim. Depending on the credit environment, this market might be closed for non-investment grade corporates and collateral may be demanded. In contrast, credit derivatives offer unconditional protection that cannot be rejected once the predefined credit event has taken place and they do not require the posting of collateral.

Prepayment discounts can not only be expensive, but they are also an inefficient hedging tool once the counterparty's credit begins to deteriorate, as distressed customers have little incentive to exercise the early payment option.

swaps (whereby the corporate periodically pays a fixed fee to the dealer in exchange for a large credit-contingent payment) presents large potential basis risk. The risk of a client defaulting on its trade obligation is hedged with an instrument that pays off in the event that such a client defaults on a bond or a loan, or suffers debt restructuring or goes bankrupt. It is clear that default could take place on the receivable side, long before any of the trigger events take place, thus leaving the hedger unhedged. An associated drawback is the issue of documentation. While banks have been pushing their standard documentation tailored for inter-dealer transactions (and thus based mostly on "borrowed money" reference assets), corporates need specific documentation tailored to their specific receivables risk (ie, "payments" basis).

At the same time, there are the issues of market depth, liquidity and cost. While credit default swaps (CDSs) may be available at a reasonable cost for investment-grade counterparties, corporates are more likely to want to hedge the risk of their less creditworthy customers (the unrated or speculative-grade customers), yet that protection is usually only available (if at all) at prohibitively expensive levels. Also, sometimes credit derivatives protection can be much more expensive than traditional credit insurance, even for well-known names. For instance, in the turbulent and bankruptcy-prone period of 2001–2002 credit swap spreads widened dramatically, but insurance premiums did not. In the early part of 2001, annual credit insurance protection costs on Enron ranged around 0.45–0.75% while the CDS traded at around 1.00–1.50%. In addition, even for those corporate names that do trade, liquidity can be quite limited. Worse yet, even for apparently liquid names, market activity can dry up very quickly. In times of stress (whether systematic or idiosyncratic), the market for a particular name can shut down completely; with liquidity returning only after the crisis has ended. In other words, for many names default swap protection is likely to be unavailable precisely at the time when it is needed most. Such episodes have taken place quite regularly in the past few years, particularly noteworthy is the case of so-called "fallen angels", that is, companies that descend from investment-grade heaven into high-yield hell. High-profile examples of cases where the credit derivatives market failed to provide any liquidity to market participants seeking to hedge their positions throughout the crisis period include the Swiss engineering company ABB (downgraded to high-yield in early 2003), the Dutch supermarket chain Ahold (also early 2003) and US tyre maker Goodyear (mid-2002).

Then there is the issue of the characteristics of the contracts themselves. Corporates find the standard, single-name, CDS unsatisfactory for several reasons. First, the most liquid 5- and 10-year swap maturities are much longer than the average trade debt, which could be for as little as one month. Second, the smallest size that can be traded in the CDS market is usually around US$10 million, making the product suitable only for the largest customer exposures. In addition, there is the issue of how much protection to buy. In the event of default, the protection buyer receives the difference between the recovery value and the par value of the reference bond, and this figure may bear little relation to the trade losses. Crucially, many financial institutions do not offer cash settled contracts, and physical settlement is obviously inconvenient for corporates as they do not often hold bonds and buying them just for the purpose of delivering them to the protection seller can be highly problematic.

Corporates are also concerned about the accounting impact of using credit derivatives to hedge the receivables risk. The new derivatives accounting standards (FAS 133 for US-listed companies, IAS 39 for those listed in Europe) force companies to mark-to-market into earnings the value of those derivatives that are deemed to be ineffective. As credit derivatives would most likely not be exempt from the new standards, and given the potential high basis risk involved in hedging receivables payments, corporates would not get good accounting treatment on their credit derivatives' positions (meaning potentially enhanced income statement volatility).

Finally, there are concerns due to the reputation of credit derivatives. Scandals involving the credit derivatives' market (be it legal disputes over the breaching of a credit event, or large losses suffered by investors) have most probably damaged the reputation of these contracts inside corporate boardrooms. High-profile comments against credit derivatives by luminaries such as Warren Baffet have not helped matters either. Many executive boards may simply not allow their finance departments to indulge in the credit derivatives market. The fear is that an involvement with these products would confer a stigma upon the corporation that investors may find unacceptable.

IT'S NOT SO BAD

In light of all these obstacles and complaints, is there any future in the application of credit derivatives by corporates? Should dealers even keep trying?

Bankers, possibly desperate to grab at least a portion of the receivables risk management pie, have started to show more flexibility and a certain commitment to cater to the tailor-made needs of corporate clients. Some companies have been able to successfully negotiate special documentation where the credit event is referenced to receivables payments, thus crucially eliminating basis risk. Others have been able to at least guarantee that the contract is cash-settled, rather than using the corporate-unfriendly standard physical settlement. Again, SFS pops up as the innovator here, having successfully achieved both results. Other examples of recent innovations that try to address some of the complaints by corporates include the development of hybrid credit products that behave like financial guarantees and thus are exempt from mark-to-market accounting treatment, the appearance of a credit correlation market that allows corporates more flexibility in managing a portfolio of credit risks, and the proliferation of so-called digital default swaps that pay a fixed known sum that is independent of recovery values, thus allowing credit protection to be extended on corporates that do not issue bonds.

While these flexibility-enhancing developments are surely welcomed and much needed, perhaps in the end the most potent convincing factor for corporates to kick-start their credit derivatives activities lies in the fact that, simply put, many of the obstacles to product usage (comprehensively highlighted in the previous section) may not be as bad as they seem at first glance.

Market depth in particular has notably increased, with the proportion of below-investment-grade and unrated names that are being traded going up significantly. According to a global survey by the rating agency Fitch, in 2002 only 8% of the overall reference entities belonged to the high-yield sector of the economy. By 2003, that figure had changed to 18%. While one explanation for this shift was lower demand for senior protection, trading flows involving high-yield credits experienced a net increase due to the expansion of the market into lower rated names. By the end of 2004, of the 100 credits in the Dow Jones North American high-yield credit derivatives index, smooth individual trading could be found for around 75 names, in sharp contrast with the situation just a year before, when only 25 names were easily available. If one counts the names not included in the index for reasons of diversity, by the beginning of 2005 there were more than 300 pure high-yield reference credits available in that market. To confirm this global trend, SFS reports a surge in sub-investment grade hedging possibilities in the last year, having done several transactions down to single B reference entities. In any case, corporates should not get too caught up in the "high-yield debate", and should not forget to pay due attention to their bigger exposures, as these are the exposures that can put them out of business (the recent defaults by large corporates emphasise the importance of this way of thinking). As has been repeatedly mentioned in this chapter, credit derivatives lend themselves very well to the purposes of hedging big name risk.

Liquidity has also seen remarkable growth. In the 2002–2004 period, bid–offer spreads on single name CDSs on corporate names declined precipitously, at all points across the credit spectrum. This is consistent with a market that is maturing and experiencing deeper liquidity. Moreover, bid–offer spreads have seen the most significant reductions at the high-yield end, with improved liquidity in this segment outpacing the market as a whole. According to Fitch, in 2002 names quoted at a spread of 250 basis points (bps) or higher traded with a bid–offer spread of 23 bps on average. By 2004, the number had declined to just 6 bps (very close, by the way, to the figure for investment-grade names). While it is true that bid–offer narrowing has been helped by a period of improving credit fundamentals, at the same time it is undeniable that new important players have entered the market in force and that trading volume has increased, both crucial factors behind an increase in liquidity. For instance, the number of trades increased dramatically by 250% between the first half of 2003 and the year before, setting the floor for bid–offer spreads at which the market has more or less settled since then.

Regarding the issue of basis risk when hedging receivables, there are two key factors that may make it look less dangerous. (1) Such risk is bound to be positive in most instances, as it is likely that most corporates will maintain payments to suppliers for as long as possible in order to operate as going concerns, and that this type of default almost always happens after bankruptcy (certainly in jurisdictions where bankruptcy is protection from creditors). Even if a receivables default occurs first, it is reasonable to assume that such an event would trigger bankruptcy, given the very likely delivery flow cut-off by suppliers as a direct consequence (this is what happened to Kmart or MG Rover, for instance). Defaults on receivables that remain unsolved would also ultimately go public and cause lenders to close their pockets, another potential bankruptcy trigger. (2) There seems to be a tendency for receivables to have higher recovery values than bonds, so in the end a corporate is more likely to be overhedged than underhedged. Research by S&P points in this direction, and notable corporate market players agree to its logic. Factors that allow companies to make such a claim include the fact that the bankrupt corporate (or its successor) will want to continue producing and this will only work if suppliers come out no worse off than debtors, and the fact that in general receivables have some security on the delivered goods. Such arguments are supported in practice by the increasing importance of the so-called "critical vendor doctrine" applied during bankruptcy-induced reorganisations, which says that those suppliers that are deemed to be essential to the survival of the company as an ongoing concern receive preferential treatment when it comes to paying pre-bankruptcy claims. Thus, critical vendors (who are unsecured creditors) get paid first to avoid a disruption in service and creditors with greater or equal priority interest just have to wait in line and hope that there is something left over for them. This, of course, is the opposite of traditional bankruptcy rules, where secured creditors always come first, and clearly favours the recovery values of trade receivables. For example, WorldCom was allowed to pay critical vendors as much as US$70 million, United Airlines was approved for US$35 million, and in perhaps one of the most significant bankruptcy court decisions regarding this issue, Kmart was authorised to make payments in excess of US$320 million (it is crucial to note that although in this case the decision was later reversed by a different court, the critical vendor doctrine was not rejected but rather made subject to heightened procedural and evidentiary standards).

The negative reputation of credit derivatives, in general, may be widely exaggerated and public perceptions may have been shaped by the widely reported losses suffered by a handful of investors. Just as it happened 10 years ago with derivatives in general, only the disasters tend to be reported and the undoubted benefits of the products tend to be sidelined. In addition, one can also find strong support for the market from high-profile endorsers. Alan Greenspan, for one, has declared his repeated and unabashed support for credit derivatives, crediting them with having saved the financial markets from disaster on more than one occasion. According to the influential Fed chairman, the world economy is more shock-resistant and flexible thanks to the use of credit derivatives by market players.

With regards to the characteristics of the contracts, corporates are able to enter into shorter-term, lower-notional transactions than the standard five-year, US$10 million trade. This applies not only to the ubiquitous SFS, but also to companies such as IBM, which since 2003 has been entering into default swaps with two-year maturities to hedge credit exposures to certain clients.

Finally, the accounting effects of using credit derivatives may be tamer than expected, for reasons already touched upon in the previous paragraphs. If the basis risk involved in hedging trade receivables with contracts for which payment is triggered by borrowed money events is not that significant (in fact, this could very well be positive for the company) then the chances that the derivative may be deemed at least partly effective would be enhanced. Also, if default swaps with shorter maturities are used then this immediately reduces the potential mark-to-market valuation swings.

LET'S MAKE A DEAL

This chapter has highlighted the many benefits that credit derivatives offer over more traditional credit risk management tools. An attempt has also been made at showing that the loud complaints coming from treasurers regarding the unfriendliness of the products may be based on somewhat flawed assumptions. While undoubtedly not claiming the whiter than white character of the market, the simple message to corporates is: credit derivatives can help you and they are not as ugly as they look.

A few companies, with Siemens leading the pack (at least in terms of media notoriety), have shown that credit derivatives can be put to good use and can add value in the critical credit hedging arena. Crucially, the German giant has proven that it is possible to convince bankers to modify the products in accordance with a corporate's specific demands. SFS's credit portfolio management division has signalled to the world that it can be done. Perhaps the conclusion, then, is that when it comes to corporate applications of credit derivatives, where there is a will, there can be a deal.

A Practitioner's View: Ralf Lierow Credit Derivatives in Risk Management: Chances for the Corporate World

Ralf Lierow is a Senior Portfolio Manager in the trade finance division of Siemens Financial Services GmbH, Munich. Coming from an investment banking background, he actively links this business to international credit markets

In the history of trade finance, for a long time only a few channels for the placement or trading of credit risk existed: factoring for short-term receivables, forfeiting for longer or more structured exposures, and credit insurance. In addition to this, securitisation has emerged in recent years as a tool to refinance assets and to offload large and diversified portfolios from balance sheets through asset-backed transactions. While the latter can be a source of cheap funding for companies with lower credit ratings, it is only of limited use when the focus is more on risk management. However, the alternative to sell the assets outright into secondary markets might not only prove to be difficult for lack of liquidity, it could also lead to frictions with the debtors, who often are long-term business partners. Many would not like to see this happening, or will even include clauses in their commercial contracts preventing the resale of their receivables.

Siemens Financial Services (SFS) is offering finance and leasing solutions for short and long term trade finance assets to both internal and external customers. SFS is not only providing funds, but also assuming the full underlying credit risk into its own books. The bulk of the business comes from Siemens operative groups, thereby causing concentration risk from certain industries in our credit portfolio. As opposed to banks, industrial companies will hardly be able to avoid this problem – most of us are only active in a limited number of segments. Furthermore, credit business at SFS has the same boundaries as that in banks: credit lines are not unlimited, but assigned according to sophisticated risk management procedures. This means we sometimes cannot do all of the business offered to us – a fact we're not ready to accept as an unavoidable luxury problem, though.

Since July 2000, SFS has used the credit derivatives market as a source to accommodate these challenges in portfolio and risk management, and it does so with credit default swaps (CDS). The objective is to hedge a portion of the credit risk in our trade finance book in order to optimise its credit profile, and to increase operational flexibility. What SFS achieves is a reduced exposure to some of our key industry segments, and higher asset purchases through synthetic credit lines on the back of CDS. Both customers and management are pleased with the results.

Why did we choose credit derivatives? We were tempted by the opportunities arising when crossing over from one segment of the financial markets to another one, which offered us a new risk management tool alongside credit insurance and forfeiting, and more counterparties to work with. My belief is each of the aforementioned is a useful instrument and that they all should be in a risk manager's tool box. Obviously, credit derivatives will still mainly work for relatively large, international debtors bearing an external rating and also issuing in the bond market. However, the range of tradeable credits has steadily increased with time. Today, there is also liquidity in sub-investment grade and niche issuers – we are now able to close deals not even dreamed of some time ago.

Many of our assets are typical for an industrial company: short term receivables with maturities of up to one year. As these simple payment obligations make rather unusual underlying for a banking product like a CDS, we took considerable time and effort before entering the market, also tapping external legal expertise, to amend standard documentation so it would work for us. Our documents are still based on the ISDA standards, but reflect specific requirements for our asset types. Another typical problem is the maturity mismatch: our book of accounts receivables tends to turn over in less than 60 days, while the CDS market doesn't get started much below 180. However, these bills are results of longer-term manufacturing and service contracts, so it is in fact possible to fore-cast some of the flow over a feasible period. We would still look to buy protection on the shorter end of the credit curve to match our asset's higher turnover, but feel comfortable with tenors offered in the market – liquidity aside the broadly traded 5–year horizon has increased significantly in recent years.

One problematic issue arises from the accounting opinion on hedge perfection embedded in IFRS and US GAAP. Derivative structures that rely on cash settlement based on post-default mar-ket prices within homogenous clusters of risk, for example refer-ring to bonds in lieu of trade receivables, can create a highly effective hedge. However, they will typically fail the tests of hedge accounting, thereby creating income volatilities. Practical evidence, including ours, doesn't seem to confirm these definitions of "ineffi-ciency" – not if deals are prudently structured, including a certain "overhedge buffer". Prices shown in markets for defaulted debt are often moving in a very common range, irrespective of the asset type – unless there is some sort of subordination, be it structural or otherwise. Companies from all industry segments are reporting problems with this artificial source of earnings volatility created via derivatives on their books (also from "classical" f/x and inter-est rate hedges), which is penalising exactly those institutions try-ing to reduce their risk profile through hedging. Unfortunately, a re-evaluation of these rules is not on the agenda, as important as it would be. In the meantime, there are only two options: take the bit-ter pill, or leave it. Those who have been active in hedging opera-tions for years are likely to continue them – strategies that have proved to be useful in risk management should not be abandoned because of changing accounting rules. Neither should those who consider implementation of derivative-based hedging strategies be deterred from doing so. It may take a while for the markets to digest the reasons for the new fluctuations, but I'm confident they will – if those are explained in the necessary detail. As paradox as it seems, under current accounting rules, some degree of income volatility is a necessary evil when using derivatives in a risk man-agement context.

To me, the credit default swap is more than a useful hedging instru-ment, it is a management tool. First of all, it is an instrument to sin-gle out credit risk in a focused way, as compared to portfolio-based alternatives, like credit insurance or securitisation. Given the counterparties have agreed on a basis documentation, a deal can be structured rather quickly, and sometimes at a comparatively low cost – portfolio solutions might be optically cheaper, but may require to extend coverage to a range of assets where it is in fact not needed. Example: if what you are ultimately concerned about is one exposure of 10 million, will it be economic to embed it into a more diversified pool of 50 million, including assets you would not sell off otherwise? Few solutions seem more adequate when dealing with concentrated risk. Second, the information obtained through these channels can be used in the purchase process on the origination side, irrespective of a need to hedge. I have often stated my belief that many corporations acting in an international context are missing out on the benefits of credit derivatives. Some of that seems due to above mentioned accounting pitfalls, some to a subliminal uneasiness with derivatives beyond the banking sector, some to structured investment banking packages of slightly over-engineered complexity. Furthermore, using the product efficiently does require a certain degree of knowledge, experience, and organisation. Even so: a knife can be used as a household tool, but also for more sinister purposes. Would anyone denounce it as a categorical threat for that reason? The key is in the way a product is used, and how it is embedded into risk management and reporting processes. Credit derivatives have come a long way from their first appearance in the markets, to develop from a niche application into one of the most liquid sectors of the credit market. Like currency and interest rate derivatives, they are here to stay. The corporate world should not only accept this fact, but embrace the opportunities it offers.

16

Beyond Receivables

What to do with credit derivatives after you have hedged non-payment risk

In the previous chapter "Addressing Concerns", we noted that the most obvious use of credit derivatives in a corporate setting was for receivables hedging. However, that does not mean that this is the only way in which treasurers can profitably use this most modern of financial engineering tools. In fact, credit derivatives offer a very rich menu of possibilities for those companies in dire need of solving complex problems and designing value-enhancing solutions. Thanks to the intelligent use of credit default swaps (CDSs), total return swaps, credit spread options, and (possibly) credit-linked notes, corporates can be positively assisted in other key areas apart from receivables risk management. First of all, there is another area of trade finance where the products can be effectively put to use, namely vendor financing. Second, and particularly noteworthy, are the possible financing applications, such as the raising of funding and the management of existing liabilities. Using the new tools, a company can synthetically repurchase outstanding bonds, forward hedge the spread risk of a forthcoming bond issue and in general reduce the cost of new financing activities. In fact, many people believe that these are the applications of credit derivatives that have the highest chance of being widely embraced by corporates. Other notable available applications are hedging the risks of emerging markets investments and managing exposures to derivatives counterparties.

The main contrast between these other corporate applications and receivables hedging is that while in the case of the latter the value of credit derivatives lies in the possibility of offering an already available service in a cheaper and more efficient way in the case of the former, credit derivatives may be providing a solution that otherwise would not have been possible. In this sense, it could be argued that treasurers have an even bigger incentive to embrace the products in these more exotic areas than in the straightforward receivables field.

WHAT DO LUCENT, XEROX AND FORD HAVE IN COMMON?

In order to facilitate transacting, many corporates the world over have for years extended vendor-financing agreements to their customers. The selling entity basically lends the buying entity the cash needed to purchase the goods. The credit risks here can be tremendously high for the lender, and thus the need for risk management. For instance, it is no secret that customer financing backfired badly on telecom equipment suppliers in the last few years.

By the end of 2000, nine telecom equipment suppliers (Alcatel, Cisco, Ericsson, Lucent, Motorola, Nokia, Nortel, Qualcomm and Siemens) had extended more than US$25 billion in vendor financing loans to telecom service providers, motivated by the new economy bubble and the then-prevalent conventional wisdom of a world of endless demand for services. Of course, as we know, things did not turn out exactly as planned. The first signs of serious trouble came in the first half of 2001, with a series of high-profile losses, including Globalstar's default of some US$800 million in vendor loans to Qualcomm and Loral, Winstar's bankruptcy at a time when it owed Lucent US$2 billion in vendor financing, 360 Network's default on US$700 million owed to Alcatel and Telsim's default on a US$720 million loan to Nokia. By mid-2003, around 90% of the largest publicly traded service providers were bankrupt, and write-offs for loans by suppliers to those companies soared as a consequence. Anywhere from a third to 80% of their loan portfolios went down the drain. Lucent Technologies and Nortel Networks stood on the brink of insolvency, while many if not all the other suppliers struggled to retain their footing.

Other examples can be drawn from different sectors of the economy. Xerox struggled under the burden of the US$11 billion it borrowed to help customers purchase its products. Boeing Capital got caught in the downdraught of United Airlines bankruptcy after financing a significant proportion of United's aircraft. Ford Motors confronted liquidity concerns because of the huge short-term liabilities it took on to finance sales in the face of low demand.

How can vendors protect themselves? It probably is not necessary for them to drop the practice of financing their sales, especially since doing so could make the difference between winning and losing the business, but they will need to scrutinise borrowers more closely and adopt better risk-management techniques. This is where credit derivatives come into play. The issues of basis risk, documentation hurdles and nasty accounting treatment are probably tamer than in the case of receivables, as both the hedged risk and the trigger event on the hedging instrument would be based on borrowed money. In fact, it is safe to say that in most cases the correlation coefficient between the credit derivative and the underlying vendor loan would be sufficiently large to deem the hedge effective.

Prior to credit derivatives, a corporate had two basic alternatives for the purpose of hedging vendor financing exposures: (1) sell the vendor loans at the prevailing market price; (2) securitisation of the loans. The first technique presents two major problems: it could create a negative mark-to-market on the vendor obligation, and it does not maintain customer confidentiality and thus may create potential relationship problems with the client. The second technique also has several drawbacks: the corporate usually has to retain the first-loss piece of the structure in order to make the deal viable (otherwise it could be prohibitively expensive), so that in practice not all credit risk is transferred to the market, and again the deal would be non-confidential as customer consent would be needed prior to assigning the loans. (This problem could be erased if the securitisation was synthetic, in which case the loans are retained on the corporate's balance sheet.)

Credit derivatives present clear advantages over both selling the loans and securitisating them as they do not subject the corporate to potential negative mark-to-market loses, offer cover for the totality of the risk and confidentiality is assured. A corporate could enter into a total return swap (TRS) where it transfers all economic risks associated with the loan (both credit and market risk) in exchange for Libor-related payments from the dealer. In this sense, the vendor loan (which might have been agreed to under pressure and against the wishes of the company) effectively disappears. In an economic sense, it is as if it had never happened. In an accounting sense, since the TRS is an off-balance sheet instrument, the loan asset would remain unmatched on the balance sheet. However, it is important to understand the key benefits for the company: it allows the company to offer vendor financing to its customers thus preserving the business relationship, it erases all economic risks from such extended financing and it guarantees a Libor return (akin to a funding cost). In this sense, for those companies whose only intention when providing vendor loans is to assure the business deal, and not to make extra profit from the loan's interest, a TRS could be a very interesting proposition.

WHAT DO CASINO, KOREA ELECTRIC AND PARMALAT HAVE IN COMMON?

Many people believe that financing-related activities are the credit derivatives applications of the future for corporates. They come in three main forms: hedging the spread risk of upcoming bond issues, reducing borrowing costs, and synthetic bond/loan repurchases.

Credit spread hedging

Regarding the first type of application, corporates have began to use credit spread options to forward hedge spread movements in advance of a bond placement by buying protection on their own names, effectively locking tight spreads. One big advantage of spread options is that the payout occurs regardless of the reason for the spread movement, and thus compensation is not contingent on events such as bankruptcy, bond default or restructuring (clearly, significant spread widening could take place even in the absence of such events).

Corporates that want to definitely protect themselves against spread widening can buy credit put options on their own name. This gives them the right, but not the obligation, to sell the reference bond to the contract counterparty at a price corresponding to the strike spread. If the spread widens above the strike level, the corporate would be compensated for the difference, and in that sense fix its new issue spread at the strike level. If the spread tightens, then the corporate would not exercise the option and would be able to take advantage and issue at the favourable market spread. The option premium is usually paid upfront, but it can also be sliced into a schedule of regular payments, thus making the option similar to a CDS (it would be identical in the case where the exercise was American-style).

One problem corporates face in using spread options is caused by the potential lack of liquidity in the underlying name, as even on some of the most liquid names you may distort the market and push spreads out if you were to buy, say, US$1 billion worth of protection ahead of a bond issue. To address this, many banks are now suggesting basket or index-based hedges, but these are really just proxy hedges as they only hedge the first-to-default or the sectoral, but not the individual risk. The basis of such a hedge could be too large to bear. In this sense, basket and index hedges would be more appropriate for those corporates that present low levels of idiosyncratic risk.

In spite of these problems, it is important to note that spread options represent an advancement over previously available spread hedging alternatives, in particular so-called spread locks. Spread locks can be seen as the forwards of the credit spread market, and as such they subject the user to potentially significant opportunity costs: if the spread tightens, the end-user would not be able to take advantage of such beneficial market conditions as it is irremediably locked at the strike spread. With options, of course, the most a corporate can lose is the premium. Crucially, in the case of spread locks the bond issue must go through no matter what, that is, even if spreads widen.

Borrowing costs reduction

Some corporates choose to sell, rather than purchase, spread options and amortise the obtained premium as lower financing costs while establishing a known floor for such costs. For instance, in mid-2004, French supermarket chain Casino launched €500 million of credit-spread warrants with the help of investment bank Dresdner Kleinwort Wasserstein. This was the first such transaction ever to take place in the global capital markets. The main idea was to monetise credit-spread volatility so that the corporate could reduce the cost of an upcoming bond issue: the premium of the sold options (calls in this case) would be utilised as a cushion against the eventual spread of the bond. Since the premium for Casino's warrants turned out to be 7 basis points (bps) per annum, this was the amount by which the bond spread would be effectively reduced. If, come issue date, the spread was below the strike (85 bps), then investors would exercise the warrants (since they could purchase bonds at a cheaper price than the market price) and Casino's net financing cost would be fixed at a spread of 78 bps (85 bps minus 7 bps). If, on the other hand, the spread is above the strike and the warrants are not exercised then Casino's financing cost would be a variable spread equal to the market's set spread minus 7 bps.

Clearly, this trade requires the corporate to have a clear view regarding its own upcoming new issue spread. If the corporate is convinced that the eventual spread will be below 78 bps, then selling the warrants would not be a good idea. If the corporate is convinced that the spread will be above 85 bps, then the collected premium would turn out to be a very welcome cushion. The key, then, is to find the right market environment that allows a corporate to sell options at attractive spreads (ie, as low as possible) while collecting a decent amount of premium. Given the historically tight credit market conditions prevalent at the time, Casino was able to obtain the combination of an attractive strike level and a decent premium (if spreads had been wider, then in order to obtain the 7 bps per annum cushion the strike would have had to be higher than 85 bps, thus implying a break-even level above 78 bps and clearly setting a higher floor for Casino's financing costs). In fact, it can be argued that the biggest advantage of issuing the warrants was that it allowed Casino to take advantage of the very favourable market conditions without having to issue the bonds right away (which could be undesirable from a balance sheet point of view). In a sense, it was a matter of not missing out on a unique opportunity. While postponing the bond issue did not allow Casino to fully capitalise on such opportunity, selling spread options assured at least some future benefits.

The bet that Casino was making was basically that spread volatility would be tame between the issue date of the warrants (May 2004) and the issue date of the new bond (December 2004). As with any option writer, the company was very much short volatility. If spreads tightened significantly then Casino's financing cost would be higher than it should have been. If spreads widened significantly, then the company would have been better off issuing the bonds earlier. This points to the paradoxical aspect of selling spread options: the strategy makes the most sense when the market is abnormally tight (since, as we saw before, this guarantees a lower spread floor for a given level of premium or upside protection), but in order to work it requires that such abnormal conditions continue unchanged for a while longer.

The rationale behind structuring the idea as a warrant and not as an option is because the former could reach a larger investor base, including those that do not buy over-the-counter (OTC) contracts. Warrants are freely transferable and, unlike options, they require no additional documentation upon transfer and carry no counterparty risk. Actually, bringing new investors to Casino was another important advantage of the trade in the company's eyes. Those people who might have been uncomfortable with Casino's credit in the past could now obtain non-linear leveraged exposure to the company with limited downside from spread widening while still maintaining the full upside from potential tightening. Of course, this scenario varies dramatically from the linear exposure afforded by simple bond positions. The warrants could also be attractive to hedge funds and proprietary traders who target volatility as an asset class in itself. Finally, investors could also see the warrant as a way of securing allocation in future issues.

A potential major drawback associated with the issuance of credit-spread warrants is the limited liquidity of the market. Corporate bond issues could easily be for amounts of US$1 billion or more, and it is not foreseeable that the credit derivatives market could absorb even half of that. A lack of investors could thus prevent corporates from hedging significant portions of upcoming issues using the new technique and make it unviable.

Finally, it must be emphasised that a corporate that sells options (warrants or OTC contracts) will have to account for their mark-to-market value in the income statement, as net sold derivatives do not qualify for hedge accounting under the new accounting standards. For some corporates, such inconvenience may outweigh the benefits of the trade (principally, getting money upfront and retaining the flexibility of not coming to market if spreads widen) and thus render the whole idea undesirable.

Another way of reducing the all-in cost of a new issue is to incorporate credit derivatives into swaps. The main idea is that concurrently with entering into the swap the corporate sells protection on the sovereign or, less habitual, on itself thus achieving savings of several basis points. The downside is that were the reference credit to default, the swap would terminate thus leaving the corporate unhedged. Obviously, such a trade would make less sense when spreads are tight, as the pick-up from selling credit protection would be small. The ideal scenario is when spreads are historically wide and the corporate does not believe that the real credit risk is as high as implied by the market. Another potential obstacle to this type of transaction arises when the corporate sells protection on its own name. As cash compensation by the corporate is usually required in case the mark-to-market of the swap is in the bank's favour when default occurs, dealers are concerned about the possibility of obtaining preferential treatment for the swap in the event of liquidation. Thus, trades may only happen if the banks are comfortable from a legal point of view.

An example of this type of structure is the deal entered into by Korea Electric Power Corporation (Kepco) in September 2002, with the assistance of JP Morgan and Deutsche Bank. The company wanted to swap its recently issued US$650 million five-year bond into a fixed yen liability. In order to obtain cost savings, the cross-currency swap was made contingent on the credit quality of the Republic of Korea. If there was a default by this sovereign, the swap would end and the ensuing settlement would depend on the swap's value at that time. If it were in the company's favour then the banks would deliver Republic of Korea bonds. If it were in the banks' favour, then Kepco would have to pay cash. Exposing itself to such contingencies earned the company 30 bps in cost savings.

It is clear that before entering into such a transaction, Kepco had to think hard about two issues: first, what are the chances that the sovereign will default? Second, what is the relationship between sovereign default and the mark-to-market of the swap? As this is no longer a vanilla cross-currency swap but a credit-contingent swap, its value depends not only on exchange rate fluctuations but also on the reference entity's credit risk. Thus, prior to default, the mark-to-market depends on the correlation between the currency rate and Korea's credit default spread. While the initial pick-up on the swap is a highly desirable feature for the company, it faces quite a lot of risk in return. If there is a default the best that the corporate can hope for is to receive defaulted securities as compensation for suddenly being unhedged and faced with a large and naked dollar liability. Given these prospects, the conclusion has to be that unless a corporate is completely certain as to the quality of the reference credit risk it probably should not enter into such trades.

Management of existing liabilities

Corporates may often be flush with cash and decide that it would be a good idea to repurchase some outstanding bonds in the open market. However, this simple strategy might run into problems. In particular, the cost may be too high and the repurchase may not be 100% successful. Credit derivatives offer a way around these obstacles, by providing a cheaper alternative that guarantees a full buyback and that may not be contingent on the amount of cash available.

There are two basic ways in which corporates can use credit derivatives to synthetically repurchase outstanding debt. The most commonly cited tool is the TRS, whereby the company would receive the bond coupon plus the change in price of the bond over the swap's life, in exchange for paying Libor (or an alternative index) plus a spread. Thus, it is economically equivalent to extinguishing the outstanding bonds today and replacing them with alternatively priced debt. It is important to emphasise that TRS are off-balance sheet instruments and thus the corporate's bond liability would not be matched by a credit derivative that replicates it on the asset side. The replication is of an economic, not accounting, nature.

The second possible strategy is to purchase self-referenced credit-linked notes (CLNs), that is, notes that are contingent on the credit of the corporate itself (the firm would be selling protection on itself, thus betting on its own credit worthiness). A CLN is an on-balance sheet non-derivative security, essentially a fixed income asset with an embedded CDS. In other words, it is a collateralised or "fully funded" CDS. The corporate posts collateral (ie, the note's principal) for the amount of the repurchase and receives a stream of payments corresponding to the market rate (Libor). At the same time, the corporate periodically receives the credit swap spread as part of the CDS. The idea is to broadly match the coupon being paid on the outstanding debt. Of course, a big assumption is that the credit spread of the company has not decreased (as otherwise the total return from the CLN would be less than the original debt cost that it is trying to replicate). If, on the other hand, the spread has increased then the corporate would effectively be overhedged.

If the company experiences a credit event, then the note is accelerated and the corporate would face loses equal to the difference between the collateral amount posted minus the recovery rate. This would mirror the losses faced by the original bondholders in case of default.

A well-known case of a corporate buying CLNs as a way to synthetically repurchase outstanding debt is that of London-based publishing house United Business Media, which in 2002 carried out some US$200 million in CLNs deals. This case is important not only as a successful example of these liability management strategies, but perhaps more for the many problems encountered by the company when trying to transact. Apparently, several dealers refused to take up the deal and those that seized on the opportunity did so in limited amounts. This highlights two key issues: on the one hand, the significant obstacles in the form of legal risks faced by the banks when entering into self-referenced CLNs; on the other hand, the lack of depth and liquidity of the market.

One key concern that is raised by the many banks that have been reluctant to enter into self-referenced deals (also raised by rating agencies), is that owning self-referenced notes may accelerate the financial downfall of a company in times of stress, as the value of the asset would decline in tandem with bad news, thus producing a double-whammy effect. In that sense, rather than providing protection in difficult times, the note creates a claim on the corporate's assets at precisely the most inopportune time.

It is undeniable that self-referenced CLNs have been involved in several high-profile corporate scandals, and many bankers may wish to walk away from such reputationally risky affairs. Perhaps the most famous of all involved failed Italian group Parmalat, which was accused of purchasing self-referenced notes as a way to forge its balance sheet (in the words of some commentators, with the goal of "conjuring up an asset out of thin air"). In addition, some corporates have been accused of using self-referenced CLNs as a way of manipulating their own credit spread. All in all, we see that these products have the capacity to expose end-users (and their bankers) to pretty bad press.

OTHER MENU ITEMS

As mentioned at the beginning of the chapter, two other possible applications of credit derivatives that may be of interest to corporates are the hedging of emerging markets' exposures as well as defaults on other derivatives contracts (and, in a related issue, the risk that counterparties credit lines may be consumed).

Emerging markets risk

Given the (arguably, on-and-off) popularity of investing in emerging markets, which represent greater credit risk, it follows that credit derivatives designed to minimise this cross-border exposure would be in demand. Some dealers report more inquiries on cross-border credit hedges than on straight receivables. Using a CDS a corporate could pay the bank a fixed-period payment in exchange for a contingent payment based on a given country's equity index or specific bonds (typically sovereign debt). These structures are subject to significant basis risk and limited to countries with identifiable reference assets with public market prices. Another application concerns lowering the cost of funding the investment. In this case, a corporate may buy protection on the emerging market itself, and pass it on to the lender. This way, the risk facing the latter is limited to the investment asset's risk and isolated from the emerging market's risk, thus lowering the financing costs that it would demand from the corporate.

Derivatives counterparties/credit lines

Corporates can use credit derivatives to manage the risk that their banking counterparties might default on other derivatives contracts, particularly swaps. If a bank defaults on an interest rate or foreign exchange derivative transaction then the company will effectively be left unhedged on those exposures. It is possible to structure credit derivatives with a protection amount linked to the market value of a swap or other derivative. At the same time, corporates, particularly the larger corporates, often have a huge amount of transactions with their preferred counterparties and thus can easily come up against line restrictions. Firms should sooner or later realise that they will have to hedge against that risk or find new counterparties (which sometimes can be difficult and time-consuming).

A famous case that illustrates the potentially negative consequences of a counterparty not fulfilling its obligations when it comes to guaranteeing a certain price/rate (which is of course the basic function of a derivative) involves Enron. As we know, on 2nd December 2001, Enron Corporation (then the largest US energy trader) filed for bankruptcy. The estimated credit exposures on the company at the time were in excess of US$30 billion, including on-balance-sheet debt and derivatives contracts. Thus, the effects of its downfall rippled through the US (and world) economy, negatively affecting many different entities. One of those victims was the Texan energy company EOTT, which itself went bankrupt in early October 2002. The trigger that set the stage for the company's death spiral was Enron's rejection of a contract guaranteeing the price of a gasoline additive that EOTT traded and that provided EOTT with much-needed revenue stability.

LET'S MAKE A DEAL (AGAIN)

In the previous chapter "Addressing Concerns", we explained how corporates account for only a small proportion of overall credit derivatives activity and we provided an extensive list of factors that so far have prevented corporates from fully embracing the new tools when it comes to hedging receivables. The fact that, as we have seen in this chapter, there are many other possible applications that would assist companies in critically important areas should soon make credit derivatives more popular inside treasury departments.

Bankers in general sound quite bullish in fact. They insist that corporates are getting more and more educated about what credit derivatives can do for them and that they have seen a pick-up in requests for information. It may be the case that corporates have not entered into credit derivatives transactions for the simple reason that they were not aware of their wide-ranging applications in the first place.

Thus, it could very well be that the market is just too young for corporate users to have fully understood its implications and possibilities, and all that is needed is a little bit of patience until they catch up. Some people embrace that idea, explaining that any derivatives activity always starts in the inter-bank market and then spreads to the corporate customer base. The credit derivatives market is in the high-growth stage for the banks. With corporates we might be simply seeing the early adoption stage.

Section 6

Weather Derivatives

17

Weather Update

How much growth has the weather derivatives market
experienced and where is it going?

Few companies around the world can claim to have a bottom line that is insensitive to the fluctuations of the weather. In fact, people have been worrying about the economic effects of weather for centuries, but could not do anything about it (though some civilisations did try offering human sacrifices as a way to placate the gods). Since the late 1990s humanity has, for the first time ever, sensible weather hedging tools at its disposal. One might conclude that the demand for such products should be huge and universal. The truth is that, while the market is certainly growing, weather derivatives still remain pretty much a mystery to many potential end-users who as of yet have not dared to venture into this new world.

For those corporates who are tired of complaining about how the weather derails their carefully designed business plans and strategies, the good news is that the weather derivatives market has reached a remarkable level of maturity. The possible applications have extended well beyond the original temperature-related structures. Liquidity has been greatly enhanced thanks to the very successful introduction of exchange-traded contracts. The departure of high-profile dealers (whether forced or voluntary) has not only failed to cause irreparable damage but has been more than compensated by new entrants.

Thus, while certain obstacles remain, it may seem as if companies could be running out of excuses not to use this utmost symbol of financial wizardry especially given the likelihood that more and more analysts and investors will not let them get away with using the weather as an excuse for disappointing results.

WHY WEATHER DERIVATIVES?

For many businesses around the world a change in the weather can result in significant bottom line effects. Agriculture, apparel, beverage, construction, energy, entertainment, gaming, production, promotions, retail, sports and transportation are all sectors clearly sensitive to the weather. Different estimates provide the same picture: the weather has critically important economic consequences. Deutsche Bank has estimated that four-fifths of all economic activity worldwide is directly or indirectly affected by the weather. The US Department of Commerce says that at least US$1 trillion of the American economy is weather dependent. Last year, investment bank ABN Amro produced the first ever study aimed at quantifying the extent to which adverse weather conditions affect industry production in Europe and North America. The report assigns weather risk ratings based on industry wide weather related losses for the period 1980–2003. The results clearly show the vast amount of production that is vulnerable to the weather. More than half of the US receives the worst possible rating, indicating weather exposure of more than 35% of overall production. No American state is assigned an exposure inferior to 20%. In Europe, the United Kingdom, Portugal, Sweden, Denmark and Holland obtain the worst rating, with Spain, Italy, Belgium and Austria having 25–30% of their production exposed to weather. The sensitivities of Germany and France are no less than 20%. One would tend to think that this kind of evidence should prompt corporate bigwigs to want to hedge their (substantial) weather risk.

Recently, a weather derivatives market has been created that enables those businesses that could be adversely affected by unanticipated weather swings to transfer this risk. Just as professionals regularly use futures and options to hedge their risk in interest rates, equities and foreign exchange, now there are tools available for the management of risk from extreme movements of nature. This sector of hedging and risk management products represents one of todays most exciting derivatives markets.

So, the quick answer to the question posed in the section header is that weather derivatives exist and are needed because so much

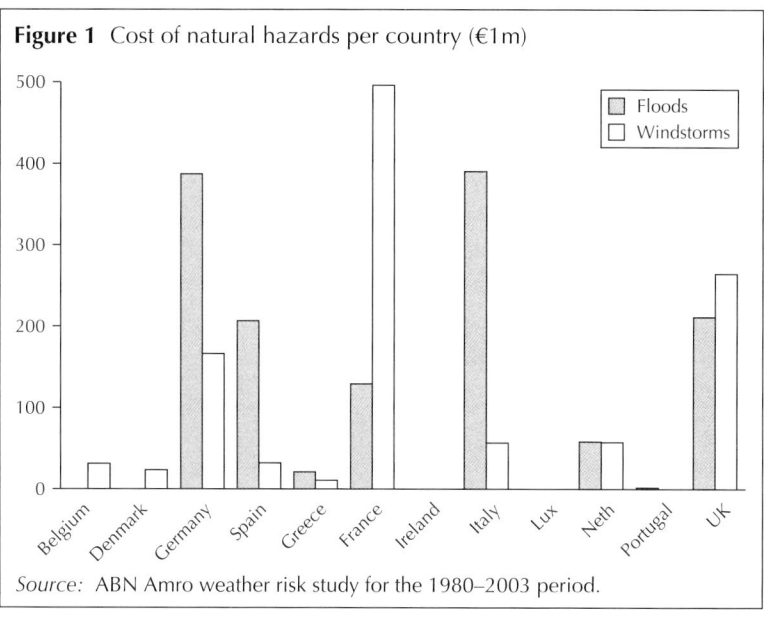

Figure 1 Cost of natural hazards per country (€1m)

Source: ABN Amro weather risk study for the 1980–2003 period.

economic activity and the fate of so many different businesses depend on whether it is hot, cold, sunny, cloudy, rainy, dry, frosty, windy, snowy or humid. Clearly, a market with so many potential customers (and which contingencies, unlike other derivatives markets, are not man-made and thus become inevitable) had to come to life at some point.

Historically, the energy and utility industries have been the most sophisticated in terms of recognising the risk they face from weather. If there is any industry that has its fortunes inextricably bound to weather, it is the energy industry. Simple fluctuations in hot and cold temperatures can affect the year-end financial balance of a company severely. In the days before deregulation, utility concerns did not really care much for risk management. Because the industry was regulated, utilities earned a fixed return on assets. If there was a loss in one year due to weather or other factors, the utility would typically be allowed to raise rates the next year to make up for it. With deregulation came an understanding that more sophisticated alternatives were needed to manage risk, especially in the area of weather. In the last few years, derivative instruments and insurance contracts have emerged as the primary tools to do so.

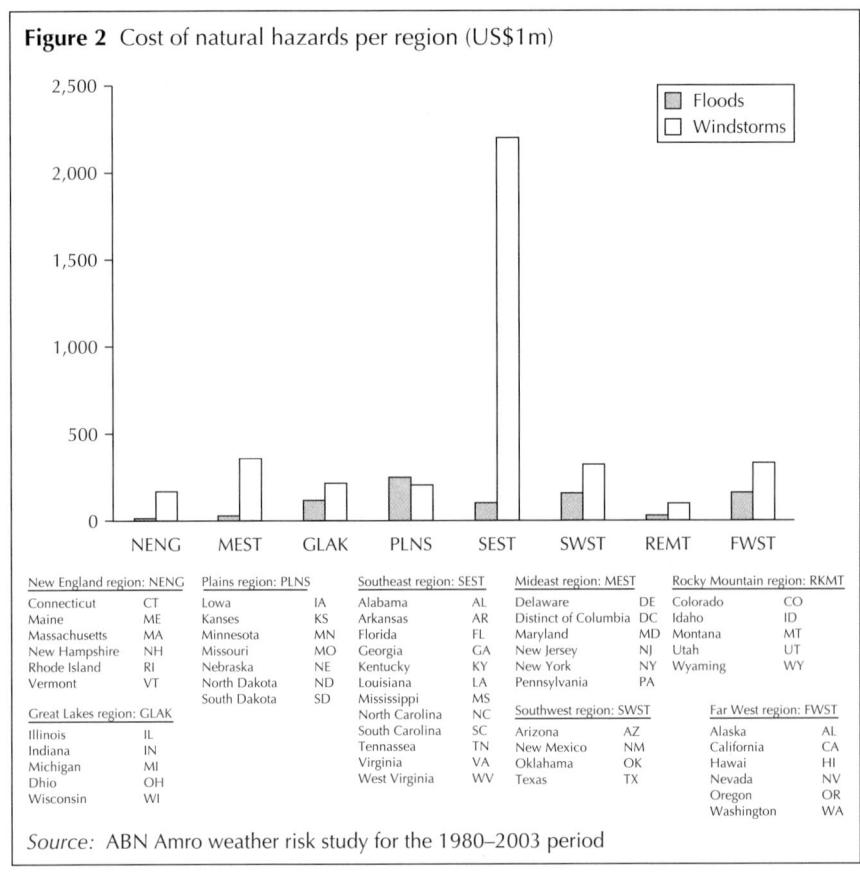

Figure 2 Cost of natural hazards per region (US$1m)

New England region: NENG		Plains region: PLNS		Southeast region: SEST		Mideast region: MEST		Rocky Mountain region: RKMT	
Connecticut	CT	Iowa	IA	Alabama	AL	Delaware	DE	Colorado	CO
Maine	ME	Kanses	KS	Arkansas	AR	Distinct of Columbia	DC	Idaho	ID
Massachusetts	MA	Minnesota	MN	Florida	FL	Maryland	MD	Montana	MT
New Hampshire	NH	Missouri	MO	Georgia	GA	New Jersey	NJ	Utah	UT
Rhode Island	RI	Nebraska	NE	Kentucky	KY	New York	NY	Wyaming	WY
Vermont	VT	North Dakota	ND	Louisiana	LA	Pennsylvania	PA		
		South Dakota	SD	Mississippi	MS				
Great Lakes region: GLAK				North Carolina	NC	Southwest region: SWST		Far West region: FWST	
Illinois	IL			South Carolina	SC	Arizona	AZ	Alaska	AL
Indiana	IN			Tennassea	TN	New Mexico	NM	California	CA
Michigan	MI			Virginia	VA	Oklahoma	OK	Hawai	HI
Dhio	OH			West Virginia	WV	Texas	TX	Nevada	NV
Wisconsin	WI							Oregon	OR
								Washington	WA

Source: ABN Amro weather risk study for the 1980–2003 period

While energy and utility companies have led the way in weather risk management, and to this day continue to be the leading players, many other different types of businesses have also jumped onto the bandwagon once they have been able to appreciate the financial benefits of hedging their weather exposure with these new products. As mentioned earlier, the number of potential end-users of weather derivatives is vast. For instance, a sports drink manufacturer might wish to minimise the impact of weather on sugar prices, its largest input cost. A derivatives structure could be designed such that it hedges the company against weather that is detrimental to the sugar industry. Similarly, an ice-cream maker may want to manage its exposure to a cool summer that limits sales. It could enter into a contract that pays out if the temperature for the July–August period was below a certain threshold. A hotel operator could stand to lose financially were the amount of rain to be heavier than expected. In this case too, a derivative could be devised that hedges such precipitation risk. There are countless other examples involving, among other businesses, ski resorts, shipbuilders, fruit growers, golf clubs and restaurants, and we will take a look at real-life deals involving some of these sectors in the following chapter.

Potential end-users are not just a large crowd; the number of things that they can do with weather derivatives is also quite amazing. The number of possible applications (and thus value-adding capabilities) of weather derivatives have been dramatically enhanced in recent years through the development of products with ever more exotic and varied underlyings. If the first member of the weather derivatives family to appear on the scene were the so-called "temperature contracts", these days they have lots of company. While temperature derivatives are by far still the most widely used type of weather derivative, accounting for around 90% of the total market volume, other younger members of the weather family are making significant strides, in a clear sign that the market is evolving. Contracts referenced to the level of rainfall, the speed of wind, the amount of snow, the frequency of typhoons, the height of waves or the level of humidity have been transacted in the market at one point or another. Some people are even suggesting the need for solar and space derivatives.

Another key development that makes weather derivatives more attractive and user-friendly has been the introduction in force of exchange-traded products. While the market originated as an over-the-counter (OTC) effort, in September 1999 the Chicago Mercantile Exchange (CME) established a weather derivatives exchange for temperature contracts referenced to US cities, adding European and Asian references in 2004 (in December 2001, the London International Financial Futures Exchange (LIFFE) followed suit by offering contracts related to the weather in London, Paris, and Berlin but it soon reversed course and ended that business). Lately, the CME has witnessed explosive growth in trading volume.

The new exchange-traded contracts facilitate dealings not simply by providing a direct transacting platform, but also by meeting the hedging needs of the OTC sector. OTC dealers are able to lay off their risk using liquid, standardised contracts with the additional benefit of the pricing transparency provided by exchange-traded markets. All this should contribute to a more liquid, transparent, sophisticated and economical OTC sector that can deliver the tailor-made solutions that many corporates demand.

So we see that weather derivatives can help companies manage a very important type of risk (and one that is not going to disappear; unlike foreign exchange or interest rates the weather's volatility cannot be regulated away), that the number of tools available is extremely wide and that significant gains in liquidity and market depth have been accomplished. Nothing, in principle, should then prevent companies from availing themselves of these innovative products. Well, not quite. Apart from specific supply–demand issues that will be addressed in the final section of the chapter, there is the minor inconvenience that weather derivatives, plainly, have a competitor in the shape of weather insurance. In this sense, it is crucial to understand the differences between both types of covers. This applies not just to potential end-users who must be able to discriminate between the two for each particular risk management exercise, but also to the dealers that cater to them as they must clearly explain in their sales pitches what the value added of derivatives is.

THE INSURANCE COMPETITION

Although derivatives and insurance to mitigate weather-related risk are often designed to accomplish the same goal, there are some fundamental differences. First of all, derivatives cover low-risk, high-probability events, while insurance covers high-risk, low-probability events (ie, much more customised protection). Derivatives are thus ideal for those companies that believe that weather deviations of even modest magnitudes (say, an increase in temperature of only a few degrees) can be financially damaging. For instance, a utility may use a weather derivative to hedge against a summer that forecasters think will be five degrees colder than the historical average (a low risk, high probability event). However, the same company would most likely purchase an insurance policy for protection from damages caused by a flood or a hurricane (a high risk, low probability event).

Another obvious difference is that while derivatives are index-based, requiring that a trigger be breached in order for payment to occur, insurance will require both an index measure as well as an actual demonstrable economic loss on the part of the purchaser.

With weather derivatives the payout is designed to be in proportion to the magnitude of the phenomenon whereas insurance pays a one-off lump sum that may or may not be proportional and hence lacks flexibility.

Also, derivatives can be cancelled or monetised at any time (usually based on mark-to-market issues). On the other hand, insurance policies are generally held for the full term (which of course means that they are not affected by market fluctuations).

Another point to consider is the credit rating of a counterparty. Within the weather markets at least, the credit rating of insurance companies could outweigh the credit rating of derivatives providers. That is, corporates may find it easier to deal with insurance companies than with pure derivatives dealers.

Buying an insurance policy to cover weather risk also does not require the creation of International Swaps and Derivatives Association (ISDA) documentation as must be done with derivatives. Those who have negotiated an ISDA with a new counterparty know that the process can be very time consuming and there is no guarantee that it would finally be signed.

Finally, there are also tax issues to consider. Premiums on a derivative must be classified as an investment and are not immediately deductible. Insurance premiums, on the other hand, are immediately deductible.

The derivatives versus insurance question is often resolved as a function of a firm's corporate culture. Those companies experienced in risk management are much more comfortable with derivatives than those who have never traded them. For those companies that do not have a history of trading, it is much easier to justify an insurance policy. Purchasing an insurance policy, a much more conventional means of managing risk, can also often be done without a board's approval.

In spite of all these apparently clear-cut differences between weather derivatives and insurance, some people have been busy trying to have the two equated, essentially by attempting to classify weather derivatives as insurance. In late 2003, the US National Association of Insurance Commissioners (NAIC) drafted a controversial white paper in which it claimed that weather derivatives are disguised insurance products and should therefore be regulated as insurance products, rather than be treated as unregulated

capital markets products. Any move in that direction would immediately close business opportunities for a number of weather dealers, given the stringent requirements implied by being a regulated
provider of insurance policies (requirements to maintain adequate
financial reserves to assure solvency, payment of state premium
taxes, rates charged would be subjected to scrutiny, etc). As has
been the case with all other derivatives markets, its unregulated
status provides weather derivatives with an edge and goes a long
way towards explaining the rationale for people dealing OTC.
Just as self-regulation has been a crucial factor behind the staggering growth of the interest rate and foreign exchange derivatives
markets in the past couple of decades, external regulation of the
weather derivatives market could essentially threaten its very
existence.

No wonder, then, that the Washington DC based Weather Risk
Management Association (WRMA), the industry's trade body,
promptly fought back. In its March 2004 response to the NAIC
draft paper, the WRMA affirmed its stance that weather derivatives
are not insurance products and should not be regulated as such. It
argued that when weather derivatives are fully analysed under
insurance law, they cannot be classified as an insurance product
and expressed its surprise at the NAIC's conclusions given the contrary precedent opinions previously laid out by the New York
Insurance Department.

The WRMA points out that while weather insurance complies
with the general definition of insurance, weather derivatives do
not. Let us briefly summarise the six elements that are generally
cited as common to insurance.

❑ A contract must be in place between two parties and run for a
   specified term or cover.
❑ The insurer must promise to compensate the insured should a
   specified future contingent event occur during the term of the
   contract.
❑ Payment of a premium (upfront or in instalments) from the
   insured to the insurer in consideration of the above promise by
   the insurer.
❑ There must be uncertainty as to the occurrence or timing of the
   specified future contingent event.

❑ The insured must have an "insurable interest" in the subject matter of the contract. This means that the insured must have an economic interest in the subject matter, and one that is lawful.
❑ The insured must suffer a loss of a pecuniary nature in relation to its insurable interest.

The typical weather insurance contract meets all these elements. The contractual nature, the payment of premium, the commitment of the insurer and the uncertainty are all obviously present. The insurable interest is also present: a farmer cannot take out annual crop insurance if he has no crop or no share in a crop that year; similarly, a sports stadium manager cannot take out raincheck insurance if he has no sport event scheduled. The requirement for loss to take place is also a feature of weather insurance: crop insurance contracts would not pay to the extent that government compensation covered crop losses for insect damage; raincheck insurance would not pay out to the extent a sporting event was cancelled because of a contractual dispute.

According to the WRMA, weather derivatives do not meet most of the six sacrosanct elements. In fact, they only meet the first one (as of course a derivative requires a signed contract). As the majority of weather derivatives are swaps and forwards (or other zero-cost products), there is no premium involved and payments could flow from each of the two parties to the other (ie, not exclusively from the insurer to the insured). This rules out elements two and three. Element four is also excluded, as payments would take place with certainty.

At this point the alert reader might have a complaint: what about options? Surely they involve a premium, payment can only go in one direction and the possibility of such payment taking place is certainly uncertain. While our inquisitive observer would have seriously threatened to derail the arguments of the WRMA the conclusion would have not changed, simply because even options won't comply with the fifth and sixth elements. A derivative contract is indifferent as to whether the acquirer has a legal economic interest in the subject matter: it pays out either way (ie, you do not need to be a farmer to get crop protection through a weather derivative, but you do need to be a farmer to obtain weather insurance). As to the element of loss, perhaps it would be best if we let the New York State Insurance Department explain it, as per its Office of Government Commerce (OGC) Opinion No 2000-26 where it notes that under a weather derivative:

"the issuer is obligated to pay the purchaser whether or not that purchaser suffers a loss. Neither the amount of the payment nor the trigger itself in the weather derivative bears a relationship to the purchaser's loss. Absent such obligations, the instrument is not an insurance contract".

The WRMA concludes its response by pointing out two grave dangers of classifying weather derivatives as insurance. First, the risk of bringing other derivative instruments (interest rate, foreign exchange, equity, credit, etc) that have not previously been considered to be insurance within the insurance realm as well; clearly this would bring about a fundamental regulatory sea change and would have very significant repercussions throughout the business community (the end of the derivatives industry?). Second, it would concentrate weather risk into just one market (namely, insurance), with the negative repercussions that such development would bring in the form of a lower number of providers (as people run away from the legal and regulatory restrictions on entities conducting insurance) and the consequent enhanced possibility of systemic risk and potentially higher costs.

While the WRMA concedes that the solvency and market regulatory benefits provided by insurance regulation is a necessary level of protection for the general insuring public, it emphasizes that this additional layer of regulation (and expense) is not necessary when it comes to purchasers of weather derivatives, who have a higher level of sophistication than the average insurance purchaser. Solvency concerns are also typically handled through the use of contractually based (ISDA) credit support arrangements, letters of credit, collateral or other methods of security common in the complex derivatives market. In this light, the WRMA argument goes, the imposition of additional burdens upon weather derivatives players is counterproductive given the existing controls and the sophistication of the market. Expansion of the insurance regulatory environment into the weather derivatives arena would thus be completely unwarranted.

The survival of the weather derivatives market may well depend on whether such counsel is heeded or not.

EVOLUTION OF THE WEATHER DERIVATIVES MARKET

As already mentioned, the trigger for the appearance of weather derivatives was the de-regulation of energy markets in the US in the 1990s. While utilities have always been exposed to changes in demand due to weather conditions (ie, electricity sales go down if winters are not harsh enough or if summers are not warm enough), regulators compensated them for possible losses in the form of offsetting rate increases the following year. In a sense, power producers enjoyed a "regulatory hedge" that made the creation of a new financial hedge unnecessary. With deregulation, utility companies were suddenly left facing two different sets of risks: price and volumetric. There was now a clear possibility that a slump in prices and volume would coincide, with no regulator picking up the tab this time. Energy suppliers needed to find ways to hedge both price risk and volume risk. While derivative products for hedging the former had existed for decades, the same was not true in the case of the latter. For energy companies, finding an effective way to deal with volumetric exposures became a top priority. That necessity became the mother of the weather derivatives invention.

In the early days of deregulation, the energy markets looked to the insurance industry for risk solutions. The insurers, however, were not receptive to the idea of providing non-catastrophic coverage. Thus, the energy sector had to effectively invent its own hedging tools if it was to survive the potential damage created by the weather. This is how companies such as Enron, Koch and Aquila developed the weather derivatives market (not only to hedge their own exposures, but also to profit from the creation of a new business with high potential).

Although several pioneering trades were done in 1996, they were not publicly discussed, and thus did not create the necessary level of awareness. The trade that is consensually credited with having jump-started the weather derivatives market took place in 1997, between Enron and Koch, based on a Milwaukee temperature index for the winter of 1997–98 (the point of the deal was basically to commence trading in the marketplace, rather than to hedge any particular risk). Additional deals that generated extensive media coverage were soon transacted between Enron, Koch and Aquila. The market was thus born.

Additional sources of liquidity were urgently needed for the market to take off, though. Soon, energy commodity brokers and big reinsurers entered the playing field in search of new sources of income. As the number of market participants grew and the underlying issues regarding data gathering and pricing were resolved, US activity exploded. In 1999, Europe and Japan began to taste the new products. In September of that year the CME launched its weather indexes on US cities.

Since then, many new players have entered the market (some have also left, as will be analysed later), new products have been created, and activity has increased by a considerable margin. Probably the most reliable source of information regarding market size is the annual reports that the WRMA has been publishing in conjunction with PriceWaterhouseCoopers since 2001. We are now going to spend a few moments analysing the revealing data that such surveys have been providing, so as to have a reliable picture of the success (or lack of) of the weather derivatives industry in establishing itself at the forefront of financial engineering.

The first survey covered the activity incurred by WRMA members between October 1997 and March 2001. Throughout that period energy companies made up 37% of the overall number of market participants, just like insurance/reinsurance firms. Banks accounted for 21%, and commodity traders for the remaining 5%. While this shows that the market had (positively) become more diverse from the original days characterised by the exclusive presence of the energy sector, notice also the (negative) absence of corporate end-users from non-energy sectors, such as agriculture, entertainment or hotels. Bringing such entities into the market would later prove to be the next stage of growth.

Another welcome development was the more global reach of the market, originally of course confined to the US. By March 2001, US institutions represented just 58% of the total, with Japanese institutions representing 21% and French firms 16%.

The notional value of trades experienced a substantial jump in the US, with the US$900 million transacted during October 1997–October 1998 paling in comparison to the US$2.9 billion recorded in the October 1999–October 2000 period. While Europe and Asia began to record activity in late 1999, by early 2001 the notional amounts still remained insignificant (less than US$100 million annual volume in both cases). The total value of all transactions entered into worldwide during the surveyed period was approximately US$7.5 billion, corresponding to some 4800 separate deals.

Originally, all trades were temperature-related. In fact, in 1997 all recorded deals (less than 100) were winter temperature-related. In 1998, summer temperature contracts started to be transacted (though winter products retained, and enhanced, their hegemony throughout). It was only in 2000 that non-temperature related derivatives made their debut, with rain-referenced contracts being especially noteworthy.

Once we have taken a brief look back at the early days of the market, it is time to fast-forward and see where weather derivatives are today. Has the initial promise been fulfilled? Have notional and deal volumes skyrocketed as predicted? Has activity in Asia and Europe picked up steam? Have contracts other than temperature gained pre-eminence?

We are going to focus on the results for the 2004 and 2005 reports, as these are the periods when trading on the CME really took off. As such, the analysis can serve the purposes of understanding both the spectacular success and consolidation of exchange-traded contracts and how this phenomenon has affected the OTC segment. The results of the July 2004 survey (containing data for the period April 2003–May 2004) yielded the following key results.

❏ The number of OTC trades reported by survey participants was 3,162 (down from 4,517 on the previous year).
❏ The average notional value for OTC contracts was US$1.2 million for winter trades and US$0.4 million for summer trades.
❏ More than 50% of OTC trades took place in the US, with Europe and Asia accounting for 30% and 20% of trades, respectively.
❏ 85% of OTC trades were in temperature-related contracts, with winter trades almost twice as prevalent as summer trades; rain, snow, and wind derivatives combined for about 10% of all trades.
❏ Energy firms accounted for 56% of OTC business inquiries, with agricultural firms representing 13%, retailers 9%, construction 7% and transportation 4%.
❏ The CME reported 21,335 trades, up from 7,239 in the previous survey.
❏ CME summer contracts more prevalent than winter contracts.

❑ The total notional value of the market was US$4.5 billion, with OTC contracts representing around US$2.75 billion and CME contracts accounting for around US$1.75 billion. It is important to note that while total notional value for CME contracts had increased significantly since the prior year's survey (by around US$1.25 billion), notional value for OTC contracts had actually declined (by around US$0.75 billion). The total combined value represented a 10% annual increase, and what was then an all-time high for the weather derivatives industry.

What are the main lessons to draw from the 2004 results? What did change with regards to the 1997–2001 pioneering efforts? Well, the OTC corporate customer base had clearly diversified, with non-energy companies representing almost half of all activity. The product range had also improved, with exotic underlyings such as snow or wind becoming clearly noticeable. However, possibly the most impacting development was the staggering growth experienced by CME trading. And not just because it signalled the coming of age of exchange-traded contracts, but especially because it seemed to have come (at least partly) at the expense of OTC transactions. The total notional value of OTC deals for the 2003–04 period was not only below 2002–03 results but also significantly below 2001–02 numbers (when the OTC market was worth more than US$4 billion) and just slightly above 2000–01. While the good health of the CME is obviously a welcome sign for OTC dealers (by providing heightened levels of liquidity and transparency, never mind hedging tools with which to cover their own positions), it could spell lower profits as customers flow to the safety and comfort of the exchanges (where dealing does not require the signing of bilateral agreements and where credit concerns are limited).

As we see, it was with a certain sense of anxiety regarding the state of the OTC market that the 2004–05 survey was carried through. Practitioners and outside observers were undoubtedly eager to find out if the decrease in both number of deals closed and total notional value had simply been a bump in the road or, worse, the beginning of a pronounced and persistent trend. They need not have worried, as the below results show.

❑ The number of OTC trades reported was 4,057, a surge in excess of 30%.

❑ The average notional value for OTC contracts was US$0.8 million for winter trades and US$1.25 million for summer trades.

❑ 60% of OTC trades took place in the US, with Europe and Asia accounting for 15% and 25% of trades, respectively.

❑ 90% of OTC trades were in temperature-related contracts (winter slightly more prevalent than summer); rain continues being the second most traded underlying, with wind catching up and with snow in third place.

❑ Energy firms accounted for 69% of OTC business inquiries, with agricultural firms representing 7%, retailers 5%, construction 4% and transportation 2%.

❑ The CME reported 223,139 trades, but it is crucial to point out that in April 2004 the contract size was changed from US$100 to US$20 (thus, the equivalent figure for 2003–04 for activity comparison purposes would be 106,675).

❑ CME winter contracts were much more prevalent than summer contracts.

❑ The total notional value of the market was US$8.3 billion, with OTC contracts representing around US$4 billion and CME contracts accounting for the remaining US$4.3 billion. The total combined value represented an 85% annual increase, obviously establishing a new all-time high for the industry.

The conclusions: the OTC market is not dead after all, the CME market seems unstoppable (the total weather volume for 2005 almost reached the staggering figure of 900,000 contracts), the number of OTC contracts traded in Europe hit a four-year low, the number of OTC contracts traded in Asia hit an all-time high and non-energy companies seem to lose relative weight.

In summary, and based on the results from the latest WRMA/PwC report, the weather derivatives market appears to be quite healthy. And this report may just be scratching the surface. The market may in fact be much larger. An alternative survey carried out by *Energy Risk* magazine in August 2004 showed that a mix of traders, brokers and end-users believed the total notional value of weather derivatives to be around 50% higher than the figure released by WRMA/PwC. The credibility of this other survey is backed by two key facts: the number of respondents was significantly larger (70 compared with only 19 in the WRMA/PwC

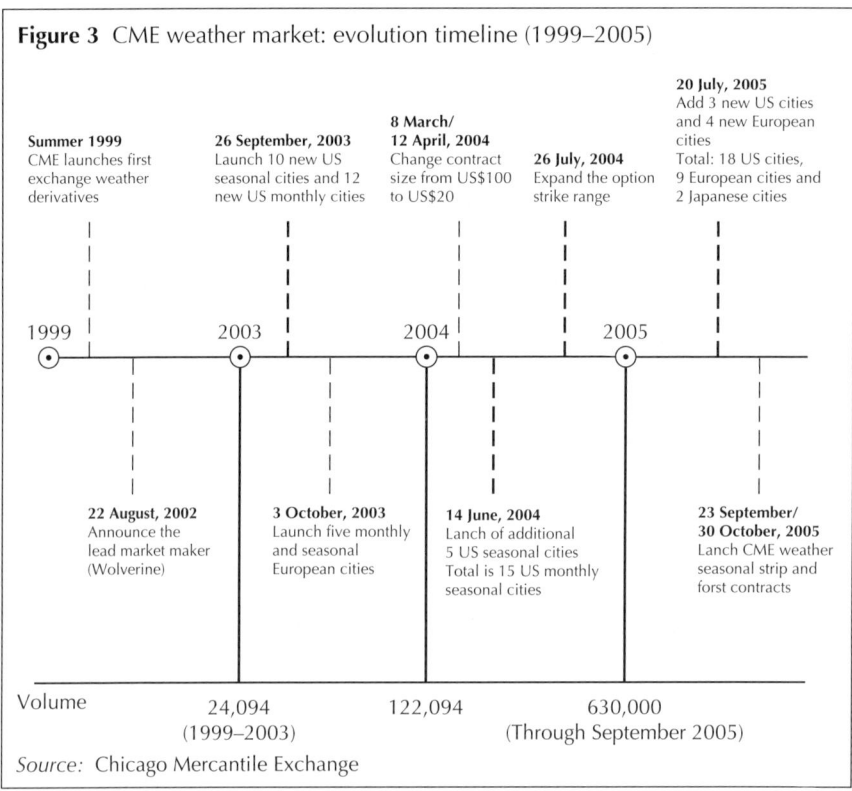

Figure 3 CME weather market: evolution timeline (1999–2005)

Summer 1999
CME launches first
exchange weather
derivatives

26 September, 2003
Launch 10 new US
seasonal cities and 12
new US monthly cities

**8 March/
12 April, 2004**
Change contract
size from US$100
to US$20

26 July, 2004
Expand the option
strike range

20 July, 2005
Add 3 new US cities
and 4 new European
cities
Total: 18 US cities,
9 European cities and
2 Japanese cities

1999   2003   2004   2005

22 August, 2002
Announce the
lead market maker
(Wolverine)

3 October, 2003
Launch five monthly
and seasonal
European cities

14 June, 2004
Lanch of additional
5 US seasonal cities
Total is 15 US monthly
seasonal cities

**23 September/
30 October, 2005**
Lanch CME weather
seasonal strip and
forst contracts

Volume   24,094   122,094   630,000
            (1999–2003)   (Through September 2005)

Source: Chicago Mercantile Exchange

study), and among those respondents were some leading dealers that are not members of the WRMA (such as Deutsche Bank and Calyon).

FUTURE PROSPECTS: WILL IT RAIN ON THE MARKET'S PARADE?

What are the prospects for the weather derivatives market? Will trading volumes continue to increase in the future? The answer to these questions will most likely depend on the evolution of supply and demand. That is, will dealers continue to enter the market and offer weather derivatives solutions? Will the range and sophistication of products continue to increase? Will the number of end-users go up? Can weather risk management really become as familiar to corporate treasurers as interest rate and foreign exchange risk management, as some claim?

On the supply side, the truth is that some players have actually exited the business. For instance, banks BNP Paribas, Société Générale (SocGen) and IntesaBCI have ceased weather trading, in all cases citing low returns on capital. When announcing in early 2002 the bank's withdrawal from the weather derivatives market, BNP's global head of risk solutions stated that:

"Weather derivatives trading was not providing the return on capital that was initially expected. Weather trading is a complex business and we review our involvement across all products regularly. We decided the resources, both in terms of capital and staff, could be better used elsewhere in the business. Weather derivatives are interesting products. However, it's a relatively time-consuming business for what on average are small transactions".

More importantly, some of the founders and leading players of the market are no longer participants, be it because of credit concerns (Aquila) or bankruptcy (Enron).

Having said that, new players have also entered the market in force, such as in the cases of investment bank ABN Amro and specialist firm XL Weather (originally staffed by former Enron and Aquila people). It is expected that new weather desks will emerge in the near future, while existing desks are likely to take larger positions. *Energy Risk's* survey found that 95% of respondents believed that there would be new entrants into the market in the short-term.

The tremendous growth of the CME's weather exchange is another definite sign of market maturity, as is the continuing expansion of its contract offerings that now include several temperature contracts based on European and Japanese locations (this has somehow compensated for the failures of LIFFE and Finland's Hex, where lacklustre demand led to business closure), Amsterdam-referenced frost days contracts, and since February 2006 snowfall contracts on Boston and New York. The CME successes provide critical aid to OTC dealers when it comes to hedging their own books.

Probably the biggest obstacles to market growth from the supply side lie on the issues of pricing, namely the lack of a single accepted valuation model and, outside the US, the extreme difficulties associated with data gathering. These issues are dealt with extensively in a final appendix at the end of the chapter.

On the demand side, it is envisaged that companies and sectors that already use weather derivatives successfully will tend to employ them more, while those that have still not hedged their weather exposures will start to do so in some measure as awareness and publicity of the market and done deals increase. The bottom line is that the contracts have so far widely proven useful to those entities that have dared to enter the market. The widely extended range of available underlyings beyond temperature should clearly be a strong draw for new corporate end-users (some visionaries are even discussing space-weather derivatives to hedge the risk that satellites or aircraft would be affected by solar winds).

Crucially, weather products could be used by companies not just as hedging instruments but also as marketing tools that may lead to higher sales. For instance, a manufacturer of snowmobiles could use a weather derivative to be able to offer its customers a money-back guarantee if there are less than a particular number of days of snow during the winter season. Similarly, a travel agent could use a weather derivative to offer a refund in case a summer holiday on a beach resort is ruined by excessive rain.

The weather derivatives gospel is being rapidly spread out of the US, with demand proving robust in Europe and Japan, and inroads being made in Australia, South Africa and even emerging markets (thanks in particular to a World Bank initiative). As the market becomes more international, companies will start to consider weather derivatives a mature industry rather than a fad or a crazy idea ("if others are doing it, shouldn't I do it?").

In any case, companies might just be forced to hedge their weather exposures, as the very existence of efficient hedging tools will make it very difficult for managers to simply blame bad results on the weather. Analysts and rating agencies will likely start to closely watch whether firms are managing their weather risk, and will punish inaction. As early as 2001, there were plenty of warnings regarding the negative consequences of not hedging against swings in the weather as well as the rewards that should accrue to those that do hedge. Analysts from top investment banks issued reports containing statements such as "investors get greater value in a company that buys protection against adverse weather than from one that remains unprotected" or "all things being equal, a company having downside weather risk will trade at a lower valuation relative to a company having deployed financial weather mitigation measures … the Street will begin to penalize businesses that don't hedge their weather exposure". Ratings analysts came to similar conclusions, with a Standard & Poor's report stating that "the prudent use of weather derivatives can only enhance credit quality as cash flows should stabilize". In fact, in early 2003 energy distributor Star Gas Partners' subsidiary Petro (the largest heating oil distributor in North America) was able to maintain its BBB rating by Fitch precisely as a direct result of putting in place a weather risk management programme using derivatives.

APPENDIX: THE PRICING AND DATA OBSTACLES

The lack of a single universal pricing model is a major hurdle to the growth of the weather derivatives market. It prevents participants from talking in the same language, with each market maker essentially developing its own pricing methodologies (which they, predictably, may not be too willing to share with outsiders). If a generally recognised pricing model were developed, this could greatly improve market transparency and would most likely enhance the number of entrants. Just as the Black–Scholes breakthrough has been a key driving factor of the explosive growth experienced by, among others, the equity and currency options markets in the last 30 years, the weather market needs a common reference.

Why is it difficult to come up with a standard weather-derivatives pricing formula? Plainly stated, because the Black–Scholes framework cannot be used in this context. While Black–Scholes modelling may be the standard approach for options pricing in many other derivatives markets, applying it to weather derivatives is hazardous. One might even say it is flat-out wrong.

The primary reason why a Black–Scholes model cannot be used to price weather options is that the model is based on an underlying tradable asset, and in weather derivatives there is of course no available underlying asset. In the natural gas market, for example, the model derives the price of the gas derivative from the price of physical gas itself. But weather doesn't have a price. The whole idea behind Black–Scholes is dynamic replication of the option by continuously trading the underlying asset. In the weather market such dynamic hedging is impossible.

Another big obstacle lies in the fact that the mathematics behind Black–Scholes cannot be applied to the weather market. Black–Scholes assumes that the underlying follows a random walk without mean reversion where the volatility increases with time. This clearly does not apply to weather (it is important to note that the maths behind Black–Scholes are also flawed when it comes to the foreign exchange or equity markets, but not as blatantly as in the case of weather). In practice, weather shows mean-reverting tendencies (tendencies to go back to its historical levels) and is reasonably predictable, at least in the short term. Also, what Black–Scholes would be implying is that the variability of temperature increases with time, so that it could wander off to any kind of levels (including infinity, or hotter than the sun).

In light of these modelling difficulties, practitioners have opted for two more hands-on, alternative methods when pricing weather derivatives, namely historical analysis and simulation.

Historical analysis, or "burn analysis", makes use of past weather data to determine the fair value of the option. This method is quite straightforward, needing only the collection of historical time series and calculating what would have been the payoff for a particular option on each past date. The price of the option should then equal the average of all those payoffs. This basic approach is often complemented with some kind of prediction of future weather. This predictive component is a proprietary tool that derivatives providers understandably like to keep secret (eg, it seems clear that the analysis should take into account the disrupting effects of global warming, which threaten to alter historical weather patterns).

One big problem associated with burn analysis is that it is totally data-dependent, that is, it makes a difference how far back in time we go to calculate the average historical payoff of the option. Using, say, 10-years data will most likely yield very different results from using 50-years data. A recent study of New York City's weather derivatives market found the following diverging figures for CDD, (three summer months) and heating HDD, (three winter months), depending on the time series considered. CDD stands for "cooling-degree-days" and HDD for "heating-degree-days" and they are both the underlyings used in temperature-related contracts; they both measure deviations of the average temperature from 65 degrees F (18 degrees C), whether on the way up (CDD) or on the way down (HDD).

Record length in years	Period	Underlying	Average of degree days (summer for CDD, winter for HDD)
10	1988–1997	CDD	934
30	1968–1997	CDD	923
50	1948–1997	CDD	906
122	1876–1997	CDD	843
10	1988–1997	HDD	2602
30	1968–1997	HDD	2733
50	1948–1997	HDD	2739
122	1876–1997	HDD	2849

It is hard to say which is the right number of years to use when working with weather data. In principle, the longer the history the more information we can capture. On the other hand, the shorter in time we travel, the more weight can be placed on recent (and more relevant) weather patterns. The industry convention seems to be the use of 10–20 years data.

Another key related issue is, of course, the availability and reliability of weather data. If there is not enough data on the past weather of a particular location, we simply cannot use burn analysis as a pricing tool. Fortunately, meteorological archives in some countries are rich with long and accurate weather records. In fact, some weather time series are longer than the series of interest rates and economic data used in the financial markets. This is the case in the US, where data is not only plentiful but, crucially, also free. In Europe, however, things are not that rosy at all. In fact, many observers attribute the relatively smallish size of the European weather derivatives market in large part to the lack of reliable, standardised and inexpensive data (it is true that in the early days of the market obtaining reliable data in Europe was extremely difficult and costly. But it is also undeniable that this is changing. National Met Offices have become more flexible and better equipped to provide weather data. In both Holland and Germany there has been a release of free data sets. Additionally, a number of private companies has helped to facilitate data access in a quick and reliable way).

Given the drawbacks associated with burn analysis, it should come as no surprise that Monte Carlo simulation seems to be the most commonly used method for pricing weather derivatives. It entails generating, with the help of a computer, a large number of simulated random future weather scenarios to determine possible option payoffs. The option premium would then be the discounted average of all those possible payoffs.

The key question, and the main difficulty associated with simulation, is how to generate the future scenarios in the first place. The answer lies in choosing an appropriate process for the underlying (temperature changes beyond an index, rainfall, wind speed, etc). As was said before, temperature is mean reverting and not a random walk (volatility stays within a reasonable range through time). Thus, the probabilistic process used for simulation purposes should take those aspects into account.

18

Weather Deals

A brief walk through some real-life high-profile transactions

This chapter is dedicated to both sceptics and nostalgics. On the one hand, it is a good idea to present a list of some of the weather derivatives deals that have been closed out there in the real world so that those who never believed that such a market could possibly exist can be proven wrong. Perhaps the best antidote against scepticism and disbelief is knowing that a Japanese ski resort has actually used a hedge referenced to snow, that a London restaurant has really used a contract to cover its exposure to rain, as has a German golf club, or that a South African fruit company has been able to take care of its exposure to frost through a tailor-made product. It is much more difficult to make fun of the weather derivatives market and to dismiss it as a crazy idea or a senseless fad that no company in their right mind would contemplate when one is presented with factual dates, names and deal descriptions.

However, revanchism and "I told you so" impulses are not the only drivers of this chapter. It is also intended as a humble homage to all those who have, through the years, made this wonder of financial engineering prowess come alive and blossom. If weather derivatives eventually become mainstream risk management tools for corporate hedgers some time in the future, much will be owed to those pioneers who innovated and (in some cases) persisted in the face of apparently insurmountable obstacles. In this light, this chapter will play the role of against-the-tide maverick and utilise this platform to say positive things about Enron, that most resented and despised entity. Enron, as everyone knows, started the whole thing. Most likely, no other segment of the derivatives business has had such a clear-cut founding father. From the trading floor in Houston led by Lynda Clemmons sprung what is now an US$8 billion market, with trades being executed all around the world by a large myriad of participants. Enron's culture has been endlessly criticised, ruthlessly dragged through the mud by countless books and newspapers articles. However, it seems that a key aspect of that culture was incentivising people to go ahead and try new things, to dare to innovate and reach new frontiers. The emergence and pre-eminence of Enron's weather derivatives desk was most certainly a direct consequence of that free-spirited entrepreneurial environment. So, as we nowadays contemplate the successful state of the market as well as take a look back at the breakthroughs of the past, it is tempting to think that, after all, perhaps something right went on inside that tall building with the "crooked E" in front.

In following pages we are going to display a chronological list of real-life weather deals involving non-financial companies. Obviously, this is by no means an exhaustive list. Only those transactions that have been publicly disclosed are covered, and even then we are probably still missing out on a lot of reported trades on which information has not been found (it is entirely possible that some data references are incorrect, given the difficulty involved in finding accurate information regarding some transactions; many deals are described exactly as they were originally reported). However, limited though the list necessarily is, it nevertheless provides a clear picture of a market that is global in scope, diverse in its corporate end-users and innovative in its product range. The hope is that after learning about these examples, other companies (perhaps competing firms of some of the names mentioned) would be tempted to contact a weather derivatives dealer and join the bandwagon. If so many other people are proving that it works, can a corporate bigwig really afford not to give it a try?

DEAL TIMELINE

❑ In 1997, the first widely publicised deal in the US took place between Enron and Koch Energy, referenced to the Milwaukee winter season; in September 1998, the first European deal between Enron and Scottish Power was made.

❑ In March 1999, SocGen and French utility Soccram made a temperature-referenced collar deal whereby the latter hedged against the consequences of excessively warm weather in the winter (October–April) and thus against the associated decline in sales during that period. If the winters of the two subsequent years displayed a temperature above a certain pre-defined point, Soccram would receive compensation. Conversely, if the weather was colder than a certain strike level, Soccram would pay SocGen. Since Soccram's business is concentrated in Paris, the raw data was temperature measurements provided by Meteo France for Orly airport. This transaction is believed to have been the first ever weather derivatives deal in France.

❑ In late 1999, Canadian snowmobile maker Bombardier entered into a snowfall contract with Enron that would allow the company to offer its customers a sales-boosting special promotion. Bombardier would pay a US$1,000 rebate to customers if snowfall levels did not reach half that of the previous three years. It funded this potential liability by purchasing snowfall digital floors structured in each major market where the promotion was offered (44 cities). Each floor would pay out US$1,000 per unit in case the strike (the average snowfall for the past three years) was breached. The period covered was November 1999–March 2000 (ie, the winter season), and the upfront premium varied depending on the reference city. "We examined insurance, but wanted a weather risk management strategy sold by an expert in the field", said Ken McLeod at the time, then Bombardier's vice president of industrial sales. "We had a tough time in several regions over the past few years", he explained. "Some areas were getting tremendous amounts of snow and others very little. Consumers were questioning whether or not to purchase our product based on snowfall. They would hold back until winter hit, and if we had marginal snowfall, they were less likely to buy". Thanks to the deal with Enron, the company could now take the earnings sting out of a snow-less winter. The hedging programme was later credited for a 40% increase in sales.

❑ In early 2000, SocGen entered into a temperature deal with an unnamed Japanese retailer that wanted protection from colder than usual post-winter weather, as under those circumstances customers would buy less summer clothing. The weather derivative sold to the retailer would pay out a lump sum of money if the weather for the upcoming month of March was particularly cool. The deal, worth roughly US$10 million, was the second Japanese weather deal to be written by SocGen. The previous summer, the bank (then the only financial institution making markets in weather derivatives) had entered into a deal with a Japanese ski resort in Nagano to protect it against low snowfall. Under that deal, the minimum number of skiing days was 15 in a period of two months between 1st December 1999 and 31st January 2000. A skiing day meant a day where snow depth was above 10 cm. For every skiing-day below 15, the resort received ¥10 million from SocGen, up to a total of ¥150 million. For skiing days above 15, the resort would then have to pay SocGen a similar amount per day (but that was supposedly offset by a rise in sales due to increased skiing potential).

❑ In October 2000, Washington-based WGL Holdings Inc, which delivers natural gas to residential, commercial and industrial customers through its Washington Gas Light Co. unit, took out a five-year contract to protect its profit against warm weather sapping demand for power. Two years later, the company, which paid US$4.25 million annually for the coverage, said it received US$14.8 million in compensation for "unusually warm weather" in winter 2001.

❑ In January 2001, London-based The White Swan pub entered into a temperature contract with SocGen. Payment was triggered by the number of cold Fridays and Saturdays during the April–July period. In particular, the pub would receive compensation if there are too few such days where the temperature was above 14°C in April and 18°C in May, and if there are too many such days where the temperature was below 18°C in June and 20°C in July. White Swan estimated that it stood to lose in excess of £15,000 per day that was too cold to drink outside.

❑ In February 2001, UK wine bar chain Corney & Barrow Wine Bars Ltd bought a weather derivative from Enron that paid £15,000 (around US$25,000) for every Thursday and Friday that the temperature failed to reach 24°C (75°F) during the summer. After all, if the weather is miserable people are less likely to hang out for a drink after work. In May 2004, Corney & Barrow returned to the weather derivatives arena, and for the same reasons. After the exceptional summer of 2003, the bar chain was keen to secure protection against the possibility of the reverse experience the following year. Paul Masters, then Group Commercial Director at Corney & Barrow said: "With the same attention to detail that drives success in our bars, we have secured a tailored financial product capable of managing the risk that abnormal weather may bring to our business".

❑ In early 2001, a Japanese leisure park management company entered into a precipitation deal, assisted by the triumvirate formed by Mitsui Sumitomo Marine, Tokyo Marine and Fire and Hiroshima Bank. The company runs about twenty parks around the country, with names such as "New Zealand Village" and "Germany Village". The concern was that the number of guests declines during rainy holidays and weekends, thus critically hitting earnings. The contract paid out if a pre-specified number of rainy days was reached during the weekends and holidays taking place in the April–November 2001 period. A rainy day was defined as that which experienced aggregate precipitation over 0.5 mm. The strikes differed depending on each particular location (between 30 and 50 rainy days), as did the compensation per unit (between ¥1.5 million and ¥3.0 million).

❑ In May 2001, the city of Sacramento in California entered into a precipitation contract with Aquila Energy. During droughts, Sacramento was to get less of its electricity from hydroelectric dams and pay higher prices for power on the open market. To ease the pain of high-cost droughts, the Sacramento Municipal Utility District (SMUD) entered a five-year contract with Aquila. Sacramento would get cash when rainfall measured at the Pollock Pines rain gauge was low, and would pay a fee when it's above normal. Also in early 2001, SMUD entered into a contract with Enron whereby the hydro generator agreed to buy a precipitation put option with a payout linked to the price of natural gas on the US benchmark Henry Hub. In the event that annual rainfall in the utility's area were to fall below 42.5" a year, SMUD would receive 18,000 times the Henry Hub gas price for each one-tenth of an inch below the strike.

❑ Also in May 2001, Elektrizitatswerk Dahlenburg, a German municipal utility, signed a contract that would protect its revenue at times of high summer rainfall, when local farmers require less power for pumps to irrigate fields. The contract was the third known weather derivatives transaction in Germany and the first international transaction for Element Re (now XL Weather), which acted as the counterparty. The deal protected Dahlenburg's revenue equal to 20% of the utility's annual profit. "Many of our customers are farmers who use electric power to pump water through periods of insufficient precipitation. The power we supply them is an important part of our total revenue projection", said Dahlenburg's then chief executive Herr Bannehr.

❑ In July 2001, another German electricity provider, Gruppen-Gas-und Elektrizitätswerk Bergstraße (GGEW), purchased protection from Dresdner Kleinwort Wasserstein covering the winter period for 2002 against temperatures below −5°C. Effectively GGEW has a limited capacity when producing electricity and has to purchase it from other suppliers once temperatures dip below –5°C. These purchases are expensive, as there is much demand for surplus capacity in cold weather. Using its arrangement, GGEW could now exercise its weather contract to receive funds to purchase electricity from other suppliers, thus protecting its profits. Apparently, GGEW's protection was a medium-sized deal in terms of notional value, but was significant in that it was one of the very first such deals in Germany. This was DKW's first weather deal and the fourth weather derivatives transaction recorded in Germany.

❑ In December 2001, Japan's Imaoka Corporation, a manufacturer of sore throat lozenges, was one of the first companies to purchase a weather derivative referenced to humidity, aimed at protecting revenues in case of an unusually humid winter. For Imaoka, sales often drop during the country's hot summer months (the soaring humidity levels lessening incidences of dry raspy coughs among the Japanese population). Conversely, as the air becomes cooler and drier, more people are struck with irritating tickly throats, prompting a spike in throat lozenge purchases. The deal, transacted with Mitsui Sumitomo Insurance, paid out once a proprietary Tokyo-based humidity index rose above a predetermined level. The nominal value, or maximum payout, was only ¥9 million (US$72,000), but the deal was highly relevant for its path-breaking creativity, not just in terms of the underlying but specifically in terms of the very particular risk that it was capable of hedging.

❏ In early 2002, Gut Apeldor golf club in Hennstedt, Germany, bought a precipitation derivative that covered it from the risk of heavy rain keeping golfers away (the weather in 2001 had been miserable in that respect). The managers of the club decided that they could put up with 50 rainy days from May to September. Once the number of days with more than 1 mm of rain passed 50, the derivatives contract started paying compensation for every wet day. The payout was doubled for weekends, when the golf course did more business and the potential loss of income due to inclement weather was greatest.

❏ In April 2002, Daiwa Bank Holdings Inc began selling to businesses contracts with payouts linked to weather conditions at the three Japanese locations where three of the soccer teams joining in the World Cup finals were to hold training camps from the following May. Under the contracts, Daiwa Bank and Asahi Bank, both under the wing of the holding company, would pay up to ¥5 million per unit contract to buyers of the contracts if it rained for more than a pre-determined number of days during the camps of up to 25 days.

❏ In May 2002, London-based restaurant The Rock Garden entered into a contract with Element Re designed to protect it against financial loss from colder-than-normal weather from 1st March to 30th June. Inclement weather during those months meant less customers. The contract would pay out when the temperature was less than or equal to 8.5°C in March, less than or equal to 11°C in April, less than or equal to 14.5°C in May, and less than or equal to 18°C in June. The number of days per month required to trigger the contract remained fixed. The payouts in the latter months were to be higher because the restaurant's sales typically increased as summer approached. This deal was believed to be the very first involving a restaurant.

❏ In October 2002, ZZ2 Ceres, one of South Africa's largest producers of fruit and vegetables, purchased protection against early-spring frost. This temperature-based transaction would pay out for days when the temperature was equal to or below 0°C during the crucial early spring phase. This was South Africa's first weather derivatives trade. "The weather is one of the big risk factors faced by our agricultural operations", declared Retief du Toit, then general manager of ZZ2 Ceres. "An early spring frost can have a devastating effect on crop yields and the product that has been structured will provide welcome financial support in circumstances that would otherwise leave us with a budget shortfall. We are looking forward to working with dealers on other weather-related structures to help us address risks that we have previously left in the hands of Mother Nature."

❑ In October 2002, Tokyo-headquartered kerosene wholesale company Sinanen entered into a dual weather and fuel derivatives contract with trading company Sumitomo Corporation to hedge its kerosene sales during the winter months. The wholesaler entered into a fuel derivatives contract to fix the domestic kerosene premium over the imported crude oil price, while also entering into a weather derivatives contract whereby Sinanen received payment from Sumitomo Corporation if the temperature exceeded an agreed strike price. The wholesaler therefore hedged the cost of imported oil in case of yen depreciation or a rise in oil prices, but also protected itself against lower kerosene consumption in case of a mild winter.

❑ In late 2002, ABN Amro entered into a frost-days derivative with an undisclosed Dutch construction company. The tranched five-year option contract was designed to hedge the construction firm's exposure to frosty conditions at Amsterdam's Schipol airport during the winter season, which prevented work from being carried out. It was believed to be the biggest weather deal up to that date. The first tranche almost resulted in a payout of €200 million, as there were only 19 frost days at Schipol during the November–March 2003 period, just one shy of the required 20 (for the purposes of this deal, a frost day is defined as a working day when the temperature drops below −3.5°C at 7am local time, −1.5°C at 10am or −0.5°C at both times).

❑ In November 2002, UK's Centrica plc announced that its subsidiary British Gas Trading had concluded a major weather hedging agreement with XL Weather designed to protect the company against variability in earnings of its gas retail business due to abnormal winter temperatures. With an aggregate limit of £40 million over the next five winter seasons, the programme stood as one of the largest weather-related end-user transactions concluded up to that point worldwide. The deal was also highly innovative as it was based on a "spread" of daily average temperatures, rather than the traditional degree day index. This spread of daily average temperatures continued the trend towards more structured solutions for weather risk management. The structure was arranged as a strip of daily options with strikes and payouts tailored to track weather-influenced earnings variations.

❑ In April 2004, Australia's Southern Hydro Partnership (SHP) entered into a three-year AUS$20 million notional contract with Credit Lyonnais Rouse, to protect itself against the risk of low rainfall. The region of Victoria had seen rainfall levels significantly below the 10-year average in recent years, and for a hydroelectric company this could be very problematic. SHP lowered the cost of the hedge by entering into a precipitation collar where they received payments if rainfall was lower than a threshold amount but pay in years where there was a lot of rainfall (in early 2003 SHP had pioneered the market by entering into what was believed to be Australia's first ever precipitation trade, with XL Weather as counterpart). Darryl Flukes, then General Manager of Energy Trading at SHP said of the deal: "Southern Hydro places a premium on cashflow and revenue stability. This transaction further protects us from production variability inherent in hydro generation." He also stated that: "the weather risk management industry again provided us with excellent service in developing a tailored solution with competitive offers from a number of providers. A significant aspect of this particular transaction is it being referenced to a more remote location (Lake Eildon, the most local weather station), rather than the traditional major cities, so eliminating any geographical basis risk."

❑ In October 2005, Tradition Financial Services (TFS), a leading over-the-counter (OTC) weather derivatives brokerage firm, completed a successful Dutch Auction on behalf of Centrica Energy, a subsidiary of Centrica plc. TFS solicited offers for a "lookback selective Asian Put option" for the period of October to December 2005, based on the average of the average daily temperature of the coldest 50 days of Q4 2005. All put offers came directly through TFS Energy and had to be received by 15:00 BST, Thursday, 22nd September 2005. The amount placed was approximately US$70,200,000 of risk. Offers were accepted in minimum tick increments of £100,000 and could be made for all or part of the total size of the option. In the event that there were multiple successful offers, all offers were filled until the entire tick/cap capacity for the structure was exhausted. All clearing offers then received the highest clearing price for their offer.

A RESOLUTION FOR WEATHER: THE REACH OF THE MARKET IS UN-LIMITED

As we see from the deals described above, the weather derivatives market can boast a very high level of innovation and creativity in terms of risks hedged, locations covered and products used. It is clear that the investment banks, energy companies and re-insurers that have dominated the market since its origins have shown themselves throughout the years to be capable of financial wizardry of the highest level. However, the most exotic transactions may be yet to come. If everything goes according to plan, in 2006 the United Nations' World Food Programme (WFP) will launch precipitation-related derivatives to help Ethiopia cope with the risks of drought and famine. The key idea is to structure a product that pays out before malnutrition sets in. This way, not only will the human cost be alleviated by ensuring that the money is ready before disaster strikes, but it could also end Ethiopia's unhealthy dependency on charitable aid (which in any case always arrives after the effects of drought have taken place). Current *ex post* approaches risk significant loss of livelihoods, even in well-funded emergency responses, and may not be able to cope. The hope is that the weather derivatives programme, with its *ex ante* approach to economic relief, will make aid more efficient and timely.

The UN's weather programme for Ethiopia, which is a pilot project that if successful would be extended to other developing countries such as Mali, aims to hedge the year's agricultural season (March–October) from the possibility of low rainfall. The original intentions of the WFP were to transfer no more than US$100 million of risk (ie, this would be the maximum payout), and to incur no more than US$8 million charges in premium (later reduced to US$2 million). The underlying of the contract would be a "livelihood losses index", representing the economic losses resulting from droughts for rural populations living in the agriculturally productive regions of Ethiopia. The relevant rainfall data would be derived

Figure 1 Total "At-Risk" household drought-related income losses in Ethiopia

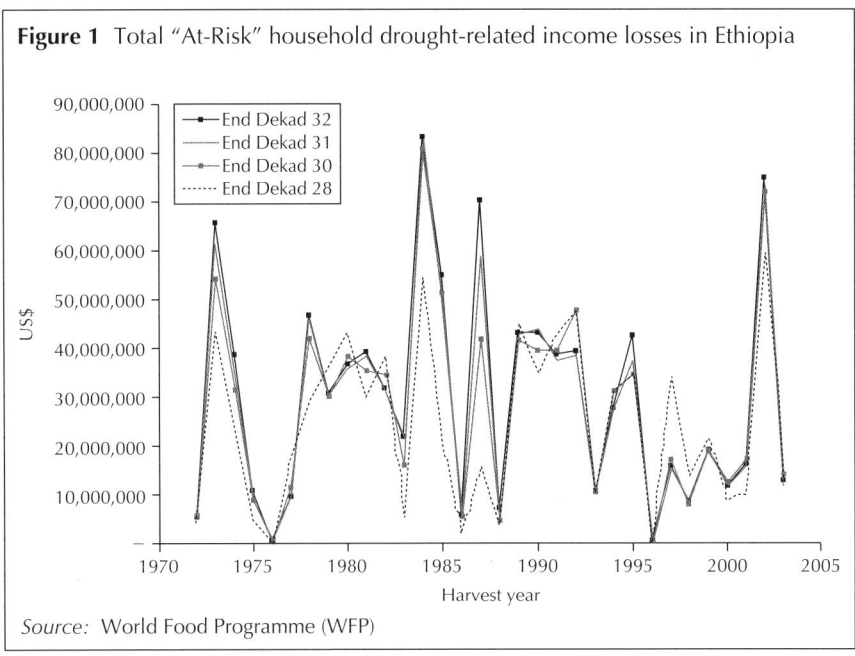

Source: World Food Programme (WFP)

from weather stations run by the Ethiopian government. Years of civil war have limited historical data for some regions, with several of them having data missing for up to five years. Nevertheless, and despite these gaps, most stations were established in the mid-1970s or earlier and some of them have complete 30-year or 50-year records. Locally obtained data would be triple-checked against satellite data and some extra source (a specialised consultancy or a European meteorological service). Once the index trigger is breached (on the way up, as the contract would be a call option on livelihood losses), payment covering the equivalent effects of a severe drought would take place with the capped payout representing a cata-strophic event (of the scale seen in the mid-1980s when one million Ethiopians died of starvation). Building the index is not straightfor-ward, as some regions are more important for food production than others and thus different weights must be assigned.

In order to obtain an understanding as to the possible levels of the underlying index, we can take a look at the livelihood-loss index calculated using rainfall data for the 1972–2003 period for the 26 weather stations that would form the index (see Figure 1).

Assuming an exchange rate of US$1 = 8.85 birr, we can see that the average loss per year was around US$30 million with quite a lot of volatility (US$23 million standard deviation). While the maximum loss was US$83 million (1984), the minimum was of just US$8,000 (1996). The term "dekad" refers to the period of the year on which losses were measured. The complete livelihood-loss index finishes at the end of the year (dekad 36), because it follows all potentially late-sowed crops to maturity; in practice, however, its value does not change from the middle of November onwards (dekad 32). The figure shows how the index changes if observed before dekad 32.

It is important to point out that events of a greater severity than 1984 or 2002 (the last big drought, with a livelihood impact of some US$75 million) are possible. The fact that they have not happened (at least in the last 35 years) doesn't mean that they will not take place in the future, especially in the context of a world dominated by climate change. To illustrate, the income losses that would be predicted by the index in case a 1984-type drought had occurred in 2002 (ie, a different geographical distribution) are US$98 million. Assuming worst-case rainfall deviation for each station from 1972–2003, the figure jumps to US$154 million.

How should the trigger for the derivative be selected? In order to answer this question, we must first determine the maturity of the contract (ie, the period when the calculation for the index ends). Since the goal of the project is to provide contingency funding for aid response (ie, to receive payment prior to fully suffering the consequences of drought), both expediency and accuracy must be carefully balanced: we want payment to be prompt but also to reflect potential real losses as closely as possible so as to minimise basis risk (which for this particular type of hedge could be measured in terms of lives lost). This led to the proposal that the calculation period be set as 31st October 2006, or dekad 30. Once this choice has been made, establishing the trigger level and the maximum payment becomes easier. The goal is that the derivative provides financing in both extreme and catastrophic drought. The first contingency can be approximated by the average historical level of the index (US$28 million for dekad 30 for 1972–2003) and the second by the maximum historical level of the index (US$80.6 million in 1984).

The Ethiopia weather derivative was expected to be tendered out competitively, and to be governed by an ISDA agreement. On the basis of the results of this tender, the project team would consult with the donors who contributed to the premium funding to ascertain whether the price is acceptable or not (in case the derivative was eventually discarded because it was found to be unacceptably costly donors would retain the risk and establish a contingency fund to be made accessible to the WFP on the same contractual basis as the derivative).

Table 1 Framework summary for the Ethiopia Pilot

Annex III: Logical Framework Summary: Pilot Development Project – Ethiopia Drought Insurance 10486.0

Hierarchy of results	Performance indicators	Assumptions and risks
Overall goal Contribute to creation of *ex ante* weather risk management system	Establishment of Government-led agricultural weather-risk management system providing protection for smallholders	The World Bank will lead policy discourse with the Government The Government will build capacity to hedge country's weather risks International capital markets will engage on Ethiopian weather risk Donors will provide reliable support to the Government to meet capacity-building and financial challenges
Outcome 1 Demonstrate feasibility of transferring Least Developed Countries (LDC) weather risks	Market transaction at acceptable premium for Ethiopian weather risk	Market players reject or charge excessive premium for newly introduced risk
Outcome 2 Price discovery for Ethiopian weather risk	Competitive tender establishes market price for Ethiopian weather risk	Markets willing to take Ethiopian risk Pricing information accepted by Government and stakeholders for development portfolio considerations

Table 1 (continued)

Annex III: Logical Framework Summary: Pilot Development Project – Ethiopia Drought Insurance 10486.0

Hierarchy of results	Performance indicators	Assumptions and risks
Outcome 3		
Setting in motion a process for *ex ante* risk management in developing countries	The Government builds *ex ante* risk management system, which is copied by other developing countries vulnerable to weather shocks, especially drought	Demonstration provides incentive for other countries to engage in the process. The Government, with assistance from the WFP and the World Bank, invests further in *ex ante* weather-risk management
Outcome 4		
Small weather hedge for the 2006 agricultural season	Weather derivative is in place no later than the end of November of 2005	Donor support for experimental transaction. Acceptable premium cost or risk retention by donor
Output 1.1		
Quantification of Ethiopia's drought risk	Credible Index based on correlation of rainfall and losses	Data available. Basis risk manageable
Output 2.1		
Derivative contract based on a rainfall Index	Contract made available to market players for transaction	Reliable data flow from Ethiopia. Third party verification agreement
Output 2.2		
Transfer of the risk to International markets or donor risk retention	Transaction on contract	Willing counterparty at acceptable price

Source: World Food Programme (WFP), October 2005.

Why should the Ethiopian deal be considered such a major breakthrough? Why does it benefit the weather derivatives market? What value does it add that has not been added already by some of the other deals described in the previous section? On top of the obvious (and welcome) humanitarian benefits of the WFP initiative, the deal presents clear benefits to weather players. Simply put, it can open the doors to a previously unexplored new market, namely the least developed of the group of least-developed countries. While the World Bank's International Finance Corporation (IFC) had earlier pioneered weather derivatives inroads into emerging economies such as Morocco (2002) and India (2003), no one had tried it before in such a hard case as Ethiopia. If the WFP manages to succeed there, it would essentially signal that it can be done anywhere. As it is difficult to underestimate the potential need for agriculture-related hedges in the most underdeveloped parts of the globe, that development should prove highly beneficial to dealers and brokers, not only for fee-generating reasons but also because these new markets could offer desirable risk diversification mechanisms. In fact, it seems that the main rationale for those re-insurers that have showed an interest in participating in the Ethiopia deal was precisely the possibility of taking exposure to equatorial and southern hemisphere climates, which are of course not strongly correlated to extremes of northern hemisphere weather. At the very least, the WFP initiative would enable price discovery in international financial markets for Ethiopian (and close proxies) weather risk. Even if the weather market for LDCs does not boom as much as expected and desired by development organisations, this deal should become a valuable benchmark for those entities that in future may wish to structure bespoke and highly exotic transactions.

Another crucially important beneficial characteristic of the WFP initiative is that it very clearly highlights the value-added that weather derivatives offer over insurance. The particular aspect of this transaction that emphasises the advantages of using derivatives is, of course, the unavoidable need for prompt payment. Recall that the whole purpose of the project is to make sure that Ethiopian farmers receive cash compensation before the most adverse effects of a drought take place. If destitution and famine are to be avoided once the level of rainfall has fallen below a certain critical level, compensation has got to be channelled to farmers without delay. There is no time for the lengthy physical assessment of damages required by insurance policies (which payment would always be subject to the possibility of full or partial refusal). Farmers may be beyond help once a final settlement decision has been reached. Derivatives, in sharp contrast, get settled within five days of the end of the contract period and the pre-agreed amount of compensation can't be reduced or refused. Thus, for drought-afflicted farmers, using derivatives instead of insurance could mean the difference between being able to keep their assets and prevent famine or having to eat their seed grain and sell their livestock in order to survive. It is difficult to think of another example that so dramatically underlines the usefulness of weather derivatives.

However, the largest impact that the Ethiopian transaction could have on the overall weather risk market would be a tremendous dose of positive publicity. Think about it. Here we could have a product that does away with famine in Ethiopia. If there is a country that is embedded in the world's psyche as a symbol of famine and its devastating effects that surely has to be Ethiopia. More than ten years ago, the shocking images of starving Ethiopian children with bloated bellies and sunken eyes shamed the planet. Anybody (anything) that decisively contributes to preventing something such as that from happening again would be hailed as a universal saint. Were the WFP livelihood index contract to perform well and provide aiding comfort immediately following a significant drought, extensive media coverage would (and should) spell the new gospel to the four corners of the globe and tell everyone that it was weather derivatives that performed the miracle. No amount of paid advertising or public relations effort on the part of the industry could top that. Soon, shareholders may be demanding from corporate bigwigs that they too embrace such wonderful tools.

APPENDIX: JUST IN! IT'S AXA RE!

On March 6th, 2006 the WFP announced that French reinsurer AXA Re had been assigned the Ethiopia livelihood index contract, after a competitive tender process that involved five different reinsurers (ie, AXA Re will be the option's writer). The amount covered turned out to be quite below original expectations, with a maximum payout of just US$7 million. Why? Simply put, because that's the best that could be afforded given the limited sums of money collected from donors. The US$7 million payout corresponds to the US$930,000 in premium that the WFP was able to raise. Apparently, the governments of the US and Ethiopia were the main donors to the project.

Further Reading

Auer, J., 2003, "Weather Derivatives Heading for Sunny Times", Deutsche Bank Research – Frankfurt Voice, February.

Brown, G. and D. Chew, 1999, *Corporate Risk* (Risk Books).

Chew, L., 1996, *Managing Derivatives Risks* (John Wiley & Sons).

Das, S., 1996, "*Exotic Options*" (IFR Publishing).

Das, S., 2004, *Credit Derivatives, CDOs & Structured Credit Products* (John Wiley & Sons).

Dunbar, N., 2000, *Inventing Money* (John Wiley & Sons).

Dunbar, N., 2004, "Lost in the Post", *Risk*, April.

Ernst & Young, 2001, "Financial Reporting Developments – Accounting for Derivative Instruments and Hedging Activities", www.ey.com, December.

Fitch Ratings, 2004, "Hedge Accounting and Derivatives Study for Corporates", www.fitchratings.com, November.

Fitch Ratings, 2004, "CDS Market Liquidity: Show me the Money", www.fitchratings.com, November.

Fitch Ratings, 2004, "Liquidity in the CDS Market: Too Little Too Late", www.fitchratings.com, June.

Fitch Ratings, 2005, "Self-Referenced CLNs Raise Questions and Concerns", www.fitchratings.com, January.

Galitz, L., 2005, *Financial Engineering – Tools and Techniques to Manage Financial Risk* (Irwin).

Hakala, J. and U. Wystup, 2002, *Foreign Exchange Risk* (Risk Books).

Kawaller, I., 2003, "Hedging with Swaps: When Shortcut Accounting Can't Be Applied", www.kawaller.com, June.

Kawaller, I., "FAS 133 Overview", www.kawaller.com

Miller, M., 1997, *Merton Miller On Derivatives* (John Wiley & Sons).

Morgan Stanley Corporate Derivatives Group, 2004, "Corporate Use of Credit Derivatives: Next Stop in Risk Management", *Risk*, May.

Nelken, I., 2000, *Pricing, Hedging, and Trading Exotic Options* (McGraw-Hill).

Partnoy, F., 2003, *Infectious Greed* (Profile Books).

Petersen, M., 2001, "The Accidental Credit Investors", *Euromoney*, August.

Pollock, A., 2005, "What Is Accounting Truth?" *Journal of Applied Corporate Finance*, Vol 17, No 3, July.

PriceWaterhouseCoopers, 2005, "IAS 39 Hedging – Aligning Theory with Practice", www.pwcglobal.com, February.

Reyman, A. and K. Toft, 2001, "Credit Derivatives: A Risk Management Tool for Nonbank Corporations" Goldman Sachs Fixed Income Research, May.

Sawyer, N., 2004, "Dabbling with Credit", *Risk*, February.

Risk, 2000, "Weather Risk Supplement", August.

Risk, 2001, "Weather Risk Supplement", August.

Teague and Solomon, 2004, "*IAS 39*: The State of Play", *Risk*, May.

Thackray, J. and Bere, C., 2000, "The Two Faces of Kevin Hudson", www.derivativesstrategy.com, November.

Thind, S., 2005, "Spain's Companies Face Accounting Test", *Euromoney*, April.

Triana, P., 2005, "The Quanto Conundrum", *Risk*, June.

Wallace, J., 2003, "Derivative Accounting & Hedging Under FAS 133", Greenwich Treasury Advisors, www.greenwichtreasury.com

Wood, D., 2005, "Living with Volatility", *Risk*, April.

Index